Investment Fund Taxation

EUCOTAX Series on European Taxation

VOLUME 59

Series Editors

Introduction

EUCOTAX (European Universities Cooperating on Taxes) is a network of tax institutes currently consisting of eleven universities: WU (Vienna University of Economics and Business) in Austria, Katholieke Universiteit Leuven in Belgium, Corvinus University of Budapest, Hungary, Université Paris-I Panthéon-Sorbonne in France, Universität Osnabrück in Germany, Libera, Università Internazionale di Studi Sociali in Rome (and Università degli Studi di Bologna for the research part), in Italy, Fiscaal Instituut Tilburg at Tilburg University in the Netherlands, Universidad de Barcelona in Spain, Uppsala University in Sweden, Queen Mary and Westfield College at the University of London in the United Kingdom, and Georgetown University in Washington DC, United States of America. The network aims at initiating and coordinating both comparative education in taxation, through the organization of activities such as winter courses and guest lectures, and comparative research in the field, by means of joint research projects, international conferences and exchange of researchers between various countries.

Contents/Subjects

The EUCOTAX series covers a wide range of topics in European tax law. For example tax treaties, EC case law, tax planning, exchange of information and VAT. The series is well-known for its high-quality research and practical solutions.

Objective

The series aims to provide insights on new developments in European taxation.

Readership

Practitioners and academics dealing with European tax law.

Frequency of Publication

2-3 new volumes published each year.

The titles published in this series are listed at the end of this volume.

Investment Fund Taxation

Domestic Law, EU Law, and Double Taxation Treaties

Edited by

Werner Haslehner

ATOZ Foundation
under the aegis of Fondation de Luxembourg

Wolters Kluwer

Published by:
Kluwer Law International B.V.
PO Box 316
2400 AH Alphen aan den Rijn
The Netherlands
E-mail: international-sales@wolterskluwer.com
Website: lrus.wolterskluwer.com

Sold and distributed in North, Central and South America by:
Wolters Kluwer Legal & Regulatory U.S.
7201 McKinney Circle
Frederick, MD 21704
United States of America
Email: customer.service@wolterskluwer.com

Sold and distributed in all other countries by:
Air Business Subscriptions
Rockwood House
Haywards Heath
West Sussex
RH16 3DH
United Kingdom
Email: international-customerservice@wolterskluwer.com

ISBN 978-90-411-9669-9

e-Book: ISBN 978-90-411-9679-8
web-PDF: ISBN 978-90-411-9670-5

Editor

Werner Haslehner is Professor of Law at the Faculty of Law, Economics, and Finance at the University of Luxembourg, where he holds the ATOZ Chair for European and International Taxation and is the Director of its LLM Programme in European Union (EU) and International Tax Law. His research focus lies at the intersection of European and international tax law, tax planning, and tax policy.

Contributors

Heribert M. Anzinger is a Professor of Business and Taxation Law at the University of Ulm, Germany.

Daniel Dürrschmidt is a Post-Doctoral Researcher at Ludwig-Maximilians-Universität München. His main area of research is German domestic, European, and international tax law.

Eric Fort is a Partner in the Tax Law and Private Wealth practices of Arendt & Medernach. He is the Head of the firm's New York office, he advises on both national and international tax issues. He has substantial experience in real estate, private equity, private wealth structuring, and finance transactions.

Daniel Gutmann is a Professor of Tax Law at the University Paris 1 Panthéon-Sorbonne, and a Partner at CMS Bureau Francis Lefebvre.

Charlène A. Herbain is a Senior Managing Lawyer in the tax policy and tax litigation practice at Law Square and a VAT specialist. She is also a Senior Lecturer at the University of Luxembourg and Adjunct Lecturer at the University of Nancy II Faculty of Law.

Philipp Jost is an Associate in the Tax Law practice of Arendt & Medernach in the firm's Luxembourg office.

Keith Lawson is Deputy General Counsel - Tax Law for the Investment Company Institute (ICI) and ICI Global, which carries out the ICI's international work serving a fund membership that includes regulated funds publicly offered to investors in jurisdictions worldwide, seeking to advance common interests and promote public understanding of regulated investment funds, their managers, and investors. www.iciglobal.org.

Claire Micheau is a Policy Officer at the European Commission. She also holds the title of Associate Professor at the University of Helsinki, Finland and is a regular Lecturer at several universities, including University Paris 1 Panthéon-Sorbonne, University of Luxembourg, and Leiden University. She is qualified as an attorney at the Paris Bar and has published various books and articles in the areas of tax law, EU law, WTO law, and competition law.

Uljana Molitor-March, Director, ATOZ Tax Advisers, Luxembourg has nine years of experience, focusing on Private Equity, Real Estate, as well as Multinational Corporations and advises a wide range of international clients on tax matters related to cross-border operations, set-up of investment structures, mergers & acquisitions, reorganizations, and divestures.

Keith O'Donnell, Partner, ATOZ Tax Advisers, Luxembourg, has twenty-seven years of experience in advising international groups on the design and implementation of global tax strategies and is President of IFA Luxembourg, Chair of the INREV Tax Committee, Chair of the ALFI Double Tax Treaties and ALFI Regulation Advisory Board commissions, and a member of key international tax groups.

Katerina Pantazatou is an Associate Professor in Tax Law at the University of Luxembourg.

Isabelle Riassetto, already professor of law in France prior to becoming professor in Commercial Law at the University of Luxembourg in 2008, is Study Director of the Faculty of Law, Economics and Finance's Master 2/LLM in European Banking and Financial Law. Her main research fields are individual and collective portfolio management law emphasizing investment funds law using a European and comparative approach.

Marie-Isabelle Richardin, a specialist in financial services VAT, has been with PwC Luxembourg's VAT practice since 2000. A regular speaker on VAT for financial services, she is Chair of the VAT Working Group of the Luxembourg Private Equity Association (LPEA) and the firm's representative in other VAT working groups.

Geoffrey Scardoni is an Avocat à la Cour and Partner at DLA Piper, Luxembourg. His practice focuses on international corporate structuring, cross-border financial products, and fund formation. He is also an assistant lecturer at the University of Luxembourg.

Jean Schaffner is a Tax Partner in Allen & Overy's Luxembourg office and has more than twenty years of extensive experience in advising institutional investors and private equity funds in cross-border investments, tax aspects for Luxembourg investments, and the structuring of international acquisitions via Luxembourg regulated and non-regulated vehicles.

Mario Tenore is a Senior Associate at Maisto e Associati, with competence in corporate taxation and European and international tax law. Holding a PhD and an Advanced LLM, he publishes extensively in the field of international and European tax law.

Dirk A. Zetzsche holds the ADA Chair in Financial Law in the Faculty of Law, Economics and Finance at the University of Luxembourg and is the author and editor of some leading English and German treatises on collective investment schemes and financial law in English and German.

Summary of Contents

Table of Contents

Introduction

Werner Haslehner

I INVESTMENT FUND TAXATION: A MULTIFACETED TOPIC

The world of taxation is changing at the international, European, and national levels: impending reforms, undertaken in the context of the OECD/G20 BEPS Project, new EU tax legislation, and shifting administrative and judicial approaches to domestic and cross-border investment fund structures will have a substantial impact on investment funds. Together, these changes will assert significant pressure on advisors, as well as national legislatures, to ensure the frictionless operation of this essential part of the financial sector. This book provides a comprehensive legal and practical analysis of the changes to the already highly complex multi-level regulatory framework concerning different types of investment funds. It is the result of a conference held at the University of Luxembourg on 17 November 2016 entitled 'The Future of Funds Taxation – Domestic Law, Tax Treaties and EU Law' under the auspices of the ATOZ Chair for European and International Taxation. The authors finalized their chapters over the course of several months following the conference and updated them in late 2017 to reflect important later developments.

The book covers the central questions arising in national law and tax policy, explores the regulatory and tax framework of the European Union (EU) and also discusses the multifaceted interactions of both national and EU law with bilateral tax treaties. Through fourteen chapters, leading academic experts and practising specialists provide decisive insight into the **regulatory regime for European investment funds**; the **tax laws and reforms in Luxembourg and Germany;** the European Commission's **State Aid practices**; case law concerning the application of **non-discrimination rules** to various investment vehicles; the impact of tax-specific EU legislation such as the **Parent-Subsidiary Directive**, the **Tax Merger Directive**, and the **Anti-Tax-Avoidance Directive**, as well as the relevant European **exchange of information regimes**; the availability of **tax treaty protection** for different collective and non-collective investment vehicles and the impact of **BEPS developments** on the taxation of cross-border investments; the **value added tax (VAT)** treatment of investment funds and their managers; and the consequences of the global drive towards **automatic exchange of information** relating to existing cross-border investment structures.

This wide array of topics is collected in three sections, each of which addresses separate aspects of investment fund regulation and taxation: national (taxation) rules, EU (taxation) regimes, and international (taxation) rules as addressed through bilateral tax treaties. Five of those chapters focus on the particular situation in Luxembourg, which acts as a showcase for common issues that arise in virtually every other jurisdiction with a sizeable fund industry. As Luxembourg is the leading centre for investment funds in Europe (and around the globe, as it is second only to the United States), Luxembourg provides an instructive model for domestic-level investment fund regulation and taxation. A sixth chapter dealing with national law – concerning the investment tax reform in Germany, which became effective in 2018 – offers an insightful explanation of the concerns and different national approaches that might be taken with respect to fund taxation, which are likely to inform future legal and policy considerations undertaken in other EU countries. The remaining chapters take a decidedly global or, at least, European-wide perspective, while covering all of the most relevant issues that have arisen, or are likely to arise, in the fast-changing world of international taxation.

II OVERVIEW OF THE CONTENTS

The book's domestic law part introduces various forms of fund structures and analyses the plethora of regulatory and tax consequences that flow not only from the funds' structural differences but also from the domestic-taxation variations that abound. In the opening chapter (Chapter 1 – Introduction to Investment Funds Law), **Isabelle Riassetto** analyses both the economic rationale and the legal framework for investment funds, with a particular focus on the EU directives that harmonize regulation of the funds industry across all Member States, and, as a concrete example of national implementation, Luxembourg's legislation.

The subsequent three chapters of the first part address the tax implications under national law on multiple levels, including taxation of the fund itself, of its investors, and of its managers or management companies. First, **Eric Fort and Philipp Jost** (Chapter 2 – Investment Funds Taxation in Luxembourg) provide a detailed synopsis of the diversity of fund vehicles operating in Luxembourg. They describe the most common forms of investment funds together with the regulatory and legal framework applicable in Luxembourg and highlight the divergent taxation regimes applicable to them. In addition, this chapter sheds light on the latest rules concerning exchange of information applicable to the investment fund industry and the reporting requirements specified therein.

Second, **Charlène Herbain and Marie-Isabelle Richardin** (Chapter 3 – VAT and Investment Funds) explore indirect tax aspects relevant to investment funds, particularly the VAT status of investment funds themselves, as well as taxation based on the relationship between the fund and the fund manager. They provide theoretical and practical answers through their review of the relevant CJEU case law and also cover most recent cases concerning the practical implementation of harmonized EU rules intended to clarify the VAT treatment of entities engaged in cross-border investment management services. Their chapter further analyses the recent administrative and judicial clarifications surrounding Luxembourg's fund taxation regime. Its innovative and extensive offer of an array of fund vehicles ensures this to be an edifying example that is, and will continue to be, relevant across the EU in the coming years.

Third, **Heribert M. Anzinger**'s chapter (Chapter 4 – Transparent, Semi-transparent, Opaque: Recent Developments in Fund Taxation in Germany) highlights the variability of direct tax regimes covering investment vehicles and introduces an important comparative perspective. Recounting the development and result of Germany's recent global investment tax reform, which entered into force in 2018, he illustrates – through the German example – the array of options available to legislatures to respond to political and legal pressures. In order to address issues of fragility, complexity, and open questions surrounding superior EU law, the new German regimes opted to create two separate systems, distinguishing between two kinds of investment vehicles; an opaque taxation system and an optional semi-transparent system for special investment funds. Whether the overall goal of improved simplicity and robustness has thereby been achieved remains, however, in doubt.

In its second part, the book discusses the three major elements of EU law that currently affect investment fund taxation. While a range of EU directives have been adopted in the fields of tax and finance, the EU has yet to adopt a common framework for taxing investment funds. This part of the book investigates why that is so, finding that the status quo is due, in part, to the vast number legal forms and highly diverse tax treatments found across the Member States. They further investigate the application of State aid law to the investment fund sector, where specific risks arise from both the investment vehicles' different treatment when compared to the general tax framework in effect for other undertakings and the existence of variations within the financial sector itself. Choosing the correct reference-framework for investment funds represents the greatest challenge when conclusively assessing the selectivity of a certain tax measure, which is the main criterion for finding illegal State aid. The EU Commission's recent heightened scrutiny of the Member States' tax regimes has brought the question to the fore, particularly after it launched formal investigations against Luxembourg, the Netherlands, and Ireland with respect to advanced tax rulings issued to Amazon, Apple, Fiat-Chrysler, Starbucks, and more recently, McDonalds', that resulted in the Commission findings of illegal State aid. In the opening chapter to the EU law section of the book, **Claire Micheau** (Chapter 5 – Taxation of Collective Investments Within the Legal Framework of State Aid) addresses special taxation regimes for various investment vehicles from a State aid law perspective. After a general introduction that recalls the criteria for illegal State aid under Article 107 TFEU and the distinctive nature of collective investment undertakings, this chapter explores the requirements of an investment fund vehicle to qualify as an 'undertaking' and elaborates on how the selectivity test has to be applied for the assessment of special regimes tailored to the investment fund industry and its various vehicles. Discussing relevant CJEU cases on

State aid and funds, it underscores the difficulty of demonstrating the existence of State aid in the fund sector, which is partly due to the various levels of taxation that all need to be taken into account. At the same time, Micheau flags the vulnerability of a legal system that introduces a variety of different regimes without a clear rationale for the distinctions it makes.

Following the assessment of a potential danger for investment structures from EU State aid law, two chapters investigate the somewhat more certain ground of the fundamental freedoms' application to investment funds. As the CJEU has already confirmed on several occasions, the operation of funds across borders may give rise to prohibited discriminatory tax treatment, in particular where withholding taxes are imposed on non-resident investment funds while similar resident investment funds are exempt from any such tax burden. The CJEU's case law, however, has not yet definitively established the preconditions for a foreign investment fund to be considered comparable to a domestic one, the essential criterion for protection against less favourable treatment. This issue is particularly difficult with respect to investment funds established in third countries, as these are entirely outside the reach of the regulatory harmonization applicable within the EU, making the potential to find relevant differences greater. **Keith O'Donnell** and **Uljana Molitor-March** (Chapter 6 – Funds Taxation and the Third-Country Dimension) investigate this particular issue, recounting a number of judgments – both by the CJEU and by the national courts – that provide important clues about the elements to be taken into account. One key to establishing objective comparability between a domestic investment fund and its foreign counterpart relies on their respective regulatory frameworks, while another key relates to the system of tax integration between the three relevant levels of taxation: the fund itself, its investors, and the taxation of its investment targets.

In the following chapter, **Mario Tenore** (Chapter 7 – Investment Fund Taxation and Fundamental Freedoms: Four Approaches to Comparability) makes a critical and detailed assessment of the CJEU's different approaches to this question of comparability. In a meticulous review of the key judgments, Tenore distinguishes four approaches to comparability, which the Court applies separately and without a clear hierarchy: The '*ACT GLT/Denkavit* Approach', the 'Distinguishing Criterion Approach', the 'Aim Approach', and the 'Regulatory Framework Approach'.

While EU law has long regulated investment funds by way of harmonizing legislation such as the UCITS and AIFM directives, no such harmonization has been forthcoming with respect to their taxation, despite the Union's increasing legislative activity in corporate taxation matters. In the last chapter of the second part, **Katerina Pantazatou** (Chapter 8 – Funds and EU Tax Directives) reviews the impact of existing directives on the taxation of investment fund activities. Describing the dearth of references to investment funds in the existing tax directives, the chapter elaborates on the consequences of this absence and potential remedies for them, in particular as it arises from the CJEU's case law on the fundamental freedoms. The exploration spans from primarily beneficial directives, such as the Parent-Subsidiary Directive and the Tax Merger Directive, to more recent regimes that impose burdens on investment funds, such as the Anti-Tax Avoidance Directive, the Administrative Cooperation Directive, and the Anti-Money Laundering Directive.

The focus of the book's third part is on tax treaty questions. It is generally understood that investment funds occupy a special place in the tax treaty context: due to their legal form and frequently tax-exempt status, many fund vehicles are routinely denied access to tax treaty benefits, whereas it is exactly their nature as flow-through entities and their function as cross-border investment facilitators that make juridical double taxation particularly harmful. The issue has recently become even more salient in the context of the OECD/G20 BEPS Project and, more particularly, its BEPS 2015 Report on Action 6, which supports the adoption of 'limitation-on-benefits' or 'principal purposes' rules to combat the problem of the *inappropriate* granting of benefits.

Approaching the subject from a background of financial law, **Dirk Zetzsche** (Chapter 9 – Non-collective Investment Funds under BEPS Action 6 Versus European Investment Fund Law) argues that tax law could take a cue from European investment fund law, since the rationale and regulatory objectives are to a large part aligned. He also argues that the EU could helpfully drive the development at the international level by adopting a harmonized taxation regime for all investment funds covered by European investment fund law, to the benefit of investors and European capital markets alike.

In the absence of such a fund vehicle's specific mention in a tax treaty, its protection from double taxation is often in doubt, as it will depend on the interpretation of the tax treaty's general terms. On the other hand, investment funds may be excluded from the personal scope of a particular double tax treaty as it may be difficult to prove their status as 'resident' as a consequence of their tax-exempt status. As the overhaul of the international tax framework is ongoing, the jury is still out on the ultimate treatment of different categories of investment funds. Three separate chapters address the question of tax treaty entitlement: **Daniel Dürrschmidt** (Chapter 10 – Treaty Entitlement of Funds in the Pre-BEPS World) discusses the application of tax treaties to Collective Investment Vehicles (CIVs) prior to the adoption of the OECD/G20 BEPS Project Action reports. The chapter analyses the meaning of standard concepts in tax treaties in light of their application to investment funds, which includes, for example, the personal scope of application of a treaty, the distributive rules relevant to funds, and the methods of avoiding double taxation. Dürrschmidt also critically reviews the relevance of special tax treaty provisions for CIVs and demonstrates their weakness, using the example of the special rules for CIVs contained in the protocol to the double tax treaty signed between Germany and Luxembourg. This last issue is of particular pertinence for countries such as Luxembourg, which puts much emphasis on the inclusion of such specific wording relating to investments funds in its tax treaties to ensure appropriate coverage and to avoid higher-tax consequences that could arise via withholding taxes or the inapplicability of reduced tax rates.

In the next chapter, **Jean Schaffner** (Chapter 11 – Funds in International Tax Law: Examples from Luxembourg's Treaties) highlights the difficulties of ensuring treaty protection for the whole variety of different investment vehicles offered by Luxembourg law and the response of the tax treaty negotiators and tax administration in the application of these treaties. The chapter provides practical examples of inclusion and exclusion of investment funds in selected double tax treaties, also referring to potential pitfalls that could arise as a consequence of the entry into force of the Multilateral Instrument (MLI). The chapter concludes with suggestions to improve the tax treaty protection of investment funds by making changes to their domestic tax regime. In light of the criticism lodged against special clauses in tax treaties, this suggestion is certainly relevant. Schaffner also points to the danger inherent in such changes from a European State aid law perspective.

Keith Lawson, then, addresses tax treaty entitlement from a post-BEPS perspective (Chapter 12 – Treaty Entitlement of Funds in the Post-BEPS World). Following a comprehensive overview over the development from the OECD's 2010 CIV Report to the final BEPS Reports, the chapter outlines the new focus and paradigm of international tax rules applied to investment funds and then contrasts this with the concerns of the fund industry and national governments. Lawson particularly highlights the need for practical and reliable solutions to minimize the distortions created by taxation.

Even in cases where no tax treaty benefits are available directly to investment funds, there are ways to prevent or minimize disadvantages from overlapping tax jurisdictions. The last two chapters of the book explore some of these routes. In the penultimate chapter (Chapter 13 – Non-discrimination of Funds and Double Taxation Relief) **Daniel Gutmann** explores potential discrimination arising from the limited tax relief available to cross-border investment funds from the perspective of both the source state and the resident state, assessing the applicability of the different non-discrimination clauses contained in Article 24 of the OECD Model. In general, a non-discrimination clause modelled after Article 24 of the OECD Model may still apply to otherwise excluded investment funds due to that provision's broader personal scope. The chapter discusses practical tests to assess the comparability of resident and non-resident funds in order to establish whether a discrimination claim can be raised and then also remarks on the possible further protection granted by the European Convention of Human Rights.

In the final chapter of the book (Chapter 14 – Practical Tax Aspects of Fund Structuring in Luxembourg), **Geoffrey Scardoni** offers key practical considerations for structuring cross-border funds in Luxembourg. Through the example of an alternative investment fund investing in real estate in Europe, the author illustrates the different legal and tax aspects arising at the levels of the investors, the funds, and the fund managers. The chapter addresses both domestic and international constraints with respect to essential factors, such as the arm's length principle, substance requirements, and other relevant operational aspects that practitioners need to keep in mind when structuring funds.

Part I Funds Taxation: National Law and Policy

CHAPTER 1

Introduction to Investment Funds Law

Isabelle Riassetto

§1.01 INTRODUCTION

There is no general legal definition of an investment fund, known at the European level as an Undertaking for Collective Investment (UCI) or Collective Investment Undertaking (CIU) - hereinafter 'UCI' - (*'organisme de placement collectif'* or *OPC*).[1] Rather, there are only criteria of investment funds in European Union (EU) investment funds law, as transposed into national laws and regulations.[2] The terminology in this field is very sensitive, because there are different meanings for the concepts used in various national laws and in practice. There is a need for clarification because the same terms do not always cover exactly the same concept or the same scope and, thus, can become a source of discrepancies and misunderstandings. At the EU level, the *summa divisio* of UCIs[3] is between Undertakings for Collective Investment in Transferable Securities (UCITS)[4] and Alternative Investment Funds (AIFs).[5] At the national level, in Luxembourg, for example, the expression UCI OPC has a more limited scope than at the EU level: it covers UCITS *and* 'other UCIs'. The latter are AIFs according to EU law. There

1. The expressions are synonyms. In the French version of the relevant EU Directives (*see infra*, §1.02[A]), there is a unified reference to *organismes de placement collectif* (OPC); the term 'collective investment schemes' (CIS) is also used to mean a UCI or CIU.
2. Regarding European investment funds law in English, *see*, notably: Claude Kremer & Isabelle Lebbe, *Collective Investment Schemes in Luxembourg* (2d ed., Oxford University Press 2014); Niamh Moloney, *EU Securities and Financial Markets Regulations* (Oxford EC Law, 2d ed., 2014); *The Alternative Investment Fund Managers Directive* (Dirk A. Zetzsche ed., International Banking and Finance Law Series, 2d ed. 2015); *Alternative Investment Funds in Europe* (Lodewijk Van Setten & Danny Busch eds, Oxford University Press, 2014); *Alternative Investment Fund* Regulation (Eddy Wymeersch ed., Wolters Kluwer, 2012).
3. Regarding the different Directives, *see infra*, §1.02[A].
4. The expression 'mutual funds', which is sometimes used as a synonym for UCITS, should be limited to its relevant field - that is, US law.
5. For the definitional criteria, *see infra*, §1.03[C][2].

are other types of Luxembourg AIFs, grounded on the different laws that created them,[6] such as Luxembourg Specialized Investment Funds (SIFs) (*'fonds d'investissement spécialisés'* or *FIS*), risk capital investment funds (*'sociétés d'investissement en capital à risque'* or *SICARs*), and Reserved Alternative Investment Funds (RAIFs) (*'fonds d'investissement alternatifs réservés'* or *FIAR*). However, some of those SIFs and SICARs do not fulfil the EU's AIFs criteria,[7] so they must be characterized as non-AIFs.[8] These national investment funds are regulated (i.e., their legal regime is grounded on a law that establishes a more or less detailed framework). An investment fund can be supervised (i.e., authorized, registered, and supervised) or not[9] by the national competent authority; in Luxembourg, that is the *Commission de surveillance du secteur financier* (CSSF). Apart from regulated investment funds, there are also unregulated[10] – and unsupervised – investment 'vehicles',[11] which are not technically investment funds within the meaning of EU law (i.e., they are not UCIs); they are structured under the provision of company law or civil contract law.[12] Investment funds must also be technically separated from Institution for Occupational Retirement Provisions (IORP), so-called pension funds,[13] and securitization vehicles,[14] even if these different vehicles are structured according to a similar legal pattern.

6. Regarding the different laws, *see infra*, §1.02[B].
7. *See infra*, §1.03[C][2].
8. *See infra*, §1.02[B].
9. For example, RAIFs.
10. The concept of an 'unregulated' fund must be handled with care, as there might be different understandings of the word, depending on what, exactly, is regulated and to what extent (e.g., the 'product' or its 'actors', such as its manager and its depositary).
11. The word 'vehicle' is preferable to the word 'fund'.
12. There are unregulated and unsupervised instruments in Luxembourg: *sociétés de participation financières* (SOPARFIs) and securitization vehicles that are neither UCITS nor AIFs nor specific investment funds. A SOPARFI is an ordinary commercial company governed by the 1915 Law on commercial companies used for managing holdings and for financing and holding venture capital and private equity investments. The securitization vehicles, which do not fall into the scope of the Law of 22 March 2004 on securitization, as amended, can be constituted either as a company under 1915 Law or as a fund under the co-ownership regime.
13. *See* Directive (EU) 2016/2341 of the European Parliament and of the Council of 14 December 2016 on the activities and supervision of institutions for occupational retirement provisions (IORPs) [2016] OJ L 354/37 (the 'IRP II Directive').
14. According to Art. 1 of the Law of 22 March 2004, securitization means:

> the transaction by which a securitisation undertaking acquires or assumes, directly or through another undertaking, risks relating to claims, other assets, or obligations assumed by third parties or inherent to all or part of the activities of third parties and issues securities, whose value or yield depends on such risks.

Securitization special purpose entities are expressly excluded from the scope of Directive 2011/61/EU of the European Parliament and of the Council of 8 June 2011 on Alternative Investment Fund Managers and amending Directives 2003/41/EC and 2009/65/EC and Regulations (EC) No 1060/2009 and (EU) No 1095/2010 (Text with EEA relevance) [2011] OJ L 174/1, as amended (hereinafter the 'AIFM Directive'), Art. 2(3)(g). It means entities whose sole purpose is to carry on a securitization or securitizations within the meaning of Art. 1(2) of Regulation (EC) No 24/2009 of the European Central Bank of 19 December 2008 concerning statistics on the assets and liabilities of financial vehicle corporations engaged in securitization transactions and other activities which are appropriate to accomplish that purpose.

At first glance, an investment fund is an entity[15] that hosts one or more portfolios. The investment fund collects money from investors and issues a corresponding number of units or shares in exchange therefore.[16] Because its units or shares are marketed on an internal or cross-border basis, an investment fund is considered by extension as an investment 'product'. The money that has been raised from the investors is collectively[17] invested by a manager,[18] on behalf and in the best - and sole - interest of the investors, in different type of assets (e.g., financial instruments and/or goods), according to the investing policy and the category in which the fund belong, and its legal regime, namely UCITS or AIF. The portfolio of investments is managed according to a defined investment policy that integrates different degrees of risk-spreading and investment strategies. The assets that comprise the fund's portfolio are obligatorily deposited with a depositary for safekeeping.[19]

Investment funds may also have different economic purposes. From an investor point of view, an investment fund is, above all, a profit-making investment 'product', even if for certain categories of funds investing according to extra-financial criteria, there is another dimension (e.g., investors in an Islamic fund may also be interested in the respect of *Sharia'h* rules). The fund units can be integrated as part of the portfolio of the investor managed on an individual and discretionary basis by a financial service provider, and such a portfolio can also be part of a wider wealth management strategy. Investment funds are also a source of project financing in different sectors of the economy. A company in need of money will proceed to a capital increase or a bond issue. The subscription of the shares or bonds by a fund will thus bring money to the company. Therefore, an important use of investment funds is venture capital and private equity. The use of long-term investment funds is another means to finance infrastructures such as transport infrastructures, sustainable energy generation or distribution, social infrastructure (schools, social housing, or hospitals). Social impact funds also make possible to finance actors of the social business sector, which may otherwise face difficulties in accessing credit. Another sector is that of microfinance, where microfinance funds invest in microfinance institutions, providing them with the money needed to grant micro-credits. This important financial role of the investment funds explains why the public authorities are so interested to control the risks of shadow banking created by certain types of funds such as money market funds (MMFs) and hedge funds[20] and in particular with regards to systemic risk.

15. Regarding its legal form, *see infra*, §1.03[A].
16. It depends on the legal form of the fund.
17. The collective dimension makes an important difference with individual/discretionary portfolio management which is a financial service under Directive 2014/65/EU of the European Parliament and of the Council of 15 May 2014 on markets in financial instruments and amending Directive 2002/92/EC and Directive 2011/61/EU (Text with EEA relevance), as amended (hereinafter 'MiFID II').
18. The external manager (a management company) of an investment fund is considered an 'actor' of the fund, in contrast to the 'product' (its units and, by extension, the entity itself). *See infra*, §1.04[B][2].
19. *See infra*, §1.04[A][2].
20. Hedge funds make use of alternative and sophisticated investment strategies by using of short selling, derivatives and increased leverage, pursuing absolute returns rather than measuring their performance to a benchmark.

According to Luxembourg for Finance, Luxembourg is the 'leading investment fund centre in Europe and second only in the world behind the United States'.[21] Regularly, the CSSF published statistics on Luxembourg investments funds. At the end of November 2017,[22] the total number of UCIs was 4,068: 1,864 UCITS, 325 other UCIs,[23] 1,591 SIFs, and 288 SICARs. As to their legal form, the breakdown was as of that date: 2,208 SICAVs, 1,527 FCPs, 45 other UCIs/SIFs, and 288 SICARs. The total assets under management were EUR 4,135.199 billion.[24]

After presenting the source of investment fund law (§1.02), it will be appropriate to specify the main rules for the creation of an investment fund (§1.03), and those relating to its life (§1.04).

§1.02 SOURCES OF INVESTMENT FUND LAW

The legal nature of the investment funds closely depends on their legal regime: regulated investment funds are structured under legal framework defined at the European [A] and national levels [B]. Apart from EU Directives and regulations, the importance of soft law from public[25] and private[26] source at the international, European, and national levels in this field must be underlined.

[A] European Union

At the EU and national level, two categories of investment funds are regulated and supervised: Undertakings for Collective Investment in Transferable Securities (UCITS) and AIFs. Both are gathered under the category of UCIs, namely investment funds. These categories coexist in national law along with domestic regulated investment vehicles that are neither UCITS nor AIFs.

21. http://www.luxembourgforfinance.com/fr/produits-services/fonds-dinvestissement.
22. *See* www.cssf.lu.
23. Part II of the Law of 17 December 2017.
24. Breakdown according to applicable law (in EUR billion): 3,469.422 for UCITS (Part I of 2010 Law), 155.343 UCIs (Part II of 2010 Law), 465.954 SIF, 45 080 SICAR; breakdown according to legal form: 3,204.085 for SICAVs, 860.164 for FCPs, 26.470 for Other UCIs/SIFs, and 45.080 for SICARs.
25. For instance, the recommendations and opinion issued by international, European, and national institution sur as IOSCO (International Organization of Securities Commissions), ESMA (Level-3 Guidelines), and by the national competent authorities (in Luxembourg, CSSF circulars).
26. *See* the governance codes and best practice recommendations issued by the 'European Fund and Asset Management Association (EFAMA)', the 'Association of the Luxembourg Fund Industry' (ALFI); 'investment company institute' (ICI) and governance codes published by management companies.

In European law, investment funds law is articulated around two Directives – under the Lamfalussy process – and their respective execution measures.[27] The Level 1 Directives are the so-called UCITS Directive[28] and the AIFM Directive.

Moreover, several stand-alone European regulations have been adopted in the field of investment funds, establishing uniform rules applicable to certain categories of investment funds: Regulation (EU) n° 345/2013 of the European Parliament and of the Council of 17 April 2013 on European venture capital funds[29] and Regulation (EU) n° 346/2013 of the European Parliament and of the Council of 17 April 2013 on European social entrepreneurship funds,[30] which lay down harmonized requirements and condition for managers and European cross-border marketing of UCIs under the designation 'EuVECA' and 'EuSEF'. Furthermore, Regulation (EU) n° 2015/760 of the European Parliament and of the Council of 29 April 2015 on European long-term investment funds[31] provides a harmonized framework for management and cross-border marketing of funds named 'ELTIFs', which are designed to procure long-term financing for infrastructure projects, unlisted companies and listed small- and mid-sized companies (SMEs) that issue equity of debt instruments. A final regulation is a transversal EU regulation applicable to UCITS, AIFs, and their managers: Regulation (EU) n° 2017/1131 of the European Parliament and of the Council of 14 June 2017 on money market funds (MMFs).[32] This harmonization regulation aims to enhance the stability of MMFs as a source of short-term financing for both the government and the corporate sectors across the Union and would also ensure that MMFs remain a reliable tool for the cash management needs of industry in the Union.

Finally, other EU Directives and regulations that are not specifically dedicated to UCIs may nevertheless be applied to them. These are, notably: MiFID II;[33] Directive 2000/31/EC (the 'Electronic Commerce Directive'); Directive (EU) 2002/65/EC (the 'Distance Marketing Directive'); Directive (EU) 2005/29/EC (the 'Unfair Commercial Practices Directive'); Directive 2014/57/EU (the 'Market Abuse Directive II' – MAD II); Directive (UE) 2015/849 (the 'Anti-Money Laundering Directive IV' or MLD); Directive (EU) 2007/36/EC, as amended (the 'Shareholders' Rights Directive'); Directive (EU) 2002/47/EC, as amended (the 'Collateral Directive'); Regulation (UE) n° 1286/2014 (the 'PRIIPs Regulation'); and Regulation (EU) n° 648/2012, as amended (the 'Securities Financing Transaction Regulation'). On the other hand, other Directives expressly or implicitly exclude UCIs or some of them from their scope. For instance, Directives (EU) 2003/71/EC as amended (the 'Prospectus Directive') and Directive 2004/109/CE as amended (the 'Transparency Directive') both exclude open-ended

27. As regard to the limited content of the present chapter, the different Level-2 execution measures (i.e., EU directives or regulations) will be referenced below when necessary.
28. Directive 2009/65/EC of the European Parliament and of the Council of 13 July 2009 on the coordination of laws, regulations and administrative provisions relating to undertakings for collective investment in transferable securities (UCITS) [2009] OJ L 302/32, as amended (hereinafter 'UCITS Directive').
29. [2013] OJ L 115/1.
30. [2013] OJ L 115/18.
31. [2015] OJ L 123/98.
32. [2017] OJ L 169/8.
33. *Supra* note 17.

funds (i.e., UCITS and certain AIFs). Directive (EU) 2005/56/EC (the 'Cross-Border Mergers Directive') expressly excludes UCITS from its scope, as that there is a specific regime in the UCITS Directive.

[B] Luxembourg

At the national level, Luxembourg UCITS are regulated by Part 1 of the Law of 17 December 2010 on Undertakings for Collective Investment, as amended, which transposes the UCITS Directive.[34] This text is completed by (a) CSSF Regulation n° 10-04 transposing Commission Directive 2010/43/EU of 1 July 2010 implementing Directive 2009/65/EC of the European Parliament and of the Council as regards organizational requirements, conflicts of interest, conduct of business, risk management, and content of the agreement between a depositary and a management company, and (b) CSSF Regulation n° 10-05 transposing Commission Directive 2010/44/EU of 1 July 2010 implementing Directive 2009/65/EC of the European Parliament and of the Council as regards certain provisions concerning fund mergers, master-feeder structures, and notification procedure.

Luxembourg investment funds that do not comply with the UCITS Directive are regulated by a different set of rules. The AIFM Directive was implemented by the Law of 12 July 2013 on alternative investment funds managers.[35] This law amends different pre-existing laws organizing a specific and tailored legal framework for some investment vehicles. These are: Part II of the Law of 17 December 2010; the Law of 15 June

34. *Loi du 17 décembre 2010 concernant les organismes de placement collectif*, as amended (hereinafter the 'Law of 17 December 2010'). All Luxembourg texts relating to UCIs are available at www.cssf.lu.

35. *Loi du 12 juillet 2013 relative aux gestionnaires de fonds d'investissement alternatifs et - portant transposition de la directive 2011/61/UE du Parlement européen et du Conseil du 8 juin 2011 sur les gestionnaires de fonds d'investissement alternatifs et modifiant les directives 2003/41/CE et 2009/65/CE ainsi que les règlements (CE) n° 1060/2009 et (UE) n° 1095/2010; portant modification: de la loi modifiée du 17 décembre 2010 concernant les organismes de placement collectif; de la loi modifiée du 13 février 2007 relative aux fonds d'investissement spécialisés; de la loi modifiée du 15 juin 2004 relative à la société d'investissement en capital à risque (SICAR); de la loi modifiée du 13 juillet 2005 relative aux institutions de retraite professionnelle sous forme de société d'épargne-pension à capital variable (SEPCAV) et d'association d'épargne-pension (ASSEP); de la loi du 13 juillet 2005 concernant les activités et la surveillance des institutions de retraite professionnelle; de la loi modifiée du 5 avril 1993 relative au secteur financier; de la loi modifiée du 12 novembre 2004 relative à la lutte contre le blanchiment et contre le financement du terrorisme; de la loi modifiée du 23 décembre 1998 portant création d'une commission de surveillance du secteur financier; de la loi modifiée du 10 août 1915 concernant les sociétés commerciales; de la loi modifiée du 19 décembre 2002 concernant le registre de commerce et des sociétés ainsi que la comptabilité et les comptes annuels des entreprises; du Code de commerce; de la loi modifiée du 4 décembre 1967 concernant l'impôt sur le revenu; de la loi modifiée du 1er décembre 1936 concernant l'impôt commercial; de la loi modifiée d'adaptation fiscale du 16 octobre 1934; de la loi modifiée du 16 octobre 1934 sur l'évaluation des biens et valeurs; et de la loi modifiée du 12 février 1979 concernant la taxe sur la valeur ajoutée*, as amended (hereinafter the 'Law of 12 July 2013').

2004 (creating SICARs);[36] the Law of 13 February 2007 (creating SIFs);[37] and the Law of 23 July 2016 (relating to RAIFs).[38] As a result, some of the regulated investment vehicles in Luxembourg are non-AIFs,[39] because they do not fulfil the criteria for an AIF.[40]

Apart from the different specific laws and regulations, Luxembourg investment funds are subjected to national so-called common law (*droit commun*) if relevant, such as company law, contract law, liability law, insolvency law, and criminal law.

§1.03 CREATION OF AN INVESTMENT FUND

The creation of an investment fund requires the fulfilment of certain conditions relating to the legal structure [A], the location of the funds [B], and to its object [C], minimal financial requirements [D], investors [E], and units or shares [F]. In addition, some of the funds may choose certain mode of organization [G], and be subjected to an authorization or registration procedure [H].

[A] Legal Structures of the Investment Fund

UCITS [1] and AIFs [2] must be distinguished on the basis of their legal structures.

[1] UCITS Legal Structures

The UCITS Directive permits only two legal structures for UCITS: either an investment company or a common fund.[41]

The legal form of a UCITS ruled by its documents of incorporation or by-laws ('*statuts*') as an 'investment company' depends closely on the national law implementing the UCITS Directive.[42] For instance, under Luxembourg's 17 December 2010 Law, an investment company is an open-ended investment company referred to as an investment company with variable capital ('*société d'investissement à capital variable*'

36. *La loi modifiée du 15 juin 2004 relative à la société d'investissement en capital à risque (SICAR)*, as amended (hereinafter the 'Law of 15 June 2014').
37. *Loi du 13 février 2007 relative aux fonds d'investissement spécialisés et portant modification de la loi modifiée du 20 décembre 2002 relative aux organismes de placement collectif, et modification de la loi modifiée du 12 février 1979 concernant la taxe sur la valeur ajoutée*, as amended (hereinafter the 'Law of 13 February 2007').
38. *Loi du 23 juillet 2016 relative aux fonds d'investissement alternatifs réservés et portant modification de: 1. la loi modifiée du 16 octobre 1934 concernant l'impôt sur la fortune; 2. la loi modifiée du 1er décembre 1936 concernant l'impôt commercial communal; 3. la loi modifiée du 4 décembre 1967 concernant l'impôt sur le revenu; 4. la loi modifiée du 5 avril 1993 relative au secteur financier; 5. la loi modifiée du 13 février 2007 relative aux fonds d'investissement spécialisés; et 6. la loi modifiée du 17 décembre 2010 concernant les organismes de placement collectif*, as amended (hereinafter the 'Law of 23 July 2016').
39. There are non-AIF SICARs and non-AIF SIFs.
40. *See infra*, §1.03[C][2].
41. UCITS Directive, Art. 1(3).
42. UCITS Directive, Art. 27(2).

or *SICAV*), which must adopt the legal form of a public limited company (*'société anonyme'* or *SA*),[43] which has legal personality. A SICAV must either appoint a management company to manage its portfolio or designate itself as 'self-managed'.[44]

The second legal structure for a UCITS is the 'contractual form' of common fund (*'fonds commun de placement'* or *FCP*). Unit trusts are assimilated to FCPs.[45] As common funds do not have the legal personality, they always require a separate management company. That management company acts on behalf of the collectivity of investors under the co-ownership regime.[46] Common funds are ruled by their 'rules' or 'regulations', which have a contractual nature.

[2] AIF Legal Structures

In contrast, AIFs may adopt any kind of legal structure:[47] they can be constituted 'under contract' as common funds or unit trust law, 'under statutes' as investment companies (e.g., a SICAV or an investment company with fixed capital (*'société d'investissement à capital fixe'* or *SICAF*), or under any other legal structure permitted under national AIF law.[48] Luxembourg AIFs may adopt different legal forms of investment company depending on the type of AIF at issue. For instance, according to Article 93 of the Law of 17 December 2010 (Part II), a UCI-SICAV must adopt the form of a public limited company (SA), but its Article 97 (and following) applies to all companies and all undertakings other than FCPs and SICAVs. According to Article 25 of the Law of 13 February 2007, Article 1 of the Law of 15 June 2004, and Article 23 of the Law of 23 July 2016, respectively, an investment company – a SICAV or other investment company – may adopt one of the following forms: a public limited company (SA), a partnership limited by shares (*'société en commandite par actions'* or *SCA*), a limited partnership (*'société en commandite simple'* or *SCS*), a special limited partnership (*'société en commandite spéciale'* or *SCSp*), a limited company (*'société à responsabilité limitée'* or *SARL*), or a cooperative in the form of a public limited company (*'société coopérative organisée sous forme de société anonyme'* or *CoopSA*).

[B] Location of the Investment Fund

UCITS must all be established in a Member State or in a member of European Economic Area (EEA).[49] The registered office of the investment company must be situated in the investment company's home Member State.[50]

43. Law of 17 December 2010, Arts 25, 27(2).
44. The SICAV managed by its own management bodies (i.e., its *conseil d'administration* (board of directors) or its *Directoire* (management board), *see infra*, §1.04[B][1].
45. UCITS Directive, Art. 1(3)(a).
46. *See* Law of 17 December 2010, Art. 5.
47. AIFM Directive, Art. 2(2).
48. *See* Law of 12 July 2013, Art. 2(1).
49. The UCITS depositary must be also established in the UCITS Member State, but not of its management company.
50. UCITS Directive, Art. 27(3).

The AIFM Directive includes both EU and non-EU AIFs in its scope:[51] the location of the AIF is irrelevant for purposes of the AIF definition. According to Luxembourg law, for instance, the Law of 17 of December 2010:

> A UCI shall be deemed to be established in Luxembourg if the registered office of the management company of the common fund or the registered office of the investment company is established in Luxembourg. The head office shall be located in Luxembourg.[52]

The same solution applies to investment companies under the legal regime of SIFs[53] and of RAIFs.[54] The solution derives from Article(1)(1)(k),[55] which defines an 'EU AIF' as:

(i) an AIF which is authorised or registered in a Member State under the applicable national law; or
(ii) an AIF which is not authorised or registered in a Member State, but has its registered office and/or head office in a Member State.

[C] Object of the Investment Fund

[1] UCITS

A UCITS is an undertaking with the sole object of collective investment in transferable securities or in other liquid financial assets of capital raised from the public and which operate on the principle of risk spreading.[56]

[2] AIF

Regarding AIFs, the AIFM Directive specifies that AIFs are CIUs that 'raise capital from a number of investors, with a view to investing it in accordance with a defined investment policy for the benefit of those investors'.[57] ESMA's *Guidelines on Key Concepts of the AIFMD*[58] provide the essential characteristics for each element of this definition. To qualify as a CIU thereunder, (a) the undertaking must not have a general commercial or industrial purpose;[59] (b) the undertaking must pool together the capital raised from its investors for the purpose of investment with a view to generating a

51. AIFM Directive, Art. 4(1)(k); In Luxembourg, *see* Law of 12 July 2013, Art. 1 (35), (40), (41).
52. Article 88 [CSSF translation].
53. Law of 13 February 2007, Art. 3.
54. Law of 23 July 2016, Art. 3.
55. *See* Law of 12 July 2013, Art. 1(40).
56. UCITS Directive, Art. 1(2)(a). *See, infra*, §1.04[B][2].
57. AIFM Directive, Art. 4(1)(a)(ii).
58. 24 May 2013 | ESMA/2013/600, Annex III (hereinafter, the 'ESMA 2013 Guidelines').
59. By commercial or industrial purpose, ESMA means:

> pursuing a business strategy which includes characteristics such as running predominantly: (i) a commercial activity, involving the purchase, sale and/or exchange of

pooled return for those investors; and (c) the undertaking's unitholders or shareholders - as a collective group - must have no day-to-day discretion or control over the undertaking.[60] Moreover, with respect to the obligation for the CIU to have the goal of generating a pool return for those investors, the term 'pool return' is defined by ESMA as:

> the return generated by the pooled risk arising from acquiring, holding or selling investment assets - including the activities to optimize or increase the value of these assets - irrespective of whether different returns to investors, such as under a tailored dividend policy, are generated.[61]

Regarding the 'raising of capital', those same guidelines specify that:

> the commercial activity of taking direct or indirect steps by an undertaking or a person or entity acting on its behalf ... to procure the transfer or commitment of capital by one or more investors to the undertaking for the purpose of investing it in accordance with a defined investment policy should amount to the activity of raising capital.[62]

The activity can take place only once, on several occasions or on an ongoing basis. The transfer or commitment of capital takes the form of subscriptions in cash or in kind. When capital is invested in an undertaking by a member of a pre-existing group, for the investment of whose private wealth the undertaking has been exclusively established (i.e., a family office[63]), this is not to be within the scope of raising capital.[64] The manager of the AIF must respect a 'defined investment policy' (i.e., the policy about how the pooled capital in the undertaking is to be managed to generate a pooled return for the investors). ESMA further specifies the factors that would, singly or cumulatively, tend to indicate the existence of such a policy, notably the investment policy is determined and fixed, at the latest by the time that investors' commitments to the undertaking become binding on them.[65] The competent authority appreciates on a case-by-case basis if the undertaking fulfils the criteria.

Some AIFMs are exempted from the scope of the AIFM Directive[66] and so are the AIFs they manage. The AIFM Directive is not applicable to AIFMs insofar as they manage one or more AIFs whose only investors are the AIFM or its parent undertakings or its own subsidiaries or the subsidiaries of its parent undertakings, provided that none of those investors is itself an AIF. Moreover, some AIFM whose assets under

---

goods or commodities and/or the supply of non-financial services, or (ii) an industrial activity, involving the production of goods or construction of properties, or (iii) a combination thereof.

Ibid., at 29.

60. 'The fact that one or more but not all of the aforementioned unitholders or shareholders are granted day-to-day discretion or control should not be taken to show that the undertaking is not a collective investment undertaking.' *Ibid.*, at 31 (para. 12(c)).
61. *Ibid.*, at 29.
62. *Ibid.*, at 32 (para. 13).
63. *See also* AIFM Directive, Recital 7.
64. *See* ESMA 2013 Guidelines, at 32 (para. 15).
65. *See ibid.*, at 33 (paras 20–22).
66. AIFM Directive, Art. 3(1).

management remain under certain thresholds[67] – a *de minimis* amount – the AIFM Directive is only partially applicable.[68] Nevertheless, an AIFM has the right to opt in for a complete application of the AIFM Directive and, thus, benefit from the passports, but when they do, they are obligated to comply with all the of the AIFM Directive's requirements.[69]

The AIFM Directive expressly excludes from its scope certain entities: (a) holding companies; (b) institutions for occupational retirement provision which are covered by Directive 2003/41/EC (including, where applicable, the authorized entities responsible for managing such institutions and acting on their behalf referred to in Article 2(1) of that Directive or the investment managers appointed pursuant to Article 19(1) of that Directive, insofar as they do not manage AIFs); (c) supranational institutions, such as the European Central Bank, the European Investment Bank, the European Investment Fund, the European Development Finance Institutions and bilateral development banks, the World Bank, the International Monetary Fund, and other supranational institutions and similar international organizations, if such institutions or organizations manage AIFs and only insofar as those AIFs act in the public interest; (d) national central banks; (e) national, regional, and local governments and bodies or other institutions that manage funds supporting social security and pension systems; (f) employee participation schemes or employee savings schemes; (g) securitization special purpose entities.[70]

[D] Minimal Financial Requirements to Create an Investment Fund

The UCITS and AIF Directives only specify the minimal financial conditions of the management companies (EUR 125,000) and the self-managed investment companies (EUR 300,000).

National laws determine the minimal financial conditions for the different type of funds. For instance, in Luxembourg, regarding UCITS, Article 23 of the Law of 17 December 2010, says that:

---

67. *Ibid.*

> (a) AIFMs which either directly or indirectly, through a company with which the AIFM is linked by common management or control, or by a substantive direct or indirect holding, manage portfolios of AIFs whose assets under management, including any assets acquired through use of leverage, in total do not exceed a threshold of EUR 100 million; or
>
> (b) AIFMs which either directly or indirectly, through a company with which the AIFM is linked by common management or control, or by a substantive direct or indirect holding, manage portfolios of AIFs whose assets under management in total do not exceed a threshold of EUR 500 million when the portfolios of AIFs consist of AIFs that are unleveraged and have no redemption rights exercisable during a period of 5 years following the date of initial investment in each AIF.

68. *Ibid.*, Art. 3(2) & (3). They are only subjected to registration and not to authorization of their home competent authority, and to provide some information on the investment strategies of the AIF they manage. Their AIF do not need to have a depositary. The Member State may nevertheless adopt stricter rules for these AIFM according to AIFM Directive, Art. 3(3).
69. AIFM Directive, Art. 3(4).
70. *Ibid.*, Art. 2(3).

> The net assets of a common fund may not be less than one million two hundred and fifty thousand euro (EUR 1,250,000). / This minimum shall be reached within a period of six months following the authorisation of the common fund. / A CSSF regulation may increase this minimum amount up to a maximum of two million five hundred thousand euro (EUR 2,500,000).

According to Article 27(1):

> The minimum capital of a SICAV which has not designated a management company may not be less than three hundred thousand euro (EUR 300,000) at the time of authorisation. The capital of any SICAV including SICAVs which have designated a management company shall reach one million two hundred and fifty thousand euro (EUR 1,250,000) within a period of 6 months following the authorisation of the SICAV. A CSSF regulation may raise those minimum amounts up to a respective maximum of six hundred thousand euro (EUR 600,000) and two million five hundred thousand euro (EUR 2,500,000).

Regarding the SIF, Article 21 of the Law of 13 February 2007 indicates that:

> The net assets of a common fund may not be less than one million two hundred fifty thousand Euro (1,250,000 Euro). /This minimum must be reached within a period of twelve months following the authorisation of the common fund. A grand-ducal regulation may increase such minimum amount up to a maximum of two million five hundred thousand Euro (2,500,000 Euro).

[E] Investors of the Investment Fund

UCITS and AIF population of investors may be distinguished according to the categories of investors [1], their number [2], even if they have the same rights [3] among the same category.

[1] Categories of Investors

UCITS are not dedicated to a certain type of investors. According to the UCITS Directive, the capital of a UCITS is raised from 'the public'.[71] Investment is not restricted to a certain category of investors. Investors can therefore be non-professional (retail) or professional – which is considered to be a professional client or may, on request, be treated as a professional client within the meaning of Annex II to MiFID II.[72]

---

71. *Ibid.*, Art. 1(2).
72. *See* MiFID II, Annex II, *Professional Clients for the Purpose of this Directive,* Section 1:

> The following shall be regarded as professionals in all investment services and activities and financial instruments for the purposes of the Directive ...
>
> 1. Entities which are required to be authorized or regulated to operate in the financial markets. ... (a) Credit institutions; (b) Investment Firms; (c) Other authorized or regulated financial institutions; (d) Insurance companies ; (e) Collective investment schemes and management companies of such schemes; (f) Pension funds and management companies of such funds; (g) Commodity and commodity derivatives dealers; (h) Locals; (i) Other institutional investors.

Some of them may also be characterized as consumers within the meaning and for application of consumer law (e.g., for unfair trade practices).

By contrast, in principle, AIFs are dedicated to 'professional investors' only. By exception, Member States may allow AIFM to market a certain type of AIF to retail investors.[73] In such case, the Member State may impose stricter requirements on the AIFM or the AIF than the requirements applicable to the AIFs marketed to professional investors in their territory in accordance with the Directive. However, the Member State shall not impose stricter or additional requirements on EU AIFs established in another Member State and marketed on a cross-border basis than on AIF marketed domestically. For instance, in Luxembourg, for the other UCIs structured on the basis of the Part II of the Law of 17 December 2010, no restrictions apply as to who may be an investor. In contrary, SIF[74] and RAIF[75] are only dedicated to 'well informed' ('*investisseurs avertis*'), a category which includes institutional investors, professional investors, and any other investor who either invest a minimum of EUR 125,000 or have been assessed by a credit institution, an investment firm, or a management company which certifies the investors' ability to understand the risks associated with investing in the fund.[76]

The national laws or fund rules/by-laws may also impose objective criteria for investor (e.g., a special amount of investment), except from discriminatory ones such as religion (even for so-called faith-based funds such as Islamic funds), age, nationality.

[2] Number of Investors

The number of investors is an important criterion of definition for the funds falling into the scope of the European Directives, since UCITS have to raise capital from 'the public'[77] and AIF from 'a number of investors'.[78] According to the ESMA Guidelines,[79] an AIFM must have at least two investors. Then, single investor structures are not part of the scope of the AIFM Directive. However, the temporary presence of a sole

2. Large undertakings meeting two of the following size requirements, on a company basis: / - balance sheet total: EUR 20 000 000; / - net turnover: EUR 40 000 000; / - own funds: EUR 2 000 000.

3. National and regional governments, public bodies that manage public debt at national or regional level, central banks, international and supranational institutions such as the World Bank, the IMF, the ECB, the EIB and other similar international organizations.

4. Other institutional investors whose main activity is to invest in financial instruments, including entities dedicated to the securitization of assets or other financial transactions.

73. That is, an investor who is not professional.
74. Law of 13 February 2007, Art. 2, *see also* Arts 1, 4, 25.
75. Law of 23 July 2016, Art. 2, *see also* Arts 1, 6.
76. The conditions are not applicable to the directors and other persons who intervene in the management of these funds.
77. UCITS Directive, Art. 1(2)(a).
78. AIFM Directive, Art. 4(1)(a)(i).
79. ESMA 2013/600 Guidelines, at 32 (paras 17–19).

investor[80] and a unique investor through it several investors invest[81] are not considered as a single investor fund and preclude the fund from the scope of the Directive.

There is no maximum number for investors in the UCITS and AIFM Directives. However, the national law or the fund's rules/by-laws can impose an upper limit (e.g., fifty investors).

[3] Investor Rights

The unit-/shareholders of an investment fund have a right to information. For UCITS it covers the pre-contractual information based on the Key Investor Information Document (KIID).[82] In addition, they must have access to the prospectus,[83] the constitutive documents (rules/documents of incorporation), the annual and half-yearly reports,[84] and to the price of the funds units.[85] The AIFM Directive also imposes an important and detailed investor information.[86] All information delivered shall be fair, clear, and not misleading.

The shareholders of a SICAV or SICAF have the right to vote attached to their shares in application of company law, which does not derogate from that of UCITS/AIF. Such a right does not exist in principle in an FCP, since there is no institutional unitholder assembly. But the FCP rules can validly establish an assembly, knowing that its implementation is nevertheless cumbersome.

The right to repurchase and redemption of the investors determines the *summa divisio* between open-ended funds and closed-ended funds. In an open-ended fund, the investors have a right to repurchase – followed by redemption[87] – at all times, at their own and discretionary request. If UCITS are always open-ended funds,[88] AIFs can be open-ended or closed-ended funds depending on national law.[89] By contrast, in a closed-ended fund (e.g., a SICAF), the investors have no right to

80. Subsequent to a sale or the decease of an investor.
81. This targets masters and feeder structures, funds of funds, and sole investor acting as an agent for more than one investor (e.g., nominees).
82. UCITS Directive, Arts 78 et seq.; Commission Regulation (EU) No 583/2010 of 1 July 2010 implementing Directive 2009/65/EC of the European Parliament and of the Council as regard key investor information and conditions to be met when providing key investor information or the prospectus in a durable medium other than paper or by means of a website [2010] OJ L 176/1. The KIID includes appropriate information about the essential characteristics of the UCITS concerned. So that they are reasonably able to understand the nature and the risks of the investment product that is being offered to them and, consequently, to make investment decisions on an informed basis.
83. UCITS Directive, Art. 75.
84. UCITS Directive, Art. 75.
85. UCITS Directive, Art. 76.
86. AIFM Directive, Art. 23.
87. On the basis of the net asset value minus the redemption fee.
88. UCITS Directive, Art. 1(2)(b), 84.
89. AIFM Directive, Art. 2(2).

repurchase/redemption during the life of the fund. The number of units or shares is fixed. They only have the right to sell them or to wait for the liquidation of the fund. One can remark that the characterization of a European closed-ended fund is related neither to the issuing of its units/shares or its number of investors nor to the existing liquidity management tools it uses, such as the suspension of the right to repurchase/redemption, gates, block periods.

Regarding the right to financial distribution, UCITS and AIF may regulate freely the distribution of dividends or other repayments or returns to their investors by way of conditions in the fund's rules/by-laws.

As a general rule of conduct,[90] the investors must in principle be fairly treated by the manager. By exception, the AIFM Directive[91] states that: 'No investor in an AIF shall obtain preferential treatment, unless such preferential treatment is disclosed in the relevant AIF's rules or instruments of incorporation.'

[F] Units or Shares of the Investment Fund

A fund can issue one or different classes of units or shares [1],[92] which are subscribed or bought by the investors on a secondary market. The units or shares can be listed or not [2].

[1] Classes of Units or Shares

An investment fund - or a compartment of an investment fund[93] - can issue different unit or share classes to investors according to the national law or the rules/incorporation documents/by-laws of the fund. They must be described in the fund's information disclosure documents (i.e., prospectus, KIID[94]). For instance, these classes may be subject to different rules for distribution or to different management, subscription, and/or redemption fees. The UCITS Directive does not provide any details as to the different unit/share classes. As a result, there is no common legal framework for them and diversity throughout EU. Therefore, to ensure a harmonized approach on it, ESMA issued an opinion on 30 January 2017 emphasizing principles to be followed.[95]

The minimum unit/share capital depends upon the particular legal form of the fund chosen.

90. UCITS Directive, Art. 14(1); Dir. 2010/43/EU, Arts 22 et seq.; AIFM Directive, Art. 12(1)(f).
91. AIFM Directive, Arts 12(1)(f), and 23(1)(j) (relating information of investors); Delegated Act (UE), n° 231/2013, Art. 23.
92. Funds under company legal form.
93. *See infra*, §1.03[G][1].
94. Key Investor Information Document (KIID) for a UCITS.
95. EMA *Opinion on UCITS Share Classes*, ESMA 34-43-296.

[2] Listed Units or Shares

The funds units/shares can be listed and traded on a stock exchange through a broker-dealer. Those funds (UCITS or AIF) are known as Exchange Traded Funds (ETFs). Most of them are Index Funds.[96]

[G] Investment Funds Specific Organization

Both UCITS and AIF can adopt a specific organization by structuring compartments of investments [1] or be part of a master and feeder structure [2] in order to pool assets, to achieve economy of scales, and to diversify their investment offer.

[1] Compartments of Investments

Irrespective of their legal structure (investment company or common fund) and regime (UCITS or AIF), investment funds can be structured as single legal funds, called 'umbrella funds', composed of several compartments of investment – also known as 'sub-funds'. The 'umbrella fund' is based on a segmentation technique that allows to juxtapose, under a single legal structure and denomination, several types of portfolios, each representing a specific asset allocation or having different management orientations. Each sub-fund constitutes by itself a portfolio of financial instruments that can be analysed as an asset allocation with no legal personality and which is held jointly by its unitholders or shareholders.

The general principle is the structural autonomy of each compartment in terms of authorization or registration – if required – investment policy, financial results, accounting, unit classes, target distribution market, etc. But as a single fund, the umbrella fund must elaborate one regulation or documents of incorporation, one prospectus, and must only appoint one management company[97] and depositary.

[2] Master Funds and Feeder Funds

A 'feeder fund' is an investment fund – or a compartment of investment – which raise capital from its investors, and invest or is exposed in another fund, referred to as the 'master fund'. A feeder fund is a sort of 'fund of fund' that invests mainly in another fund. Under the UCITS Directive, the feeder UCITS must invest at least 85 % of its assets in units or shares of another UCITS.[98] According to the AIFM Directive, a 'feeder AIF':

> means an AIF which: / (i) invests at least 85 % of its assets in units or shares of another AIF (the 'master AIF'); / (ii) invests at least 85 % of its assets in more than

96. *See infra*, §1.04[B][2].
97. If the fund is not a self-managed investment company.
98. UCITS Directive, Art. 58(1).

one master AIFs where those master AIFs have identical investment strategies; or / (iii) has otherwise an exposure of at least 85 % of its assets to such a master AIF.[99]

In order to make it easier for regulators to monitor them, in particular in a cross-border context, a feeder UCITS cannot invest in more than one master UCITS (i.e., the feeder can only have one master). This prohibition is not applicable to AIF.

The master fund is a fund, which has among its unitholders at least one feeder fund.[100] Regarding UCITS, the master fund cannot be itself a feeder in order to prevent cascades or funds. The master fund cannot hold units of a feeder UCITS, either.[101] There are no equivalent rules in the AIFM Directive.

Information-sharing agreements between the depositaries or the auditors, respectively, of the feeder fund and the master fund should ensure the flow of information and documents that is needed for them to fulfil their duties.[102]

As a general principle of functioning, the feeder fund follows the course of its master fund in terms of liquidation and of suspension of the repurchase/redemption or subscription of the units.

[H] Authorization or Registration of the Investment Fund

The authorization delivered by the competent authority of the fund – in Luxembourg the CSSF – makes also a huge difference between UCITS and AIF. UCITS must always be authorized by the competent authority,[103] while AIF can be authorized or not, registered or not,[104] depending on national law. For instance, in Luxembourg, AIF under Part II of the Law of 17 December 2010 Law[105] and the Law of 13 February 2007[106] must be authorized, but RAIFs are not subject to CSSF approval before they are launched.[107]

But, both have the benefit of the European passport for the marketing of their units on a cross-border basis within the EU without any restriction except from a simple notification procedure.[108]

99. AIFM Directive, Art. 4(1)(m).
100. UCITS Directive, Art. 58(3).
101. *Ibid.*
102. Regarding UCITS, *see* UCITS Directive, Art. 58.
103. UCITS Directive, Art. 5.
104. AIFM Directive, Art. 4(1).
105. Law of 17 December 2010, Art. 129, referring to said Art. 87.
106. Law of 13 February 2007, Art. 42.
107. Law of 23 July 2016, Art. 34. The constitution of the fund shall be recorded in a notarial deed within five working days of its constitution.
108. UCITS Directive, Arts 93 et seq.; Commission Regulation (EU) No 584/2010 of 1 July 2010 implementing Directive 2009/65/EC of the European Parliament and of the Council as regard the form and content of the standard notification letter and UCITS attestation, the use of electronic communication between competent authorities for the purpose of notification, and procedures for on-the-spot verifications and investigations and the exchange of information between competent authorities [2010] OJ L 176/16; AIFM Directive, Arts 31, 32, 35.

§1.04 LIFE OF THE INVESTMENT FUND

The UCITS and AIFM Directives contain numerous provisions related to the investment fund life concerning the assets [A], the funds management [B], administration [C] and supervision [E], and the marketing of the funds units or shares [D]. On the contrary, they contain few rules relating to the investment funds end of life [F].

[A] Assets of the Investment Fund

Each UCITS/AIF comprises a portfolio, which is owned by the fund or collectively by the unitholders depending whether the UCITS/AIF has or not the legal personality. The portfolio, which is an undivided collection of assets, contains as a whole the assets that have been subscribed or bought with the capital raised from the investors. The assets must be kept by a depositary [2]. However, not all types of assets are eligible for a UCITS/AIF portfolio [1].

[1] Eligible Assets

The kind of assets an investment fund is allowed to invest in depends on its legal regime, namely UCITS or AIF, and on its investment policy.[109]

Regarding UCITS, the eligible assets in portfolio are clearly defined in the UCITS Directive as: transferable securities (shares, bonds and any other instruments offering the right to acquire these securities through subscription of exchange), money market instruments, units of UCITS and UCIs,[110] bank deposits and cash. For the purpose of investor protection and to insure the investors' repurchase/redemption rights, all the assets must be liquid.[111] Under certain conditions, UCITS may make use of financial derivatives instruments, such as futures, options, swaps based on an eligible UCITS assets or an approved financial index. The UCITS Directive, which defines eligible assets in general terms,[112] has been explained in a Level 2 Directive[113] in order to ensure a common understanding of eligible assets and criteria. For investor protection, the Directive prohibits investment in goods and in precious metals or certificates representing them.[114] However, an investment company (SICAV) may acquire movable or immovable property which is essential for the direct pursuit of its business.[115]

109. In the fund's prospectus.
110. That makes possible the creation of a 'fund of funds'.
111. The liquidity is part of the UCITS definition. Art. 1(2) of the UCITS Directive states that the term 'UCITS means an undertaking: / (a) with the sole object of collective investment in transferable securities or in other liquid financial assets referred to in Article 50(1)'.
112. UCITS Directive, Art. 50. In Luxembourg, *see* Law of 17 December 2010, Art. 41.
113. Commission Directive 2007/16/EC of 19 March 2007 implementing Council Directive 85/611/EEC on the coordination of laws, regulations and administrative provisions relating to undertaking for collective investment in transferable securities (UCITS) as regard the clarification of certain definitions; CESR's guidelines concerning eligible assets for investment by UCITS, March 2007, Ref: CESR/07-044.
114. UCITS Directive, Art. 50(2). In Luxembourg, *see* Law of 17 December 2010, Art. 41(2).
115. UCITS Directive, Art. 50(3). In Luxembourg, *see* Law of 17 December 2010, Art. 41(3).

The Directive either prohibits certain transactions. These are: short selling,[116] loans (with exception),[117] leverage,[118] and personal guarantees.[119]

By contrast, there is no special requirement regarding the eligible assets of an AIF in the AIFM Directive, which does not regulate the product (AIF). In theory, all goods in trade can be eligible to an AIF portfolio: movable assets such as financial instruments, art, wine, commodities, precious metals or stones etc., immovable properties (for real estate funds), derivatives. The only element is the duty of the manager to specify the level of leverage of its funds under management.[120] National laws may - or may not[121] - demand different types of assets (e.g., financial instruments, goods, or commodities) for different types of AIF (e.g., hedge funds, private equity funds, real estate funds, art funds, and cinema funds).

[2] Safekeeping of the Assets

Every investment fund has to appoint a single depositary among a list of eligible entities, such as credit institutions,[122] investment firms having their registered office in the Union, or another category of institution that is subject to prudential regulation and ongoing supervision, etc.[123] determined at the EU level by the UCITS and AIFM Directives implemented in the national law related to investment funds.[124] In order to avoid conflicts of interest, no company may act as both manager/SICAV and depositary.[125]

The UCITS Directive - as amended by the Directive 2014/91/EU of the European Parliament and of the Council of 23 July 2004, so-called UCITS V Directive - and the AIFM Directive, and their respective Level 2 execution measures,[126] precisely define the functions of the depositary: safekeeping, oversight, and cash monitoring.[127]

116. UCITS Directive, Art. 89. In Luxembourg, *see* Law of 17 December 2010, Art. 52.
117. UCITS Directive, Art. 88(1). In Luxembourg, *see* Law of 17 December 2010, Art. 51(1).
118. UCITS Directive, Art. 51(3) ('A UCITS shall ensure that its global exposure relating to derivative instruments does not exceed the total net value of its portfolio.')
119. UCITS Directive, Art. 88(1). In Luxembourg, *see* Law of 17 December 2010, Art. 51(1).
120. UCITS Directive, Art. 15. In Luxembourg, *see* Law of 12 July 2013, Art. 14.
121. For instance, in Luxembourg there is no specification.
122. In Luxembourg according to the Law of 17 December 2010, only a credit institution can be appointed as for UCITS and UCIs structured on the basis of this text (*see* Arts 1, 17, 33, 88(3)).
123. For more information regarding UCITS depositaries, *see* UCITS Directive, Art. 23; regarding AIF depositaries, *see* AIFM Directive, Art. 21(3).
124. In Luxembourg, *see* Law of 17 December 2010, Arts 1, 17, and 33 (UCITS) and Art. 88-3 (other UCIs); Law of 2013, Art. 19(3); Law of 12 July 2013, Art. 19(5); Law of 13 February 2017, Arts 19, 34, 81; Law of 26 July 2016, Art. 5(3).
125. Regarding UCITS, *see* UCITS Directive, Art. 25; regarding AIF, *see* AIFM Directive, Art. 21(4). In Luxembourg, for instance regarding UCITS, *see* Law of 17 December 2010, Arts 20, 37; for AIFs, *see* Law of 12 July 2013, Art. 19(4).
126. Commission Delegated Regulation (EU) 2016/438 on 17 December 2015, supplementing Directive 2009/65/EC of the European Parliament and of the Council as regard to obligations of depositaries; The Commission Delegated Regulation (EU) No 231/2013 of 19 December 2012 supplementing Directive 2011/61/EU of the European Parliament and of the Council with regard to exemptions, general operating conditions, depositaries, leverage, transparency and supervision.
127. As regard to oversight and cash monitoring duties, *see infra*, §1.04[E][2].

Safekeeping[128] means two different things according to the nature of the fund's assets. For financial instruments that can be held in custody – physically or in a financial instruments account – the depositary must hold them in custody. It must ensure that all financial instruments that can be registered in a financial instrument's account are registered in the depositary's books within segregated accounts in accordance with the principles set out in Article 16 of Directive 2006/73/EC, opened in the name of the management company acting on behalf of the common fund, so that they can be clearly identified as belonging to the common fund in accordance with the applicable law at all times. For 'other assets' such as cash, derivatives contracts, goods, the safekeeping duty of the depositary is limited to the ownership verification and a record keeping of those assets. The depositary must provide the management company, on a regular basis, with a comprehensive inventory of all of the assets of the investment fund. The depositary of AIF shall not reuse the assets without the prior consent of the AIF or the AIFM acting on behalf of the AIF.[129] By contrast, the depositary of a UCITS cannot reuse the assets, except if the reuse is executed for the account of the UCITS on the instructions of its management company and for the benefit of the UCITS or its unitholders and the transaction is covered by high-quality and liquid collateral received by the UCITS under a title transfer arrangement.[130]

Safekeeping is the only function that a depositary can delegate to a third party according to the provisions of the UCITS and AIFM Directives.[131] These Directives detailed the regime of the delegation.[132]

The depositary's liability regime depends on the type of loss suffered by the UCITS/AIF and/or the investors. In case of loss of financial instruments held in custody,[133] the depositary has to return instruments of identical type or the corresponding amount to the UCITS/AIF without undue delay.[134] The only way to escape from its liability is to invoke an 'external event'.[135] The depositary is also liable for any other

128. Regarding UCITS depositaries, *see* UCITS Directive, Art. 22(5); Del. Reg. (UE) n° 2016/438, Art. 13; regarding AIF depositaries, *see* AIFM Directive, Art. 21(8); Del. Reg. (UE) n° 231/2013, Art. 88. In Luxembourg, regarding UCITS depositaries, *see* Law of 17 December 2010, Art. 18(4), 34(3); regarding AIF depositaries, *see* Law of 12 July 2013, Art. 19(8); regarding SIFs, *see* Law of 13 February 2007, Arts 16, 33.
129. AIFM Directive, Art. 21(10)(3). In Luxembourg, *see* Law of 12 July 2013, Art. 19(10), clause 3.
130. UCITS Directive, Art. 22(7). In Luxembourg, *see* Law of 17 December 2010, Art. 18(6).
131. Regarding UCITS depositaries, *see* UCITS Directive, Art. 22a; Del. Reg. (UE) n° 2016/438, Art. 15; regarding AIF depositaries, *see* AIFM Directive, Art. 21(11); Del. Reg. (UE) n° 231/2013, Art. 98. In Luxembourg law, regarding UCITS depositaries, *see* Law of 17 December 2017, Arts 19(a) and 34(a); regarding AIF depositaries, *see* Law of 12 July 2013, Art. 19(11).
132. Regarding UCITS depositaries, *see* UCITS Directive, Art. 22; Del. Reg. (UE) n° 2016/438, Art. 15; regarding AIF depositaries, *see* AIFM Directive, Art. 21(11); Del. Reg. (UE) n° 231/2013, Art. 98. In Luxembourg, regarding UCITS depositaries, *see* Law of 17 December 2017, Arts 18, 34; regarding AIF depositaries, *see* Law of 12 July 2003, Art. 18.
133. For the definition of the loss, regarding UCITS depositaries, *see* Del. Reg. (UE) n° 2016/438, Art. 18; regarding AIF depositaries, *see* Del. Reg. (UE) n° 231/2013, Art. 100.
134. Regarding UCITS depositaries, *see* UCITS Directive, Art. 22a; regarding AIF depositaries, *see* AIFM Directive, Art. 21(11). In Luxembourg, regarding UCITS depositaries, *see* Law of 17 December 2010, Arts 19(1) and 35(1); regarding AIF depositaries, *see* Law of 12 July 2013, Art. 19(11).
135. 'External event beyond its reasonable control, the consequences of which would have been unavoidable despite all reasonable efforts to the contrary'; For the definition of the 'external

loss[136] suffered (e.g., moral wrong, loss of chance) as a result of any breach of its duties (e.g., ownership verification).[137] The liability of a UCITS depositary cannot be contractually limited or excluded.[138] The depositary's liability shall not be affected by the fact that it has entrusted all or some of the assets in its custody to a third party.[139] An AIF depositary is expressly[140] allowed to discharge itself of liability subject to a contractual transfer of such liability to that third party, pursuant to a written contract between the depositary and the AIF or the AIFM acting on behalf of the AIF, in which such a discharge is objectively justified, and that the third party can be held liable for the loss based on a contract between the depositary and the third party, the depositary should be able to discharge itself of liability if it can prove that it has exercised due skill, care and diligence and that the specific requirements for delegation are met. By imposing the requirement of a contractual transfer of liability to the third party, the AIFM Directive aims to attach external effects to such contract, making the third party directly liable to the AIF, or to the investors of the AIF, for the loss of the financial instruments held in custody. In addition, the depositary may also incur administrative sanctions[141] or criminal penalties[142] in case of infringement of the provision of the UCITS/AIFM law.

[B] Management of the Fund

Collective management - UCIs management - includes the management of the portfolio [2] and the management of the risk and liquidity [3]. Those functions represent the heart of the task of an investment fund manager [1].

event', regarding UCITS depositaries, *see* UCITS Directive, Art. 24(1); Del. Reg. (UE) n° 2016/438, Art. 19; regarding AIF depositaries, *see* AIFM Directive, Art. 21(12); Del. Reg. (UE) n° 231/2013, Art. 101). In Luxembourg, regarding UCITS depositaries, *see* Law of 17 December 2010, Arts 19(1) and 35(1); regarding AIF depositaries, *see* Law of 12 July 2013, Art. 19(11). For criteria, regarding UCITS, *see* Del. Reg. (UE) n° 2016/438, Art. 19; regarding AIFs: Del. Reg. (UE) n° 231/2013, Art. 101. A depositary should not, for example, be able to rely on internal situations such as a fraudulent act by an employee to discharge itself of liability.

136. Regarding UCITS depositaries, *see* UCITS Directive, Art. 22a; regarding AIF depositaries, *see* AIFM Directive, Art. 21(11). In Luxembourg, regarding UCITS depositaries, *see* Law of 17 December 2010, Arts 19(1), 35(1); regarding AIF depositaries, *see* Law of 12 July 2013, Art. 19(11).
137. Investor's right to claim for damage is the same, irrespective of the legal form of the UCITS/AIF (SICAV or FCP).
138. UCITS Directive, Art. 24(3). In Luxembourg, *see* Law of 17 December 2010, Arts 19(3), 35(3).
139. Regarding UCITS depositaries, *see* UCITS Directive, Art. 24(2); regarding AIF depositaries, *see* AIFM Directive, Art. 21(13). In Luxembourg, regarding UCITS depositaries, *see* Law of 17 December 2010, Arts 19(2), 35(2); regarding AIF depositaries, *see* Law of 12 July 2013, Art. 19(11).
140. AIFM Directive, Art. 21(13) & (14). In Luxembourg, *see* Law 12 July 2013, Art. 19(13) & (14).
141. Regarding UCITS management companies, *see* UCITS Directive, Arts 99 et seq.; regarding AIFMs, *see* AIFM Directive, Art. 48. In Luxembourg, regarding AIFMs, *see* Law of 12 July 2013, Arts 51 and 52.
142. In Luxembourg, regarding UCITS management companies, *see* Law of 17 December 2010, Arts 165 et seq., regarding AIFMs, *see* Law of 12 July 2013, Art. 59.

[1] Manager of the Fund

The manager of a UCITS/AIF may be either an external or an internal manager.[143] The external manager is the legal person appointed by the UCITS/AIF or acting on behalf of the UCITS/AIF and which through this appointment is responsible for managing the UCITS/AIF.[144] For UCITS, the external manager is called 'management company'. The external manager is the only possible manager for a common fund or FCP. Where the legal form of the UCITS/AIF permits internal management of the portfolio and where the UCITS/AIF's governing body, namely its board of directors (*conseil d'administration*) or management board (*directoire*) chooses not to appoint an external manager, the UCITS/AIF itself, the UCITS/AIF is self-managed by its governing body.

The fund manager must fulfil specific conditions laid down by the both UCITS and AIFM Directives,[145] implemented into national laws,[146] especially for its authorization granted by the competent authority. It must set up and respect in permanence organizational conditions,[147] notably to manage risks,[148] and conflicts of interests.[149] Moreover, the fund manager must respect legal rules of conduct while performing its tasks: acting professionally in the best/exclusive interest of the investors[150] and to treat them equally,[151] and for its remuneration.[152]

Their functions are described in the respective Annexes II and I and their Article 6 of the UCITS and AIFM Directive. Regarding the fund 'collective management', the

143. Regarding UCITS management companies, *see* UCITS Directive, Arts 7, 29; regarding AIFMs, *see* AIFM Directive, Arts 4, 7 et seq. In Luxembourg, regarding UCITS management companies, *see* Law of 17 December 2010, Arts 27, 101 et seq.; regarding AIFMs, *see* Law of 12 July 2013, Arts 4, 6 et seq.
144. And not for the day-to-day management of the company, which lays on its governing bodies.
145. Regarding UCITS management companies, *see* UCITS Directive, Arts 7, 29; regarding AIFMs, *see* AIFM Directive, Arts 7 et seq.
146. Regarding UCITS management companies, *see* Law of 17 December 2010, Arts 27, 101 et seq.; regarding AIFMs, *see* Law of 12 July 2013, Arts 6 et seq.
147. Regarding UCITS management companies, *see* UCITS Directive, Art. 12; regarding AIFMs, *see* AIFM Directive, Arts 12, 17. For both Directives, Level-2 measures explain in detail the conditions. In Luxembourg, regarding UCITS management companies, *see* Law of 17 December 2010, Art. 109; regarding AIFMs, *see* Law of 12 July 2013, Arts 11 and 16.
148. *See infra*, §1.04[B][3].
149. Regarding UCITS management companies, *see* UCITS Directive, Art. 14(1)(d); regarding AIFMs, *see* AIFM Directive, Arts 12(1)(d) and 14. For both Directives, level 2 measures explain in detail the conditions. In Luxembourg, regarding UCITS management companies, *see* Law of 17 December 2010, Arts 109 and 111; regarding AIFMs, *see* Law of 12 July 2013, Arts 11(1)(f) and 13.
150. Regarding UCITS management companies, *see* UCITS Directive, Art. 14(1)(b); regarding AIFMs, *see* AIFM Directive, Art. 12(1)(b). In Luxembourg, regarding UCITS management companies, *see* Law of 17 December 2010, Art. 111(b); regarding AIFMs, *see* Law of 12 July 2013, Art. 11(1), b).
151. Regarding UCITS management companies, *see* UCITS Directive, Art. 14(1)(d); regarding AIFMs, *see* AIFM Directive, Art. 12(1)(f). In Luxembourg, regarding UCITS management companies, *see* Law of 17 December 2010, Art. 111(d); regarding AIFMs, *see* Law of 12 July 2013, Art. 11(1), f).
152. Regarding UCITS management companies, *see* UCITS Directive, Art. 14a; regarding AIFMs, *see* AIFM Directive, Art. 13, and Annex II. In Luxembourg, regarding UCITS management companies, *see* Law of 17 December 2010, Art. 111a; regarding AIFMs, *see* Law of 12 July 2013, Art. 12.

'heart' of their function, these are: regarding UCITS managers, (1) Portfolio management, namely making investment decision according to the investment policy; (2) administration of the fund[153] and (3) marketing of the fund units;[154] regarding AIFMs, (1) Investment management functions which an AIFM shall at least perform when managing an AIF: (a) portfolio management; (b) risk management. (2) Other functions that an AIFM may additionally perform in the course of the collective management of an AIF: (a) Administration; (b) Marketing; (c) Activities related to the assets of AIFs.[155] These functions may be delegated to third parties according to the provision of Article 13 of the UCITS and Article 20 of the AIFM Directive, but they cannot be delegated to the extent that, in essence, the management company of a UCITS of an AIFM becomes a letter-box entity.[156] These functions can be performed on a cross-border basis through the EU passport of the managers.[157] Investment companies shall manage only assets of their own portfolio and shall not, under any circumstances, receive any mandate to manage assets on behalf of a third party.[158]

By way of derogation, in addition, the UCITS/AIF managers may be authorized to provide individual portfolio management, and as non-core services: investment advice and safekeeping and administration in relation to units of CIUs. AIFMs may also in addition be authorized to provide as a non-core service the reception and transmission or orders. All those services must be performed according to MiFID II provisions.

In case of breaches of duties, the manager is liable - tort or contract liability - according to the national law. There is no specific provision in both Directives regarding the civil liability of a fund manager,[159] except the rule stating that the UCITS/AIF manager's liability toward the UCITS/AIF and its investors shall not be affected by the UCITS/AIF has delegated function to a third party (or by any further sub-delegation - regarding AIFMs).[160] In addition, the manager incurs administrative

153. *See, infra*, §1.04[B][2].
154. *See, infra*, §1.04[D].
155. Namely the services necessary to meet the fiduciary duties of the AIFM, facilities management, real estate administration activities, advice to undertakings on capital structure, industrial strategy and related matters, advice and services relating to mergers and the purchase of undertakings and other services connected to the management of the AIF and the companies and other assets in which it has invested.
156. Regarding UCITS management companies, *see* UCITS Directive, Art. 13(2); regarding AIFMs, *see* AIFM Directive, Art. 20(3). In Luxembourg, regarding UCITS management companies, *see* Law of 17 December 2010, Art. 110; regarding AIFMs, *see* Law of 12 July 2013, Art. 18(3). Article 82 of the Delegated Regulation (EU) n° 231/2013 specify a battery of criteria of the letter-box entity.
157. Regarding UCITS management companies, *see* UCITS Directive, Arts 16 and 17; regarding AIFMs, AIFM Directive, Arts 33, 34, 37. In Luxembourg, regarding UCITS management companies, *see* Law of 17 December 2010, Arts 113 et seq.; regarding AIFMs, *see* Law of 12 July 2013, Arts 32, 33 and 36.
158. Regarding UCITS, *see* UCITS Directive, Arts 28, 30(2); regarding AIFMs, AIFM Directive, Art. 6(3). In Luxembourg, regarding UCITS management companies, *see* Law of 17 December 2010, Art. 25; regarding AIFMs, *see* Law of 12 July 2013, Art. 5(3).
159. Comp. with the fund depositary, *see supra*, §1.04[A][2], *infra*, §1.04[E][2].
160. Regarding UCITS' management companies, *see* UCITS Directive, Art. 13(2); regarding AIFMs, *see* AIFM Directive, Art. 20(3). In Luxembourg, regarding UCITS management companies, *see* Law of 17 December 2010, Art. 110; regarding AIFMs, *see* Law of 12 July 2013, Art. 18(3).

sanctions[161] or criminal penalties[162] in case of infringement of a provision of the UCITS/AIFM law.

[2] Management of the Portfolio

The management of a UCITS or an AIF can be passive or active depending on the fund investment strategy. In passive management, also known as index management, the management objective of the fund is to replicate as closely as possible the return of an index. Such funds are therefore indexed funds whose composition is frozen *ab initio* and whose assets are bought for a long-term conservation purpose. In contrast, in active management, the manager of the fund has more flexibility to compose the portfolio and make relevant investments decisions relying on research (financial theories), forecasts, and their own experience, in order to take advantage of market opportunities and to attempt to 'beat' an index.

The criteria of selection of the UCITS/AIFs must respect at all times the eligible assets legal rules - if any - and the contractual investment policy of the fund. The manager must perform due diligence duty while selecting the assets. The selection is based on financial and/or extra-financial criteria (e.g., for faith-based funds such as Islamic funds, SRI fund based on ESG criteria, social impact funds).

The investment policy takes into account a risk-spreading principle, which varies with the type and the legal regime of the fund. A UCITS must respect a principle of strong diversification, which is part of its definition.[163] This pursues the objective of avoiding excessive concentration of assets and reduces investment risk. A minimum level of diversification of investment in different type of assets and issuers is required. Article 50 and following of the UCITS Directive[164] contain rules of diversification based on the principle of risk spreading. There are two different sets of limits. First, these are rules of diversification based on the UCITS portfolio composition which impose on the UCITS maximum limits of holding of certain categories of financial instruments and ratios expressed as a percentage of securities of the same issuer.[165] The second rules are adjusted according to the target companies whose securities are eligible for the assets of the UCITS (i.e., issuers in which the UCITS invest): these rules correspond to the idea that the investment of the UCITS must not lead to a control or a takeover of the targeted issuer. The manager of the UCITS must respect at all times the investment policy of the fund complying with the rules of the UCITS Directive implemented in Luxembourg Law of 17 December 2010. Because the AIFM Directive does not harmonize the product,

161. Regarding UCITS management companies, *see* UCITS Directive, Arts 99 et seq.; regarding AIFMs, *see* AIFM Directive, Art. 48. In Luxembourg, regarding AIFMs, *see* Law of 12 July 2013, Arts 51 and 52.
162. In Luxembourg, regarding UCITS management companies, *see* Law of 17 December 2010, Arts 165 et seq. regarding AIFMs, *see* Law of 12 July 2013, Art. 59.
163. UCITS Directive, Art. 1(2)(a).
164. In Luxembourg, Law of 17 December 2010, Art. 43.
165. For instance, in Luxembourg, regarding UCITS, *see* Part I of the Law of 17 December 2010, Arts 43 et seq.; regarding UCIs, *see* Part II of the Law of 17 December 2010, Arts 89, 91, 93, 96; regarding SIFs, *see* Law of 13 February 2007, Art. 4.

there is no special requirement about risk spreading in it. National law regarding AIFs may have differed degrees of diversification.

[3] Risk and Liquidity Management

One of the most important tasks of a fund manager, especially for AIFM, is risk management.[166] For UCITS, it has been decided to allow management companies some flexibility in structuring the organization of their risk management. Where it is not appropriate or proportionate to have a separate risk-management function,[167] the management company should nevertheless be able to demonstrate that specific safeguards against conflicts of interest allow for an independent performance of risk-management activities.[168] UCITS/AIF managers must establish and maintain a permanent risk-management function functionally and hierarchically separated from the operating units, including from the functions of portfolio management. AIFMs must implement adequate risk-management systems in order to identify, measure, manage, and monitor appropriately all risks relevant to each AIF investment strategy and to which each AIF is or may be exposed. Moreover, AIFMs shall set a maximum level of leverage which they may employ on behalf of each AIF they manage as well as the extent of the right to reuse collateral or guarantee that could be granted under the leveraging arrangement.

In addition, the Directives require UCITS/AIF managers to set up and employ an appropriate and proportionate liquidity risk-management process,[169] 'liquidity risk' means 'the risk that a position in the UCITS portfolio cannot be sold, liquidated or closed at limited cost in an adequately short time frame and that the ability of the UCITS to comply at any time with (UCITS Directive) is thereby compromised'.[170] Especially, the AIFM Directive requires the AIFM to employ, for each AIF it manages, that is not an unleveraged closed-ended AIF, an appropriate liquidity management system and to adopt procedures that enable it to monitor the AIF's liquidity risk and to ensure that the liquidity profile of the AIF's investments complies with its underlying obligations. The AIFM Delegated Regulation[171] specifies that the liquidity management systems and procedures should allow AIFMs to apply tools and arrangements necessary to cope with illiquid assets in order to respond to redemption requests.[172] AIFMs must conduct

166. Dir. 2011/61/EU, Art. 15; Del. Reg. (EU), n° 231/2013, Arts 38–45. In Luxembourg, regarding AIFMs, *see* Law of 12 July 2013, Art. 14.
167. Regarding requirements for risk management, *see* Commission Directive 2010/43/EU of 1 July 2010 implementing Directive 2009/65/EC of the European Parliament and of the Council as regard organizational requirements, conflicts of interest, conduct of business, risk management and content of the agreement between a depositary and a management company [2010] OJ L 176/42, Arts 12, 40.
168. Dir. 2010/43/EU, Recital 12.
169. AIFM Directive, Art. 16, In the UCITS Directive, the liquidity management is part of the risk management. *See* Dir. 2010/43/EU, Art. 40. In Luxembourg, *see* Law of 12 July 2013, Art. 15.
170. *See* Dir. 2010/43/EU, Art. 1(8).
171. Del. Reg. (EU), n° 231/2013, Arts 46–49.
172. Such arrangements may include 'special arrangements' such as 'side-pockets'.

stress tests at least annually, under normal and exceptional liquidity conditions, in order to assess the liquidity risk of the AIFs and to monitor it accordingly.

[C] Administration of the Investment Fund

The administration of an investment fund is one of the tasks relating to the activity of collective portfolio - UCITS/UCIs - management according to Annex II of the UCITS Directive and Annex I of the AIFM Directive.[173] It corresponds to 'back-office' functions. It covers: legal and fund management accounting services; customer inquiries; valuation of the portfolio and pricing of the units/shares (including tax returns); regulatory compliance monitoring; maintenance of unit-/shareholder register; unit/shares issues and redemptions; contract settlements (including certificate dispatch); record keeping. The Level 2 execution measures (Directive and Regulation) explain the operating conditions.[174] These obligatory administrative tasks are incumbent on the manager of the fund, but they can be delegated to third parties.

Regarding fund accounting, both Directives impose the accounting information given in the UCITS/AIF annual report to be audited by one or more persons empowered by law to audit accounts in accordance with Directive 2006/43/EC. The auditor's report, including any qualifications, shall be reproduced in full in the annual report.[175]

[D] Marketing of the Investment Fund's Units or Shares

> Luxembourg is the uncontested leader in the cross-border distribution of undertakings for collective investment (UCI). Three out of every four undertakings for collective investment in transferable securities (UCITS) sold into at least three countries are domiciled in Luxembourg.[176]

Article 4(1)(x) of the AIFM Directive defines marketing of the fund units/shares as:

> a direct or indirect offering or placement at the initiative of the AIFM or on behalf of the AIFM of units or shares of an AIF it manages to or with investors domiciled or with a registered office in the Union.

Although there is no definition of marketing in the UCITS Directive, there is no reason for a different definition.

The fund distributor has no special status neither in UCITS Directive nor in AIFM Directive. The marketing of the UCITS/AIFs is one of the functions relating to collective management incumbent to the fund manager, according to Annex II of the UCITS Directive and Annex I of the AIFM Directive. Then the 'natural' distributor of a fund is

173. Article 6 of both UCITS and AIFM Directives make reference to the annex.
174. Regarding UCITS, *see* Directive 2010/43/UE; Regarding AIF, *see* Del. Reg. (UE) n° 231/2013.
175. UCITS Directive, Art. 73; AIFM Directive, Art. 22(2)(2).
176. http://www.luxembourgforfinance.com/en/products-services/investment-funds/fund-administration.

its management company (closed architecture). In practice, fund managers make use of different distribution channels of UCITS/AIF, such as bank branch networks, independent financial advisors, life insurance companies, distribution agents,[177] fund supermarkets. In Luxembourg, a distributor of UCIs must obtain the status of Professional of the Financial Sector (PSF) according to the Law of 5 April 1996 on the financial sector.

The reception and transmission of orders relating to UCITS/AIF units or shares by a distributor which is not the management company of the fund is submitted to MiFID II requirements.

[E] Supervision of the Investment Fund

An investment fund is supervised at two levels: that of the competent authority [1] and that of the depositary [2].

[1] The Competent Authority's Supervision

Except for funds that are regulated but not supervised (such as RAIFs in Luxembourg[178]), each investment fund is subjected to ongoing supervision by a competent authority from its constitution to its liquidation. In Luxembourg, that is the CSSF.

[2] Depositary's Supervision

Apart from its safekeeping function, the depositary has an important function of supervision, which covers two aspects harmonized at the European level. Both UCITS and AIMD Directives contain the same provisions detailed in the Level 2 EU delegated regulations issued by the European Commission.

First, the depositary must perform an oversight duty,[179] which consists in an ex post compliance duty on the UCITS/AIFs with applicable law, regulations, and UCITS/AIF's rules and by-laws/instruments of incorporation. From this function derives five uniform duties irrespective of the legal form of the UCITS/AIF (investment company or contractual fund) and of its legal regime (UCITS or AIF): control of issue, repurchase, redemption, and cancellation of units; control of the net asset value (NAV) calculation; control that the consideration to the fund's transactions is remitted within the usual time limits; compliance with the investment restriction, and control that the UCITS/AIF's income is applied correctly.

Second, the depositary is also in charge of the cash flow monitoring of the UCITS/AIF and in particular it must ensure that all UCITS/AIF's cash regarding the

---

177. Acting as simple intermediary (*mandataire*) or nominee of the investors.
178. Law of 23 July 2016, Art. 34.
179. Regarding UCITS depositaries, *see* UCITS Directive, Art. 22(3); Del. Reg. (UE) n° 2016/438, Arts 3-8; regarding AIF depositaries, *see* AIFM Directive, Art. 21(9); Del. Reg. (UE) n° 231/2013, Arts 92-97. In Luxembourg, regarding UCITS depositaries, *see* Law of 17 December 2010, Arts 18(1), 34(1); regarding AIF depositaries, *see* Law of 12 July 2013, Art. 19(9).

portfolio and the units are received and properly registered in segregated accounts in the name of the UCITS/AIF or its manager.[180]

The depositary is liable for any 'other loss'[181] suffered (e.g., moral wrong, loss of chance) as a result of any breach of its supervision duties.[182] The liability of a UCITS depositary cannot be contractually limited or excluded.[183] Regarding, AIF, the AIFM Directive limits the possibility of contractual limitation or exclusion to delegation of the safekeeping duties, but do not prohibit them in another context. The validity of such a clause depends on the public order character of the rule imposing the duty.

[F] Investment Funds End of Life

The life-cycle of an investment funds ends with its liquidation [1] or a merger [2].

[1] Investment Fund Liquidation

There is no special regime for the liquidation of UCITS/UCIs in both UCITS and AIFM Directives. Also, the rules of investment funds liquidation should be found in national UCITS/UCIs laws. In Luxembourg, for instance, Articles 143 and following in Part II of the Law of 17 December 2010 and Articles 20 and 46 and following of the Law of 13 February contain specific provisions regarding the conditions and proceedings for the liquidation of a UCI and an SIF, respectively, which can be a judicial or a non-judicial liquidation.

[2] Investment Fund Mergers

Only the UCITS Directive has drawn up a framework for mergers of UCITS. In its Articles 37–48, the Directive laid down a minimum harmonized but nevertheless detailed framework for cross-border mergers of UCITS that have been implemented in Articles 59 and following of the Luxembourg Law of 17 December 2010.[184] This Directive has introduced a 'right to' cross-border merger for UCITS – and their

---

180. Regarding UCITS depositaries, *see* UCITS Directive, Art. 22(4); Del. Reg. (UE) n° 2016/438, Arts 9–11; regarding AIF depositaries, *see* AIFM Directive, Art. 21(7); Del. Reg. (UE) n° 231/2013, Arts 85–87. In Luxembourg, regarding UCITS depositaries, *see* Law of 17 December 2010, Arts 18(2), 34(2); regarding AIF depositaries, *see* Law of 12 July 2013, Art. 19(7).
181. Regarding UCITS depositaries, *see* UCITS Directive, Art. 22a; regarding AIF depositaries, *see* AIFM Directive Art. 21(11). In Luxembourg, regarding UCITS depositaries, *see* Law of 17 December 2010, Arts 19(1), 35(1); regarding AIF depositaries, *see* Law of 12 July 2013, Art. 19(11).
182. Investor's right to claim for damage is the same irrespective of the legal form of the UCITS/AIF (SICAV or FCP).
183. UCITS Directive, Art. 24(3). In Luxembourg, *see* Law of 17 December 2010, Arts 19(3) and 35(3).
184. These provision are completed with Commission Directive 2010/42/EU of 1 July 2010 implementing The UCITS Directive of the European Parliament and of the Council as regard certain provisions concerning fund mergers, master-feeder structures and notification procedure [2010] OJ L 176/28.

compartments of investment and for some 'domestic mergers'. 'Cross-border merger' means a merger of UCITS: (a) at least two of which are established in different Member States, or (b) established in the same Member State into a newly constituted UCITS established in another Member State. 'Domestic merger' means a merger between UCITS established in the same Member State where at least one of the involved UCITS has activated its European passport for cross-border marketing its units or shares.

By contrast, the AIFM Directive, which does not harmonize the product, is silent about mergers of AIF. In Luxembourg, there is no special merger AIF regime neither in Part II of the Law of 17 December 2010 nor in the Laws of 13 February 2007, 15 June 2004, or 26 July 2016. Then, the merger regime must be found in 'common law'. In this respect, some AIFs under the investment company legal form can make use of the company law rules (i.e., Directive (EU) 2005/56/EC, the so-called Cross-Border Mergers Directive) if they are part of its scope, and the Luxembourg Law of 1915, as amended. For 'common funds' they can either transform them into investment company before merging or use the civil rules for the transmission of assets.

CHAPTER 2

Investment Funds Taxation in Luxembourg

Eric Fort & Philipp Jost

§2.01 INTRODUCTION

The tax treatment of investment funds depends on the legal and regulatory framework under which the investment fund is set up by its promoter(s). As a general rule, which applies to the vast majority of investment funds, Luxembourg tax law applies the so-called tax neutrality principle to Luxembourg-based investment funds and non-Luxembourg-based investment funds that have their effective place of management in Luxembourg.

Generally speaking, the tax neutrality principle can be achieved through different approaches: first, the tax legislature may, basically, choose to exempt the investment vehicle from taxation in its jurisdiction. This method is commonly referred to as the 'subjective exemption' method. Second, tax law may also exempt (certain items of) income received by an otherwise fully taxable person from taxation – this is known as the 'objective exemption' approach – that is, the taxpayer itself is still subject to tax, but only (certain types of) income are exempt from taxation and therefore will not be recognized in the taxable basis of the relevant taxpayer.[1] Third, tax law can make certain deduction methods available to taxpayers, allowing for the lowering of the tax base.[2] Ordinary tax rates are applied to the (fundamentally) reduced tax base. A fourth method to grant tax neutrality to taxpayers can be achieved by applying tax transparency at the level of the investment vehicle, meaning that the vehicle itself is not subject to taxation but its investors – as partners in the vehicle – are taxed on their proportionate share of the vehicle's income.

---

1. Luxembourg and Germany's participation exemption regimes, which exempt, *inter alia*, received dividends under certain conditions from taxation, are examples of an objective exemption method.
2. This approach, for instance, has been taken by Belgium.

The Luxembourg legislature decided, in principle,[3] to follow the subjective exemption approach with respect to most investment fund structures, thereby exempting such investment funds from income taxation and wealth taxation. Although, according to Article 159 of Luxembourg's income tax law or LIR,[4] an investment fund, in general, is considered to be a Luxembourg resident taxpayer if the investment fund either has its registered office or its central administration located in Luxembourg, investment funds that fall within the scope of special legislation for investment funds are exempt from taxation pursuant to Article 161(1)no. 10 LIR. Nevertheless, certain types of investment funds may also fall within the scope of general taxation principles. Before considering both taxation methods in more detail, this chapter first gives a historical background regarding the development of the taxation of investment funds in Luxembourg. In order to be in a position to clearly differentiate the application of these taxation methods, it then goes on to describe the legal and regulatory framework for investment funds in Luxembourg that is the basis for the relevant taxation treatment.

§2.02 HISTORICAL BACKGROUND OF TAXATION OF INVESTMENT FUNDS

The first investment funds - *fonds d'investissement*, in French and now commonly referred to as 'undertakings for collective investment' or UCIs[5] - were established in Luxembourg during the 1950s. By Grand Ducal Decree,[6] UCIs were then placed under the supervision of the Banking Commissioner. In the early days of regulation, there were two main legislative initiatives relating to UCIs, both of which have since been abrogated: the first was enacted in 1983 (the '1983 UCI Law')[7] and the second in 1988 (the '1988 UCI Law').[8]

The 1983 UCI Law created, for the first time in Luxembourg, a specific legal form for UCIs on a purely contractual basis, which is known as *fonds commun de placement* or FCP. In addition, it introduced a new type of corporate UCI in the form of an investment company with variable share capital, Luxembourg's *société*

3. For example, a *société d'investissement en capital à risque* (SICAR) may benefit from an objective exemption because certain items of income arising from funds held pending their investment in risk capital do not constitute taxable income for SICARs. This exemption is however only applicable for a maximum period of twelve months preceding the investment in risk capital and where it can be established that the funds have effectively been invested in risk capital.
4. *Loi modifiée du 4 décembre 1967 concernant l'impôt sur le revenu (texte coordonné au 1er janvier 2018)* (www.impotsdirects.public.lu/content/dam/acd/fr/legislation/LIR/LIR2018.pdf (last visited 29 December 2017) (hereinafter 'LIR').
5. The term 'UCI' is typically used to mean regulated investment funds. For this chapter, however, the term 'investment funds' includes both regulated and non-regulated investment funds.
6. *Arrêté grand-ducal du 22 décembre 1972 ayant pour objet le contrôle des fonds d'investissement* (abrogated 1983).
7. *Loi du 25 août 1983 relative aux organismes de placement collectif*, abrogated 1988 (hereinafter, the '1983 UCI Law'.
8. *Loi du 30 mars 1988 relative aux organismes de placement collectif*, abrogated 2003 (hereinafter, the '1988 UCI Law').

d'investissement à capital variable or SICAV.[9] The 1988 UCI Law replaced the 1983 UCI Law to bring Luxembourg law in line with the first UCITS Directive.[10]

Historically, UCIs enjoyed favourable tax treatment compared to the tax treatment of corporations under national Luxembourg law. In the early beginnings of the set-up and taxation of UCIs in Luxembourg, the tax treatment of UCIs basically followed the tax provisions applicable to Luxembourg's 1929 holding companies.[11,12] Following the tax system for 1929 holding companies prior to the 1983 UCI Law, UCIs were, in principle, excluded from general taxation and only subject to a capital duty (*droit d'apport*)[13] and a subscription tax (*taxe d'abonnement*);[14] in other words, such UCIs were treated as 1929 holding companies).

---

9. In addition, Luxembourg's *Loi du 19 juli 1991 concernant les organismes de placement collectif dont les titres ne sont pas destinés au placement dans le public* (abrogated 2007), introduced the possibility of creating UCIs having units or shares that could be reserved to one or several institutional investors - this concept for well-informed investors is basically the predecessor of the present and commonly used specialized investment funds.
10. Council Directive 85/611/EEC of 20 December 1985 on the coordination of laws, regulations and administrative provisions relating to undertakings for collective investment in transferable securities (UCITS) (abrogated 2011).
11. *Loi du 31 juillet 1929 sur le régime fiscal des sociétés de participations financières (Holding companies)* (abrogated 2006). In 2006, the European Commission decided that Luxembourg's tax regime for its 1929 holding companies was in violation of EU State-aid rules (Commission Decision of 19 July 2006 on aid scheme C 3/2006 implemented by Luxembourg for '1929' holding companies and 'billionaire' holding companies, [2006] OJ L 366/47). On 22 December 2006, the Luxembourg Parliament adopted a law abolishing the regime for the 1929 holding companies (*Loi du 22 décembre 2006 abrogeant: la loi modifiée du 31 juillet 1929; l'arrêté grand-ducal modifié du 17 décembre 1938 concernant les sociétés holding; l'arrêté grand-ducal modifié du 17 décembre 1938 sur le régime fiscal des sociétés de participations financières (Holding Companies); la loi modifiée du 12 juillet 1977; le règlement grand-ducal du 29 juillet 1977; et la loi du 21 juin 2005*), which provided a transitionary that ended on 31 December 2010. During that period, previously established 1929 holding companies were allowed to benefit from continued special tax rules, provided the shares of the company had not been transferred.
12. For further details, *see* Bernard Delvaux, *Questions actuelles concernant la loi de 1929 sur le régime fiscal des sociétés de participations financières*, 16 Pasicrisie Luxembourgeoise 145, 156 (1956).
13. Capital duty was introduced by the *Loi du 29 décembre 1971 concernant l'impôt frappant les rassemblements de capitaux dans les sociétés civiles et commerciales et portant révision de certaines dispositions législatives régissant la perception des droits d'enregistrement* as amended (abrogated 2008), which law transposed into national law Council Directive 69/335/EEC of 17 July 1969 concerning indirect taxes on the raising of capital [1969] OJ L 249/25, as amended by Council Directive 85/303/EEC of 10 June 1985 amending Directive 69/335/EEC concerning indirect taxes on the raising of capital [1985] OJ L 156/23.
14. In principle, Luxembourg's annual subscription tax is an indirect annual tax created by the *Loi du 23 décembre 1913 concernant la révision de la législation qui régit les impôts dont le recouvrement est attribué à l'administration de l'enregistrement et des domaines*, as amended. Originally, the subscription tax consisted of a tax imposed on the transfer of securities of all kinds and was levied on the owner of the securities. However, in practice, it was basically impossible for the tax authorities to track changes in ownership of bearer shares. Consequently, pursuant to the *Loi du 7 août 1920 portant majoration des droits d'enregistrement, de timbre, de succession*, etc., as amended, the subscription tax became a kind of inclusive tax payable on the basis of the right to transmit securities, the amount thereof generally being levied on the amount of the share capital of the relevant company based on the average value during the preceding year. In 1986, the subscription tax was abolished with respect to debentures and, again in 1990, with respect to all company shares, except for shares in 1929 holding companies and UCIs.

[A] The System of Capital Duty and Subscription Tax

Generally speaking, both Luxembourg's capital duty and its subscription tax qualify as a kind of registration duty on the transfer of assets. In the context at hand, the capital duty was levied on the capital contribution of an investor in a Luxembourg-based, non-commercial company (*société civile*) or commercial company (*société commerciale*). The contribution of funds to a company in such an exchange scenario occurs at the level of the company, with the funds going directly from the investor to the company and the company then issuing new shares to that investor. The subscription tax - a registration duty as well - accrues in the context of the transfer of company securities and is intended to tax such transfer on the basis of a certain percentage (a lump-sum payment) tied to the value of the securities.

With respect to UCIs, capital contributions to investment companies, on the one hand, and capital contributions to the management companies of FCPs,[15] on the other hand, both fall within the scope of capital duty and are taxable at the rate applicable for holding companies. Subscription tax, however, was levied on the investment companies and the FCPs themselves.[16] Investment companies were subject to the subscription tax at a rate of 0.20% per year, calculated in accordance with the value of the issued shares over the past year. An FCP's net asset value was taxed at a lower rate of 0.06% under the subscription tax regime.

[B] An Independent Tax System for UCIs under the 1983 UCI Law

The 1983 UCI Law marked a significant change with respect to fund taxation and introduced an independent tax system for UCIs detached from the taxation of 1929 holding companies.[17] That new tax system for UCIs brought a major shift in tax policy: under the new law, UCIs were no longer treated in the same way as 1929 holding companies, which brought, *inter alia,* a major advantage for UCIs because, under the new regime, they could - potentially - claim benefits of Luxembourg's double tax treaties (DTTs),[18] whereas holding companies were historically excluded therefrom.

Although taxation of UCIs was still based on the collection of capital duty and subscription tax, while being excluded from income taxation, the computation of the

---

15. An FCP is founded on a contractual basis and has no legal personality. It must be managed by an authorized management company which is regulated by the *Commission de Surveillance du Secteur Financier* or CSSF.
16. For a general overview, *see* Claude Kremer & Isabelle Lebbe, *Collective Investment Schemes in Luxembourg*, Recitals 11.06 et seq. (2009).
17. Introducing a separate tax system for UCIs, one completely independent from the taxation of 1929 holding companies, was also influenced by mounting criticism of the advantageous tax treatment they received under the 1929 holding regime.
18. Whether a particular investment fund has access to treaty benefits must be determined on a case-by-case basis. Some DTTs expressly exclude investment funds from their scope (e.g., the Switzerland/Luxembourg DTT), while others are silent with respect to their application to investment funds. Still other DTTs expressly include some, but not necessarily all, types of investment funds (e.g., the German/Luxembourg DTT).

taxation basis had since been altered fundamentally.[19] The tax system and its principles, introduced by the 1983 UCI Law, basically remained unchanged[20] and were adopted for the taxation of so-called Specialized Investment Fund or SIF[21] governed by the 2007 SIF Law.[22]

The general taxation principles, as laid out in the 1983 UCI Law, for all funds having their registered office (or, in the case of FCPs, the registered office of their management companies) in Luxembourg had been reproduced in the 1988 UCI Law that replaced it, and were governed by its Articles 105–109.[23] The Luxembourg legislature thereby introduced a sui generis fiscal regime for UCIs. Article 105(1) 1988 UCI Law provides that:

> Apart from the capital duty levied on the contribution of capital to civil and commercial companies and the subscription tax mentioned in Article 108 below, no other tax shall be payable by the undertakings for collective investment referred to in this law. (author translation).

Further, Article 105(2) 1988 UCI Law states that amounts distributed by such undertakings shall not be subject to deductions at source and are not taxable, if they are received by non-residents. Of course, the exemption established by Article 105 1988 UCI Law did not apply to other indirect taxes, in particular, the value added tax

19. The annual subscription tax is levied on the total net assets of a UCI, valued on the last day of each trimester. However, a derogation is applied to take account of the date of the UCI was entered or removed from the list: the tax for that period is calculated on the basis of the number of days between the time of the entry of the UCI on the list and the end of the first trimester, or the number of days between the commencement of the final trimester and the time of the removal of the UCI from the list, as the case may be. This exception, however, does not apply to the creation or dissolution of a compartment within a UCI, as multi-compartment UCIs constitute one entity.
20. The *Loi du 23 décembre 1994 concernant le budget des recettes et des dépenses de l'État pour l'exercice 1995*, as amended, lowered the rate of the annual subscription tax to be levied on UCIs from 0.06% to 0.03% for those UCIs investing solely in money market instruments, cash, or subscriptions. The *Loi du 24 décembre 1996 portant modification de certaines dispositions en matière des impôts directs et indirects*, as amended, further lowered the subscription tax rate to 0.01% for certain institutional UCIs and Luxembourg-based UCIs investing in money market instruments or demand or time deposits. Further, subscriptions by UCIs resident in Luxembourg in other UCIs resident in Luxembourg were fully exempted from the subscription tax. Subsequently, the *Loi du 21 décembre 2001 portant réforme de certaines dispositions en matière des impôts directs et indirects*, the general subscription tax rate was reduced from 0.06% to 0.05%.
21. *Fonds d'investissement spécialisés*, in French.
22. *Loi du 13 février 2007 relative aux fonds d'investissement spécialisés et portant modification de la loi modifiée du 20 décembre 2002 relative aux organismes de placement collectif, et modification de la loi modifiée du 12 février 1979 concernant la taxe sur la valeur ajoutée*, as amended (hereinafter the '2007 SIF Law'). For an overview of SIF tax treatment, *see* Alain Goebel & Bruno Gasparotto, *Specialised Investment Funds, in Tax Aspects of SIFs*, 148 et seq. (Arendt & Medernach ed., 2007).
23. With the introduction of the 1983 UCI Law, the first coherent legal framework was given to UCIs. The sui generis fiscal regime introduced by its Art. 62 derived the tax treatment from the regime governing 1929 holding companies. The 1988 UCI Law reproduced, in its Arts 105–109, the 1983 UCI Law's Arts 62–66.

(VAT).[24] At that time, the fiscal regime applied equally to all types of UCIs,[25] irrespective of their legal form (contractual or corporate), their status, their structure (single or multi-compartment), the origin of their promoters, or any other classification (institutional funds, real estate funds, etc.).

§2.03 OVERVIEW: LUXEMBOURG INVESTMENT VEHICLES

To be able to fully understand Luxembourg's taxation principles for the various types of investment funds, especially when dealing with a regulated UCI or a non-regulated investment fund, it is necessary to briefly summarize their legal and regulatory background. A Luxembourg-based *regulated* UCI, in principle, must be built on the following three characteristics: (1) its exclusive object must be the collective investment of savings (2) that are invested in assets (transferable securities or other assets) in accordance with the principle of risk spreading, and (3) funds being used for the collective investment have been raised from the public (i.e., a number of investors).[26] Moreover, Luxembourg investment funds are categorized according to the nature of assets to be collectively invested, the type of eligible investor,[27] the marketing method adopted,[28] or the geographical area in which the fund is marketed.[29]

[A] The Corporate-Product Level

Basically, two fund categories have to be distinguished at corporate-product level: undertakings for collective investment in transferable securities or UCITS,[30] on the one hand, and alternative investment funds or AIFs,[31] on the other hand.

24. *See* the 1988 UCI Law's Parliamentary Documents, Law Project No. 3172, Opinion of the *Conseil d'État*, 14.
25. However, one distinction was made with respect to the level of taxation based on the classification of the assets held by the UCI.
26. Kremer & Lebbe, *supra* note 16, Recital 1.01.
27. That is private investors, informed, qualified, or institutional investors.
28. That is private placement, direct distributions, distributors, or stock exchange.
29. For instance, the European Economic Area (hereinafter 'EEA').
30. UCITS are governed by Part I of *Loi du 17 décembre 2010 concernant les organismes de placement collectif*, as amended (the '2010 UCI Law').
31. As defined by Art. 1(39) of the *Loi du 12 juillet 2013 relative aux gestionnaires de fonds d'investissement alternatifs et portant transposition de la directive 2011/61/UE du Parlement européen et du Conseil du 8 juin 2011 sur les gestionnaires de fonds d'investissement alternatifs et modifiant les directives 2003/41/CE et 2009/65/CE ainsi que les règlements (CE) n° 1060/2009 et (UE) n° 1095/2010; portant modification: de la loi modifiée du 17 décembre 2010 concernant les organismes de placement collectif; de la loi modifiée du 13 février 2007 relative aux fonds d'investissement spécialisés; de la loi modifiée du 15 juin 2004 relative à la société d'investissement en capital à risque (SICAR); de la loi modifiée du 13 juillet 2005 relative aux institutions de retraite professionnelle sous forme de société d'épargne-pension à capital variable (SEPCAV) et d'association d'épargne-pension (ASSEP); de la loi du 13 juillet 2005 concernant les activités et la surveillance des institutions de retraite professionnelle; de la loi modifiée du 5 avril 1993 relative au secteur financier; de la loi modifiée du 12 novembre 2004 relative à la lutte contre le blanchiment et contre le financement du terrorisme; de la loi modifiée du 23 décembre 1998 portant création d'une commission de surveillance du secteur financier; de la loi modifiée du 10 août 1915 concernant les sociétés commerciales; de la loi modifiée du 19 décembre 2002*

[1] UCITS

A UCITS is subject to Directive 2009/65/EC[32] and falls under the scope of Part I of Luxembourg's 2010 UCI Law.[33] The sole purpose of UCITS is the collective investment in transferable securities and/or in other liquid financial assets of capital raised from the public operating on the principle of risk spreading with units that are, at the request of holders, repurchased, directly or indirectly, out of the undertaking's assets.

[2] AIFs

AIFs are also collective investment undertakings that raise capital from a number of investors with a view to investing that capital, but AIFs do so in accordance with a defined investment policy for the benefit of those investors and do not require authorization pursuant to Article 5 of Directive 2009/65/EC and are not covered by Part I of the 2010 UCI Law. Investment vehicles that are subject to the approval and supervision of Luxembourg's financial-market regulator, the *Commission de Surveillance du Secteur Financier* or CSSF, are called 'product-regulated AIFs'. Such product-regulated AIFs are generally referred to as 'regulated investment funds' (i.e., UCIs); non-UCITS investment funds qualify as AIFs in the following scenarios:

- They fall within the scope of Part II of the 2010 UCI Law and invest in assets other than those mentioned in Directive 2009/65/EC (so-called Part II UCIs).
- They are SIFs governed by the 2007 SIF Law[34] and, although the nature of their investments is not restricted, they are required to only raise capital from well-informed investors (i.e., institutional investors, professional investors, or other investors who have declared, in writing, that they are well-informed investors and either invest a minimum of EUR 125,000 or they present an appraisal from a bank, an investment firm or a management company certifying their respective appropriate expertise, experience and knowledge).
- They are a *Société d'investissement en capital à risque* or SICAR, designed for private equity and venture capital investments, and are subject to the 2004 SICAR Law.[35] As opposed to SIFs, there are no investment diversification obligations nor lending or leverage restrictions on SICARs.

---

concernant le registre de commerce et des sociétés ainsi que la comptabilité et les comptes annuels des entreprises; du Code de commerce; de la loi modifiée du 4 décembre 1967 concernant l'impôt sur le revenu; de la loi modifiée du 1er décembre 1936 concernant l'impôt commercial; de la loi modifiée d'adaptation fiscale du 16 octobre 1934; de la loi modifiée du 16 octobre 1934 sur l'évaluation des biens et valeurs; et de la loi modifiée du 12 février 1979 concernant la taxe sur la valeur ajoutée, as amended (hereinafter the '2013 AIFM Law').

32. Directive 2009/65/EC of the European Parliament and of the Council of 13 July 2009 on the coordination of laws, regulations and administrative provisions relating to undertakings for collective investment in transferable securities (UCITS) (recast) (Text with EEA relevance) [2009] OJ L 302/32, as amended (hereinafter 'Directive 2009/65/EC').
33. As defined *supra* note 30.
34. As defined *supra* note 22.
35. *Loi du 15 juin 2004 relative à la Société d'investissement en capital à risque (SICAR) et portant modification de la loi modifiée du 4 décembre 1967 relative à l'impôt sur le revenu, la loi modifiée*

In addition, investors may also choose for their investment so-called manager-regulated AIFs (i.e., investment vehicles that are not themselves subject to the direct supervision of a regulatory authority, but which appoint a regulated AIFM). Hence, the manager itself is subject to supervision of the CSSF. Commonly such AIFs are referred to as non-regulated investment funds and occur in the following constellations:

- A reserved alternative investment fund or RAIF is an investment vehicle governed by Luxembourg's 2016 RAIF Law[36] having the sole objective to collectively invest the funds raised in assets under risk spreading considerations. Similar to SIFs, RAIFs are reserved for well-informed investors and must be managed by an authorized AIFM within the meaning of the 2013 AIFM Law.[37]
- Furthermore, non-regulated investment funds can also qualify as AIF to the extent the very broad definition under Article 1(39) 2013 AIFM Law[38] is fulfilled. Such investment vehicles are not subject to the approval and supervision of the CSSF. The term 'non-regulated investment funds', of course, does not mean that the vehicle is not governed by any law: for example, *Sociétés de participations financières* or SOPARFIs[39] are governed by Luxembourg's 1915 Company Law.[40] Non-regulated AIFs may be set up in the form of a partnership (a *société en commandite simple* or SCS) or *société en commandite spéciale* or SCSp) or in corporate form, such as a public limited company (*société anonyme* or SA), a private limited company (*société à responsabilité limitée* or SARL), or a partnership limited by shares (*société en commandite par actions* or SCA). In contrast thereto, regulated AIFs are either incorporated under the SICAR regime or under the SIF regime.

---

du 16 octobre 1934 concernant l'impôt sur la fortune, la loi modifiée du 1er décembre 1936 concernant l'impôt commercial communal, la loi modifiée du 12 février 1979 concernant la taxe sur la valeur ajoutée, et la loi modifiée du 20 décembre 2002 concernant les organismes de placement collectif, as amended (hereinafter the '2004 SICAR Law').

36. *Loi du 23 juillet 2016 relative aux fonds d'investissement alternatifs réservés et portant modification de: 1. la loi modifiée du 16 octobre 1934 concernant l'impôt sur la fortune; 2. la loi modifiée du 1er décembre 1936 concernant l'impôt commercial communal; 3. la loi modifiée du 4 décembre 1967 concernant l'impôt sur le revenu; 4. la loi modifiée du 5 avril 1993 relative au secteur financier; 5. la loi modifiée du 13 février 2007 relative aux fonds d'investissement spécialisés; et 6. la loi modifiée du 17 décembre 2010 concernant les organismes de placement collectif,* as amended (hereinafter the '2016 RAIF Law').
37. As defined *supra* note 31.
38. Non-regulated AIFs may either appoint an AIFM or elect to be self-managed. In the latter case, the AIF itself will be considered the AIFM. Any Luxembourg AIFM meeting the managed-funds thresholds defined in the 2013 AIFM Law is required to be authorized by the CSSF. The thresholds are set at EUR 100 million or EUR 500 million, but only if the underlying AIFs are unleveraged and have no redemption rights exercisable during a period of five years. Any AIFM not meeting such thresholds is subject to a lighter registration regime.
39. The term 'SOPARFI' is a generic term used to designate companies whose purpose is hold and manage participating interests in affiliated undertakings. In addition to such holding activities, SOPARFIs may carry out other activities (e.g., commercial, real estate, or industrial activities).
40. *Loi du 10 août 1915 concernant les sociétés commerciales,* as amended and as consolidated in *Règlement grand-ducal du 5 décembre 2017 portant coordination de la loi modifiée du 10 août 1915 concernant les sociétés commerciales* (hereinafter the '1915 Company Law').

The choice of the regulatory regime depends on the choice of the targeted asset classes, given that certain types of investment funds can only invest in a limited range of asset classes. For example, hedge funds, private equity funds, and real estate investment strategies can only be pursued in one of the above-mentioned AIF regimes.

Furthermore, the type of investors to which the relevant investment fund is intended to be marketed also has an influence on the choice of the regulatory regime. Indeed, UCITS can be marketed to retail investors throughout the European Union (EU) and beyond, while an AIFM benefits from a passport for marketing either regulated or non-regulated AIFs to professional investors. The extent to which AIFs can be sold to non-professional investors must be assessed on a country-by-country basis.

[3] Legal Structure

In principle, and as already indicated above, the following legal structures are available to investors:

- a *société d'investissement à capital fixe* or SICAF (an investment company with fixed capital); or
- a *société d'investissement à capital variable* or SICAV (an investment company with variable capital); or
- a *fond commun d'investissement* or FCP (a common investment fund).

Both the SICAF and the SICAV may be self-managed, but if not, a management company must be appointed. All of the aforementioned structures can be set up as a standalone investment fund having a single investment portfolio. Alternatively, such funds can also be structured as a multiple-compartment fund,[41] which creates separate sub-funds (the compartments) under the umbrella of a single legal entity. These sub-funds function as independent entities, each with its own investment policy, target distribution market, and investor profile. Two structures are reserved for well-informed investors only – SIFs and SICARs.

The choice of the specific investment fund vehicle (i.e., whether to establish the investment fund in company form (either the SICAF or SICAV) or contractual form (the FCP)) is primarily based on tax motives as well as operational and marketing considerations.

A SICAF, on the one hand, is a fixed capital investment company that allows for the pooling of assets. The SICAF is an open- or closed-end investment company with fixed capital whereby its authorized capital can only be increased by its shareholders. Any amendments to the SICAF's capital within its authorized capital require notification and publication. SICAFs are allowed to repurchase their own shares. Further, SICAFs can be established in almost any legal form: including an SA, SE, SARL, SCA, SCS, or SCSp.

A SICAV, on the other hand, is a variable capital investment company that allows for the pooling of assets. It is established under a company form with its own legal

41. Commonly referred to as an 'umbrella fund'.

personality and its registered office in Luxembourg. A SICAV's capital is constantly equal to its net assets. Hence, its capital automatically increases or decreases with subscriptions and redemptions, as well as by deviating valuations of its net asset value. There are no formalities required for the increase or decrease in capital. SICAVs may be either self-managed or appoint a management company. If a SICAV intends to qualify as a UCITS, it must be organized as an SA or SE. If a SICAV intends to qualify as an SIF, it can be incorporated in either a corporate form (as an SA, SE, SARL, or SCA) or as a partnership (an SCS or SCSp).

Finally, an FCP is simply a collection of assets held under joint ownership. It is governed by a contractual agreement and has no legal personality. Thus, it must be managed by a Luxembourg management company on behalf of the joint owners. The co-ownership is established under Luxembourg law by its constitutional document. The joint owners' liability is limited to the amount they have contributed and their rights are represented by units.

§2.04 FISCAL REGIME FOR LUXEMBOURG REGULATED AND NON-REGULATED INVESTMENT FUNDS

First and foremost, the tax treatment of a Luxembourg-based investment fund will depend on its concrete structure (i.e., whether the investment vehicle is regulated or non-regulated under the applicable laws in Luxembourg).

In general, and as already indicated above, Luxembourg-based UCIs and those non-Luxembourg-based UCIs that have their effective place of management in Luxembourg are not subject to Luxembourg's *impôt sur le revenu des collectivités* (corporate income tax or CIT),[42] its *impôt commercial communal* (municipal business tax or MBT),[43] or its *impôt sur la fortune* (net wealth tax or NWT)[44] and, therefore, essentially exempt from the general direct taxation principles. However, registration duty and annual subscription tax will be levied on UCIs (instead). There is however no stamp duty on the issuance of shares or the transfer of shares.

From a systematic standpoint, in the area of direct taxation of investment funds it has to be differentiated between the following phases and potential scenarios:

(1) Taxation at the time of the constitution of an investment fund.
(2) Taxation during the course of the existence of an investment fund.
(3) Taxation of an investment fund in the event of dissolution, merger, demerger, conversion of legal form, or any similar circumstances.
(4) Taxation of the management companies.
(5) Taxation of the investor(s).

42. *See* Arts 159 et seq. LIR.
43. *Gewerbesteuergesetz (la loi modifiée du 1er décembre 1936 concernant l'impôt commercial)*, as amended (hereinafter the '1936 MBT Law').
44. *Vermögensteuergesetz* (*loi sur l'impôt sur la fortune du 16 octobre 1934*).

[A] Taxation at the Time of the Constitution of an Investment Fund

At the time of constitution, investment funds incorporated as investment companies are subject to a registration duty of EUR 75[45] on the date of incorporation as well as in case of the modification of the articles of incorporation. Registration duty of the same amount will also be levied when a non-Luxembourg-based investment fund transfers its effective place of management or registered office to Luxembourg. In contrast thereto, investment funds established as FCPs (i.e., constituting an undivided pool of assets) are not subject to registration duty.

[B] Taxation During the Course of the Existence of the Investment Fund

The distinguishing feature for Luxembourg-based regulated investment funds is that, under certain conditions, they are not subject to any income taxation or wealth taxation imposed on ordinary corporations. Their ordinary revenue, received from domestic or foreign sources, and their capital gains (both realized and unrealized), in principle, may be exempt from taxation. In contrast thereto, non-regulated investment funds, however, under certain conditions, may not be exempt from income taxation and wealth taxation, but might be subject to tax in accordance with general taxation principles.

Taxation during the course of the existence of the relevant investment fund varies depending on its concrete set-up. Regulated UCIs, in general, have in common that the only tax they have to pay is the subscription tax, based on the particular UCI's net asset value. Whether or not the fund makes distributions or capitalizes all or part of its income has no effect on the subscription tax. From a procedural perspective, the Luxembourg legislator recently introduced electronic filing for tax returns. UCIs are now obliged to file their tax declarations electronically from 1 January 2018 onwards.

[1] UCITS and Part II UCIs

UCITS and Part II UCIs may be set up as FCP or SICAV/SICAF. Such investment funds do fall within the scope of Articles 172 through 179 2010 UCI Law and are in general subject to an annual subscription tax at a standard rate of 0.05%.[46] According to Article 173(1) 2010 UCI Law, and without prejudice to the collection of a registration fee and transcription and implementation of national legislation on VAT, there is no other tax payable by UCIs located or established in Luxembourg within the meaning of the 2010 UCI Law.

The taxable basis for the annual subscription tax is calculated on the aggregated net assets of the specific UCI, valued as of the last day of each calendar quarter during the fiscal year. On the date of incorporation of the UCI, the subscription is calculated on

45. The registration duty is fixed in the amount of EUR 75 and does not change if different compartments are used in an umbrella fund structure.
46. Article 174(1) 2010 UCI Law.

a pro rata basis with respect to the date of incorporation and the end of the following calendar quarter. The subscription tax is payable on a quarterly basis.

Article 174(2) 2010 UCI Law grants a reduced rate of 0.01% in the following cases:

- undertakings whose sole object is collective investment in money market instruments and placing of deposits with credit institutions;
- undertakings whose sole object is collective investment in deposits with credit institutions; and
- individual compartments of UCITS/UCIs with multiple compartments as well as for individual classes of securities issued within a UCITS/UCI or within a compartment of a UCITS/UCI with multiple compartments, provided that the securities of such compartments or classes are reserved to one or more institutional investors.

Several exemptions from subscription tax are available under Article 175 2010 UCI Law for:

- the value of the UCIs' assets represented by units held in other UCIs, provided that such units have already been subject to the subscription tax provided for in Article 174 2010 UCI Law, Article 68 2007 SIF Law, Article 46 2016 RAIF Law;
- UCIs, as well as individual compartments of UCIs with multiple compartments, whose (i) securities are reserved for institutional investors, (ii) sole object is collective investment in money market instruments and placing of deposits with credit institutions, and (iii) weighted residual portfolio maturity does not exceed ninety days, and (iv) that have obtained the highest possible rating from a recognized rating agency. Where several classes of securities exist within the UCI or the compartment, the exemption only applies to those classes of securities reserved to institutional investors;
- UCIs whose securities are reserved to (i) institutions for occupational retirement pension or similar investment vehicles, set up on one or more employers' initiative for the benefit of their employees and (ii) companies of one or more employers investing funds they hold to provide retirement benefits to their employees;
- UCIs, as well as individual compartments of UCIs with multiple compartments, whose main objective is investment in microfinance institutions;
- UCIs, as well as individual compartments of UCIs with multiple compartments, whose (i) securities are listed or traded on at least one stock exchange or another regulated market operating regularly, recognized and open to the public, and (ii) exclusive object is to replicate the performance of one or more indices. If several classes of securities exist within the UCI or the compartment, the exemption only applies to classes fulfilling the condition of sub-point (i).

Withholding tax on the amounts distributed by UCITS and Part II UCIs will not be levied.

[2] SIFs

Pursuant to Article 66 2007 SIF Law, no tax – other than the subscription tax described in Article 68 2007 SIF Law – shall be payable by SIFs. The annual subscription tax amounts to 0.01% of the aggregate net asset value of the SIF as evaluated on the last day of each calendar quarter during the fiscal year and is payable on a quarterly basis.

The following exemptions from subscription tax are available under Article 68(2) 2007 SIF Law for:

- the value of the assets represented by units held in other UCIs provided that such units have already been subject to the subscription tax provided for by Article 68(1) 2007 SIF Law, Article 174 2010 UCI Law, or Article 46 2016 RAIF Law;
- SIFs, as well as individual compartments of SIFs with multiple compartments, whose (i) sole objective is collective investment in money market instruments and placing of deposits with credit institutions and (ii) weighted residual portfolio maturity does not exceed ninety days, and (iii) that have obtained the highest possible rating from a recognized rating agency;
- SIFs whose securities or partnership interests are reserved for (i) institutions for occupational retirement provision, or similar investment vehicles, set up on one or more employers' initiative for the benefit of their employees and (ii) companies of one or more employers investing funds they hold, in order to provide retirement benefits to their employees;
- SIFs as well as individual compartments of SIFs with multiple compartments whose main objective is the investment in microfinance institutions.

The amounts distributed by SIFs are generally not subject to a withholding tax.

[3] RAIFs

Article 45(1) 2016 RAIF Law states that RAIFs are – *inter alia* with the exception of VAT and subject to Article 48 2016 RAIF Law – not liable to other taxes apart from the subscription tax. Article 46(1) 2016 RAIF Law, read in conjunction with Article 46(3) 2016 RAIF Law, limits the annual subscription tax to 0.01% of the aggregate net asset value of the RAIF as evaluated on the last day of each calendar quarter in the fiscal year. The subscription tax is payable on a quarterly basis.

Article 46(2) 2016 RAIF Law exempts the following from subscription tax:

- the value of its assets represented by units held in other UCIs provided that such units have already been subject to the subscription tax provided for by this provision, Article 174 2010 UCI Law, or Article 68 2007 SIF Law;
- RAIFs, as well as individual compartments of such funds with multiple compartments, whose (i) sole objective is collective investment in money market instruments and placing of deposits with credit institutions or (ii)

weighted residual portfolio maturity does not exceed ninety days, and (iii) that have obtained the highest possible rating from a recognized rating agency;

- RAIFs, as well as individual compartments and individual classes of such funds, whose securities or partnership interests are reserved to (i) institutions for occupational retirement provision, or similar investment vehicles, set-up on one or more employer's initiative for the benefit of their employees and (ii) companies of one or more employers investing funds they hold in order to provide retirement benefits to their employees;
- RAIFs, as well as individual compartments of such funds with multiple compartments, whose investment policy provides that at least 50% of their assets shall be invested in one or more microfinance institutions.

The amounts distributed by RAIFs are not subject to withholding tax.

[4] SICARs

A SICAR, which cannot be established in the form of a common fund, may either be set up in the form of a corporate entity or a partnership. Therefore, a SICAR may take the legal form of, *inter alia,* an SA, SARL, or SCA. On the other hand, a SICAR may also be established as an SCS or SCSp.

From a direct tax perspective, corporate entities, such as SAs, SARLs, and SCAs, are considered to be separate legal entities having their own tax liability, whereas partnerships, such as SCSs or SCSps, are deemed to be transparent entities for the purpose of CIT.[47] Consequently, the following description is divided into two subsections.

[a] Corporate Form

Unlike UCIs, a SICAR in a corporate form is not liable to the annual subscription tax. Rather, its business profits are fully subject to CIT and MBT at ordinary rates,[48] in the same manner as those of any other ordinary Luxembourg company.[49] However, income derived from its private equity and venture capital activities are excluded from its tax base for CIT and MBT purposes.

A corporate-form SICAR benefits from a partial objective exemption, according to which the following income is excluded from its tax base:

- income derived from portfolio items consisting of securities, as well as capital gains derived from such securities upon transfer, contribution, liquidation or

47. Pursuant to Art. 34(1)(a) 2004 SICAR Law, Art. 14(1) LIR was amended to state that SICARs organized as ordinary limited partnerships cannot be considered commercial companies.
48. Cf. Art. 174(1) LIR and § 16 1936 MBT Law.
49. However, a SICAR is not eligible for the CIT's consolidation regime, which permits, under certain conditions, companies to consolidate their tax liability with subsidiaries in which it holds, directly or indirectly, at least 95% (cf. Art. 164*bis*(5) LIR).

any other disposal thereof.[50] The term 'securities' should be broadly interpreted to include shares, bonds, and other debt instruments, as well as other negotiable instruments giving a right to acquire such securities;
- income derived from a temporary investment in liquid assets held for a maximum period of twelve months before their investment in risk capital.[51] Investment in 'risk capital' means providing funds, directly or indirectly, to an entity for the purpose of its launch, development, or listing on a stock exchange.

In order to avoid a double exemption, realized losses, losses resulting from the transfer of transferable securities, and unrealized losses accounted for on the reduction of the value of these assets cannot be deducted from the taxable income of the company pursuant to Article 34(2) 2004 SICAR Law.

Although a corporate-form SICAR is not liable to NWT, the recently enacted minimum NWT or MNWT will apply to a corporate-form SICAR.[52] As from 1 January 2016, an MNWT is levied on companies having their statutory seat or central administration in Luxembourg. For entities for which the sum of fixed financial assets, transferable securities, and cash at bank exceeds 90% of their total gross assets and EUR 350,000, the MNWT is set at EUR 4,815. For all other companies having their statutory seat or central administration in Luxembourg which do not fall within the scope of the EUR 4,815 MNWT, the MNWT ranges from EUR 535 to EUR 32,100, depending on the company's total gross assets.

In general, CIT for a corporate-form SICAR is levied at an effective maximum rate of 20.33% (inclusive of 7% surcharge for Luxembourg's employment fund). The MBT is levied at a variable rate according to the municipality in which the company is located; it was 6.75% for Luxembourg City in 2017. Consequently, the maximum aggregate CIT and MBT rate was 27.08% in Luxembourg City in 2017. As of 1 January 2018, the CIT rate will be reduced from 19% to 18%, which would imply a reduction of the CIT and MBT maximum aggregate rate to 26.01% in Luxembourg City for 2018.

Dividends distributed by a SICAR are exempt from withholding tax.

[b] Partnership

For income tax purposes,[53] a partnership is not considered to have a distinct legal personality from its partners. Therefore, both SCSs and SCSps are considered tax-transparent entities for income tax purposes; as such, they are not liable to CIT in

---

50. Article 34(2) 2004 SICAR Law.
51. Article 34(3) 2004 SICAR Law.
52. Pursuant to Art. 35 2004 SICAR Law, § 3(1)(5) of the *Loi sur l'impôt sur la fortune du 16 octobre 1934 - (Vermögenssteuergesetz)*, as amended (hereinafter the '1934 NWT Law') was further amended: SICARs organized under the form of a partnership limited by shares, a cooperative in the form of a public limited company, a private limited company, or a public limited company governed by Luxembourg law are exempt from NWT, except from MNWT determined in accordance with the requirements of § 8(2) 1934 NWT Law.
53. Article 175(1) LIR; *see also* §11*bis* of the *Loi d'adaptation fiscale du 16 octobre 1934 (Steueranpassungsgesetz)*, as amended.

Luxembourg. Any profits realized by such partnerships are, instead, directly taxable at the level of the partners, irrespective of any distribution thereof.[54] In the same manner, any losses are, in principle, directly deductible from the partner's other taxable income.

According to Article 57 LIR, each of the partners is deemed to run his own, separate enterprise to the extent of his proportionate interest in the partnership. From a direct tax perspective, the partnership itself merely bundles together the separate balance sheets of its partners and their respective separate enterprises: this principle is commonly referred to as *Bilanzbündeltheorie*, which has its origin in the case law of the *Bundesfinanzhof* (the German Federal Tax Court).

Moreover, for MBT purposes, a partnership itself can be subject to tax, if it realizes or is deemed to realize business profits, even absent any business activity. According to the *Geprägetheorie* (commonly translated as the 'business-taint theory'),[55] the partnership's profits are deemed to be business profits and, thus, are subject to MBT even without any genuine business activity, so long as the general partner is a *société de capitaux* (i.e., a company limited by share capital), such as an SA or SARL, and that entity owns at least 5% of the economic interest in the partnership. However, the *Geprägetheorie* does not apply to SICARs, such that any risk of a business-profit characterization pursuant to the *Geprägetheorie* is avoided.[56]

[5] Non-regulated Investment Funds

Non-regulated investment funds may be set up in the form of either a corporate entity or a partnership under the SOPARFI regime for holding companies. These investment funds are not subject to the beneficial treatment provided to regulated UCIs (i.e., only applying subscription tax) but rather fall within the scope of the general taxation principles as follows.

[a] Corporate Form

The term 'SOPARFI' refers to an ordinary, unregulated Luxembourg resident corporate entity which is fully subject to CIT, MBT, and NWT, whose main activity is to hold shares in subsidiaries benefiting from the participation exemption regime pursuant to Article 166 LIR. A typical SOPARFI adopts the form of an SA, SARL, or SCA.

In principle, any dividend and liquidation proceeds received by a Luxembourg corporate entity are generally taxable and, consequently, are included in its taxable base. A tax credit is, in principle, available for Luxembourg or foreign withholding tax retained by the distributing company. The same applies to liquidation proceeds. Capital gains, in general, are regarded as ordinary business income and, consequently, are also included in the taxable base for CIT and MBT purposes.

54. Marc Schmitz & Philip J. Warner, *Luxembourg in International Tax*, 201 et seq. (3d ed. 2015).
55. Article 14(4) LIR.
56. Pursuant to Art. 36 2004 SICAR Law, the 1936 MBT Law was further amended to add a new paragraph (4) to §2(2) thereof, essentially excluding SICARs in the form of a common limited partnership from § 2(2)(3) 1936 MBT Law.

However, Article 166 LIR provides that dividend income and liquidation proceeds derived by a Luxembourg company from its participation in subsidiaries should be tax exempt, by virtue of the participation exemption, provided that a subsidiary is an eligible entity and that, at the time the income is made available, the Luxembourg company has held or commits to hold directly for an uninterrupted period of at least twelve months a participation of at least 10% in the distributing entity or with an acquisition price of at least EUR 1.2 million.

In this context, it should be noted that Luxembourg introduced an anti-hybrid and a general anti-abuse rule (GAAR) in its domestic provisions[57] regarding the revised version of the EU Parent-Subsidiary Directive or PSD.[58]

In a nutshell, the benefit of participation exemption rules could be denied:

> in the framework of an arrangement or a series of arrangements which, having been put in place for the main purpose or one of the main purposes of obtaining a tax advantage that defeats the object or purposes of the PSD (so-called motive test), are not genuine having regard to all relevant facts and circumstances (so-called substance test). An arrangement or a series of arrangements shall be regarded as not genuine to the extent that they are not put in place for valid commercial reasons which reflect economic reality.[59]

The 2015 GAAR Law does not provide guidance as to the meaning of the GAAR concepts mentioned therein. That being said, it should be noted that GAAR is intended to establish a common minimum standard among the EU Member States for situations of misuse of the PSD. The wording is intentionally expansive, in order to give broad discretion to the Member States' tax authorities, such that it is difficult to indicate which 'arrangements or series of arrangements' fall within its scope and which distributions are at risk of being denied the benefits thereof.

Capital gains are, generally, taxable upon realization. However, as in the context of dividends and liquidation proceeds, capital gains realized by a Luxembourg company in connection with its subsidiaries will be exempt from CIT and MBT provided that a subsidiary is an eligible entity[60] and that, at the time of disposal of the

57. *See* the *Loi du 18 décembre 2015 Loi du 18 décembre 2015 portant transposition: - de la directive 2014/86/UE du Conseil du 8 juillet 2014 modifiant la directive 2011/96/UE concernant le régime fiscal commun applicable aux sociétés mères et filiales d'États membres différents; de la directive 2015/121/UE du Conseil du 27 janvier 2015 modifiant la directive 2011/96/UE concernant le régime fiscal commun applicable aux sociétés mères et filiales d'États membres différents; portant modification: de la loi modifiée du 4 décembre 1967 concernant l'impôt sur le revenu; de la loi modifiée du 16 octobre 1934 sur l'évaluation des biens et valeurs; de la loi modifiée du 1er décembre 1936 concernant l'impôt commercial; de la loi générale des impôts modifiée du 22 mai 1931 ('Abgabenordnung'); et de la loi modifiée du 24 décembre 1996 portant introduction d'une bonification d'impôt sur le revenu en cas d'embauchage de chômeurs,* as amended (hereinafter the '2015 GAAR Law').
58. Council Directive 2011/96/EU of 30 November 2011 on the common system of taxation applicable in the case of parent companies and subsidiaries of different Member States [2009] OJ L 345/8, as amended by Council Directive 2014/86/EU of 8 July 2014 amending Directive 2011/96/EU on the common system of taxation applicable in the case of parent companies and subsidiaries of different Member States, [2014] OJ L 219/40 (hereinafter the 'PSD').
59. Cf. Art. 166(2*bis*) LIR.
60. *See* Art. 166 LIR with respect to the participation exemption for dividends and liquidation proceeds.

shares, the Luxembourg company has held or commits itself to hold directly for an uninterrupted period of at least twelve months a participation of at least 10% or with an acquisition price of at least EUR 6 million in a subsidiary.[61]

However, the participation exemption regime contains some rules intended to avoid double benefits.[62] Should the capital gain realized by a Luxembourg company upon disposal of its participation in a subsidiary be exempt under the participation exemption regime, that exemption would not apply to the algebraic sum of related expenses (i.e., business expenses in direct economic relationship with the exempt capital gains) and value adjustments that decreased the tax result in the current or preceding years (this is referred to as the 'recapture rule' for previous deductions). To the extent that the participation in the subsidiary is equity-funded, the recapture rule has little practical relevance.

[b] Partnership

A SOPARFI set up as a tax-transparent entity (e.g., an SCS or SCSp) is not subject to CIT or NWT. Profits, however, may still be subject to MBT if the partnership either carries out a business activity or, by virtue of the business-taint theory, if the partnership's general partner owns 5% or more of the interests in the partnership.[63]

Business income may derive from a genuine business activity, as defined in Article 14(1) LIR. Based on the said provision, a genuine 'business activity' is defined as any (i) independent, (ii) profit-driven activity that is (iii) exercised in a permanent manner and (iv) participates in general economic life. Activities not fulfilling these four criteria, concomitantly, are not business activities and should rather qualify as *Vermögensverwaltung* (private wealth-management activities) for tax purposes. These four criteria however are not defined in the relevant statutes. Luxembourg case law analyses on a case-by-case basis, whether the activity at hand, if it had been performed by an individual, would have constituted the mere management of his/her private wealth or if the activities go beyond this scope and notably impact the substance of his/her wealth. Thus, provided that the activity of the partnership does not go beyond the mere management of its private wealth, it should not be subject to MBT.

In this regard, the Luxembourg tax authorities issued, on 9 January 2015, a circular[64] with respect to the taxation of, for example, income realized by a Luxembourg SCS or SCSp and providing additional guidance as to what would be considered

61. This is governed by Art. 166(9) LIR and *Règlement grand-ducal du 21 décembre 2001 portant exécution de l'article 166, alinéa 9, numéro 1 de la loi modifiée du 4 décembre 1967 concernant l'impôt sur le revenu.*
62. Article 166(5) LIR.
63. Recall that, according to *Geprägetheorie* (the business-taint theory), a partnership's profits are deemed to be business profits subject to MBT even absent a genuine business activity, if the general partner is a company limited by share capital (e.g., an SARL) that owns at least 5% of the economic interest in the partnership. In other words, if the general partner owns less than 5% thereof, the business-taint theory does not apply.
64. *Circulaire du directeur des contributions, LIR n° 14/4 du 9 janvier 2015: Objet: Imposition des revenus réalisés par une société en commandite simple ou une société en commandite spéciale* (hereinafter the '2015 Circular').

to exceed the normal management of private wealth. In particular, the 2015 Circular provides that an activity will be considered as private wealth management if the acquisitions and sales are only auxiliary and incidental to the main activity, which is the enjoyment of the fruits (*Fruchtziehung*) of private wealth, the substance of which is broadly maintained. On the contrary, the exploitation of the substance of a taxpayer's wealth through the transfer (*Umschichtung*) of substantial elements of its wealth would in principle exceed the limits of the normal management of private wealth. Accordingly, a high number of investments (e.g., trading activity) that are acquired and traded within a short timeframe could indicate that an enterprise is conducting a business activity. Repeated short-term transactions on substantial portions of the assets could therefore in general be seen as business activity. Also, when determining whether a partnership is a business enterprise, the extent or importance of the wealth under management is thus not conclusive. More than the nature of the investment, it is the investment strategy that needs to be considered in order to determine whether a partnership may be exempt from MBT.

The fact that, in a fund scenario, the partnership is often administered by external professional asset managers is not an indication that it is performing a commercial activity. With regards to investment strategies, the 2015 Circular specifies that if a partnership qualifies as an AIF within the meaning of the 2013 AIFM Law, it is automatically deemed to not be carrying out a commercial activity, as its sole purpose is an investment purpose, rather than a commercial purpose. Thus, provided that the partnership limits its activities to activities that are normally carried out by AIFs (e.g., long-term investments and private equity investments), it should not, according to the 2015 Circular, be viewed as carrying out a business activity.

[6] NWT

As previously mentioned, Luxembourg imposes an NWT on resident corporate taxpayers[65] at a rate of 0.5% applied on net assets as determined for NWT purposes on a taxable base of up to EUR 500 million and a rate of 0.05% on any portion of the taxable base that exceeds EUR 500 million.[66] For the purposes of the 1934 NWT Law, 'net worth' means the *valeur unitaire* (unitary value), as typically determined on 1 January of each year. The unitary value is calculated as the difference between (i) assets estimated at their fair market value (*valeur estimée de réalisation*), and (ii) liabilities vis-à-vis third parties.[67] In that respect, third-party liabilities in relation to exempt assets are not deductible in computing the unitary value. The amount of NWT due for

65. For the purposes of the 1934 NWT Law, *supra* note 52, partnerships are also viewed as tax-transparent entities and, as such, are not liable to the NWT. NWT treatment at the level of the partners, however, depends on their personal status.
66. Cf. § 4 1934 NWT Law.
67. Cf. §§ 73 through 77 Evaluation Law (*loi du 16 octobre 1934 concernant l'évaluation des biens et valeurs - Bewertungsgesetz*).

any given year, however, can be reduced up to the amount of CIT payable for the prior tax year, subject to the creation and maintenance of a specific reserve therefor).[68]

However, UCIs governed by the 2010 UCI Law, the 2004 SICAR Law, the 2007 SIF Law, or the 2016 RAIF Law are basically exempt from NWT and – apart from the SICAR – the MNWT will not be levied, either.

Unregulated investment funds are exempt from the NWT if the conditions of the participation exemption regime applicable to dividends are fulfilled (other than the holding period, which is not required). However, although the participation exemption is applicable (or would be applicable but for the holding period), as of 1 January 2016, the MNWT will be levied on companies having their statutory seat or central administration in Luxembourg. An RAIF vehicle opting for the treatment as a venture capital vehicle under the 2016 RAIF Law, despite being exempt (in whole or in part) from CIT, remains subject to the MNWT.

[C] Taxation of a UCI in the Event of Dissolution, Merger, Demerger, Conversion of Legal Form, or Any Similar Circumstances

In general, the dissolution of a UCI is in principle tax neutral and does not have particular tax consequences under Luxembourg tax law.[69] The distribution of the liquidation surplus, if any, is not subject to withholding tax at source, either.[70]

Mergers and demerges of UCIs, or their sub-funds, are also not taxable in Luxembourg. A change of legal form (i.e., when a contractual UCI is converted into a UCI in a corporate form) is also not subject to taxation.[71]

However, in contrast to the aforementioned tax neutrality in cases of a UCI's dissolution, merger, demerger, conversion of legal form, the general taxation principles of Article 169 LIR et seq. do apply when a non-regulated investment fund in a corporate form under the SOPARFI holding-company regime is subject to such a transaction. For instance, under Article 169 LIR, a merger is assimilated to a liquidation of the absorbed company. A merger is generally carried out at the *valeur d'exploitation* (the going-concern value), leading to the taxation of hidden reserves (i.e., the difference between the going-concern value and the book value) of the absorbed company. Such hidden reserves are in general subject to CIT and MBT at ordinary rates, with the maximum aggregate rate in 2017 in Luxembourg City being 27.08% (including a contribution to the employment fund). As of 1 January 2018, the CIT rate was reduced from 19% to 18%, which implies a reduction of the CIT and MBT maximum aggregate rate to 26.01% in Luxembourg City. As an exception, however, certain mergers can be carried

68. Cf. § 8a 1934 NWT Law.
69. Kremer & Lebbe, *supra* note 16, Recital 11.83.
70. For example, Art. 34(2) 2004 SICAR Law.
71. From the implementation of the Council Directive 2003/48/EC of 3 June 2003, on taxation of savings income in the form of interest payments (hereinafter 'EU Savings Directive') into Luxembourg law pursuant to the Law of 21 June 2005 until its repeal effective 1 January 2016, mergers of UCIs, compartments and share classes may have been subject to the application of the EU Savings Directive.

out at book value (i.e., without realizing the hidden reserves);[72] consequently, they are tax neutral at the level of the absorbed company. In order for a non-regulated investment fund in corporate form to benefit from such a tax neutral merger, the following conditions, set out in Articles 170 and 171 LIR, must be met (cumulatively):

- the absorbing company is a Luxembourg fully taxable resident company;[73]
- the transfer of the absorbed company's assets to the absorbing company needs to be carried out against the issuance of shares in the absorbing company to the absorbed company's shareholders and, as the case may be, a cash payment not exceeding 10% of the nominal value of the shares of the absorbed company;[74] and
- the transfer is carried out in a way that ultimately ensures the taxation of the hidden reserves of absorbed company's assets in Luxembourg.[75]

[D] Taxation of Management Companies

Luxembourg management companies are established in corporate form (usually as SA or SARL) and are subject to general taxation principles.[76] As a tax resident in Luxembourg, management companies are in general subject to NWT at the rate of 0.5% (or 0.05% for the upper tranche of the net worth exceeding EUR 500 million) applied on net assets as determined for NWT purposes. However, the participation of a management company, if any, in another company will be considered an exempt asset for NWT tax purposes to the extent that the conditions of the Luxembourg participation exemption regime are met (except that the management company must merely hold the qualifying participation at the end of the previous accounting year).

As a rule, dividends paid by the management company to its shareholders are subject to a 15% withholding tax, unless a reduced rate or an exemption applies under an applicable DTT or by virtue of Luxembourg's participation exemption regime.[77]

Further, Luxembourg resident companies may be subject to MNWT. The MNWT is set at EUR 4,815 for Luxembourg companies whose financial assets, receivable against related companies, transferable securities, and cash deposits exceed, cumulatively (i) 90% of their total balance sheet and (ii) EUR 350,000. All other companies

72. Cf. Art. 170 LIR.
73. Article 170(2) LIR.
74. Article 170(2)(1) LIR).
75. Article 170(2)(2) LIR.
76. As for 2017, the maximum aggregate CIT and MBT rate amounts to 27.08% in Luxembourg City. As of 1 January 2018, the maximum aggregate CIT and MBT rate amounts to 26.01% in Luxembourg City.
77. As already described above, under Luxembourg's participation exemption regime, dividend payments paid by a fully taxable Luxembourg company may be exempt from withholding tax if, at the time the income is made available, the recipient, which must be an eligible recipient, has held or commits itself to hold, directly, for an uninterrupted period of at least twelve months, a participation of at least 10% or with an acquisition price of at least EUR 1.2 million in the share capital of the distributing entity. The benefit of the participation exemption on outbound dividends remains subject to the 2015 GAAR Law, *supra* note 57.

which do not meet the aforementioned conditions are subject to MNWT on the basis of their total balance sheet according to a progressive tax scale varying from EUR 535 to EUR 32,100.

[E] Taxation of Investors

With respect to taxation of an investment fund's investors[78] in Luxembourg, the above-drawn differentiation between regulated UCIs and non-regulated investment funds has to be taken into account as well.

[1] UCIs

Generally, an investor or shareholder in a Luxembourg-based investment fund will not become a resident for income tax purposes, nor be deemed to be a tax resident in Luxembourg, only by reason of holding such shares, or by the execution, performance, delivery, and/or the enforcement of rights and obligations under the shares. As already indicated above, regulated investment funds are in general not required to withhold withholding tax.

[a] Income Taxation of Investors Qualifying as Luxembourg Non-residents

Investors or shareholders who are non-residents of Luxembourg and who have neither a permanent establishment nor a permanent representative in Luxembourg to which or to whom the shares are attributable are not liable to any Luxembourg income tax on income received or capital gains realized upon the sale, disposal, or redemption of such shares or interests in a Luxembourg-based investment fund.

Non-resident corporate shareholders in a Luxembourg-based investment fund that have a permanent establishment or a permanent representative in Luxembourg to which the shares in the investment fund are attributable must include any income received, as well as any gain realized on the sale, disposal, or redemption of shares, in their taxable income for Luxembourg tax-assessment purposes. The same inclusion applies to non-resident individuals acting in the course of the management of a business undertaking, if they have a permanent establishment or a permanent representative in Luxembourg to which or to whom the shares are attributable.

Taxable gains are determined as being the difference between the sale, repurchase, or redemption price and the lower of the cost or book value of the shares sold or redeemed.

78. Individuals are subject to progressive income tax rates (in 2017 with a top marginal rate of 45.78%, including the contribution for the employment fund).

[b] *Income Taxation of the Investors Qualifying as Luxembourg Residents*

Any dividends received, and other payments derived, from shares in a Luxembourg-based investment fund by individuals who are Luxembourg tax residents and are acting in the course of either their private wealth-management activity or their professional or business activity are subject to income tax at Luxembourg's progressive ordinary rates.[79]

Capital gains realized upon disposal of shares in Luxembourg-based investment funds by Luxembourg tax-resident individuals, acting in the course of the management of their private wealth, are not subject to income tax, unless said capital gains qualify either as speculative gains or as gains on a 'substantial participation'.[80] Capital gains are deemed to be speculative, and are thus subject to income tax at ordinary rates, if the shares are disposed of less than six months after the acquisition thereof,[81] or if their disposal precedes their acquisition. A shareholding is a 'substantial participation' in only limited cases, in particular if (i) the shareholder has held, either alone or together with his spouse or partner and/or his minor children, either directly or indirectly, at any time within the five years preceding the realization of the gain, more than 10% of the share capital of the fund, or (ii) the taxpayer acquired free of charge, within the five years preceding the transfer, a participation that was constituting a substantial participation in the hands of the alienator (or the alienators in case of successive transfers free of charge within the same five-year period).[82] Capital gains realized on a substantial participation more than six months after the acquisition thereof are subject to income tax according to the half-global rate method (i.e., the average rate applicable to the total income is calculated according to progressive income tax rates and half of the average rate is applied to the capital gains realized on the substantial participation).[83] A disposal may include a sale, an exchange, a contribution, or any other kind of alienation of the shareholding.

Capital gains realized on the disposal of the shares in Luxembourg-based investment funds by an individual Luxembourg tax resident, who acts in the course of the management of his or her professional or business activity, are subject to income tax at ordinary rates. Taxable gains are the difference between the price for which the shares have been disposed of and the lower of their cost or book value.

79. In the case of a transparent investment fund (e.g., an FCP), the fund itself is considered fiscally transparent from a Luxembourg tax perspective, meaning that any income and gains received by the fund are generally taxed at the interest holder's level as soon as it is received by the fund. Although an FCP is, in principle, treated as a tax-transparent entity, the Luxembourg tax authorities – for practical purposes – follow a 'distribution approach', instead, for Luxembourg resident interest holders, meaning that the FCP's distribution of profits qualify as the taxable event. Corporate resident interest holders which are fully taxable companies are in general subject to CIT, MBT tax as well as the solidarity surcharge on income and gains from the interest.
80. Article 99, Art. 99*bis* and Art. 100 LIR.
81. Article 99*bis*(1) no. 1(b) LIR.
82. Article 100(2) LIR.
83. Article 132(2) no. 2 and Art. 131(1)(c) LIR.

Luxembourg resident corporate shareholders must also include any income received, as well as any gain realized on the sale, disposal, or redemption of shares, in their taxable income for Luxembourg income tax-assessment purposes.

[2] Non-regulated Investment Funds

As described above,[84] non-regulated investment funds may be set up in the form of either a corporate entity or a partnership under the SOPARFI regime.

For an investment fund vehicle that qualifies as a corporate entity (e.g., an SA or SARL), dividends paid by such an entity to its shareholders, as a rule, are subject to a 15% withholding tax, unless a reduced rate or an exemption applies under an applicable DTT or by virtue of Luxembourg's participation exemption regime.[85]

Distributions made by a partnership (e.g., an SCS or an SCSp.) to its partners are not subject to withholding tax in Luxembourg. Indeed, the partnership is deemed to be tax-transparent and distributions are performed for corporate reasons only, but are disregarded from a tax perspective, as any income and loss derived at the level of the partnership is directly attributable to its partners. Any Luxembourg non-resident partners will not become a tax resident, nor be deemed to be a tax resident, in Luxembourg solely by reason of the subscription, holding, and/or disposal of their interests in the partnership or the execution, performance, or enforcement of that partner's rights thereunder. From a Luxembourg tax perspective, a partner holding interests in the partnership is deemed to be holding a direct interest in the underlying investments of the partnership.[86] In such a look-through scenario, Luxembourg's participation exemption regime, pursuant to Article 166(3) LIR, may be applicable under certain circumstances.[87] Any Luxembourg non-resident partner, who has neither a permanent establishment nor a permanent representative in Luxembourg to which or to whom its interests in the partnership are attributable, should generally not be liable to Luxembourg income taxes (except in limited cases).

---

84. *See* §2.04[B][5]
85. Article 147 LIR. For further details, *see* §2.04[B][5][a], *supra*.
86. Article 175(1) LIR; *see also* §11*bis* of the *Loi d'adaptation fiscale du 16 octobre 1934 (Steueranpassungsgesetz)*, as amended.
87. For further details, *see* §2.04[B][5][a], *supra*.

CHAPTER 3

VAT and Investment Funds

Charlène A. Herbain & Marie-Isabelle Richardin

---

§3.01 INTRODUCTION

In the European Union (EU) value added tax (VAT) Directive,[1] special investment funds are covered by one provision.[2] This sets up an exemption for the management of special investment funds and covers a rather broad range of services.

But, minimalism is not synonymous with simplicity. The fact that only one provision of the EU VAT Directive relates to the investment-fund industry, and that this provision was adopted in the VAT legislation without prior discussion, as if it was an obvious 'no-brainer',[3] does not mean that the matter is simple. To the contrary, the questions relating to the VAT status of investment funds, as well as the scope of the VAT exemption, generally, are not straightforward. New types of funds appear on the market and certain services are not eligible for the VAT exemption. Furthermore, there are different interpretations of the scope of the exemption across the Member States, and there is a growing volume of more-or-less consistent case law on the subject from the Court of Justice of the European Union (CJEU).

The VAT treatment of the investment-fund industry is a concern not only for the investment funds themselves, but also for all the suppliers gravitating around them (management companies, central administration suppliers, depositaries, etc.) that

1. Council Directive 2006/112/EC of 28 November 2006 on the common system of value added tax, [2006] OJ L 347/1, as amended (hereinafter the 'EU VAT Directive'). The VAT Directive recast the Sixth Council Directive 77/388/EEC of 17 May 1977 on the harmonization of the laws of the Member States relating to turnover taxes – Common system of value added tax: uniform basis of assessment, [1977] OJ L 145/1 (hereinafter the 'Sixth Turnover Tax Directive'].
2. Article 135(1)(g) VAT Directive.
3. It was originally adopted in the Sixth Turnover Tax Directive without having been present in the Proposal for a sixth Council Directive on the harmonization of legislation of Member States concerning turnover taxes – Common system of value added tax: uniform basis of assessment, COM(1973)950 FINAL.

have to deal with numerous complex questions, such as the treatment of their services to said investment funds or the recovery of the VAT incurred on their purchases.

The developments discussed below are not exhaustive – a manual dedicated to the subject would be required to give such a list – but they do represent the legislation and the critical case law that highlight the areas of the matter that are most important to Luxembourg-based industry.

§3.02 VAT STATUS OF INVESTMENT FUNDS

[A] Directive and CJEU Case Law

The EU VAT Directive determines the taxable status of an operator based on the activity it performs and the remuneration it receives for it.[4] A 'taxable person'– that is, a person who is responsible for charging, collecting, and paying VAT to the tax authorities – means any person who, independently, carries out, in any place, any economic activity.[5] Any business activity is regarded as an 'economic activity'.[6] The purpose or results of such an activity do not influence the qualification of the activity, but it needs to consist of the exploitation of tangible or intangible property for the purposes of obtaining income therefrom on a continuing basis.[7]

The VAT status of holding entities cast doubt as to whether the activity of investment funds could qualify as an economic activity. Without prejudice to shareholder's rights, companies holding shares without getting involved, either directly or indirectly, in the management of the companies whose shares they held (so-called passive holdings), are not considered to be performing an economic activity for VAT purposes and, as such, are not regarded as a VAT-taxable person.

In that context, then, the taxable status of investment funds was not crystal clear: the intervention of the CJEU was needed for clarification.

In 2004, in the *BBL* case,[8] the CJEU ruled on the VAT status of SICAVs.[9] Based on the nature of their activities, which consist of raising capital from the public, purchasing securities, assembling portfolios, and managing such portfolios, as well as the existence of remuneration received therefor (i.e., a fee),[10] the CJEU held SICAVs to be VAT-taxable persons.[11] The reasoning of the Court was that these types of activities were going beyond the out-of-scope activity of acquisition and sale of securities to such an extent that it was, in fact, an economic activity within the meaning of the EU VAT Directive.

4. Article 9 VAT Directive.
5. Article 9 of the EU VAT Directive.
6. Article 2 of the EU VAT Directive.
7. Article 9(1) of the EU VAT Directive.
8. *BBL*, C-8/03, Judgment, EU:C:2004:650.
9. Open-ended investment companies.
10. Per Art. 1(2) of the amended Directive 85/611/EEC (abrogated). *See BBL*, C-8/03, para. 42.
11. *BBL*, C-8/03, paras 43–44.

In 2006, in the *Abbey National* case,[12] the CJEU used the same language to describe the activity and remuneration of a UCIs in transferable securities (UCITS) as it had used in *BBL* for SICAVs:

> the transactions carried out by UCITS consist in the collective investment in transferable securities of capital raised from the public. With the capital provided by subscribers when they purchase shares, UCITS assemble and manage, on behalf of the subscribers and for a fee, portfolios consisting of transferable securities.[13]

Therefore, and to the extent the *BBL* Court based VAT status on the nature and remuneration of the activities the entity performed, the conclusion drawn for SICAVs also applies to UCITSs in general:[14] they are to be considered taxable persons for VAT.

[B] Luxembourg Tax Authorities' Analysis

In Luxembourg, until the above-mentioned CJEU decisions, undertakings for collective investment (UCIs) were largely assimilated to passive holdings; as such, they were in principle deemed not to be taxable persons but, on a case-by-case basis, according to their effective activities, they could be recognized to be taxable persons. Performing an about-face, Luxembourg's VAT authority – the *Administration de l'Enregistrement et des Domaines* (AED) – published, in December 2006, a circular recognizing the automatic taxable status for UCIs.[15] Circular 723 generally provides that the status of 'VAT person' must be recognized for all entities that benefit from the VAT exemption applicable to fund-management services by virtue of Article 44(1)(d) of the VAT law.[16] This statement relies on a syllogism:

- Investment funds are taxable persons.
- The management of qualifying investment funds is exempt.
- Therefore, every entity that has its management exempt under the provision dedicated to investment funds management services is a taxable person.

The syllogism, like Circular 723, relies on the following underlying premises: the taxable status of investment funds is based on the nature of its output activities.[17] The exemption for VAT is granted to input costs when these are allocated to a specific output realized through the economic activity of a UCI. Therefore, whenever an input is exempt, it necessarily implies the existence of a qualifying output and it can, as such, determine the taxable status of an investment fund.

12. *Abbey National*, C-169/04, Judgment, EU:C:2005:523.
13. *Ibid.*, para. 61.
14. *Ibid.*
15. Direction de l'Enregistrement et des Domaines, *Circulaire N° 723 du 29 décembre 2006: Incidence des arrêts BBL et ABBEY NATIONAL de la Cour de Justice des Communautés européennes*, January 2007 (hereinafter 'Circular 723'), at http://www.aed.public.lu/actualites/2007/01/03_circulaire_723/index.html (last visited 3 January 2018).
16. *Ibid.*
17. The exemption of fund-management services is relying on the nature of the services rendered and the allocation of such services to the UCI's business.

This being said, it should be noted that both the CJEU's case law and Circular 723 define the UCIs' activity as the collective investment in transferable securities of capital raised from the public for a fee paid by the subscribers. This stance on the output is not well founded as, in practice, UCIs do not necessarily receive a fee from their investors, but rather dividends, interest, or gain from the investment activity itself. Therefore, in theory, a case-by-case analysis, relying on the VAT concept of 'consideration', is required to ascertain the correct VAT status of each UCI.[18] In practice, no such analysis is performed and, as soon as an entity has its management services exempt by virtue of Article 44(1)(d) of the VAT Law,[19] it is deemed to be a VAT-taxable person.

[1] The Entities

All investment funds whose management is exempt under the VAT Law are VAT-taxable persons.[20] As of the release of Circular 723 recognizing the automatic taxable status to UCIs, the practical impact of this rule has evolved with the scope of the exemption for the management of investment funds in the VAT Law.

At the time of the release of Circular 723, turning its back on a definition relying on a list of entities, a rather generic definition was used by the VAT Law.[21] It targeted: UCIs and pension funds otherwise supervised by Luxembourg's *Commission de Surveillance du Secteur Financier* (CSSF), its financial sector supervisory commission, or its *Commissariat aux Assurances* (CAA), its insurance supervisory authority; *Société d'investissement en capital à risque* or SICARs;[22] securitization vehicles;[23] and *fonds d'investissement spécialisés* or specialized investment funds (SIFs).[24] Then, in 2013

18. Michel Lambion, *Les Exonérations de TVA en Matières Financière au Luxembourg : Concepts et Interprétation, in Droit Fiscal Luxembourgeois: Livre Jubilaire de l'IFA Luxembourg,* 619 (André Elvinger et al., eds, 2008).
19. *Loi modifiée du 12 février 1979 concernant la taxe sur la valeur ajoutée concernant la taxe sur la valeur ajoutée,* as amended (hereinafter the 'VAT Law').
20. *See,* §3.04[A], *infra.*
21. The reference to a generic definition dates back to 2003. For a historical look at this issue, *see* Michel Lambion, *TVA: Inclusion des Fonds d'Investissement Alternatifs dans l'Article 44(1)(d) : Une Longue Marche,* 9 ACE 21 (2014).
22. Article 38, *Loi du 15 juin 2004 relative à la Société d'investissement en capital à risque (SICAR) et portant modification de la loi modifiée du 4 décembre 1967 relative à l'impôt sur le revenu, la loi modifiée du 16 octobre 1934 concernant l'impôt sur la fortune, la loi modifiée du 1er décembre 1936 concernant l'impôt commercial communal, la loi modifiée du 12 février 1979 concernant la taxe sur la valeur ajoutée, et la loi modifiée du 20 décembre 2002 concernant les organismes de placement collectif,* as amended (hereinafter the '2004 SICAR Law') added SICARs to the list of entities targeted by the VAT exemption.
23. Article 52(3), *Loi du 22 mars 2004 relative à la titrisation et portant modification de la loi modifiée du 5 avril 1993 relative au secteur financier; la loi modifiée du 23 décembre 1998 portant création d'une commission de surveillance du secteur financier; la loi du 27 juillet 2003 sur le trust et les contrats fiduciaires; la loi modifiée du 4 décembre 1967 relative à l'impôt sur le revenu; la loi modifiée du 16 octobre 1934 concernant l'impôt sur la fortune; et la loi modifiée du 12 février 1979 concernant la taxe sur la valeur ajoutée,* as amended (hereinafter the '2004 Securitization Vehicle Law') added securitization vehicles situated in Luxembourg to the list of entities targeted by the VAT exemption.
24. Article 73, *Loi du 13 février 2007 relative aux fonds d'investissement spécialisés et portant modification de la loi modifiée du 20 décembre 2002 relative aux organismes de placement*

and in response to Directive 2011/61/EU on Alternative Investment Fund Managers (AIFM),[25] the Luxembourg legislature amended the VAT Law by the 2013 AIFM Law;[26] the scope of the VAT exemption changed profoundly. The legislature extended the range of funds qualifying for the VAT exemption, as well as the geographical scope of that exemption. The new format of Article 44(1)(d) of the VAT Law stating the exemption in respect of the management of investment funds and, thus, establishes the qualification of VAT-taxable persons, is an entities' enumeration followed by a generic definition. The applicability of the fund-management exemption extends to non-Luxembourg vehicles and Alternatives Investment Funds (AIFs). These additions came with the attribution of VAT-taxable status to these vehicles.

We refer the reader to the section below (§3.04 *infra*) on the matter of the exemption for further details about the entities.

[2] Points of Attention

While there is no doubt that the VAT definition of a 'taxable person' was not forged by civil law concepts, it should be mentioned that, in the case of an investment fund that has no legal personality, determining if it is a VAT-taxable person might raise some issues.

Both *fonds commun de placement* or FCPs (common investment funds) and *sociétés en commandites spéciales* or SCSps have no legal personality, but might still be investment funds. An FCP is an undivided collection of assets and necessarily qualifies

---

collectif, et modification de la loi modifiée du 12 février 1979 concernant la taxe sur la valeur ajoutée, as amended (hereinafter the '2007 SIF Law') added specialized investment funds to the list of entities targeted by the VAT exemption.

25. Directive 2011/61/EU of the European Parliament and of the Council of 8 June 2011 on Alternative Investment Fund Managers and amending Directives 2003/41/EC and 2009/65/EC and Regulations (EC) No 1060/2009 and (EU) No 1095/2010 (Text with EEA relevance) [2011] OJ L 174/1, as amended (hereinafter the '2011 AIFM Directive'). *See* §3.03, *infra*.
26. Article 1(39) *Loi du 12 juillet 2013 relative aux gestionnaires de fonds d'investissement alternatifs et - portant transposition de la directive 2011/61/UE du Parlement européen et du Conseil du 8 juin 2011 sur les gestionnaires de fonds d'investissement alternatifs et modifiant les directives 2003/41/CE et 2009/65/CE ainsi que les règlements (CE) n° 1060/2009 et (UE) n° 1095/2010; portant modification: de la loi modifiée du 17 décembre 2010 concernant les organismes de placement collectif; de la loi modifiée du 13 février 2007 relative aux fonds d'investissement spécialisés; de la loi modifiée du 15 juin 2004 relative à la société d'investissement en capital à risque (SICAR); de la loi modifiée du 13 juillet 2005 relative aux institutions de retraite professionnelle sous forme de société d'épargne-pension à capital variable (SEPCAV) et d'association d'épargne-pension (ASSEP); de la loi du 13 juillet 2005 concernant les activités et la surveillance des institutions de retraite professionnelle; de la loi modifiée du 5 avril 1993 relative au secteur financier; de la loi modifiée du 12 novembre 2004 relative à la lutte contre le blanchiment et contre le financement du terrorisme; de la loi modifiée du 23 décembre 1998 portant création d'une commission de surveillance du secteur financier; de la loi modifiée du 10 août 1915 concernant les sociétés commerciales; de la loi modifiée du 19 décembre 2002 concernant le registre de commerce et des sociétés ainsi que la comptabilité et les comptes annuels des entreprises; du Code de commerce; de la loi modifiée du 4 décembre 1967 concernant l'impôt sur le revenu; de la loi modifiée du 1er décembre 1936 concernant l'impôt commercial; de la loi modifiée d'adaptation fiscale du 16 octobre 1934; de la loi modifiée du 16 octobre 1934 sur l'évaluation des biens et valeurs; et de la loi modifiée du 12 février 1979 concernant la taxe sur la valeur ajoutée*, as amended (hereinafter the '2013 AIFM Law').

as a UCI. From a VAT standpoint, it has been a longstanding practice that the FCP's management company is deemed to be the taxable person on behalf of the FCP.

The case of SCSps was not that clear. One of the uncertainties is caused by its lack of automatic status as an AIF,[27] since an SCSp may only benefit from the exemption (and, therefore, automatically recognized as a VAT-taxable person) when it is an AIF. Whether a UCI is an AIF is not a straightforward question, because there is no official status of AIF, neither in Luxembourg nor abroad, but only some requirements provided by law. In Luxembourg, to qualify as an AIF, the entity must raise capital from a number of investors with a view to investing that capital in accordance with a defined investment policy based on the principle of risk spreading for the benefit of those investors and must not need to be supervised according to Article 5 of the UCITS Directive.[28,29] Therefore, AIFs are not restricted to regulated undertakings, to Luxembourg vehicles, or even to EU vehicles and undertakings that wonder if they qualify as an AIF have to self-assess their status. Moreover, as there is a specific exclusion from AIF status for holding companies,[30] a further complication arises when an undertaking is not investing directly, but via a special purpose vehicle.

More uncertainty concerns a situation in which an SCSp is a VAT-taxable person. There are several questions that arise: How does its lack of legal personality impacts recognition of its VAT status at the level of the SCSp? Is its general partner deemed to be the taxable person as the representative of the SCSp? When an SCSp has more than one general partner, particularly one from a non-EU country, which one should prevail if VAT-taxable status is to be granted to the general partners?

These SCSp characteristics were prone to create issues from a VAT perspective and prompted some practitioners to argue in favour of the recognition of distinct taxable persons for the SCSp and its general partners. The argument obviously succeeded, based on the fact that VAT status is now determined by the activities performed and an SCSp can perform economic activities. The argument also relied on the fact that even though it has no legal personality, an SCSp is different from an FCP to the extent it is a contractual entity and not an 'undivided collection of assets' and that similar types of entities have been granted VAT-taxable status.

The AED confirmed that an SCSp should be considered as a VAT-taxable person, on its own and distinct from its general partners, to the extent the SCSp's activities qualify as economic activities conferring the status of VAT-taxable person.[31]

27. Article 88-1 of the *Loi du 17 décembre 2010 concernant les organismes de placement collectif*, as amended (the '2010 UCITS Law'). It is only when an AIF is a Part II UCI under the 2010 UCI Law that it automatically qualifies as an AIF.
28. Directive 2009/65/EC of the European Parliament and of the Council of 13 July 2009 on the coordination of laws, regulations and administrative provisions relating to undertakings for collective investment in transferable securities (UCITS) (recast) (Text with EEA relevance) [2009] OJ L 302/32, as amended (hereinafter the 'UCITS Directive').
29. *Supra* note 26
30. *Ibid.*, Art. 2(2).
31. Informal confirmation in November 2016. https://www.pwc.lu/en/private-equity/docs/pwc-private-equity-lux-limited-partnership.pdf l (last visited 10 January 2018).

§3.03 THE CONSEQUENCES OF VAT STATUS

[A] Registration and Compliance Obligations

In principle, all taxable persons, investment funds included, must register for VAT with the Luxembourg authorities.[32]

As an exception, taxable persons whose economic activity is entirely exempt, without any entitlement to recover input VAT (like most investment funds), benefit from a simplification measure and are released from the VAT registration's obligation.[33]

Leaving aside said exception and re-entering the main track, if such a taxable-but-exempt person receive non-exempt services from suppliers established outside Luxembourg for which it is liable to account for Luxembourg VAT, it is obliged to register for VAT and file VAT returns in order to report and collect the VAT due for these services to the AED.[34] In that same vein, a taxable-but-exempt person - such as an investment fund that receives, in Luxembourg, goods above the annual threshold of EUR 10,000 from other Member States - must self-assess Luxembourg VAT and, therefore, to register for VAT.[35]

VAT registration, once performed, triggers an obligation to fulfil certain compliance reporting. In a case where an investment fund has no right to input VAT deductions and cannot benefit from the simplification measure, its reporting is limited to a yearly, simplified VAT return.

On a related matter, one should note that FCPs are not VAT registered under their own name, but through their management company. The consequence is that the VAT returns of the management company include both the management company's own transactions and the FCP's transactions. In the case of a Luxembourg FCP whose management company is established outside Luxembourg, the FCP is deemed to have the seat of its economic activity[36] outside Luxembourg and, typically, is not determined to be a Luxembourg VAT-taxable person. As for VAT registration and compliance for SCSps, the matter was recently clarified. Now that SCSps can be considered as performing an economic activity from a VAT perspective, they may VAT register in their own names in cases where they qualify as a VAT-taxable person established in Luxembourg.

32. *Règlement grand-ducal du 1er décembre 2009 relatif à la déclaration de commencement, de changement ou de cessation de l'activité économique en matière de taxe sur la valeur ajoutée et à l'attribution d'un numéro d'identification TVA*, as amended (hereinafter '2009 VAT GDR'). Under the VAT Law, taxable persons whose annual turnover does not exceed EUR 30,000, are not, in principle, required to register for VAT purposes, but can request a VAT number on a voluntary basis. Article 57 VAT Law.
33. Article 2(d) 2009 VAT GDR.
34. *See* Arts 61(5), 62(2), 62(5)(b) VAT Law.
35. *See ibid.*, Arts 62, n. 2, 61(2), 62(3), 62(5).
36. *Stoppelkamp*, C-421/10, Judgment, EU:C:2011:640.

[1] Place of Supply

The 'place of supply' is at the cornerstone of EU VAT rules in the context of cross-border transactions. Once ascertained, it determines the Member State in which VAT is to be charged and paid. That Member State is entitled to levy VAT (or to exempt from a VAT levy), to decide on the applicable VAT rate, on the invoicing requirements, and on the deduction specificities.[37]

For most services supplied to Luxembourg-based investment funds, the place of supply follows the so-called general rule,[38] according to which a supply of services between businesses (B2B) is localized for VAT purposes at the recipient's place of establishment.[39] The VAT Law, therefore, applies to services provided to Luxembourg-based investment funds by foreign-based suppliers. The Luxembourg-based fund, being the service recipient, is obliged to account for VAT under the reverse-charge mechanism, except if a specific VAT exemption applies.

In this regard, one should note that VAT-taxable status shall not be confused with a VAT registration. The concept of a taxable person covers both taxable persons that are - and that are not - identified for VAT purposes. However, without proper VAT registration and subsequent communication of one's VAT identification number to foreign-based suppliers, it is highly unlikely that such suppliers would make use of the reverse-charge mechanism (i.e., that it would issue its invoices without adding on his locally due VAT). Their unwillingness may stem from the risk they incur if the customer fails to account for the VAT due under any such reverse-charge transaction, if the invoice did not reference the customer's VAT identification number as requested by the EU VAT Directive.[40] As shown by the case law of the CJEU, EU law does not prevent Member States from refusing to grant the exemption, or imposing penalty payments and fines, for cross-border transactions for which irregular invoices have been issued.[41] Even if, at the end of the day, the principles of VAT neutrality and proportionality require such a challenge to be rejected if the substantive requirements are satisfied,[42] which - to the extent the VAT status can be established by other means than by way of an identification number[43] - should be feasible more often than not, the proof of such substantive requirements come along with specific costs to establish the accurate place of supply.

37. *See* Guido De Wit & Danièle Buchler, *Le lieu de taxation: un sujet en plein mouvement*, *in TVA – Taxer, Déduire, Exonérer et Punir. État des Savoirs, Enjeux et Perspectives*, 23, 25 (Charlène A. Herbain ed., 2015).
38. Some supplies depending on the nature of the services may be subject to special rules affecting their place of supply.
39. Article 17.1(b) VAT Law.
40. Article 226(4) EU VAT Directive.
41. For example, *R*, C-285/09, Judgment, EU:C:2010:742; *Transport Service*, C-395/02, Judgment, EU:C:2004:118, para. 30; *Schmeink & Cofreth and Strobel*, C-454/98, Judgment, EU:C:2000:469, para. 62.
42. *Collée*, C-146/05, Judgment, EU:C:2007:549, para. 31.
43. *VSTR*, C-587/10, Judgment, EU:C:2012:592; *Mecsek-Gabona*, C-273/11, Judgment, EU:C:2012:547.

§3.04 SCOPE OF THE VAT EXEMPTION

Article 135(1)(g) of the EU VAT Directive provides that 'Member States shall exempt ... the management of special investment funds as defined by Member States.' Thus, the EU VAT Directive grants the Member States the power to define, in their domestic law, the funds that meet the definition of 'special investment funds' and the services that fall within the scope of the concept of 'management of special investment funds'. However, this freedom is controlled by the national courts and the CJEU, which has had the opportunity to make various judgments on the matter.

If the management of special investment funds is VAT-exempt, it means that such an activity does not entitle Luxembourg managers to recover VAT on their expenses related to their management services.

[A] Investment Funds Covered by the VAT Exemption

[1] CJEU Principles

Although Article 135(1)(g) of the EU VAT Directive grants the Member States the power to define, in their domestic law, the funds that meet the definition of 'special investment funds', the CJEU has indicated that this power must be exercised consistently with the objectives pursued by the EU VAT Directive and in accordance with the principle of fiscal neutrality. The purpose of exempting transactions connected to the management of special investment funds is primarily to facilitate investment in securities by means of investment undertakings by excluding the cost of VAT, thus ensuring that the common VAT system is neutral as regards the choice between direct investment in securities and investment through UCIs.[44]

The CJEU has also specified that funds that constitute UCITSs within the meaning of the UCITS Directive are special investment funds.[45] Their characteristics are as follows:

- their sole objective is the collective investment in transferable securities of capital raised from the public;
- they operate on the principle of risk spreading; and
- their units, at the request of holders, are repurchased or redeemed, directly or indirectly, out of the undertakings' assets.

Investment funds that, without being UCIs within the meaning of the UCITS Directive, display characteristics identical thereto and, thus, carry out the same types

44. *JP Morgan Fleming Claverhouse Investment Trust and The Association of Investment Trust Companies*, C-363/05, para. 45; *Galioto*, C-464/11, Order, EU:C:2013:79; *Wheels Common Investment Fund Trustees and Others*, C 424/11, para. 19; and *ATP PensionService*, C-464/12, Judgment, EU:C:2014:139, para. 43.
45. *Deutsche Bank*, C-44/11, Judgment, EU:C:2012:484, para. 32; *Wheels Common Investment Fund Trustees and Others*, C-424/11, para. 23; and *ATP PensionService*, C-464/12, Judgment, EU:C:2014:139, para. 46.

of transactions (or at least display features that are sufficiently comparable for them to be in competition therewith) must also be regarded as special investment funds.[46]

[2] Funds Covered by the VAT Exemption According to the VAT Law

Article 135(1)(g) of the EU VAT Directive was transposed into Article 44(1)(d) of the VAT Law, which lists all the vehicles whose management is covered by the VAT exemption.[47] The list provided by the VAT Law is formal and the case law confirmed that the types of investments of the undertaking are irrelevant.

On 9 December 2015, the CJEU decided the *Fiscale Eenheid X*[48] case. One of the questions referred to the Court was whether a company that was set up by more than one investor for the sole purpose of investing assets in immovable property could be regarded as a special investment fund. The Court ruled that investment companies must satisfy the following two conditions to qualify as special investment funds within the meaning of Article 135(1)(g) of the EU VAT Directive:

(1) the company must be subject to specific state supervision; and
(2) it must display characteristics identical to UCIs within the meaning of the UCITS Directive and carry out the same types of transactions or at least display features that are sufficiently comparable for them to be in competition therewith such undertakings (i.e., pooling of assets, existence of several investors, willing to obtain maximum profit from the assets, investment risks borne by the unitholders, and transferability of the certificates to third parties).

This decision confirms that the form of investments made by FCPs, SICAVs, SICARs, SIFs, and AIFs (i.e., transferable securities or immovable property) is irrelevant. In Luxembourg, the fact that the qualifying vehicles invest directly in real estate assets does not prevent the VAT exemption from applying to the management of them.

[a] UCITS, SIFs, SICARs, and Pension Funds Subject to the Supervision of a Luxembourg Regulator

The management of the following Luxembourg investment funds is VAT-exempt:

- UCIs covered by the 2010 UCITS Law;
- SIFs covered by 2007 SIF Law;
- SICARs covered by the 2004 SICAR Law;

46. *Abbey National*, C-169/04, paras 53–56; *JP Morgan Fleming Claverhouse Investment Trust and The Association of Investment Trust Companies*, C-363/05, paras 48–51; *Wheels Common Investment Fund Trustees and Others*, C-424/11, para. 24; and *ATP PensionService*, C-464/12, para. 47.
47. *See* §3.02[B][1], *supra*.
48. *Fiscale Eenheid X*, C-595/13, Judgment, EU:C:2015:801.

- SEPCAVS and ASSEPS covered by the 2005 SEPCAV/ASSEP Law and subject to CSSF supervision;[49]
- pension funds covered by the Insurance Law[50] and subject to CAA supervision.

Regarding the question of the VAT exemption of management services supplied to pension funds, several decisions were made by the CJEU in 2013 and 2014.[51] In the *ATP Pension Service A/S* case, the Court held that the term 'special investment funds as defined by Member States' could benefit 'defined contribution pension schemes'. According to the Court, the essential characteristics of a 'special investment fund' are the pooling of assets of several beneficiaries and the spreading of risk borne by them over a range of securities. The CJEU distinguished these special investment funds from those considered in its *Wheels Common Investment Fund Trustees and Others* case, where the members of the 'defined benefit scheme' did not bear the investment risk. In Luxembourg, the VAT Law does not make such a distinction between pension funds. While this observation does suggest that the VAT exemption is applicable to defined-benefit pension funds, it is certainly not intended to say that the issue is resolved, either.

[b] Vehicles Similar to the Ones Referred to in Point [a] Established in Another EU Member State and Subject to Supervision by a Supervisory Body

Article 44(1)(d) of the VAT Law applies to the management of undertakings similar to the ones referred to in Point [a], *supra*, of other EU Member States and subject to supervision by a supervisory body from another EU Member State similar to the CSSF or the CAA. However, the management of non-EU vehicles remains excluded from this exemption.

The historical reason for the extension of the exemption's geographical scope relates to a dispute between a Luxembourg investment manager of an Irish fund and the Luxembourg VAT authority, the AED.

At the time, the exemption provided by Article 44(1)(d) of the VAT Law only covered the management of UCIs subject to supervision by the CSSF and did not explicitly cover the management of UCIs in other Member States that were subject to supervision by their relevant local authority.

In the case at issue, an investment-management agreement was concluded in 2007 between a Luxembourg investment manager and an Irish fund similar to a SICAV,

49. *Loi du 13 juillet 2005 relative aux institutions de retraite professionnelle sous forme de société d'épargne-pension à capital variable (SEPCAV) et d'association d'épargne-pension (ASSEP) et portant modification de l'article 167, alinéa 1 de la loi modifiée du 4 décembre 1967 concernant l'impôt sur la revenue*, as amended (hereinafter the '2005 SEPCAV/ASSEP Law').

50. *Loi du 6 décembre 1991 sur le secteur des assurances*, abrogated and replaced by *Loi du 7 décembre 2015 sur le secteur des assurances*, as amended (hereinafter the 'Insurance Law').

51. *ATP PensionService*, C-464/12; *PPG Holdings*, C-26/12; and *Wheels Common Investment Fund Trustees and others*, C-424/11.

according to which the fund delegated to the investment manager full investment discretion to manage, invest, and reinvest its assets, and to execute purchases and sales of its assets. In remuneration for these services, the fund paid a fee to the investment manager. In accordance with the agreement, the investment manager was authorized to delegate some or all of its investment rights, duties, and powers. In 2009, the investment manager concluded an investment-management delegation agreement with a United States (US) company. The delegate investment manager was in charge of managing, investing, and reinvesting the Irish fund's assets. In remuneration for the services rendered, the Luxembourg investment manager paid a fee to the US-delegate investment manager.

Both transactions (i.e., the management services supplied by the US-delegate investment manager to the Luxembourg investment manager, and the management services supplied by the Luxembourg investment manager to the Irish fund) were supplies of services between two taxable persons falling within the scope of VAT. The place of taxation of the first transaction (services between the US-delegate investment manager and the Luxembourg investment manager) was Luxembourg, and the VAT had been self-assessed in Luxembourg by the Luxembourg investment manager. As the place of taxation of the second transaction (services between the Luxembourg investment manager and the Irish fund) was Ireland, the Luxembourg investment manager did not charge any Luxembourg VAT thereon.

The main issue was whether the input VAT on the services supplied by the US-delegate investment manager to the Luxembourg investment manager was deductible on the grounds of Article 49(2)(b) VAT Law. According to this Article, a taxable person is entitled to deduct VAT on its purchases when the goods and services acquired are used for the purpose of activities performed abroad that would have otherwise given rise to a right to deduct input VAT if the same activities had been performed in Luxembourg.

The AED denied the input VAT recovery. The case went first to the *Tribunal d'Arrondissement* (the Court of First Instance), which confirmed the rejection of the deduction of the relevant VAT.[52] The *Tribunal's* reasoning was as follows: if the management services supplied by the Luxembourg investment manager were rendered in Luxembourg by applying the 'fiction' offered by Article 49(2)(b) of the VAT Law, the Irish fund would have had to have been set up as a CSSF-regulated UCITS, and the management services supplied to it, consequently, would have been exempt with no right to deduct VAT based on Article 44(1)(d) of the VAT Law.

The *Tribunal's* decision was appealed before the Luxembourg *Cour d'Appel* (its appellate court), which gave its decision on 10 August 2016.[53] The *Cour d'Appel* did not follow the *Tribunal's* position and, rather, concluded that, since UCIs established in Ireland are not subject to CSSF supervision, the management of such funds cannot fall within the scope of the VAT exemption of Article 44(1)(d) of the VAT Law, as amended by the 2007 SIF Law. Consequently, the VAT paid by the Luxembourg investment

52. Luxembourg *Tribunal d'Arrondissement, Jugement civil 75/2012 (première chambre), numéro 131106 du rôle,* 21 mars 2012.
53. Luxembourg *Cour d'Appel, Arrêt n° 148/16 – II – CIV, numéro 39533 du registre,* 10 août 2016.

manager for the services subcontracted to the US-delegate investment manager was deductible.

In order to avoid similar disputes, the Luxembourg legislature, in 2013, decided to amend the wording of Article 44(1)(d) of the VAT Law to explicitly include the management of regulated investment funds located in other EU Member States in the scope of its exemption, with no right to recover VAT.[54]

[c] Securitization Vehicles

Within the scope of the VAT exemption, and pursuant to an amendment thereto by the 2004 Securitization Vehicle Law, Article 44(1)(d) of the VAT Law now exempts the management of securitization vehicles covered thereby, particularly as it was amended to carry out securitization transactions within the meaning of Article 1(2) of Regulation (EC) No 24/2009 of the European Central Bank of 19 December 2008 concerning statistics on the assets and liabilities of financial vehicle corporations engaged in securitization transactions.[55] The exemption applies irrespective of the location of the securitization vehicle (i.e., within or outside the EU).

The question as to whether a particular vehicle carries out securitization transactions within the meaning of the relevant European Central Bank regulation[56] is a legal/regulatory one - one that requires a legal expert to answer.

[d] Alternative Investment Funds (AIFs)

The management of an AIF, as defined in Article 1(39) of the 2013 AIFM Law, is also VAT-exempt pursuant to Article 44(1)(d) of the VAT Law. According to the 2013 AIFM Law, an AIF is a UCI that (i) raises capital from a number of investors with a view to investing it in accordance with a defined investment policy for the benefit of those investors and (ii) does not require authorization pursuant to Article 5 of the UCITS Directive. Article 44(1)(d) of the VAT Law covers both the management of regulated and unregulated AIFs, since the management of regulated AIFs (Part II UCIs and, potentially, SIFs and SICARs) is also covered by the exemption.

It should be noted that where the management of certain unregulated investment vehicles is VAT-exempt in Luxembourg (i.e., securitization vehicles and AIFs can be either regulated or unregulated), one cannot exclude the possibility that the Luxembourg VAT exemption for these two types of vehicles will be repealed or amended in the future as a result of the CJEU's judgment in the *Fiscale Eenheid X* case.[57] In that case, the Court ruled that one of the conditions for this VAT exemption is that the

54. Loi du 12 juillet 2013 relative aux gestionnaires de fonds d'investissements alternatifs.
55. This part of the 2004 Securitization Vehicle Law should be amended, because the European Central Bank Regulation it was based upon was repealed as of 1 January 2015. That regulation was replaced by Regulation (EU) No 1075/2013 of the European Central Bank of 18 October 2013 concerning statistics on the assets and liabilities of financial vehicle corporations engaged in securitization transactions.
56. The same is true for both the former regulation 24/2009 and/or the current one No 1075/2013.
57. *Fiscale Eenheid X*, C-595/13.

relevant Member State made the companies subject to specific state-level supervision. Whether that supervision condition may be met at another level than at the fund or investment-vehicle level remains unconfirmed.

[3] Services Covered by the VAT Exemption

The concept of 'management of special investment funds' is not clearly defined, either in the VAT Law or in the EU VAT Directive. However, both the AED and the CJEU have clarified the content of this notion.

[a] Services Falling Within the Scope of the VAT Exemption

The AED confirmed to the Luxembourg Bankers' Association (ABBL) the manner in which Article 44(1)(d) of the VAT Law should be interpreted, following discussions between the two entities in 1992. The non-exhaustive list of exempt services was published in a letter from the ABBL on 15 January 1993.[58] This list includes:

- daily portfolio management;
- research and investment advice;
- accounting in an electronic format;
- net asset value (NAV) calculation;
- issuing and redeeming funds' shares/units, and administrative services relating to this, such as domiciliation; and
- depositary banking activities, including safekeeping the securities owned by the UCI.[59]

Further, the CJEU has also interpreted the concept of 'management of investment funds'. In the *Abbey National* judgment,[60] the CJEU stated:

> the transactions covered by the exemption ... are those which are specific to the business of undertakings for collective investment. Therefore, apart from tasks of portfolio management, those of administering undertakings for collective investment themselves, such as those set out in Annex II to Directive 85/611, as amended, under the heading 'Administration', which are functions specific to undertakings for collective investment, come within the scope of [Article 135(1)(g) of Directive 2006/112/EC].[61]

---

58. Letter from Betty Pauly, Chargée d'analyses & Fernand Grulms, Conseiller de la Direction, The Luxembourg Bankers'Association, to All Its Members, *TVA sur gestion d'OPC* (15 January 1993) (with attached telefax from Romain Faust, Direction de l'Enregistrement et des Domains, to Fernand Grulms, The Luxembourg Bankers'Association, Confirming the interpretation of the Administration de l'Enregistrement et des Domaines, Minister of Finance regarding Art. 44(1)(d) of the VAT Law (13 January 1993) (copy on file with the author).
59. This is an unofficial translation of the French text.
60. *Abbey National*, C-169/04.
61. *Ibid.*, paras 63-64.

The virtually identical Annex II of the current UCITS Directive (Annex II) states that the following functions are included in the 'activity of collective portfolio management':

- investment management;
- administration;
- legal and fund-management accounting services;
- customer inquiries;
- valuation and pricing (including tax returns);
- regulatory-compliance monitoring;
- maintenance of unit-holder register;
- distribution of income;
- unit issues and redemptions;
- contract settlements (including certificate dispatch);
- record-keeping;
- Marketing.[62]

According to the *Abbey National* judgment, the said list is not exhaustive.

Moreover, in this case, the CJEU stated that the exempt management services include the services of third-party managers 'if, viewed broadly, they form a distinct whole and are specific to, and essential for, the management of those funds. ... Mere material or technical supplies, such as the making available of a system of information technology, are not covered by [the exemption]'.[63] The AED subsequently acknowledged this approach in Circular 723 and a follow-on circular thereto,[64] which emphasized that, in the context of fund-management services outsourced to third-party managers, the supply of only one, isolated service remained outside the scope of the VAT exemption.

Thereafter, in the *ATP Pension Service* case,[65] the CJEU established a potentially broader interpretation of services that could constitute fund management for VAT purposes that had been used up to that point, one that could trigger an extension to certain technical services. In that case, on the basis of information received from the employer, ATP Pension Service A/S (ATP) opened an account for each pension customer who was a member of one of the pension funds included in the pension scheme managed by ATP. The employer informed ATP of the pension contributions payable for each of its employees and transferred a single amount, representing the total sum of those contributions, to the pension fund's account at a financial institution. The amount attributable to each employee by the employer under the collective agreement or company agreement was then credited by ATP to the employee's account in the pension-scheme system managed by ATP.

62. UCITS Directive, at [2009] OJ L 302/88.
63. *Abbey National*, C-169/04, paras 70–71.
64. Circular 723, *supra* note 15, and Direction de l'Enregistrement et des Domaines, *Circulaire 723bis du 30 avril 2010*.
65. *ATP PensionService*, C-464/12, *supra* note 51.

The pension customers (i.e., the employees) had access to their pension accounts at any time through the pension fund's home page. ATP updated all accounts regularly with the amounts to be credited and withdrawn, so that the balance of any account was equal to the amount of the employee's accumulated retirement benefit (excluding income earned but not yet credited). ATP also initiated withdrawals of amounts from the accounts of pension customers who were members of a particular pension fund, by issuing instructions to a financial institution to pay such amounts to those customers.

The pension funds themselves invested the contributions paid into the retirement schemes. ATP, thus, carried out the following tasks on behalf of pension funds:

- administrative tasks, consisting, *inter alia*, in the provision of information and specific advice to employers and employees (i.e., pension customers) in relation to the retirement schemes provided by the pension funds;
- system maintenance and development in relation to the development and maintenance of the platform from which ATP provided its services to pension funds; and
- services related to payments into and disbursements from pension funds.

The Court held that:

> the term "management of special investment funds" covers services by means of which an undertaking establishes the rights of pension customers vis-à-vis pension funds through the opening of accounts in the pension scheme system and the crediting to such accounts of the contributions paid. That term also covers accounting services and account-information services such as those listed in Annex II to Directive 85/611.[66]

Based on this judgment, it seems possible to argue that the VAT exemption should also apply to services of a more technical nature. Indeed, in a second follow-on circular to Circular 723,[67] the AED took the position that risk-management services supplied to qualifying investment funds covered by Article 44(1)(d) of the VAT Law are also VAT-exempt as they are part of their management.

The CJEU provided a further interpretation of management services in the *GfBK* case.[68] In that case, the Court held that outsourced investment advice is VAT-exempt to the extent that the services provided are intrinsically connected to the characteristics of a manager, such that they have the effect of performing the specific and essential functions of the management of a special investment fund.

On 30 September 2016, the AED released Circular 781 on the VAT status of directors.[69] Admittedly, Circular 723 did not indicate whether the fund-management VAT exemption provided by Article 44(1)(d) of the VAT law could apply to directors on the boards of qualifying investment funds and/or to management companies managing these funds; but, even if Circular 723 intended to ensure a broad VAT application to

66. *ATP PensionService*, C-464/12, *supra* note 51, para. 76.
67. Direction de l'Enregistrement et des Domaines, *Circulaire N° 723ter du 7 novembre 2013*.
68. *GfBK*, C-275/11, Judgment, EU:C:2013:141.
69. Direction de l'Enregistrement et des Domaines, *Circulaire N° 781 du 30 septembre 2016 : Activité d'administrateur de sociétés.*

directors' activities, the VAT exemption should not be challenged insofar as the directors' duties are specific and essential to the management of these funds.

[b] Services Excluded from the Scope of the VAT Exemption

Below are examples of typical services that are not, generally, VAT-exempt in Luxembourg:

- marketing (in the sense advertising) services;
- depositary oversight functions;
- advisory services that do not constitute investment advice;
- legal advice;
- audit;
- tax services;
- domiciliation services for the management company of incorporated funds;
- supplying information (e.g., Bloomberg and Reuters reports);
- IT services;
- software licences;
- certain publication services (e.g., prospectuses, key investor information documents); and
- preparing and translating prospectuses.

In its *Abbey National* judgment,[70] the CJEU found that the exemption did not cover the functions of UCIs depositaries. According to the CJEU, those functions do not fall under the management of UCIs, but instead fall under the control and supervision of their activities, as their aim is to ensure that UCIs are managed in accordance with law.

In the *Fiscale Eenheid X* case,[71] the CJEU also excluded services related to immovable property management from the VAT-exemption. In that case, a company provided services to Dutch companies that were incorporated by pension funds with the aim of investing in and operating immovable property. Said company was in charge of the following tasks:

- acting in the capacity of a director of the companies;
- activities of an executive nature arising from statutory requirements, company statutes, regulations, and administrative decisions;
- managing the assets, in particular the companies' immovable property (including monitoring the immovable property and how it was used, maintaining contracts with tenants, engaging estate agents when properties were empty, assessing tenants, inspecting premises, collecting rent, debt management, etc.);
- financial reporting, data processing, and internal audits;

70. *Abbey National*, C-169/04 para. 65.
71. *Fiscale Eenheid X*, C-595/13, para. 79.

- dealing with the companies' assets, including the acquisition and sale of immovable property; and
- finding shareholders or certificate holders.

The CJEU determined that where the assets of a fund consist of immovable property, the services that can benefit from the VAT exemption include:

- services relating to the selection, purchase, and sale of immovable property; and
- administrative and accounting tasks, in particular services such as computing income and the price of units or shares, valuing assets, accounting, preparing statements for the distribution of income, providing information and documentation for periodic accounts or tax, statistical and VAT returns, and preparing income forecasts.

In contrast, the actual management of the immovable property cannot benefit from the VAT exemption insofar as it is not specific to the management of special investment funds.

§3.05 VAT RECOVERY

It follows, from Article 168 of the EU VAT Directive and from the settled case law of the CJEU,[72] that the right to deduct VAT, in principle, is granted to taxable persons for the costs they incur as a component of their taxable transactions. The recognition of the relationship between input costs and output transactions is based on a finding of the existence of a direct link between said costs and taxable transactions or, in the absence of such link, by an observation that the costs form part of the general overhead charges incurred for their taxable transactions.

However, things are different for investment funds based in Luxembourg. As early as 2006, in Circular 723, the AED had expressed its position and has never (officially) reversed it. It is still of the opinion that all Luxembourg-based vehicles whose management is VAT-exempt under the 'management of special investment funds' provision, carry out a VAT-exempt activity with no right to deduct related input VAT. Consequently, such funds bear, as a final cost, the VAT they incur on non-exempt inputs.

It is only when the fund is not a 'special investment fund' for VAT purposes that the VAT on its input costs may be deductible per his deduction right.[73]

Such a generic rule for special investment funds undermines the principle of VAT neutrality, which promotes the application of similar VAT treatment to similar transactions disregarding the structure chosen.[74] Such discrimination occurs when the effective output activities of an investment fund would have opened a recovery right if it was not a special investment fund for VAT purposes. In the case of a special

72. *Midland Bank*, C-98/98, Judgment, EU:C:2000:300, para. 24.
73. *Wheels Common Investment Fund Trustees and Others*, C-424/11.
74. *The Rank Group*, Joined Cases C-259/10 and C-260/10, Judgment, EU:C:2010:470.

investment fund that owns income-producing real estate for which the VAT option has been called illustrates the issue, as such an entity is not entitled to deduct the input VAT, but any other entity not qualifying as a special investment fund, but performing the exact same real estate activity, would be able to do so.

In fairness, it must be recognized that, despite this official situation, general practice has shown that the AED demonstrates a certain tolerance to a case-by-case analysis of the output activities of investment funds, leading – on occasion – to its recognition of a recovery right. Moreover, given the breadth of the exemption available, the vast majority of the costs incurred by investment funds are not bearing any VAT.

On another point, AIFs are recognized by the VAT Law as vehicles whose management is exempt under the management of special investment funds' provision. As such, they typically do not benefit from a deduction right.

With respect to the VAT-recovery right for investment funds, the position of Luxembourg-based suppliers of management services to non-Luxembourg undertakings deserve to be addressed.

The AED refuses the right to deduct input VAT incurred in relation to the management of an investment fund subject to prudential control by a regulatory authority in one of the Member States. Therefore, when a Luxembourg supplier provides management services to a foreign fund, it will deem that its service is not opening a deduction right when said fund is regulated under its domestic law.

Even if that logic is easily perceptible, a question arises nonetheless: Is this method in line with the Luxembourg test that, in principle, is applicable and according to which a taxable person may deduct the VAT incurred in Luxembourg if its foreign activity would have opened a deduction right should it have been realized here? An affirmative response thereto is questionable, as services would have been rendered to a vehicle that may or may not have qualified as a special investment fund for VAT purposes under Luxembourg criteria. Instead, the criteria of another Member State are assimilated by the AED to Luxembourg criteria to determine the deduction right of its domestic taxpayer.

§3.06 CONCLUSION

Despite a number of EU cases in recent years, there are still areas of uncertainty when it comes to the VAT position of investment and pension funds and the VAT treatment of services rendered to these funds.

Moreover, with the development of regulatory and reporting developments, such as MIFID II[75] and PRIIPs,[76] funds have to purchase new services or existing services

75. Directive 2014/65/EU of the European Parliament and of the Council of 15 May 2014 on markets in financial instruments and amending Directive 2002/92/EC and Directive 2011/61/EU (recast) (Text with EEA relevance), [2014] OJ L 173/349.
76. Regulation (EU) No 1286/2014 of the European Parliament and of the Council of 26 November 2014 on key information documents for packaged retail and insurance-based investment products (PRIIPs) (Text with EEA relevance), [2014] OJ L 352/1.

need to be amended, and these changes may have uncertain VAT consequences. One example of this relates to research fees that, until now, had usually been bundled with brokerage services, but now will likely have to be identified separately under MIFID II. This will most certainly trigger new VAT questions as to the treatment of these services, not only in Luxembourg but also across the EU.

In Luxembourg, recent developments around the VAT treatment of directors' fees have underscored questions bearing on specific VAT consequences, particularly as to the identification of directors' functions that are specific and essential for the management of investment funds.

Finally, it is also worth noting that, as of today, the EU Commission's VAT Action Plan[77] does not include any proposals in relation to financial services. With the withdrawal of the draft directive relating to financial services in 2016,[78] it might be worth considering an extension of the VAT Action Plan to these services.

77. COM(2016) 148 final.
78. Withdrawal of Commission Proposals (2016/C 155/04), [2016] OJ C 115/3.

CHAPTER 4

Transparent, Semi-transparent, Opaque: Recent Developments in Fund Taxation in Germany

Heribert M. Anzinger

§4.01 INTRODUCTION

In July 2016, German tax law broke with an almost 100-year-old legal tradition regarding investment taxation.[1] As of 1 January 2018,[2] mutual retail funds (i.e., professionally managed investment schemes targeting the investing interests of individual investors) will no longer be taxed in accordance with the principle of tax transparency. Instead, most common legal forms of German investment funds will be transformed from a 'tax-exempt tax subject' to a 'taxable-corporate tax subject'. Furthermore, in a kind of risk diversification, the German legislature split a previously unified investment taxation regime into two separate systems. It implemented a new, opaque regime for all former semi-transparent investment funds, which is mandatory for mutual retail funds, and established an option for semi-transparent taxation for special investment funds, targeting the investing interests of institutional investors. Additionally, it modified traditional semi-transparency to restore its conformity with European Union (EU) Law. Both actions have a huge impact on business and law and challenge fundamental understandings of investment taxation.[3]

1. For the history of German fund taxation, *see* §4.02, *infra*.
2. For transition rules, *see* §4.07, *infra*.
3. For an overview of the reform, *see* Heribert M. Anzinger, *Wesen, Reformbedürfnis und Reformoptionen des Investmentsteuerrechts*, 98 Finanz-Rundschau 101 (2016); Marcus Helios & Alexander Mann, *Das Gesetz zur Reform der Investmentbesteuerung – Darstellung, Meinung und Handlungsempfehlungen*, Sonderausgabe No. 01/2016 Der Betrieb 69 (2016); Heinz Kußmaul et al.,

This chapter presents the core elements of the 2016 reform in three steps. First, it will recall the structures of the pre-reform investment taxation regime in Germany and explain the motivations for the reform. Then, it will present the new, opaque regime of mutual retail funds, with its complex investor-taxation rules. Subsequently, it presents the new structure of modified transparency, which will remain an option for special purpose vehicles. Throughout this section, the scope of the new rules as well as the transitions rules is discussed. Connected questions, such as treaty entitlement, CFC Rules, and new anti-avoidance provisions that come along with the German Tax Reform Act are only addressed tangentially.

§4.02 HISTORY OF GERMAN FUND TAXATION

[A] Corporate Taxation: Transparency or Double Tax Burden

One of the first collective investments in Germany is said to have been the Brandenburg-African Company. It was founded through an electoral edict in 1682 with the business purpose of overseas trade with West Africa.[4] Private stockholders contributed the necessary capital and invested their assets together. With no interest in the purpose of the common undertaking exceeding their individual capital investment, their influence on the business remained low. Their motives were focused on risk diversification, dividends and capital gains in their collective investment.

Similar motives drove the members of an unincorporated association founded in 1923: the Zickert'sche Kapitalverein. Different from the Brandenburg-African Company, its purpose was not trade in pepper, ivory, gold, or slaves, but it shared a similar wish for a collective investment of assets and equity without any interest in conducting a common business.[5]

Like other collective investment associations in the early twentieth century, the Zickert'sche Kapitalverein was challenged by a burdensome corporate-tax regime.[6] At that time, corporations were unrestrictedly taxed at the level of the corporation and – without taking that into account –again at the level of the shareholders. The consequence was that indirect investments were discriminated against as compared to direct

Investmentbesteuerung vor der Zeitenwende – Grundlegende Systemänderungen in der konzeptionellen Besteuerung von Publikums-Investmentfonds, 9 Die Unternehmensbesteuerung 596 (2016).

4. 2 Richard Schück, *Brandenburg-Preußens Kolonial-Politik unter dem Großen Kurfürsten und seinen Nachfolgern (1647-1721)* 134–312 (Grunow 1889); Malte Stamm, *Das Koloniale Experiment. Der Sklavenhandel Brandenburg-Preußens im transatlantischen Raum 1680-1718*, 59, 116 (PhD dissertation, University of Düsseldorf 2011) at https://d-nb.info/1036727564/34 (accessed 9 January 2018).
5. Karlheinz Heeb, *Hermann Zickert - Der deutsche Börsenpionier*, 127–134 (2009); Thomas A. Jesch, Ulf Klebeck & Christopher Bragrock, *Einführung in das deutsche Investmentrecht inkl. historischer Bezüge, in Investmentrecht*, 2 (Thomas A. Jesch, Ulf Klebeck & Günther Dobrauz eds, Verlag C.H. Beck 2014).
6. Karl-Joachim Henkel, *Die steuerliche Behandlung der Investmentgesellschaften*, 22 (PhD dissertation, Frankfurt am Main 1961).

investments.[7] To avoid that discrimination, some early funds were structured as tax-transparent fractional shares in equity,[8] and others - where possible - as tax-transparent partnerships, while still others suffered the double tax burden silently.

[B] Semi-transparency and Special Tax Regimes

The discrimination of indirect investment through a two-tier taxation of corporations had been recognized by the German legislature early. Section 10 of the Corporate Income Tax Act (KStG) 1934[9] authorized the issuance of ordinances granting tax exemptions in favour of asset management companies. But, this authority was never used.[10]

In fact, the first investment taxation regime was introduced in Germany in 1957, together with a regulatory law intended to foster collective investment (*Gesetz über Kapitalanlagegesellschaften* or KAGG).[11] Since then, the core principle of the current German investment taxation scheme has been the so-called semi-transparency (*Semi-transparenz*).[12] Most domestic mutual retail funds are structured as unincorporated separated equity, also known as tax-transparent fractional equity (*Sondervermögen*). In the current investment tax law, this is deemed to be subject to Corporate and Trade Tax according to Section 11(1), clause 1 Investmentsteuergesetz 2003 (hereinafter 'InvStG 2004').[13] But in the same provision of that law, its income is exempt from those taxes (Section 11(1), clause 2 InvStG 2004), in which German law introduced 'Tax-Exempt Tax Subjects'. What has been called 'transparency' for nearly sixty years is not transparency in a technical sense, but represents a fiction of a tax subject and its tax exemptions. If the whole investment tax law were to be abolished in Germany, unincorporated investment funds would be treated as tax-transparent fractional equity. Therefore, the aim of the KAGG 1957 was not to introduce tax transparency, which already existed for the most common legal form of investment funds at that time, but to shape tax transparency for the convenience of the tax administration with respect to requalification of income and to promote German investment funds by granting them funds privileges connected with semi-transparency.

With the following statute on the distribution of foreign investment funds units and the taxation of income from foreign investment funds units (*Gesetz über den Vertrieb ausländischer Investmentanteile und über die Besteuerung der Erträge aus ausländischen Investmentanteilen, AuslInvestmentG*) of 28 July 1969,[14] domestic and foreign funds were put on an equal footing.

7. Dirk A. Zetzsche, *Prinzipien der kollektiven Vermögensanlage*, 304 (Mohr Siebeck 2015).
8. RFH of 11.3.1930, II A 104/30, RFHE 26, 248.
9. RGBl. I 1934, 1031.
10. Jesch, Klebeck & Bragrock, *supra* note 5, at 4.
11. BGBl. I 1957, 378.
12. Jesch, Klebeck & Bragrock, *supra* note 5, at 6.
13. Investmentsteuergesetz of 15 December 2003 (BGBl. I 2003, 2676, 2724) last amended by Art. 2 Act of 19 December 2016 (BGBl. I 2016, 1730).
14. BGBl. I 1969, 986.

Since then, investment tax law in Germany has only experienced two major changes over the past sixty years. In 2003, regulatory law and taxation law of mutual investment funds were split into two legal acts.[15] Regulatory law was separated into an Investment Act (*Investmentgesetz* or InvG). The Investment Tax Law contained in the former KAGG and the *AuslInvestmentG* was condensed into the Investment Tax Act (*Investmentsteuergesetz* or InvStG).[16] Since 2013, with the implementation of the 2011 AIFM Directive,[17,18] regulatory law for Undertakings for Collective Investment in Transferable Securities (UCITS) and Alternative Investment Funds (AIFs) has been moved and was concentrated in a new Investment Code (*Kapitalanlagegesetzbuch* or KAGB) with a broader scope on either open-ended or closed-ended funds. Investment Tax Law followed that broader scope in a revised Investment Tax Act by introducing the categories of Investment Funds (*Investmentfonds*) and Investment Companies (*Investitionsgesellschaften*). Major changes in the taxation of either Investment Funds or Investment Companies were not contained in the reform or in the new categories. Apart from the introduction of purely formal concepts such as *Investmentvermögen* and *Investitionsgesellschaften*, there were no major changes in the investment taxation regime. The semi-transparency that characterizes German investment tax law has remained untouched, as has the tax law relating to closed-end funds, which are still treated like partnerships according to general tax law.[19]

The Private Equity Companies Act (*Unternehmensbeteiligungsgesellschaftengesetz* or UBGG) of 17 December 1986[20] was unaffected by the recent reform. It, however, does not provide a complete special tax regime for private equity funds, but only an exemption of trade tax (*Gewerbesteuer*) for a certain legal type of *Unternehmensbeteiligungsgesellschaft*. As most private equity funds use the structure of a non-trading partnership, which is not within the scope of the trade tax, the relevance of UBG has remained low in practice.[21] Another attempt of the German legislature to promote Private Equity Funds, the Act on Promoting Venture Capital Funds (*Gesetz zur Förderung von Wagniskapitalbeteiligungsgesellschaften* or WKBG),[22] which was supposed to introduce a new legal form of a *Wagniskapitalgesellschaft* failed. The European Commission identified some of the provisions as prohibited State aid and, thus, incompatible with Article 107 TFEU.[23]

In summarizing the history of investment tax law and embedding it into the general tax regime, it becomes clear that there are three reasons why a special

15. *Investmentmodernisierungsgesetz* of 15 December 2003, BGBl. I 2003, 2676.
16. Anzinger, *supra* note 3, at 105.
17. Directive 2011/61/EU of 8 June 2011 on Alternative Investment Fund Managers [2011] OJ L 174/1, as amended (the '2011 AIFM Directive').
18. *Gesetz zur Umsetzung der Richtlinie 2011/61/EU über die Verwalter alternativer Investmentfonds (AIFM-Umsetzungsgesetz)* of 4 July 2013 (BGBl. I 2013, 1981).
19. Anzinger, *supra* note 3, at 105.
20. BGBl. I 1986, 2488.
21. Jesch, Klebeck & Bragrock, *supra* note 5, at 15.
22. Art. 1 *Gesetz zur Modernisierung der Rahmenbedingungen für Kapitalbeteiligungen (MoRaKG)* of 12 December 2008, BGBl. I 2008, 1672.
23. Commission Decision of 30 September 2009, C 2/09 [2010] OJ L 6/32. The *Wagniskapitalbeteiligungsgesetz* was withdrawn by *AIFM-StAnpG* v. 18 December 2013 (BGBl. I 2013, 4318).

investment tax law is necessary, even if its aim is transparent investment taxation: (1) defining fund privileges; (2) streamlining administration; and (3) ensuring neutrality among different legal structures of investment funds. Not all kinds of mutual funds are structured as transparent fractional equity (*Sondervermögen*). Some are incorporated, such as investment stock companies (Investment-Aktiengesellschaft).

To understand what caused the recent radical reform, a quick look at the mechanics of the current system might be helpful.

§4.03 CURRENT FUND TAXATION RULES

[A] Separation and Transparency

The idea of a tax-exempt tax subject, which characterizes the current German fund-taxation rules, was born out of a desire to achieve neutrality among legal forms. If an investment fund is not a tax subject according to general tax law, such as with transparent fractional equity, it is deemed to be a tax-exempt tax subject, according to Section 11(1), clause 1 InvStG 2004.[24] This is followed by tax exemptions (Section 11(1), clause 2 InvStG 2004), an artificially reshaped characterization of income, and a shift of taxable profits between time periods. First, the income of the fund is separated from the investor, then assessed, and calculated at the level of the fund. Next, the earnings of the fund are assigned to the investors independent of whether or not they have been distributed. That two-step approach leads to profit determination at the level of the fund and reporting requirements allow proper taxation at the level of the investor.[25]

[B] Income Qualification and Time Shift

Taking tax transparency seriously would mean assigning the income of the fund to the investor as the investor's own income in the same time period while maintaining its characterization as flowing to the fund. That is not the case, however, in current German investment law. Rather, according to general German tax law, there are at least

24. For more detail on the purposes of that fiction, *see* Joachim Englisch, *§ 11 InvStG, in Investmentgesetz, Investmentsteuergesetz: InvG InvStG*, margin no 13 (Hanno Berger, Kai-Uwe Steck & Dieter Lübbehüsen eds, Verlag C.H. Beck 2010); Sabine Kirchmayr, *Besteuerung von kollektiven Vermögensanlagen, in Einkommen aus Kapital*. Vol. 30 DStJG, 235, 245 (Wolfgang Schön ed., Dr. Otto Schmit KG 2007); Peter Schäfer, *Zweckvermögen; Steuerbefreiung; Außenprüfung, in InvStG* 731, margin no 33 (Joachim Moritz & Thomas A. Jesch eds, Deutscher Fachverlag GmbH 2015).

25. For more on the former system, *see* Stefan Altfelder, *Investmentfonds - endlich verständlich - Plädoyer für ein prinzipiengeleitetes Steuerrecht*, 82 Finanz-Rundschau 299 (2000); Dominik Engl, *Erträge aus Investmentvermögen. Verfassungs- und europarechtskonforme Besteuerung nach dem Transparenzprinzip*, 28 (Vol. 15 Steuerwissenschaftliche Schriften, Nomos & C.H. Beck 2009); Karl Küpper, *Das System des Investmentsteuergesetzes*, 99–130 (Shaker 2007); Stefan Thiems, *Die Verwirklichung des Transparenzprinzips im deutschen und österreichischen Investmentsteuerrecht*, 1-76 (2013); Stefan Trencsik, *Was von einer Idee übrig blieb - Analyse systematischer Defizite der Investmentbesteuerung vor dem Hintergrund aktueller Reformüberlegungen*, 91 Steuer und Wirtschaft 266 (2014).

eight different schedules for differently treated income: domestic dividends, foreign dividends, interest, current income from domestic real estate, gains from domestic real estate with a holding period of less than ten years, income from foreign real estate, capital gains from 'old' securities (i.e., acquired before 1 January 2009), and capital gains from 'new' securities (i.e., acquired after 31 December 2008). These schedules are treated differently for private and business investors according to general tax law. Through investment tax law, these schedules are partly amalgamated and some of those amalgamated parts, such as capital gains from the disposal of securities, are not taxed until they are distributed by the fund.[26] That time lag is known as the 'little funds privilege' (*Kleines Fondsprivileg*). Like a tax exemption on capital gain on long-term real estate holdings, these benefits are justified by the intent to provide a level playing field for direct and indirect investments. According to the former law (i.e., InvStG 2004), investment funds were not transparent. They act like a relay station. That is an important point to keep in mind, as the question of treaty entitlement will be discussed later on in this chapter.

[C] Withholding Tax

As domestic investment funds are corporate tax subjects while being fully tax exempt, their domestic income must not be subject to a withholding tax (WHT) withheld for their account. Consequently, German domestic funds receive dividends and interest free of a prior WHT charge or may claim a reimbursement according to Section 11(2) clause 1 InvStG 2004. That advantage is technically linked to a fund-level WHT on distributed dividends, interest, and real estate income. As the kind of income and the type of investor have to be taken into account, by raising the WHT at fund level, the tax withholding procedure has become extremely complex. That complexity is mirrored in Section 7 InvStG.

Foreign funds are not granted a source-level WHT exemption on domestic dividends. That seems logical, because foreign funds cannot be obliged to levy a German WHT at the fund level. But, that effect causes major EU Law concerns: domestic funds receive unreduced dividends, while foreign funds do not.[27]

[D] Reporting Requirements and Lump Sum Taxation

In order to apply the semi-transparent taxation system, tax administrations need detailed information about the income of the fund. Its complexity derives from the complexity of the German taxation system in general. Capital income is taxed in different schedules and, with the number of income types, the complexity in linking sources at the fund level with the investors rises. A fund must keep records of its source income, and report the different sources to its investors, which it may not even know.

26. Dieter Lübbehüsen, *§ 1 InvStG, in* Berger, Steck & Lübbehüsen eds, *supra* note 24, margin no 41.
27. *See* §4.04, *infra*.

Moreover, a fund must separate its so-called new from old stocks and its disposals of domestic real estate by holding period (either less or more than ten years).

According to Section 5 InvStG 2004, domestic and foreign investment funds are obliged to report once a year, and with every distribution, all of the different types of income they received, in a detailed form with up to thirty-three categories, and the reports must be certified by a certified accountant, according to Section 5(1)(3), clause 1, and 5(1a) InvStG 2004. Foreign funds have to prove their accuracy by translated documents on demand of the tax authorities according to Section 5(1)(4) and 5(1)(5) InvStG.

Non-compliance with these reporting requirements leads to lump-sum taxation for the investor, according to Section 6 InvStG 2004. The tax base therefore consists of the fund's distributions, plus interim gains, plus 70% of the gain in redemption price during the calendar year, with a minimum tax base equal to 6% of the last redemption price of the calendar year. There has been a doctrinal dispute over whether that lump-sum taxation should be characterized as punitive taxation or as a method of tax estimation.[28] In the past, it had been shown that foreign founds miss those reporting requirements more often, without its domestic investors being able to influence that situation. It follows that foreign funds are less attractive for German investors, which results in obvious conflict with the free movement of capital guaranteed in Article 63 TFEU.

§4.04 REASONS FOR REFORM

While investment fund managers had arranged themselves with the complexity of the current system in mind, the German tax administration started to distrust its own capacity to ensure compliance with its complex rules and procedures. The reasons for the reform arose from the following concerns.

[A] Fragility

There were three main reform reasons for a major change listed in the first discussion papers on the reform. Tax authorities stressed the vulnerability of the current system for aggressive tax planning and tax evasion.[29] In fact, investment funds often are found in the spotlight of innovative tax structures. And, there is a strong correlation between investment funds and Cum-/Ex- and Cum-/Cum-Trades, Bond stripping, and Bull-Bear Transactions. The complex rules on income equalization were utilized to circumvent the German interest-deduction limit. Package deals were used to link tax-free earnings

28. Underlining its punitive character, *see* John Büttner & Ulf Mücke, *§ 6 InvStG Kapitalanlagegesellschaften, in* Berger, Steck & Lübbehüsen eds, *supra* note 24, margin no. 7; Michael Kreft, *§ 6 Besteuerung bei fehlender Bekanntmachung, in* Moritz & Jesch eds, *supra* note 24, margin nos 2, 6. Mentioning its simplifying effects, *see*: Steffen Gnutzmann & Robert Welzel, *in* 2 Auflage *InvStG*, § 6 margin no. 162 (Haase ed., 2015).
29. Bundesministerium der Finanzen (hereinafter 'BMF'), *Diskussionsentwurf des Bundesministeriums der Finanzen: Entwurf eines Gesetzes zur Reform der Investmentbesteuerung*, 37 (21 July 2015).

with taxable losses through investment funds.[30] Funds privilege is said to have been abused. But, very few of the famous tax-evasion and tax-planning schemes are rooted in investment tax law. Investment funds were just utilized to leverage the advantages of loopholes in the WHT system or the arbitrage effect between dividends and capital gains or foreign and domestic capital income. Most of the loopholes had been closed outside investment taxation law.

[B] Complexity

From the perspective of the German tax administration, the main problem of the former system (i.e., InvStG 2004) has been its complexity.[31] The tax authorities no longer felt able to ensure compliance, and some tax offices around the country were unable to cope with thirty-three reported items and twelve loss schedules. The error-correction procedures were identified as ineffective.[32] Investment funds had been closed and liquidated before abusive tax structures were discovered. Regarding the fund level, an information gap was identified as was a growing imbalance between the tax authorities and tax experts with the increasing complexity of the tax system. Few tax officers were well-trained experts in investment tax law. Things were even worse at the investor level. A core problem arose from the decentralized organization of German tax authorities. There are currently 546 tax offices, each of them locally responsible, oftentimes, for very few investors in their district. Tax officers in most tax offices, thus, are not experienced with the complex investment funds structures that typically comprise foreign investment funds. German tax authorities had to decide whether to increase personnel and training expenses, to centralize tax administration in the field of investor taxation, or to reduce complexity in investment fund taxation, at least for the vast majority of retail fund investors. There might have been the fourth solution: to reduce the complexity of capital income taxation in general and to foster quality in the reports made pursuant to Section 5 InvStG, by strengthening the liability of the accountants certifying that report pursuant to Section 5(1)(3), clause 1 InvStG. But, that way would have been much harder to push through the political decision-making process. Oddly enough, it proved far easier to undertake a technically radical reform of the investment law to secure the necessary political majorities.

[C] EU-Law Uncertainties

After all, the most compelling reason for the reform was the legal uncertainty arising out of potential and real conflicts between the current investment taxation regime and EU Law. A clear conflict had been identified with the lump-sum penalty taxation of investors of funds that did not fulfil their reporting obligation according to German

30. Christian Völker, *Optimierung der Fonds-Aktiengewinns durch 'Kopplungsgeschäfte'*, 5 Deutsches Steuerrecht 265 (2016).
31. Alexander Mann, Anhang 2, in Weitnauer, Boxberger & Anders eds, Anhang 2 margin no. 361 (Beck'sche Kurz-Kommentare 2014).
32. BMF, *supra* note 29, at 38.

investment tax law. The German legislature had to react to the *Van Caster* decision handed down by the Court of Justice of the European Union (CJEU).[33] Its ruling clearly indicated a conflict of the reporting requirement of Section 5 InvStG 2004 and the sanction of a flat tax in Section 6 InvStG 2004:

> Article 63 TFEU must be interpreted as precluding national legislation, such as that at issue in the main proceedings, which provides that the failure by a non-resident investment fund to comply with the obligations to communicate and publish certain information required by that legislation, which are applicable without distinction to resident and non-resident investment funds alike, resulting in the flat-rate taxation of the income which the taxpayer earns from that investment fund, since that legislation does not allow the taxpayer to provide evidence or information that could prove the actual size of that income.[34]

But, to meet the requirement of free movement of capital guaranteed by Article 63 TFEU, no major reform would have been necessary. According to the ruling of the CJEU, tax authorities and tax jurisdictions acknowledge that it would have been sufficient to amend Section 6 InvStG 2004 to add a provision that allows an investor to declare and to provide the information that was not reported by the fund itself.[35] The legislature went that way; it amended Section 6 InvStG with the Investment Tax Reform Act (*Investmentsteuerreformgesetz* or InvStRefG) of 19 July 2016.[36]

Another not-so-clear conflict was identified in the privileges of domestic funds through a WHT-exemption that was not applied to foreign funds. With their limitation to domestic funds for the benefits provided by Section 11(1) and 11(2) InvStG, a violation of the basic European freedoms appears to exist.[37]

The CJEU's decisions in *Orange European Smallcap Fund*[38] and *Aberdeen Property Fininvest Alpha*[39] seemed to be far away from the German model of investment taxation. But, after the CJEU ruled in the case of *Santander*[40] (regarding French investment tax law) that the privileged treatment of domestic funds formed a violation of free movement of capital and had rejected the justification of coherence in the case of *Emerging Markets*[41] (regarding Polish investment tax law in relation to a third-country), existing EU-Law concerns became serious doubts. While one might not succeed in constructing a direct link between the tax exemption and the taxation at the investor level to activate the justification of coherence in current law, every dividend distributed to a foreign fund must be tax exempt and no WHT should be withheld.

---

33. *van Caster*, C-326/12, Judgment, EU:C:2014:2269.
34. *Ibid.*, para. 58.
35. BFH of 17 November 2015 – VIII R 27/12, BStBl. II 2016, 539; BMF v. 4 February 2015 und v. 28 July 2015, Verfahren bis zu einer gesetzlichen Umsetzung des EuGH-Urteils*Van Caster*, C-326/12, BStBl. II 2015, 135 and 610.
36. BGBl. I 2016, 1730.
37. Dirk Zetzsche, *Analoge Anwendung von § 11 InvStG auf ausländische Investmentfonds wegen ungleichen Quellensteuerabzugs auf inländische Dividenden! - Eine Nachlese zum Emerging Markets-Urteil des EuGH*, 24 Internationales Steuerrecht 8 (2015).
38. *Orange European Smallcap Fund*, C-194/06, Judgment, EU:C:2008:289.
39. *Aberdeen Property Fininvest Alpha*, C-303/07, Judgment, EU:C:2009:377.
40. *Santander Asset Management SGIIC*, C-338/11, Judgment, EU:C:2012:286.
41. *Emerging Markets Series of DFA Investment Trust Company*, C-190/12, Judgment, EU:C:2014:249.

There are some good reasons that this different treatment might be justified by coherence in the German investment tax law. But, the legal uncertainty about that point, as they are connected with the budgetary risks, offered enough reasons to think about a radical reform, with the EU-Law uncertainties being the most urgent argument therefor.[42]

§4.05 DISCUSSED REFORM OPTIONS

[A] Minimally Invasive Surgery

[1] Clarifying the Link Between Tax Exemption and Tax Burden

Until autumn 2015, it was not quite clear which direction the German reformed investment tax law would take.[43] There were strong arguments for a minor reform that would strengthen the link between fund taxation and investor taxation to stress the coherence of the German system and eliminate EU-Law uncertainties.[44] There also were some thoughts on full transparency of investment funds. At the beginning, the idea of tax-opaque investment funds came from the tax administration,[45] which faced opposition by the investment funds industry.[46] Different associations suggested slight amendments and new formulations of Sections 7(3), clause 1, 11(1), and 11(2) InvStG 2004 to clarify the systematic link between the tax exemption on the fund's entrance side and the mandatory WHT on the fund's output side.[47] Thereby, the necessity of the limitation of the tax exemption on domestic funds should have been justified – comprehensibly – with the aim of achieving coherence of the national investment tax system. It has been argued that, by the standards and the reasoning applied in the CJEU's decision in *Emerging Markets,* a hard link between tax exemption and tax burden would meet the requirements of the justification of coherence. These arguments were carefully discussed in the doctrinal debate.[48] Yet, in the light of an unstable interpretation of the CJEU on the requirements of the coherence justification for

42. BMF, *supra* note 29, at 36.
43. *See* Andreas Richter & Berthold Welling, *Tagungs - und Diskussionsbericht zum 57: Berliner Steuergespräch 'Die Reform der Investmentbesteuerung'*, 98 Finanz-Rundschau 111 (2016).
44. BVR u.a., *Neuordnung der Investmentbesteuerung, Stellungnahme v. 3.9.2014*; aba/ABV/AKA/BDI/ZIA, *Stellungnahme v. 13.11.2014*; IDW, *Stellungnahme zum Diskussionsentwurf eines Gesetzes zur Reform der Investmentbesteuerung,* 8 Die Unternehmensbesteuerung 556 (2015).
45. Bund-Länder-Arbeitsgruppe, *Bericht der Arbeitsgruppe 'Neukonzeption der Investmentbesteuerung' – ENTWURF,* 24 February 2012, 6, reprint in DB 2012, Issue 12 23 March 2012; for the history, *see* Mann, *supra* note 31, margin no. 365.
46. BVR u.a., *supra* note 44; aba/ABV/AKA/BDI/ZIA, *supra* note 44, at 1; IDW, *supra* note 44, at 556.
47. BDI/DSGV/BVI/BdB/BVR/GDV/VÖB, Eckpunkte zur partiellen Anpassung des InvStG v. 2 July 2015, briefly reflected in IDW *supra* note 44, at p. 557. The idea for this proposal was developed by Trencsik, *supra* note 25, at 296.
48. Zetzsche, *supra* note 37, at 9; Helmut Rehm & Jürgen Nagler, *Fallstricke bei der geplanten Reform der Investment-Besteuerung,* 21 Betriebs-Berater 1248, 1250 (2015).

discrimination, serious doubts remain along the path to achieve the aim of location-friendly certainties in investment tax law and a successful deconstruction of all discrimination.

[2] Tax Credit Instead of Tax Exemption at the Entrance Level

An attempt to maintain the current investment tax regime had been connected to the idea of substituting the tax exemption at the fund's entrance side through a tax credit.[49] According to that proposal, a WHT would be levied on all domestic dividends, whether distributed to domestic or foreign investment funds. At the fund's output side, at the investor level, this WHT would be credited, like a chargeable foreign WHT. This proposal was criticized for its proposed benefits for small savers, especially its definition thereof, and for non-profit investors. Although the proposal has not been adopted, its elements have been implemented to maintain the semi-transparent taxation of special investment funds.

[3] Simplification of the Current System

Scholars convincingly pointed out that the aims of simplification and robustness could have been reached without a radical reform.[50] The reporting requirements of Section 5 InvStG could have been reduced, as fragile fund privileges (in the form of tax deferrals) were dispensable, and, at the fund's output side, income of the investors could have been condensed into a unique category of income. The latter, however, would have had simplifying effects only if that unique type of income would have been treated as uniform income. That was not suggested and would have raised questions regarding the justification for such typification.

[B] Fundamental Reform Ideas

[1] Deferred, Final Levy of Tax at Disposal of Units

The most radical reform option that was discussed materialized in the idea of a complete tax exemption at the fund level and the implementation of the accrual principle at the investor level.[51] According to that proposal, only distributions and gains realized at the disposal of the units should be taxed at the investor level. The idea's advantage obviously lies in the waiver of any taxation and declaration requirements at the fund level. And, as foreign and domestic funds are treated equally in that proposal, known conflicts with EU Law would have been eliminated. However, the disadvantages are obvious. The proposed regime invites tax evasion, as long as gains

49. BDI/DSGV/BVI/BdB/BVR/GDV/VÖB, *supra* note 47.
50. Trencsik, *supra* note 25, at 296.
51. Markus Terhürne & Frank Otto, *Reformansätze zur Weiterentwicklung des InvStG im Rahmen der privaten Kapitalanlage*, 39 Deutsches Steuerrecht 2037, 2039 (2013).

are only taxed by the residence state according to domestic and treaty law. The same problem arises with the proposal to extend the tax exemptions in the former tax system provided by Section 11(1) InvStG 2004 to foreign funds.

[2] Approximation and Rejection of the Tax-Transparency Principle

Initial unpublished thoughts of the tax administration had been to foster tax transparency and treat all legal forms of investment funds more like partnerships than corporations to address EU-Law concerns. This idea was rejected early with a view to the rising complexity of an undamped transparent tax regime in an unchanged system with multiple schedules for the taxation of capital income.

The final proposal of the tax administration culminating in a discussion draft of 21 July 2015[52] was a rejection of the tax-transparency principle. The core idea had been to abolish the tax exemption for domestic funds' entrance side and to abandon the concept of the funds as tax-exempt tax subjects, at least partially. The rising problems of tax deferral on undistributed income and the double tax burden at both the fund and investor levels were addressed by an advance tax on the minimum interest on undistributed gains and a partial release of the distributed income that takes account of the prior charge of taxes.[53]

The new approach was intensively discussed by scholars.[54] It was criticized for describing an internationally uncommon regime and that it could lead to a competitive disadvantage for German funds when compared to foreign funds. Although the German Ministry of Finance had carried out an impact study,[55] it remained unclear as to the impact the reform might have on the overall tax burden for investors. The quotas for partial tax release at the investor level seemed to be arbitrary. Overall doubts existed on the question of whether such a reform would reduce complexity. As the new approach was proposed to be mandatory only for mutual retail funds and some

52. BMF, *supra* note 29, at 1.
53. For an overview, *see* Helios & Mann, *supra* note 3, at 2.
54. Martin Haisch, *Investmentsteuerreform – Wird jetzt alles gut?*, 5 Recht der Finanzinstrumente 294 (2015); Rehm & Nagler, *supra* note 48, 1248; Helmut Rehm & Jürgen Nagler, *Der jüngste Diskussionsentwurf eines Investmentsteuerreformgesetzes im Fokus des Unionsrechts*, 70 Betriebs-Berater 2006 (2015); Rainer Stadler & Jann Jetter, *Der Diskussionsentwurf zum Investmentsteuerreformgesetz (InvStRefG)*, 33 Deutsches Steuerrecht 1833 (2015); André Kral & Anne-Kathrin Watzlaw, *Die geplante Reform der Investmentbesteuerung – Praxishinweise und Handlungsbedarf aus Sicht einer depotführenden Stelle*, 70 Betriebs-Berater 2198 (2015); Jan Dyckmans, *Der Diskussionsentwurf des BMF zum Investmentsteuerreformgesetz: Ende der eingeschränkten Transparenz*, 8 Die Unternehmensbesteuerung 531 (2015); Johannes Höring, *Der Diskussionsentwurf zum Investmentsteuerreformgesetz ('InvStRefG')*, 21 Deutsche Steuerzeitung 835 (2015); Franz Wassermeyer, *Investmentsteuerreform*, 19 Europäische Zeitschrift für Wirtschaftsrecht (EuZW) 841(2016); Richter & Welling, *supra* note 43, at 111; Bela Jansen & Veronika Greger, *Reform der Investmentbesteuerung – erste Analyse des Referentenentwurfs*, 98 Finanz-Rundschau 116 (2016).
55. Copenhagen Economics, *Volkswirtschaftliche Auswirkungen einer Reform der Investmentbesteuerung auf den Kapitalmarkt, den Finanzstandort und die Altersvorsorge in Deutschland* (2014).

exceptions were implemented for pension funds and charitable investors, the multiplication of options had been identified early as a new source of complexity and fragility and as a new opportunity for tax structuring.

§4.06 CORE ELEMENTS OF THE REVISED GERMAN INVESTMENT TAX LAW

[A] Materials and Implementation

The new approach was developed in 2011 and 2012 in a working group of representatives from federal and state tax authorities, which published its results in a draft report dated 15 December 2011 and a final report dated 24 February 2012.[56] Those proposals were based on the concept of new opaqueness, which was founded on the idea of a modified corporate tax. It was approved as the favoured solution by the federal and states finance ministers as of 1 June 2012.[57] An impact study by the consultancy Copenhagen Economics was published on 17 November 2014, which concluded that no significant impact on tax burden should be expected and level playing field would be provided.[58] It was followed by the controversially disputed discussion draft of the Federal Ministry of Finance dated 21 July 2015.[59] Nevertheless, since November 2015, it seemed that the majority of the stakeholders accepted the new approach.[60] On 16 December 2015, the Federal Ministry of Finance published a draft bill,[61] and on 16 February 2016, the federal government introduced its legislative proposal with its reasoning therefor,[62] which was subject to a public hearing in the German Bundestag in May 2016. In an amended version,[63] the proposal was adopted by the Bundestag on 9 June 2016[64] and by the Federal Council (Bundesrat) on 9 July 2016[65] and published in the Official Gazette of 26 July 2016.[66] From the first draft of the Federal Ministry of Finance to the Official Gazette, only some minor changes had been made.

---

56. Bund-Länder-Arbeitsgruppe, *supra* note 45; zur Entstehungsgeschichte: Mann, *supra* note 31, margin no. 365.
57. Helios & Mann, *supra* note 3, at 2.
58. Copenhagen Economics, *supra* note 55.
59. BMF, *supra* note 29, at 1.
60. Richter & Welling, *supra* note 43, at 115.
61. Tillman Kempf & Julius Hirtz, *Schwerpunkte des Referentenentwurfs eines Gesetzes zur Reform der Investmentbesteuerung*, 1-2 Deutsches Steuerrecht 1 (2016).
62. BR-Drucks. 119/16; BT-Drucks. 18/8045; BT-Drucks. 18/8345; Johannes Höring, *Entwurf eines Gesetzes zur Reform der Investmentbesteuerung ('Investmentsteuerreformgesetz – InvStRefG')*, 10 Deutsche Steuerzeitung 383 (2016); Höring, *supra* note 54, at 835; Rainer Stadler & Martin Mager, *Der Regierungsentwurf des Gesetzes zur Reform der Investmentbesteuerung*, 12-13 Deutsches Steuerrecht 697 (2016).
63. Beschlussempfehlung und Bericht des Finanzausschusses (7. Ausschuss) of 8 June 2016 zu dem Gesetzentwurf der Bundesregierung – Drucksachen 18/8045, 18/8345, 18/8461 Nr. 1.6, BT-Drucks. 18/8739.
64. BT-Prot. 18/176, 17400D.
65. BR-Prot. 947, TOP 4, S. 289A – 289D.
66. BGBl. I 2016, 1730.

[B] Scope and Concept of Investment Funds

The change from semi-transparency to a new, opaque regime in German investment tax law seems to be a radical reform. But, on a closer look, that reform might turn out to be less radical and more like a superficial reconstruction. What now is called an 'opaque' tax regime might actually be less opaque then it seems.

The new German fund taxation regime refers to the well-known German term *Investmentfonds* in a new sense to describe its scope. Basically, its scope is now linked to regulatory law. By a reference in Section 1(2), clause 1 InvStG 2018, it addresses collective investment schemes within the meaning of Section 1(1) German Capital Investment Act (*Kapitalanlagegesetzbuch* or KAGB). Therefore, the revised InvStG is applicable to every kind of undertaking for collective investments that collect capital from a number of investors with the object of investing that capital according to a defined strategy for the (sole) benefit of the investors and which is not an operationally active company. That broad definition, however, is narrowed by settled administrative practice that excludes managed accounts and debt instruments therefrom, such as certificates.[67]

Beyond the scope of the regulatory law, the Investment Tax Act additionally includes a one investor investment vehicle (Section 1(2)(2)(1) InvStG 2018) - a tax-exempt asset-management corporation - that is not allowed operational activities (Section 1(2)(2)(2) InvStG 2018), like the Luxembourg *société de gestion de patrimoine familial* (SPF), and affiliated investment funds of capital management companies in group structures (Section 1(2)(3) InvStG 2018).

Special purpose vehicles (Section 1(3)(1) InvStG 2018; Section 2(1) and (2) KAGB) remain outside the scope of the new investment tax regime, which comprise - in a broad sense - true sales and synthetic securitization, independent from tranching.[68] Also excluded are: partnerships, if they are not UCITSs or pension schemes (Section 1(3)(2) InvStG 2018); companies according to the German participation companies act (*Unternehmensbeteiligungsgesellschaften*, Section 1(3)(3) InvStG); public funded participation companies (Section 1(3)(4) InvStG 2018); and German REITS (Section 1(3)(4) InvStG 2018). The exclusion of partnerships from the scope of the new investment tax law seems to be a major change in relation to former investment tax law, where partnerships were inside the scope and addressed as *Investitionsgesellschaften* in Section 18 InvStG 2004. In fact, there is no material change, because Section 18, clause 3 InvStG 2004 referred to the general tax rules that now become applicable by the exclusion of partnerships (except UCITS and pensions schemes) from the special tax regime on investment funds. Even the distinction between corporations and partnerships follows the general tax rules that have a settled administrative practice.[69] Therefore, private equity funds organized as partnerships, like the Luxembourg *société en commandite simple* (SCS), *société en commandite spéciale* (SCSp) and the Delaware

67. Helios & Mann, *supra* note 3, at 4.
68. *Ibid.*, at 7.
69. *Ibid.*

Limited Partnership (LP), do not fall within the scope of the new investment tax regime.

[C] Domestic and Foreign Funds

Both domestic and foreign funds are corporate tax subjects under the new law and are basically treated equally. There are no additional investment requirements for foreign mutual retail funds. Section 2(3) InvStG 2018 provides a distinction between domestic and foreign funds following the regulatory approach. Only the applicable regulatory law will be relevant, not the statutory seat the principal place of management, or the existence of a permanent establishment. That alternative linking rule does make sense, as foreign funds are deemed to be corporate tax subjects in the sense of Section 2(1) Corporate Income Tax Act (CIT, *Körperschaftsteuergesetz* or KStG), according to Section 6(1), clause 2 InvStG 2018. It is relevant with regard to provisions on the merger of investment funds, such as Sections 23(4) and 54(2) InvStG 2018 and the declaration and reporting requirements set out in Section 51(3)(2) InvStG 2018. Other references to foreign funds, such as a treaty override of exemptions of WHT covered by Section 16(4) InvStG 2018 and Section 34(3) InvStG 2018, need to be interpreted according to the linking rules provided by general corporate tax law. As domestic and foreign mutual retail funds are only liable to corporate tax on a limited basis (according to the source principle provided by Section 6(2) and 6(3) InvStG 2018) and special investment funds remain tax-exempt tax subjects, neither the fund's statutory seat nor its principal place of management are relevant for corporate tax purposes.

[D] Two Systems in One Code

Following the reform, German investment tax law will be addressed according to two different taxation principles: the new basic rule of opaqueness for all kinds of investment funds and the new optional semi-transparency for special investment funds. First, the new investment tax law introduces the separation principle as a new basic rule applicable to either mutual retail funds or special investment funds. As in the current law, investment funds are subject to corporate tax but are not fully tax exempt anymore. Instead, they are liable to corporate tax on their domestic income according to Section 6(2) and 6(3) InvStG 2018. Fund privileges were modified and a base-yield lump-sum taxation was introduced. The potential for double taxation at the fund and investor levels will be compensated by partial exemptions. Second, for specialized investment funds, the new law provides a check-the-box option. Fund managers may opt out of the new opaque regime and alternatively choose modified transparency based on the current regime of semi-transparency. The new investment law does not allow any changes between the new opaque regime and the semi-transparent regime. Even if the additional requirements of a special investment fund are met later on, it is not possible to switch once an investment fund has been chosen to be taxed according to one or the other principle.[70] If the requirements for special investment funds are no longer fulfilled, the fund is deemed to be dissolved (Section 52(1), clause 1 InvStG 2018).

[E] Basic Principles of Investment Fund Taxation

[1] Corporate and Trade Tax

As mentioned above, mutual retail funds are qualified as corporate and trade tax subjects. Both domestic and foreign funds are taxed within their limited tax liability at the regular corporate tax rate of 15%, plus the solidarity surcharge, resulting in an overall tax rate of 15.825% (Section 6(2) InvStG 2018). On income that has been subject to a WHT (e.g., domestic dividends), that overall tax rate is reduced to 15% (Section 7(1), clause 3 InvStG 2018). As a consequence of the final WHT on incoming dividends, no tax declaration is required at the fund level, if the fund only receives domestic dividends (Section 7(2) InvStG 2018).

Investment funds may be subject to trade tax (Section 15(1) InvStG 2018) under the new investment tax law. But, as long the fund does not undertake any material trade, it is exempt from German trade tax (Section 15(2) InvStG 2018). According to settled administrative practice, the 'material' threshold is 10% of the overall earnings.[71] Regardless of this, Section 15(3) InvStG 2018 states that the requirement of 'no material trade' is deemed to be met if the earnings from operational activities do not exceed 5% of the overall earnings of the fund per year. Otherwise, the operational activities of the fund are separated from its mere investment activities, the income from those activities being determined according to the accrual principle and taxed according to the general trade tax rules (Section 15(4) InvStG 2018). According to Section 9(3) Gewerbesteuergesetz (GewStG), only domestic income is assessed. Participation in a real estate company within the meaning of Section 1(9)(22) KAGB is deemed to be non-operational activity (Section 15(2), clause 2 InvStG 2018).

For foreign mutual retail funds that receive dividends from German companies that are subject to the 15% WHT under the current law, the reform, with its new approach, will not lead to a significant change in taxation. The new opaque principle might be identified as a new design of the former, deemed-distributed income WHT.

[2] Investor-Related Tax Exemptions

One of the most complex areas of the new opaque regime relates to tax exemptions that refer to the tax status of the investors. According to Section 8(1) InvStG 2018, the fund's income is exempt from corporate tax – on request – in proportion to the share of tax-preferred investors it has. Two groups of preferred investors have to be distinguished. A proportional tax exemption on all domestic income is granted with regard

70. *Ibid.*, at 8.
71. *Ibid.*, at 13.

to domestic and foreign charitable institutions, churches, foundations with their statutory seat or principal place of management in States providing official and administrative assistance comparable to the Mutual Administrative Assistance Directive,[72] and certified pension schemes. A second group is formed by domestic public entities, which do not hold investment units in a tax-exempt business and tax-exempt foreign and domestic public corporations with their statutory seat or principal place of management in Member States that adhere to the Mutual Administrative Assistance Directive. Investors from that second group are only entitled to a proportional tax exemption on income from domestic real estate (Section 8(2) InvStG 2018). Basically, the technical precondition for investor-related tax exemptions is the separation of funds with favoured investors (Section 10(1), clause 1 InvStG 2018). Meeting that precondition is essential to obtain a full tax exemption. Alternatively, mixed-investor funds are possible, following a pro rata tax exemption (Section 8(3) InvStG 2018).

[3] Tax Base

The tax base of the new fund taxation regime is strictly limited to domestic sources and structured into three types of income. The first type is formed by domestic participation income (Section 6(3) InvStG). This consists out of dividends from corporate entities with statutory seat or place of management in Germany, manufactured dividends and securities lending fees. There is no tax exemption for dividends under Section 8b KStG, even if the 10% threshold is exceeded (Section 6(6) InvStG 2018), but there is an exemption for capital gains on shares. During the legislative process, it had been rigorously debated whether dividends from shareholdings above the threshold of 10% should be exempt.[73] Tax authorities referred to the low practical relevance of substantial shareholdings above 10% for investment funds and the difficulties of administration. Domestic participation income is taxed limited to a rate of 15%. The current solidarity surcharge either is not levied or is credited back to the fund (Section 7(1) InvStG 2018).

The second type of income includes income from domestic rentals and realized capital gains on domestic real estate. Basically, the latter are taxable irrespective of the holding period (Section (6)(4), clause 2 InvStG 2018). But, there is an open-ended transition rule for dispositions of real estate made ten years or more after acquisition. All (unrealized) capital gains accrued before 1 January 2018 are exempt (Section 6(4), clause 3 InvStG 2018). The law does not answer the question of how these former capital gains are to be determined. All expenses and loss carry-forward are taken into account (Section 6(7), clause 3 InvStG 2018). Income from domestic real estate is taxed at a rate of 15% (as corporate tax) plus the current solidarity charge, so effectively 15.825% (Section 6(2) InvStG 2018).

---

72. Council Directive 2011/16/EU of 15 February 2011 on administrative cooperation in the field of taxation and repealing Directive 77/799/EEEC, OJ L 61/1 of 11.3.2011.
73. Helios & Mann, *supra* note 3, at 11.

The third type of income is formed by other domestic income within the scope of limited taxation, as defined by the patchy catalogue of Section 49(1) EStG (*Einkommensteuergesetz* or EStG), with the exception of profits from the disposition of significant shareholdings according to Section 17 EStG (Section 6(5) InvStG 2018). That third type of income includes interest from mortgage-backed loans (Sections 49(1)(5)(c) and 5(aa) EStG). Other domestic income levied through a WHT is taxed at a comprehensive rate of 15% according to Section 7(1) InvStG 2018 or, in all other cases, at a rate of 15.825%.

All other types of domestic income, such as interest, capital gains from domestic and foreign shareholdings (i.e., the proceeds from the disposition of stocks), foreign dividends, income from foreign real estate, and earnings from forward transactions are not included in the tax base in general. Therefore, the so-called fund privileges in the shape of deferred taxation can be recognized in the new law.

[4] Treaty Entitlement

The concept of semi-transparency and the idea of an investment fund as a tax-exempt tax subject have always led to the question whether collective investment vehicles can claim treaty entitlement.[74] At first glance, the new approach - with its concept of a taxable tax subject - should have removed most doubt, as investment funds are treated as a taxable person. But, with the new German investment law and especially with its limited tax base, new questions arose.

According to Section 6 InvStG 2018, investment funds are only liable to tax on their domestic income. That tax-base limitation could match the provision of Article 4(1)(2) OECD Model,[75] which excludes tax subjects with limited tax liability from the scope of treaty provisions:

> Article 1 (Persons Covered):
>
> This Convention shall apply to persons who are residents of one or both of the Contracting States.

74. *See* Dietmar Aigner, *Kapitalanlagefonds im Recht der Doppelbesteuerungsabkommen*, 91 (Linde 2001); L.J. Ed & P.J.M. Bongaarts, *Taxation of Investment Funds*, General Report, 82b Cahier de Droit Fiscal International 21 (1997); Stefano Grilli, *Treaty Entitlement of Investment Funds*, 74 Diritto e pratica tributaria 863 (2004); Florian Haase, *Treaty Entitlement of Investment Funds: The German Perspective*, 39 Intertax 337 (2011); David Kleist, *Treaty Entitlement of Tax Exempt Entities*, 36 Intertax 262 (2008); OECD, *The Granting of Treaty Benefits with Respect to the Income of Collective Investment Vehicles*, 1 (2010); Ulrich Sorgenfrei, *Steuerliche Transparenzgrundsatz und DBA-Berechtigung deutscher offener Investmentfonds*, 3 Internationales Steuerrecht 465 (1994); Hein Vermeulen, *Suggested Treaty Benefits Approaches for Collective Investment Vehicles CIV's and Its Investors under the OECD MTC 2010 update*, 39 Intertax 248 (2011); Tomi Vittala, *Taxation of Investment Funds in the European Union* 71 (IBFD 2005); Wolf Wassermeyer, *Ausländische Investmentfonds im Internationalen Steuerrecht*, 20 Internationales Steuerrecht 193 (2001).
75. OECD, Model Tax Convention on Income and on Capital 2014 (Full Version) (2014) (hereinafter the 'OECD Model'), available at http://dx.doi.org/10.1787/9789264239081-en (last accessed 18 December 2017).

Article 4 (Resident):

1. For the purposes of this Convention, the term 'resident of a Contracting State' means any person who, under the laws of that State, is liable to tax therein ... This term, however, does not include any person who is liable to tax in that State in respect only of income from sources in that State or capital situated therein.[76]

Depending on the interpretation of the new approach of the reformed investment law, the new questions on treaty entitlement of investment funds are more or less hard to answer. According to one interpretation, Section 6(2), clause 1 InvStG 2018 only subjects domestic income to tax.[77] From that perspective, German investment funds, arguably, may have lost their treaty entitlement. The only solution would be amendments to all German tax treaties. More convincing, however, is another view, which identifies the two-step approach of the new opaque tax regime as a partial tax exemption. The first step, Section 6(1) InvStG 2018, provides unlimited tax liability for domestic investment funds by referring to Section 1(1) KStG. Then, the second step, per Section 6(2) KStG, determines the tax base by cutting it down to domestic income.

[F] Investor Taxation

[1] Distributions, Dispositions, and Redemptions

The key objective of the reform had been to simplify the taxation procedures for the majority of investors in mutual retail funds. Their tax base was supposed to be determinable without assistance or information from the funds. Therefore, the new investment tax regime for mutual funds follows the cash-flow taxation principle. Every payment accruing to investors, including repayments of capital (with the exception of the liquidation of funds) is taxed according to the time of its reception. Outside a period of liquidation, the new investment law does not distinguish between the distribution of gains and such repayments (Section 17 InvStG 2018).

To avoid a lock-in effect – through the incentive of avoiding taxable distributions – the former concept of deemed-distributed income (*Ausschüttungsgleiche Erträge*) is substituted with a base-yield lump sum as a pre-determined tax base (*Vorabpauschale*). Finally, realized capital gains on the investor's interest in investment funds are taxed at the time of disposition or redemption of its units therein.

As distributions of investment funds are qualified as capital income (Section 20(1)(3) EStG 2016), and remain subject to WHT, domestic private investors are taxed with their accrual income at their WHT rate (Section 32d EStG). Business and corporate investors are not granted the advantage of partial income taxation according to Section 3(40) EStG, or given a corporate-tax exemption according to Section 8b InvStG (Section 16(3) InvStG 2018). Instead, special partial exemptions were introduced with the new investment tax regime to avoid double taxation at the fund and investor levels, which are described *infra*. As distributions from investment funds were not included in the

---

76. *Ibid.*, Arts 1 and 4.
77. Helios & Mann, *supra* note 3, at 11; Tillmann Kempf & Julius Hirtz, *supra* note 61, at 2.

catalogue of source income set out in Section 49 EStG, non-resident investors with limited tax liability are not taxed on the distributed income; it simply does not qualify as domestic income. The former WHT has been substituted by the corporate tax at the fund level.

[2] Treaty Override

Distributions by foreign funds to domestic investors are frequently tax exempt according to tax treaty provisions. Germany's new investment tax regime introduces a new subject-to-tax clause with Section 16(4) InvStG 2018, self-characterized as a treaty override. According to Section 16(4) InvStG 2018, tax exemptions through tax treaty provisions presuppose a nominal profit tax at a rate of at least 10% in the residence state (Section 16(4), clauses 1(1) and 2 InvStG 2018). Furthermore, the distribution has to be based on at least 50% non-tax-exempt income of the fund (Section 16(4)(2) InvStG 2018).

[3] Base-Yield Lump Sum (Pre-determined Tax Base or **Vorabpauschale***)*

With a base-yield lump sum or 'pre-determined tax', as the German term *Vorabpauschale* also has been translated, a permanent tax deferral is avoided and it ensures that, at a minimum, the risk-free interest rate is taxed at the investor level. The deemed-minimum rate is the average return on long-term government bonds, published annually by the Federal Ministry of Finance. As of 2016, the rate was 1.1%. The applicable rate is reduced by 30%, which is justified as a lump sum for administrative costs,[78] with reference to the first redemption price at the beginning of the year. The upper limit for the result is the gain in value of the interest in the investment fund before distributions during the year and later reduced by distributions.[79] The result is further diminished by partial exemptions justified by the partial income method. The final result is deemed to be received in the immediately following calendar year. It follows that the pre-determined tax base only becomes effective if the distributions of the fund do not reach the minimum interest rate. It is taxed at the investor level like distributions. As the pre-determined tax base does not qualify as domestic income (due to a missing reference in Section 49 EStG), non-resident investors are not liable to tax on the pre-determined tax base. The same applies to domestic tax-exempt investors. Finally, the pre-determined tax base is deductible from realized gains from the disposal or redemption of investment units. That justifies the capitalization of deferred tax assets in the investor's balance sheet.

---

78. Helios & Mann, *supra* note 3, at 15.
79. But not below zero. *See* BR-Drucksache 119/16, at 99.

[4] *Partial Income Method (Partial Exemptions)*

As the income of the fund is taxed at the fund level and the new investment tax regime is not supposed to lead to an overall increase in the tax burden, double burdens through taxation at both the fund and investor levels have to be avoided. This is achieved by the partial income method, which takes the prior charge of the income and burden that would have realized through a direct investment into account. The new law standardizes the prior tax impositions on earnings through three classes of funds.

The first class is formed by equity funds, which are qualified through investments in capital interests (stock holdings) with a continuous share of at least 51%. The basic partial exemption is 30%. It is increased to 60% if the interests are qualified as business assets of natural persons and to 80% if the interests are assets of a taxable corporate entity, with the exception of assets for trading by financial service providers according to Section 8b(7)–(8) KStG. But, the tax-exemption rate remains at 30% for WHT; otherwise, the fund has to qualify the character of its investors (Section 20(1) InvStG 2018).

The second class is formed by real estate funds that continuously invest at least 51% of their assets in real estate. Their basic partial exemption is 60%, which increases to 80% in the case of investments in foreign real estate or foreign real estate companies (Section 20(3) InvStG 2018).

Mixed funds form the third class standardized by the law; these are characterized by continuous investment of at least 25% of the assets in capital interests. The partial exemption rate for mixed funds is one-half of the partial exemption of equity funds (Section 20(2) InvStG 2018).

Funds of funds are addressed in Section 2(8)–(9) InvStG 2018. The interests of a fund in equity funds are deemed to be 51% investment in equity; accordingly, interests of a fund in real estate funds are deemed to be 51% investment in real estate. It follows that, if funds of funds are not investing solely in one of those categories, they will qualify as mixed funds.

The partial income method, however, raises further issues regarding private equity investments, trade tax, transition rules, and the provision of evidence through investors, which, due to the limitation of space, cannot be presented in detail here.[80]

[5] *EU-Law Conformity*

There had been some concerns raised in German doctrinal discussions that the partial-income exemption method might be incompatible with EU Law, as it would favour domestic investors.[81] That view is based on the thought that taxation at the fund level is only partially neutralized by the partial income method, which only applies to domestic investors and that corporate taxation at the fund level, therefore, results in a higher burden for foreign investors than for domestic investors. In response, it has been

80. *See* Helios & Mann, *supra* note 3, at 16.
81. Haisch, *supra* note 54, at 302; Rehm & Nagler, supra note 54.

convincingly argued that the investment income of foreign investors is not taxable at all in Germany and, without any tax burden, no discrimination can be identified.[82]

[G] Special Investment Funds

[1] Taxation-Related Product Regulation

Although the new opaque regime is the new basic principle of German investment tax law, the old concept of semi-transparency remains an exceptional option, but only for special investment funds. The new investment tax law establishes its own concept of special investment fund law independently from existing regulatory law and the option of semi-transparency; such qualification of special investment funds presupposes three requirements.

First, according to Section 27 InvStG 2018, special investment funds are restricted to a short list of legal forms consisting of fractional shares in equity (*Sondervermögen*) and investment corporations (i.e., investment entity with legal personality), with variable capital. Investment corporations with fixed capital and open-ended limited investment partnerships are excluded. They are limited to one hundred direct or indirect investors with partnerships investors counted according to a look-through approach (Section 26(8), clause 1 InvStG 2018). Natural persons (i.e., individuals) can invest therein only if they hold their interests as business assets, and if the participation of natural persons is required for regulatory reasons or an indirect participation of natural persons has been acquired before 9 June 2016 (Section 26(8), clause 2 InvStG 2018). Finally, the fund or the fund manager has to be subject to investment regulation. Therefore, unregulated funds that are managed by managers authorized under the AIFM Directive[83] meet the formal requirements, which might be the case for the Luxembourg *société de gestion patrimoine familial* or SPF.

Second, the investment fund has to qualify for a trade-tax exemption according to Section 15(2) and (3) InvStG 2018 (Section 26, clause 1 InvStG 2018). Therefore, it must not perform material business activities according to settled administrative practice and the threshold provided by Section 15(3) InvStG 2018.

Third, special investment funds are subject to a tax-related product regulation, which means that at least 90% of the fund's net asset value is invested in defined assets as listed in a catalogue in Section 26(4) InvStG 2018, which was introduced by the implementation of the AIFM Directive and further product-related requirements in Section 26(5)–(7) InvStG 2018 are met. The investment practice of the fund must not materially violate those rules (*nicht wesentlich*). The undefined legal concept of *nicht wesentlich* in Section 26, clause 1 InvStG has to be substantiated through a case-by-case

82. Helios & Mann, *supra* note 3, at 18.
83. Directive 2011/61/EU of the European Parliament and of the Council of 8 June 2011. on Alternative Investment Fund Managers and amending Directives 2003/41/EC and 2009/65/EC and Regulations (EC) No 1060/2009 and (EU) No 1095/2010, OJ L 174/1 of 1.7.2011.

analysis of the circumstances surrounding the violation and its consequences.[84] A significant violation of the investment rules set out in Section 26 InvStG 2018 will lead to the dissolution of the fund (Section 52 InvStG 2018). While Section 26(4) InvStG 2018 provides a list of eligible assets, Section 26(6) InvStG 2018 still provides an equity-interest cap of 10% for direct and indirect investments in corporations, which might be exceeded without limits for participation in real estate companies, public-private partnership-project corporations and corporations in the business of generating renewable energies. According to Section 29(3) InvStG 2018, exceeding that cap must not lead to benefits usually granted to participations greater than 10% in general tax law or tax treaty law.

[2] The Transparency Option

For the taxation of investment funds that meet the requirements of special investment funds, the same principles applicable to mutual retail fund generally apply (Section 29(1) InvStG 2018). However, one difference is that special investment funds qualify for the transparency option according to Section 30(1) InvStG 2018. Choosing that option affects tax exemption at the fund level and leads to taxation at the investor level, which corresponds to the former regime of semi-transparency.

The procedure for exercising the transparency option depends on the type of assets held by the special investment fund and refers to its types of income, not to the fund itself. Regarding income from equity investments that is subject to a WHT, the fund manager must irrevocably declare to the WHT-obliged parties that they will not issue tax certificates in favour of the special investment fund, but instead issue them in favour of its investors. Under that condition, Section 30(1), clause 2 InvStG 2018 rules that the WHT on income received at the fund level is deemed to have been withheld for the account of its investors and not for the account of the fund. With the design of that 'bypass,' transparency and the connection between tax exemption and WHT at the investor level is strengthened, addressing EU-Law concerns regarding the former tax regime.

For income from real estate and other income that is not subject to a WHT, Section 33 InvStG 2018 provides an alternative procedure to opt into the tax-transparency option. To obtain a tax exemption at the fund level, the fund has to impose a WHT on distributed and undistributed (i.e., deemed distributions or *ausschüttungsgleiche Erträge*) domestic income for the account of its investors and must, accordingly, issue WHT certificates in favour of their investors (Section 33(1) and (3) InvStG 2018).

Within the transparency option, only the investors are taxed and never the fund's income itself. Regarding the WHT, the investors are deemed to be a creditor of the fund and the debtor of the taxes withheld for their account (Section 30(1), clause 2 InvStG 2018). According to the wording thereof, only the gross income, and not the fund's

84. Examples at BMF of 23.10.1994 - IV C 1-S 1980-1/13/10007, 52 Deutsches Steuerrecht 2346, margin nos 4, 6 (2014).

administrative costs, is assigned to the investors. That might lead to a loss at the fund level that cannot be rebalanced until the redemption of the asset.[85] The tax base at the investor level consists of the distributed income, any deemed-distributed income, and capital gains from dispositions and redemptions of interests in the investment fund (Section 34(1) InvStG 2018). In general, the tax base corresponds to the current investment taxation regime. But, as parts of the income are directly assigned to the investors, due to the strengthened transparency offered by the transparency option, the parts of the fund income that are assigned directly to the investors have to be deducted from such distributed and deemed-distributed income (Section 36(1), clause 2 InvStG 2018).

Accumulated writer premiums (*Stillhalteprämien*), capital gains from dispositions and forward transactions (shares, debt instruments), and gains from the disposal of investment participation in other investment funds will still be granted a tax deferral with loss carry-forward (Section 36(2) InvStG 2018). Only two of the former fund privileges were slightly reduced. First, the new special-investment-fund tax regime does not provide an exemption for undistributed realized gains in real estate withholding periods of ten years or more, which the previous law did (Section 36(1)(2) InvStG 2018). Second, the so-called permanent tax deferral on undistributed-yet-realized capital gains in stocks and other financial instruments is limited to fifteen years. After that period, the accumulated undistributed realized capital gains are to be deemed-distributed income (Section 36(5), clause 1 InvStG 2018).

Income from special investment funds is qualified as capital income according to Section 20(1)(3a) EStG 2016 or prior business income (Section 20(8) EStG 2016) and is taxed at the ordinary tax rate without exception as the WHT rate is excluded (Section 34(2) InvStG 2018).

[3] Default Opaque Tax Regime

If a special investment fund does not choose the transparent regime, it will be taxed according the basic rules of the new opaque regime. Thus, its tax rate (as of this writing) will either be 15% or 15.825% depending on its types of income (Section 29(1) and (6) InvStG 2018).

At the investor level, the partial exemption rates are modified vis-à-vis the basic exemption rates applied to mutual investment funds. Section 42(4), clause 1 InvStG 2018 provides a 60% general-partial exemption for all investment income. It is increased to 100% if the investor is subject to corporate income tax and cannot claim a reduction of WHT according to tax treaty provisions below a rate of 15% (Section 42(4), clause 2 InvStG 2018). Income from domestic real estate and other domestic income is subject to a partial exemption rate of 20% (Section 42(5) InvStG 2018).

85. Haisch, *supra* note 54, at 302.

[4] No Need for a Reform?

The new option for special investment funds to stay in the transparent regime leads to the question of why transparency is still possible, despite all the enunciated problems relating to such transparency that were used to justify the reform.

There are some reasons why transparency might still work for special investment funds, while it cannot work for mutual investment funds. First, a limited number of investors is less complex to administer and easier to audit. Second, a limited number of funds and investors allows a concentration of expertise in a few, select tax offices. An investment tax regime with a narrow scope is also less vulnerable to aggressive tax planning, as it is easier to monitor. Third, with regard to EU-Law conformity, the new, strengthened transparency convincingly clarifies the pass-through concept. Remaining limitations on the free movement of capital, consequently, are justified by coherence.

§4.07 TRANSITION RULES

The new law came into effect on 1 January 2018 (Section 56(1), clause 1 InvStG 2018). At the funds level, deviating fiscal years are deemed to have ended as of 31 December 2017, which affects the determination of the investment funds' deemed-distributed profits.

At the investor level, the new law deems that there was a disposition of all investment participations as of 31 December 2017 under the previous investment tax regime and that, as of 1 January 2018, such investment participations were acquired under the new investment tax law. All gains and losses were determined as of those transition dates, but are not subject to tax at that moment (Section 56(2) InvStG 2018). Rather, taxation thereof will be deferred until the interest in the funds are disposed of or redeemed (Section 56(3), clause 1 InvStG 2018). Custodian banks will have to determine all of such deemed gains and losses as of 31 December 2020 and thereafter declare them as of 31 December 2021 (Section 56(4) and (5) InvStG 2018).

Section 56(6) InvStG further offers a limited renewal of the grandfathering of privately held interests acquired before 1 January 2009. Those gains and losses remained tax-exempt until 31 December 2017. As of 1 January 2018, all changes in value will be taxed at the time of disposal, as long as the overall gain from the disposal of shares acquired before 1 January 2009 exceeds EUR 100,000 (Section 56(6) InvStG).[86] The grandfathering of the AIFM-AnpG 2013[87] was extended until 31 December 2017 (Section 22(2), clause 1 InvStG 2004).

86. For the history thereof, *see* Helios & Mann, *supra* note 3, at 22.
87. Gesetz zur Apassung des Investmentsteuergesetzes und anderer Gesetze an das AIFM-Umsetzungsgesetz (AIFM-Steuer-Anpassungsgesetz – AIFM-StAnpG) v. 18.12.2013 (BGBl. I 2013, 4318).

§4.08 CONCLUSIONS

What Eric M. Zolt once described as a triangle of the income taxation of investment funds in developing and transition countries is just as true for globally connected, industrialized countries:

> the choice of tax rules for investment funds requires balancing three objectives: first, not to hamper the development of financial intermediaries, such as investment funds; second, to advise tax rules that are comparable to those that apply to other investments; and, third, to adopt tax rules that can be administered and enforced.[88]

From a European perspective, one would like to add that investment funds are an important product of the financial industry and national tax rules are an instrument of regional economic policy. Hence, Zolt's triangle has to be extended to a square that is even more difficult to balance.

From an academic lawyer's perspective, with a bird's-eye view of the overall tax system, a purely transparent tax regime would be the best choice to reach the aims of equal treatment and comparability with other ways to tax direct and indirect capital investments. From a domestic fund manager's point of view, the competition between different financial centres and different types of financial intermediaries have to be taken into account. From a variety of perspectives, the level playing field mostly seems to be sloppy. Strong interests led to privileges in the former investment tax system, which also increased the complexity thereof. Tax authorities, in particular, suffer from this complexity. It is far more worthwhile for the tax industry to invest in research and development in national and international investment tax law than it is for tax authorities. And, a transparent tax system is much more difficult to administer and monitor than an opaque concept that piles up different layers and reduces complexity in that way.

Zolt implicitly discouraged developing countries from implementing a transparent 'pass-through' tax regime by noting that its administration requires a highly developed tax administration.[89] German tax authorities, on the other hand, are highly developed, but have been trapped in the semi-transparency embedded in a capital income taxation regime suffering from a multitude of contradictions and over-complexity. It is easy to say that it might have been better to simply reform that capital income taxation regime instead of changing the principles of investment tax law. But, capital income taxation is a highly political topic, while investment taxation is seen as a more technical matter and, thus, much easier to revise. With the reform, the German legislature tried to simplify the existing regime by reducing complexity. One may doubt if its attempt will turn out to be successful. On the contrary, the new dualism of the new opaque regime and semi-transparency, the design of investor taxation, and the number of exceptions made, give rise to the fear that the new investment tax regime is no less

88. Eric M. Zolt, *Taxation of Investment Funds*, *in* Vol. 2 *Tax Law Design and Drafting* 969 (Victor Thuronyi ed., International Monetary Fund 1998).
89. *Ibid.*, at 969, 983, 985.

complex than the old one. Moreover, it brings transition costs, unknown concerns, and compatibility conflicts in tax treaty law. Nevertheless, to conclude with some positive aspects, the German new opaque regime is a brave experiment, which will enrich comparative tax law with a new model of investment taxation. In fact, it might not only reduce reporting requirements and administrative costs for mutual investment funds but also provide tax engineers with a new toolkit. With respect to the latter, the first amendments to the reform are already under discussion.

Part II Funds Taxation and European Union Law

CHAPTER 5

Taxation of Collective Investments Within the Legal Framework of State Aid

*Claire Micheau**

§5.01 INTRODUCTION

Investment funds play an ever-growing role in the economic landscape of the internal market. The taxation framework governing investment funds - such funds being domestic or cross-border structures - has to be applied consistently with European Union (EU) law across the Member States. It is within this context that the issue of compliance with State-aid law commands attention. State-aid rules applied to tax matters have grown in importance and in complexity over the last years: they currently occupy a key position within the regulatory policies and legislation of domestic tax systems.

Various questions emerge from the application of State-aid rules to the regulatory context of tax regimes for investment funds. On the one hand, there is a need to consider the nature of collective funds, which act as intermediary pools of assets. On the other hand, the peculiar nature of these taxation regimes brings consideration on State-aid rules to the fore. Against this legal backdrop, how should the rules governing State aid apply to such investments? Which limits should the tax regulator consider when devising and implementing tax regimes available only to collective investments? What are the lines that both the case law of the Court of Justice of the European Union (CJEU) and the Commission's practice have drawn when reviewing these tax regimes?

* Any opinions expressed by the author are strictly personal and do not reflect the views of any institution or organization.

In light of these considerations, the chapter seeks to analyse the extent to which tax regimes for collective investments can be consistent with State-aid rules.[1] After drawing the broad outlines of State-aid law, the contribution focuses on a relevant feature which characterized investment collective funds (i.e., their very nature as intermediaries). The chapter then examines in greater depth the assessment of the notion of State aid applied to collective funds from two angles: the notion of undertaking as an entity performing an economic activity and the core issue of selectivity.

§5.02 BRIEF OVERVIEW OF STATE-AID RULES

The law of State aid, which is set forth in Articles 107 through 109 TFEU, is governed by the principle of prohibition of State aid: any aid is in principle considered to be incompatible with the internal market. The TFEU, however, provides rules which allow the aid to be compatible with the market. The compatibility grounds can directly stem from the TFEU and be de jure applicable (Article 107(2) TFEU) or they can be subject to the Commission's discretionary assessment (Article 107(3) TFEU). In tax matters, however, one has to keep in mind that the compatibility analysis with the internal market plays a limited role; cases where a tax aid was found to be compatible with the internal market remain rare.[2] Despite these limited examples, State aid in tax matters are in general regarded as operating aids (i.e., aid that is 'intended to relieve an undertaking of the expenses which it would itself normally have had to bear in its day-to-day management or its usual activities').[3] These tax aids are in principle

1. This chapter focuses exclusively on an analysis of the very notion of State aid within the meaning of Art. 107(1) of the Treaty on the Functioning of the European Union, as consolidated in [2012] OJ C 326/47 and amended (hereinafter 'TFEU'), disregarding thereby any compatibility assessment. However, it is noteworthy that the Commission provides rules regarding compatibility with the internal market, in particular in the context of the General Block Exemption Regulation (which remains limited to fiscal incentives targeted at investors who are natural persons). Moreover, the Commission set out further provisions concerning the compatibility of tax incentives for corporate investors to finance eligible undertakings. *See* Communication from the Commission: Guidelines on State aid to promote risk finance investments [2014] OJ C 019/04, para. 120.
2. *See*, e.g., Commission Decision of 20 September 2011 on the measure C 35/10 (ex N 302/10) which Denmark is planning to implement in the form of duties for online gambling in the Danish Gaming Duties Act (notified under document C(2011) 6499), [2012] OJ L 68/3. The decision, which was adopted within the context of liberalization of the gambling market, took the view that liberalizing the market allowed supervision of the online gambling market and thereby strengthened control over gambling addiction and reinforced the protection of minors and other vulnerable persons.
3. *Siemens v. Commission*, T-459/93, Judgment, EU:T:1995:100, para. 48. In the same line, the outdated Commission Notice on State-aid rules that applied to measures relating to direct business taxation 'are not linked to the carrying-out of specific projects and reduce a firm's current expenditure without it being possible to assess the precise volume involved when the Commission carries out its ex ante examination'. Commission Notice on the application of the State-aid rules to measures relating to direct business taxation [1998] OJ C 384/3, para. 32.

prohibited; the Court confers a presumption for operating aids to affect the market: 'in principle, operating aid ... distorts the conditions of competition'.[4]

That being said, the key analysis of State-aid analysis in taxation focuses on the very notion of State aid. The core question is whether the measure fulfils the criteria of State aid as provided for under EU law. Article 107 TFEU lays down four criteria to qualify a measure as State aid: (i) the measure should provide for an advantage; (ii) it should be granted by or through State resources; (iii) it should be selective inasmuch as it favours certain undertakings or the production of certain goods; and (iv) it should be capable of distorting competition and affecting trade between Member States.[5]

In order to provide clarification on the concept of aid and its interpretation by the European judicature, the Commission has recently adopted the 2016 State-Aid Notion Notice,[6] which focuses exclusively on the substantive criteria to define a State aid within the meaning of Article 107(1) TFEU, disregarding thereby the compatibility grounds pursuant to Article 107(2) and (3) and Article 106(2) TFEU – which is for the Commission to assess. The 2016 State-Aid Notion Notice was adopted in order to take stock of the extensive case law developed by the Court's case law over the last sixty years and the long-standing practice of the Commission.

As stressed in the 2016 State-Aid Notion Notice, the key element for tax measures is an analysis of selectivity. The Court's case law has emerged with a test of selectivity which is threefold:

(1) the system of reference must be identified;
(2) it must be demonstrated that a given measure constitutes a derogation from that system insofar as it differentiates between economic operators who, in light of the objectives intrinsic to the system, are in a comparable factual and legal situation; and
(3) it must be established that the derogation is justified by the nature or the general scheme of the (reference) system.

In view of these broad outlines of the rules governing State aid, the question arises as to whether fund taxation regimes comply with State-aid rules. The application of State-aid disciplines to collective funds deserves close scrutiny with regard to the notion of an undertaking and that of selectivity. This chapter, therefore, focuses on these aspects.

---

4. *Germany v. Commission*, C-156/98, Judgment, EU:C:2000:467, para. 30; *see also Comitato 'Venezia vuole vivere' and Others v. Commission*, Joined Cases C-71/09 P, C-73/09 P, and C-76/09 P, Judgment, EU:C:2011:368, para. 136.
5. Although two TFEU criteria, competition distortion and trade affectation, are separately mentioned, they are usually analysed together, as the Court has consistently maintained that they are 'inextricably linked', *see*, e.g., *Regione autonoma Friuli-Venezia Giulia v. Commission*, T-288/97, Judgment, EU:T:2001:115, para. 41; *Alzetta and Others v. Commission*, Joined Cases T-298/97, T-312/97, T-313/97, T-315/97, T-600/97 to 607/97, T-1/98, T-3/98 to T-6/98 and T-23/98, EU:T:2000:151, para. 81).
6. Commission Notice on the notion of State aid as referred to in Art. 107(1) of the Treaty on the Functioning of the European Union [2016] OJ C 262/1 (hereinafter the '2016 State-Aid Notion Notice'), 1–50.

§5.03 THE DISTINCTIVE FEATURE OF COLLECTIVE INVESTMENT VEHICLES

As a preliminary comment, it is important to first define the term of 'undertaking for collective investment'. For the purpose of this chapter, undertakings for collective investments are defined as vehicles pooling assets from individuals and legal entities with the aim of developing a larger, diversified portfolio.[7]

Undertakings for collective investments present the distinctive feature of operating as intermediary bodies between, on the one hand, the investors – who are the third party – and, on the other hand, the target companies. It is this very feature which makes the analysis of their tax treatment with regard to State-aid law of particular interest. More specifically, when applying State-aid law, one has to take into account the rationale for investment vehicles. Should they be taxed as any other undertaking? Or, should they rather be subject to a tax liability that takes into account their founding rationale – that is, acting as an intermediary, if not transparent, vehicle (i.e., an investment-pool-developing portfolio)?

In that respect, and as a general principle, EU law endorses the view that undertakings for collective investments should be taxed at an appropriate level.[8] In the light of this principle, it is noteworthy that one of the main issues encountered by tax regulators when designing domestic taxation systems is the absence of specific tax rules governing investment funds. This may result in the tax authorities treating investment funds as any other taxpayer. Such a tax treatment leads to an additional tax layer on the intermediary, the investment fund. In other words, the investment's profits or gains are subject to a higher taxation level than the one that would have applied in the absence of the investment fund. It is in the context of tackling such adverse tax effects that the Member States seek to implement tax frameworks that ensure a single layer of taxation or at least tend to apply a final tax burden that applies irrespective of the form of the investment vehicle used.

In this regard, as pointed out by the tax literature, the Member States have to encompass three main objectives in designing tax rules governing investment vehicles:

> the choice of tax rules for investment funds requires balancing three objectives:
>
> - first, not to hamper the development of financial intermediaries, such as investment funds;
> - second, to devise tax rules that are comparable to those that apply to other investments; and

7. In line with the 2016 State-Aid Notion Notice (fn. 237), this notion encompasses 'undertakings for collective investment' or UCIs subject to Directive 2009/65/EC of the European Parliament and of the Council of 13 July 2009 on the coordination of laws, regulations and administrative provisions relating to undertakings for collective investment in transferable securities (UCITS) (recast) [2009] OJ L 302/32, as amended, as well as other types of collective investment undertakings, such as Alternative Investment Funds as defined by Directive 2011/61/EU of the European Parliament and of the Council of 8 June 2011 on Alternative Investment Fund Managers and amending Directives 2003/41/EC and 2009/65/EC and Regulations (EC) No 1060/2009 and (EU) No 1095/2010 [2011] OJ L 174/1, as amended.
8. 2016 State-Aid Notion Notice, para. 161:

- third, to adopt tax rules that can be administered and enforced.[9]

From a State-aid perspective, of particular relevance is the second objective: tax rules should, to the extent possible, ensure that they do not unduly hamper or preclude the development of investment vehicles. It is in the light of this consideration that the following sections address the specific issues of State-aid law.

§5.04 ECONOMIC ACTIVITY FOR INVESTMENT FUNDS UNDER STATE-AID LAW

In order to apply State-aid law, the entity should be an undertaking within the meaning of Article 107(1) TFEU. In that respect, the CJEU has consistently held that undertakings should be defined as entities engaged in an economic activity, notwithstanding their legal status or the way in which they are financed.[10] To this end, in a continuous line of jurisprudence, the Court's case law holds that any activity that consists in offering goods and services on a market is an economic activity.[11]

With regard to investment funds, one can debate whether they perform an economic activity. In this regard, the so-called *Fineco* case[12] is of relevance. Interestingly, in order to assess investment funds as performing economic activities, the Commission, in its 2005 Italian Small- and Mid-Cap Commission Decision,[13] relied on the CJEU's judgments adopted within the context of VAT: it noted that 'the Court recently held that transactions carried out by SICAVs and consisting in the collective investment in transferable securities constitute an economic activity carried out by taxable persons within the meaning of ... the Sixth VAT Directive'.[14] On this basis, the Commission came to the conclusion that the tax measure applicable to 'investors investing in specialized investment vehicles favours the vehicles themselves as undertakings when they have corporate form or the undertakings managing such vehicles when they have contractual form'.[15] In this regard, the *BBL* case is noteworthy: in this case dealing with the VAT treatment applicable to SICAVs, the Court reiterated that it is settled case law that 'the mere acquisition and holding of shares in a company is not

9. Eric M. Zolt, *Taxation of Investment Funds, in 2 Tax Law Design and Drafting*, 969 (Victor Thuronyi ed., 1998).
10. *Cassa di Risparmio di Firenze SpA and Others*, C-222/04, Judgment, EU:C:2006:8, para. 107; *Pavlov and Others*, Joined Cases C-180/98 to C-184/98, Judgment, EU:C:2000:428, para. 74.
11. *Commission v. Italy*, C-118/85, Judgment, EU:C:1987:283, para. 7; *Commission v. Italy*, C-35/96, Judgment, EU:C:1998:303, para. 36; *Pavlov and Others*, Joined Cases C-180/98 to C-184/98, para. 75.
12. *Associazione italiana del risparmio gestito and Fineco Asset Management v. Commission*, T-445/05, Judgment, EU:T:2009:50 (hereinafter, '*Fineco*').
13. Commission Decision of 6 September 2005 on the aid scheme implemented by Italy for certain undertakings for collective investment in transferable securities specialized in shares of small- and medium-capitalization companies listed on regulated markets (notified under document number C(2005) 3302) [2005] OJ L 268/1, (hereinafter the '2005 Italian Small- and Mid-Cap Commission Decision').
14. *Ibid.*, para. 38.
15. *Ibid.*, para. 39.

to be regarded as an economic activity within the meaning of the Sixth [VAT] Directive'.[16]

The 2005 Italian Small- and Mid-Cap Commission Decision was challenged before the General Court.[17] Of particular interest is the subtle position taken by the Court: it tempered the Commission's reference to its VAT jurisprudence by stressing that the Commission's interpretation 'may in some aspect appear questionable or unambiguous' and it 'must not be read out of context but in the light of the contested decision'.[18] It confirmed, however, that some investment vehicles can be qualified as undertakings. Unfortunately, the Court did not provide further development on the analysis to carry out.

In the same vein, the EFTA Surveillance Authority endorsed the view that investment funds can be regarded as undertakings inasmuch as they perform economic activities based on the VAT jurisprudence. In the *Liechtenstein Taxation of Investment Undertakings* case,[19] the Authority followed the CJEU's case law and the Commission's stance by relying on the VAT directive:

> The Authority finds, in line with the Commission's case practice in this area that this jurisprudence can also be applied when assessing the existence of an economic activity under the State-aid provisions of the EEA Agreement. Investment companies and the fund direction for an investment fund under Liechtenstein law ... are active in assembling and managing the assets of various investors with the intention of making profits via various fees related to the placements.[20]

16. *BBL*, C-8/03, Judgment, EU:C:2004:650, para. 38. The Court continued, stating:

> The mere acquisition of financial holdings in other undertakings does not amount to the exploitation of property for the purpose of obtaining income therefrom on a continuing basis because any dividend yielded by that holding is merely the result of ownership of the property and is not the product of any economic activity within the meaning of that directive.

See also, *EDM*, C-77/01, Judgment, EU:C:2004:243, para. 65 ('interest received by a holding company in consideration of loans granted to companies in which it has shareholdings cannot be excluded from the scope of VAT, since that interest does not arise from the simple ownership of the asset, but is the consideration for making capital available for the benefit of a third party').

17. *Fineco*, T-445/05. Juan Jorge Piernas López, *Annotation on Cases T-424/05 and T-445/05: Indirect Advantage and Selectivity Revisited*, 9 EStAL 10, 219–228(2010); Raymond Luja, *Investment Funds, Tax Planning and State Aid*, 46 Eur. Tax'n 565–569 (2006); Raymond Luja, *Tax Related Difficulties of State Aid Rules*, EATLP Helsinki 2007 Conference – Discussion paper (2007); Raymond Luja, *Fiscal Autonomy, Investment Funds and State Aid: A Follow-Up*, 49 Eur. Tax'n 369–374 (2009); Christophe Giolito, *Aides d'États*, 2009/2 Concurrences 158–160 (2009); Laurence Idot, *Secteur financier et avantage indirect*, 2009/5 Revue Europe 23 (2009).
18. *Fineco*, T-445/05, para. 96.
19. EFTA Surveillance Authority Decision No 416/10/COL of 3 November 2010 on the taxation of investment undertakings under the Liechtenstein Tax Act (Liechtenstein) [2012] OJ L 261/21 (hereinafter, the '*EFTA Liechtenstein Taxation of Investment Undertakings* case'.
20. EFTA Surveillance Authority Invitation to submit comments pursuant to Art. 1(2) in Part I of Protocol 3 to the Agreement between the EFTA States on the Establishment of a Surveillance Authority and a Court of Justice on State aid with regard to taxation of investment undertakings according to the Liechtenstein Tax Act [2009] OJ C 236/6, 15 (citations omitted). *See also* the *EFTA Liechtenstein Taxation of Investment Undertakings* case, *supra* note 19.

Hence, the Authority concluded that the investment companies under review should be regarded as undertakings.

It follows from the foregoing considerations that an investment vehicle can carry on an economic activity and, thereby, fall within the scope of State-aid rules inasmuch as they are more than a mere pool of assets, but they perform more than the mere acquisition and holding of shares, but also the assembly and the management of shares. To this end, the reasoning held in the context of the VAT Directive can be considered, but it should not be taken as a founding case law for State-aid purposes. Above all, the assessment has to be carried out on a case-by-case basis.

§5.05 THE KEY ISSUE OF SELECTIVITY

As pointed out, the criterion of selectivity is at the core of the analysis of State aid in the regulatory context of tax measures. As aforementioned, this criterion is assessed by means of a three-step analysis: (1) defining the general reference framework; (2) assessing the derogatory treatment from the general reference framework; and (3) determining whether the derogatory treatment can be justified by the logic of the tax system. These three steps of the assessment, which deserve emphasis, are examined in greater depth in the following sections.

[A] Defining the General Reference Framework

The first step of the selectivity analysis consists in defining the reference framework (i.e., the generally applicable tax system against which the measure is assessed). This can be fraught with difficulties, as it requires defining the dividing line between the generally applicable measure and the specific measure.[21] This issue can be all the subtler in practice, since the fact that some undertakings or producers of goods benefit more than others from the measure does not systematically mean that the tax measure should be regarded as a State aid.[22]

That being said, with regard to tax regimes in favour of investment funds, the question arises as to whether the reference tax framework can be the generally applicable corporate tax system or the applicable tax regime. On this key point, the *Fineco* case[23] commands attention. The Commission was faced with an Italian regime applicable to collective investment funds. As the tax legislation stood, Italy was imposing a tax rate of 12.5% for collective investments that was a substitute for the normal corporate tax rate. However, in 2004, the government enacted a tax scheme reducing the substitute tax from 12.5% to 5% for qualifying collective investment

21. This issue has been widely commented in the literature; for an overview made by the author, *see* Claire Micheau, *Tax Selectivity in European Law of State Aid: Legal Assessment and Alternative Approaches*, 40 Eur. L. Rev. 323, 326 fn. 15 (2015).
22. *See*, e.g., Commission Decision of 3 May 2000, Denmark, Modification of a scheme for flat-rate taxation for experts, N 41/9 [2000] OJ C 284/4.
23. *Italy v. Commission*, T-424/05, Judgment, EU:T:2009:49; *Fineco*, T-445/05 (upheld the 2005 Italian Small- and Mid-Cap Commission Decision).

vehicles (i.e., undertakings for collective investment in transferable securities specialized in shares of small- and medium-capitalization companies – 'small- and mid-caps' – listed on a regulated market in the EU[24]).

In this case, the Commission came to the conclusion that the tax rate in favour of the qualifying investment vehicles was a selective advantage that was assessed against the substitute rate applicable to all the other investment vehicles. The case was brought before the General Court which upheld the Commission's findings. Accordingly, the tax measure provided for a selective advantage when being assessed against the substitute tax regime for investment vehicles.

This case is of great interest since it raises the issue of the reference framework, the underlying question being whether the reference framework is the general corporate tax system or rather the substitute tax regime. Interesting, it is noteworthy that there has not been much discussion or debate in the scant legal literature on this issue. With regard to the Commission's decision itself, some argue that the 'the Commission seems to affirm that it is possible to maintain a "normal" tax regime for investment vehicles and their investors'.[25] However, that author tempered his stance by pointing out that the Commission, as a matter of fact:

> did not give any indication whatsoever as to on what grounds it considered the normal substitute to be the proper benchmark. The Commission did not say why the general substitute tax rate itself was out the scope of the prohibition contain in [Art. 107 §1 TFEU], although the author admits that this was not the object of the Commission's investigation.[26]

When analysing the wording of the European judicature, at first glance, it may seem that the reference framework to be taken into account would be that applicable to investment vehicles and not that applicable to all other undertakings under the general corporate tax system. However, upon a closer look, the reasoning used by the Court merits scrutiny.

One can agree that the wording of the Court is not of dogmatic clarity. However, at one point, the Court states that the reference framework cannot be that of the general corporate tax system. It only reviews the Commission's decision. Since the reasoning accepted by the Commission in its decision focuses on a comparison of the tax treatment applicable to the qualifying investment funds, on the one hand, and the remaining part of investment vehicles, on the other hand, it is consistent for the Court to use the tax regime for non-specialized investment vehicles as the reference framework.

It is equally interesting to note that the Court then added that the tax advantage applies to the entire financial sector and, thereby, is 'an exception to the general tax

24. Specifically, these companies had to have capital of less than EUR 800 million and were regarded as 'specialized' if they were holding stock of 'small- and mid-caps' for a total amount which corresponded to at least two-thirds of the value of their assets held during the year.
25. Luja (2006), *supra* note 16, at 567.
26. *Ibid.* Along the same lines with regard to the Commission's decision, the same author takes the view that the Commission's stance is 'rather equivocal' (Luja (2007), *supra* note 16, at 5).

scheme'.[27] After drawing a comparison between the beneficiary managing undertakings and that of undertakings in the financial sector that do not perform management operations for specialized investment vehicles, the Court concluded that 'the measure at issue is thus *also* selective in respect of managing undertakings of specialised investment vehicles'.[28] This statement leaves room for interpretation. It seems that the Court recognizes that there is a second selectivity that takes place at another level. However, with regard to the analysis of this other selectivity, the Court appears to focus its assessment on the indirect beneficiaries (i.e., beneficiary managing undertakings) against the tax system generally applicable to the financial sector. Regrettably, the Court did not elaborate any further on the general corporate tax system as a reference framework.

[B] Derogation from the Reference Framework

The second step of the selectivity assessment consists in determining whether the tax measure constitutes a derogation from the general tax framework. For this purpose, according to settled case law, one should assess whether the measure favours certain undertakings 'in comparison with other undertakings which are in a legal and factual situation that is comparable in the light of the objective pursued by the measure in question'.[29]

Turning to the tax regime for collective investments, the issue is to examine whether the collective investments and the other investors are in a comparable legal and factual situation in light of the objective of the tax reference system. Applied, for instance, in the *Fineco* case, the analysis focuses on assessing whether investment funds for qualifying investments and the other investment funds are in a comparable legal and factual situation in light of the objective of the tax system (i.e., taxing profit or gains generated by the investments).

[C] The Relevance of the Justification by the Logic of the Tax System

Once the derogation from the general reference framework has been established, the tax measure is deemed to be prima facie selective. This prima facie selectivity, however, can be justified by the logic of the tax system or the nature and general scheme of the system. Such a justification is important in taxation because it allows the internal mechanisms and the guiding principles of the tax system to be taken into account. If the measure is regarded as justified, it is not selective and, thus, falls outside the scope of State-aid rules.

This notion of justification, albeit not referred to in the TFEU, constitutes a significant aspect of the selectivity, which has its roots in the Court's jurisprudence.

27. *Fineco*, T-445/05, para. 156.
28. *Ibid* (emphasis added).
29. *Adria-Wien Pipeline and Wietersdorfer & Peggauer Zementwerke*, C-143/99, Judgment, EU:C:2001:598, para. 47. *See also, e.g., Spain v. Commission*, C-409/00, Judgment, EU:C:2003:92, para. 47; *Portugal v. Commission*, C-88/03, EU:C:2006:511, para. 54.

Originally introduced as a mere obiter dictum in the *Italian Textile* case,[30] the Court has since turned this justification into a well-established stance.[31] Justification by the logic of the tax system was recently enshrined in the 2016 State-Aid Notion Notice.[32]

It is important to point out that only the internal tax mechanism can be taken into account to assess the justification of the measure. In a consistent line of jurisprudence, the Court has systematically refuted objectives that are external to the measure (such as social,[33] security,[34] fiscal[35] or environmental[36] objectives). The measure must derive exclusively from the internal basic or guiding principles of the reference framework; in other words, the justification can only be based on reasons intrinsic to the tax system itself, being the inherent outcome of the mechanisms necessary for the functioning and effectiveness of the system (i.e., the fight against fraud or tax evasion, the necessity to take into account specific accounting requirements or the progressive nature of income tax and its redistributive purpose).[37]

With regard to tax regimes for investment funds, selectivity justification-by-tax neutrality commands attention. It appears to be the most relevant of those that have been raised. Tax neutrality can be defined as treating taxpayers 'the same way whether they invest in assets, such as government securities and the shares of joint-stock companies, directly or indirectly through investment funds'.[38] When applied to investment funds, the rationale is based on avoiding an excessive economic-tax liability: the favourable tax measure can be justified inasmuch as it aims to reduce the double economic taxation based on the overall design and principles inherent in the tax system. As mentioned above, one of the main features of tax regimes for collective investments lies in the need to design rules that ensure that their tax treatment remains comparable to those applicable to other investments. In other words, they can be governed by the necessity to avoid an additional layer of taxation. Therefore, the justification of tax neutrality can be accepted for tax regimes applicable to collective investments designed for tax transparency purposes, but only inasmuch as they aim to reduce double economic taxation.

In this regard, the 2010 Commission REIT Decision[39] is an interesting illustration of justification-by-tax neutrality. At stake was a tax exemption in favour of Finnish

30. *Italy v. Commission*, C-173/73, Judgment, EU:C:1974:71, para. 15.
31. *See e.g., Adria-Wien Pipeline and Wietersdorfer & Peggauer Zementwerke*, C-143/99, para. 52; *Portugal v. Commission*, C-88/03, para. 81; *Paint Graphos and Others*, Joined C-78/08 to C-80/08, Judgment, EU:C:2011:550, paras 69 and 70; *P Oy*, C-6/12, Judgment, EU:C:2013:525, paras 27 et seq.
32. 2016 State-Aid Notion Notice, paras 138 et seq.
33. *France v. Commission*, C-241/94, Judgment, EU:C:1996:353, paras 20–21.
34. Regarding road safety improvement, *see Spain v. Commission*, C-409/00, para. 46; *CETM v. Commission*, T-55/99, Judgment, EU:T:2000:223, para. 53.
35. For an example regarding exempting social security charges, *see Italy v. Commission*, C-173/73, para. 28.
36. *British Aggregates v. Commission*, C-487/06 P, Judgment, EU:C:2008:757, para. 92; *Adria-Wien Pipeline and Wietersdorfer & Peggauer Zementwerke*, C-143/99, para. 52.
37. 2016 State-Aid Notion Notice, para. 139.
38. *Ibid.*, para. 162.
39. Commission Decision, State Aid No. N131/2009, Finland, Residential Real Estate Investment Trust (REIT) scheme, 12 May 2010, C(2010) 2974 final (hereinafter the '2010 Commission REIT

Residential Real Estate Investment Trusts (REITs). Under the notified scheme, the Finnish authorities planned to implement a tax regime whereby REITs would not be taxed at the corporate level, but at the level of the shareholders, to whom at least 90% of the profits would be distributed as dividends. The Commission took the view that the tax measure, a derogatory treatment from the general corporate tax system, was justified by the logic of the tax system on the basis of tax neutrality. The exemption from corporate tax was directly related to the immediate distribution of annual profit to shareholders, the latter being subject to tax. Imposing tax liability at the level of the REIT and at that of the shareholders would have otherwise led to a quasi-double taxation:

> the exemption of REITs from the corporate income tax provided that at least 90% of the annual profits are distributed to the shareholders is indeed justified by the need to put an investment in a REIT at a par with a direct investment in real estate by an individual investor or a tax transparent investment vehicle such as a partnership or a collective real estate investment fund.[40]

The Commission, therefore, took the view that the measure was justified since 'the fiscal treatment of REITs is the same as the one for direct investments by an investor or for other comparable tax transparent investment vehicles provided by the Finnish tax system'.[41]

It is also noteworthy that the Court's case law and Commission's practice have adopted a restrictive interpretation of the justification-by-tax neutrality. For instance, the Commission has consistently rejected that justification when the tax measure was limited to well-defined investment vehicles that were subject to specific requirements. This was, for instance, the case for tax regimes favouring long-term or social-impact investment funds to the detriment of EU-harmonized funds (such as EuVECA,[42] EuSEF,[43] and ELTIF[44] funds). Another noteworthy example can be found in the *Fineco* case. The Commission endorsed the view that the tax measure could not be justified since it only favoured specialized collective investments in shares of small- and mid-caps listed on regulated markets, leaving aside collective investments in other companies and individual investments in non-listed companies.[45] Therefore, the argument of tax neutrality, applicable to all investment companies, did not hold. It is

---

Decision'). This measure was introduced to support investment in the Finnish rental housing market and to increase the supply of affordable rental housing.

40. *Ibid.*, para. 36.
41. *Ibid.* With regard to the reserve of 10% of annual profit, the Commission took the view that this tax deferral could be justified by the need for the REITs to have recourse to self-financing (*ibid.*, para. 32).
42. 2016 State-Aid Notion Notice, n. 242; Regulation (EU) No 345/2013 of the European Parliament and of the Council of 17 April 2013 on European venture capital funds [2013] OJ L 115/1, as amended.
43. 2016 State-Aid Notion Notice, n. 243; Regulation (EU) No 346/2013 of the European Parliament and of the Council of 17 April 2013 on European social entrepreneurship funds [2013] OJ L 115/18, as amended.
44. 2016 State-Aid Notion Notice, n. 244; Regulation (EU) 2015/760 of the European Parliament and of the Council of 29 April 2015 on European long-term investment funds [2015] OJ L 123/98.
45. 2005 Italian Small- and Mid-Cap Commission Decision, para. 43.

interesting to note that in that case, the Court reiterated its line of jurisprudence according to which one cannot take into account external objectives of the measure:

> It should be borne in mind in that regard that, if it were to be considered that a specific measure could escape Article [107(1) TFEU] if it pursued an economic or industrial policy objective, such as the promotion of investment, that provision would have no practical effect.[46]

The *EFTA Liechtenstein Taxation of Investment Undertakings* case[47] also serves as an example of the application of justification by the logic of the tax system. As presented above, that case concerned a tax regime in favour of investment undertakings. A distinction had to be made between, on the one hand, the tax treatment applicable to investment undertakings as such and, on the other hand, the management of the investment fund manager's own assets. With regard to the management of such assets, the Authority took the view that the logic that applied to the special tax regime for investment funds could not apply to the management companies' own assets, since they must be subject to the general corporate regime applicable to fund direction of investment funds. The Authority, therefore, held that 'the tax relief for the management company's own assets falls neither within the logic of the general tax system in Liechtenstein, nor within any specific logic of the taxation of investment undertakings'.[48]

Another point worth mentioning is compliance with the principle of proportionality. When justifying a tax advantage by the logic of the tax measure, it is important to ensure that the tax advantage is not disproportionate and does not go beyond what is necessary to achieve the objective of tax neutrality. This step was added by the Court in the so-called *Italian Cooperative* case,[49] in which the Court stated that the tax measure should respect the principle of proportionality inasmuch as it should not go beyond what is necessary to reach the legitimate goal. Applied to tax regimes for investment funds, one should, therefore, ensure that the tax measure is proportionate to the principle of tax neutrality or, in other words, there are no less far-reaching measures that could attain the same objective (i.e., of avoiding excessive and additional taxation layer).[50]

§5.06 CONCLUSION

In the nutshell, the application of State-aid rules to taxation raises interesting issues that are open to debate and command attention. In particular, the question related to

46. *Fineco*, T-445/05, para. 170.
47. *EFTA Liechtenstein Taxation of Investment Undertakings* case, *supra* note 19.
48. *Ibid.*, 25.
49. *Paint Graphos and Others*, Joined cases C-78/08 to C-80/08, para. 73.
50. A concrete example of the application of the proportionately principle within the context of the justification can be found in the abovementioned REITs case. The Commission allows the reserve of 10% of annual profit not to be distributed. Accordingly, this tax deferral can be justified by the necessity for the REITs to have recourse to self-financing (*see* para. 32). The rationale behind this reasoning is that the tax measure, despite the 10% of tax deferral, remains proportionate to the objective of tax neutrality.

the definition of 'undertaking' with regard to investment funds brings reflections on the very notion of economic activity to the fore. Moreover, the choice of the reference tax framework to apply the derogation test merits close scrutiny, as does justification-by-tax neutrality. At the core of the analysis of a tax regime applied to collective investment, the key point is to determine the extent to which the tax regulator, when designing the tax regime, planned to avoid an additional tax layer on the intermediary funds and aimed to ensure that these intermediary funds would not to be subject to a higher tax burden than any other form of investment. That being said, such an analysis can be fraught with difficulties, given the piecemeal nature of different tax regimes applied by the Member States, the distinct purposes served by investment funds (e.g., targeting geographic regions or industry sectors) and the wide-ranging forms they take (e.g., mutual funds, exchange-traded funds, hedge funds and private equity funds).

A related consideration to the intricate analysis of State-aid rules is the determination of the beneficiary under review. This chapter has focused on the investment funds themselves as the direct beneficiaries of the tax regime. There can be, however, indirect beneficiaries at a second level, such as the undertakings managing the funds or the companies targeted for investment.[51] With regard to these latter actors, one can acknowledge that there is an indirect advantage granted to the companies that are the target of the investment vehicles that benefit from favourable tax regimes.[52] However, from a State-aid perspective, this can be subtle. One of the main issues, then, would lie in the determination of the amount of indirect aid which is being granted; there may be indeed discussions as to how to determine the profits generated by these indirect beneficiaries based on the investments made by the funds that the latter would not have made in the absence of the aid measure.

These issues reflect the difficulties in applying competition rules within the specific and subtle context of investment funds. Within such an analysis, two elements are pivotal: the rationale for the tax regime and the level of the economic advantage assessed. On this basis, some approaches have to be clarified, if not refined, while some lines need to be further drawn.

51. For an analysis of the double level of beneficiaries (i.e., the targets of the investment vehicles and the investment vehicles themselves), *see* Luja (2009), *supra* note 16, at 373-374.

52. For instance, in *Fineco*, the Italian legislation provided for a favourable tax treatment for funds investing in specific SMEs. These SMEs were therefore the indirect beneficiaries of the aid. There is therefore a second level of economic advantage.

CHAPTER 6

Funds Taxation and the Third-Country Dimension

Keith O'Donnell & Uljana Molitor-March

§6.01 INTRODUCTION

The fundamental freedoms form part of the corner stones of the European Union (EU). This chapter will look into the free movement of capital in Article 63 of the Treaty of the Functioning of the European Union ('TFEU'; hereinafter 'Article 63 TFEU'), but more specifically, the third-country dimension of Article 63 TFEU.

The third-country dimension can be illustrated by a simple example: a company in Country X ('XCo') pays out a dividend to an investment fund resident in Country X; it is obligated to withhold 0% withholding tax on the dividend payment, based on a specific exemption in the tax law of Country X. However, when paying out a dividend to an investment fund in a third country, XCo is obliged to withhold a 25% withholding tax on the same dividend payment.

While, to a student of EU law, this will appear to be obviously discriminatory, it is surprising how many Member States have had, and still have, discriminatory legislation of this type.

The third-country dimension of Article 63 TFEU in the investment fund context is interesting for two reasons:

(1) The volumes invested by non-EU investment funds, particularly US investment funds, are vast and the amounts of withholding tax concerned run into billions of euros. According to the Investment Company Institute, US-registered investment companies had assets under management of in excess of USD 19,000 billion as of year-end 2016.[1]

1. ICI, 2017 Factbook, page 8.

(2) The withholding tax claims that arise under Article 63 TFEU are not well understood by European States. The impression of the authors is that the entitlement of non-European funds to receive refunds with no reciprocal entitlement for European funds is seen by many States as an unfair unilateral advantage or an unintended consequence of previous EU policy.

The article concerned reads as follows:

Article 63 TFEU

(ex Article 56 TEC)

1. Within the framework of the provisions set out in this Chapter, *all restrictions* on the *movement of capital* between Member States and between Member States *and third countries shall be prohibited.*
2. Within the framework of the provisions set out in this Chapter, all restrictions on payments between Member States and between Member States and third countries shall be prohibited.

The initial intention of this clause was to foster cross-border transactions and to open up the capital markets to attract foreign investments and free up capital on the market to facilitate the raising of capital within the European market.

This idea of opening up the common capital market dates back to the 1960s and has been a long-term work in progress. With the initiation of the euro, the shared currency fostered cross-border transactions as the foreign exchange impact for those countries participating had been removed. This ensured that one more obstacle had been removed from achieving a real integration and a truly common market.

The common market and equal treatment for investors opened up new opportunities to raise money for investments in Europe on the one hand and, on the other hand, for foreign investors to invest on a level playing field with local investors

The interesting part of Article 63 TFEU is that it specifies that restrictions are prohibited, both towards States forming part of the EU ('Member States') and towards third countries ('Non-Member States'). This vastly expanded the scope of Article 63 TFEU and has led to some discussion with Member States often arguing against this third-country aspect, on the basis that third countries receive a benefit without any reciprocity.[2] This lack of reciprocity reappears in the comments made by national governments in the multiple Court of Justice of the European Union ('CJEU' or the 'Court') cases that have been decided over the last few years, some of which will be discussed below.

The TFEU does foresee certain exceptions/derogations under Articles 64 TFEU and 65 of the TFEU, which are often used by governments to attempt to avoid or mitigate the effect of Article 63 TFEU. Below, for reference, are Article 64 TFEU and Article 65 TFEU of the TFEU:

2. *A*, C-101/05, Judgment, EU:C:2007:804, para. 38 (hereinafter *A*).

Article 64

(ex Article 57 TEC)

1. The provisions of Article 63 shall be *without prejudice to the application to third countries of any restrictions which exist on 31 December 1993* under national or Union law adopted in respect of the movement of capital to or from third countries *involving direct investment* - including in real estate - establishment, the provision of financial services or the admission of securities to capital markets. In respect of restrictions existing under national law in Bulgaria, Estonia and Hungary, the relevant date shall be 31 December 1999.
2. Whilst endeavouring to achieve the objective of free movement of capital between Member States and third countries to the greatest extent possible and without prejudice to the other Chapters of the Treaties, the European Parliament and the Council, acting in accordance with the ordinary legislative procedure, shall adopt the measures on the movement of capital to or from third countries involving direct investment - including investment in real estate - establishment, the provision of financial services or the admission of securities to capital markets.
3. Notwithstanding paragraph 2, *only the Council*, acting in accordance with a special legislative procedure, *may unanimously*, and after consulting the European Parliament, *adopt measures which constitute a step backwards in Union law as regards the liberalisation of the movement of capital to or from third countries*.

Article 65

(ex Article 58 TEC)

1. The provisions of Article 63 TFEU shall be *without prejudice to the right of Member States*:
   (a) to *apply the relevant provisions of their tax law* which distinguish between taxpayers who are not in the same situation with regard to their place of residence or with regard to the place where their capital is invested;
   (b) to *take all requisite measures to prevent infringements of national law* and regulations, *in particular in the field of taxation* and the prudential supervision of financial institutions, or to lay down procedures for the declaration of capital movements for purposes of administrative or statistical information, or to take measures which are *justified on grounds of public policy or public security*.
2. The provisions of this Chapter shall be *without prejudice to the applicability of restrictions on the right of establishment* which are compatible with the Treaties.
3. The measures and procedures referred to in paragraphs 1 and 2 *shall not constitute a means of arbitrary discrimination or a disguised restriction* on the free movement of capital and payments as defined in Article 63.
4. In the absence of measures pursuant to Article 64(3), the Commission or, in the absence of a Commission decision within three months from the request of the Member State concerned, the Council, may adopt a decision stating that restrictive tax measures adopted by a Member State concerning one or more third countries are to be considered compatible with the Treaties in so far as they are justified by one of the objectives of the Union and compatible with the proper functioning of the internal market. The Council shall act unanimously on application by a Member State.

These, therefore, are the exceptions to Article 63 TFEU, which would allow discrimination. However, these are to be interpreted strictly, especially as Article 65(3) TFEU ensures that arbitrary discrimination or disguised restrictions on the free movement of capital are prohibited.[3] The idea is to restrict the exceptions upon which discrimination would be accepted, as otherwise, Article 63 TFEU would most likely lose its meaning.

There are exceptions that show up with regards to the discrimination that may be allowed under Article 63 TFEU. The Court generally acknowledges that a difference in tax treatment is permitted either if a situation is not objectively comparable or if it is justified by an overriding reason in the public interest.[4] Generally, the following reasons justifying a difference in tax treatment regularly crop up in CJEU cases:

- targeting of wholly artificial arrangements;
- balanced apportionment of power to tax;
- preservation of the coherence of the tax system;

Article 63 TFEU effectively obliges Member States that provide a tax exemption for dividends paid to its resident companies by other companies resident in the same Member State, to accord the equivalent treatment to dividends paid to companies resident in other Member States and even to companies resident in non-Member States.[5]

There is no official definition of a transaction that should be defined as being a 'movement of capital' for purposes of Article 63 TFEU, so generally the Court has decided that it can be defined as follows:

> direct investments, that is to say ... investments of any kind undertaken by natural or legal persons and which serve to establish or maintain lasting and direct links between the persons providing the capital and the undertakings to which that capital is made available in order to carry out an economic activity.[6]

As we will see below, there are still multiple cases in which the question is argued as to whether discriminatory withholding tax suffered on dividends is to be considered as violating the free movement of capital or the freedom of establishment. This question is important as freedom of establishment is not extended to third countries whereas free movement of capital is extended to third countries. Therefore, predictably perhaps, Member States often try to argue that such a discriminatory treatment should be considered as only falling into the freedom of establishment principle.[7]

---

3. Emphasized in *Emerging Markets Series of DFA Investment Trust Company*, C-190/12, Judgment, EU:C:2014:249, paras 55–56 (hereinafter '*Emerging Markets*').
4. *Santander Asset Management SGIIC*, Joined Cases C-338/11 to C-347/11, Judgment, EU:C:2012:286 para. 23 (hereinafter '*Santander*'), and *Emerging Markets*, C-190/12, para. 57.
5. *Emerging Markets*, C-190/12, para. 59.
6. *Orange European Smallcap Fund*, C-194/06, Judgment, EU:C:2008:289, para. 100 (hereinafter '*Orange Smallcap*').
7. For example, *Emerging Markets*, C-190/12, paras 33–34.

§6.02 KEY CJEU DECISIONS

A key initial case, *Aberdeen*,[8] sets the principle that a Member State, X, could not levy taxes on a dividend paid by a Member State X tax-resident company, to an investment fund tax resident in another Member State, Y, if the same withholding tax was not applied to a dividend paid to a 'local' investment fund tax resident in Member State X. As a policy matter, many Member States had in fact exempted dividends from withholding tax when paid to a local investment fund, often on the basis that the local investment funds were tax-exempt savings vehicles for local investors with tax, if any, being levied at final investor level only. The same exemption did not exist for a comparable EU fund however. This rather blatant discrimination was surprisingly common,[9] perhaps highlighting a lack of awareness of domestic policy makers as regards EU law, a lack of awareness that has been evident also in subsequent cases involving third-country investment funds.

Over the last few years, since *Orange Smallcap*, *Aberdeen*, and *Santander* (all analysed below), it has further been established in various CJEU decisions that dividends paid to third-country investment funds should not be taxed more heavily than dividends paid to comparable local funds. In order to provide insight into the various issues by the CJEU within these cases, we have made a brief summary of key CJEU decisions.

[A] Orange Smallcap

In *Orange Smallcap*, the CJEU ruled, on 20 May 2008, on a case brought forward by Orange European Smallcap Fund NV against the Dutch government. The case concerned the relief system provided by Dutch tax law and its difference concerning dividends received by Dutch collective investment funds and foreign companies. The peculiarity was also that a Dutch national, being resident in Belgium, was receiving a worse return than when he had been resident in the Netherlands.

The Dutch tax system foresaw a mechanism by which, for private investors, the tax burden on investment proceeds through fiscal investment enterprises was the same as that on direct investments. This was ensured by taking into account the foreign tax withheld from dividends. This resulted in a less favourable answer for non-resident funds.

The Court held that the freedom of movement of capital does not mean that there will be no discrepancy between the different tax systems and that if a company decides to move to another Member State, it may have an impact – for the better or worse. This is due to the right of fiscal sovereignty that each Member State has.[10] Therefore, free

8. *Aberdeen Property Fininvest Alpha*, C-303/07, Judgment, EU:C:2009:377 (hereinafter '*Aberdeen*').
9. Germany, France, Italy, Spain and the Netherlands, to name but a few of the larger States, all had this form of discrimination.
10. *Orange Smallcap*, C-194/06, para. 37.

movement of capital does not require a harmonization of systems so as to ensure that in all circumstances disparities are removed from national tax rules.

Here, the Dutch tax system had treated foreign sourced dividends less favourably than those paid by a Dutch company. This essentially restricted the freedom of movement of capital as it would discourage foreign investment and it would restrict the raising of capital in the Netherlands by foreign companies.[11]

The Court repeated that if a Member State has a system of preventing/mitigating a series of tax charges or economic double taxation for dividends paid to residents by resident companies, it must treat dividends paid to residents by non-resident companies in the same way.[12]

The Dutch system at the time worked in such a manner that the collective investment vehicle was allowed to credit any withholding tax suffered. However, the credit was only awarded in proportion to the ratio of Dutch shareholders. This reduced the collective amount available for distributions at the level of the collective entity when non-Dutch persons were investors. Therefore, the investment vehicles would prefer to have more Dutch investors than non-Dutch. This would effectively mean a restriction on the free movement of capital.[13] As the Dutch tax system granted a concession for the tax deducted abroad and taxed all dividend distributions, whether they were paid to resident or non-resident shareholders, the tax system needed to grant the same concessions to non-residents as to residents.[14]

Furthermore, the discrimination could not be justified by the need to guarantee the effectiveness of fiscal supervision as the refusal of a concession is not based on the fiscal treatment of those shareholders in the third countries.[15]

In summary, the system would provide on top of the visible discrimination, a hidden discrimination in the form that funds would prefer to have Dutch investors and to invest in Dutch companies rather than have foreign investors and invest abroad.

Orange Smallcap was also interesting in that the Dutch government sought to distinguish between EU and non-EU investors. The Court, referring to its decision in *A*, dismissed a series of arguments including:

- the need to avoid a reduction in taxes must be capable of being a justification for a restriction on movement of capital with third countries as, unlike within the EU, taxation problems with third countries cannot be resolved by the harmonization of taxes at the EU level;
- the need to guarantee the effectiveness of fiscal supervision was capable of justifying a restriction in the case of third countries;
- loss of negotiation power due to a unilateral liberalization.[16]

11. *Ibid.*, para. 26.
12. *Ibid.*, para. 39.
13. *Ibid.*, para. 74.
14. *Ibid.*, para. 79.
15. *Ibid.*, para. 92.
16. *A*, C-101/05, para. 38.

The Court did however leave the door partly open, recalling that movements of capital with third states take place in a 'different legal context',[17] such that EU and non-EU situations were not always comparable. In subsequent cases, various efforts were made to distinguish EU and non-EU investment funds without success, suggesting that quite a high level of difference is required, which in the case of investment funds, is not visible in practice.

[B] Aberdeen

In 2009, in *Aberdeen*,[18] the Court issued its decision on the case brought by Aberdeen Property Fininvest Alpha Oy against the Finnish government.

The Finnish Supreme Administrative Court raised preliminary questions to the CJEU in relation to withholding tax suffered on a dividend paid to a non-resident parent company, a Luxembourg-resident SICAV, owning a 100% shareholding in a Finnish company. Specifically, questions were raised concerning the freedom of establishment[19] and the freedom of movement of capital.[20]

When a Finnish resident company distributed a dividend to a Finnish investment fund or a Finnish company, no withholding tax would be levied. However, when a dividend was distributed to a similar non-Finnish company, a 28% withholding tax applied.

Based on European law, Member States retain the power to define, either individually or by treaty, their powers of taxation, especially in relation to eliminating double taxation.[21] However, this has to be exercised within the parameters of European law.

Certain national measures restricting the freedom of establishment are permitted if they target wholly artificial arrangements, which do not reflect economic reality.[22] Any measure taken needs to be strictly interpreted and specifically target such artificial arrangements; should this not be the case, then the exception to the freedoms cannot be accepted.[23]

The CJEU determined that the Finnish withholding-tax rules did not specifically target artificial arrangements and, therefore, this exception could not be relied upon.[24]

An alternative exception is the balanced apportionment of the power to tax, which is permitted in the case where a certain conduct risks the right of a Member State to exercise its tax jurisdiction concerning activities upon its territory.[25] The CJEU

17. *Orange Smallcap*, C-194/06, para. 89.
18. *Aberdeen*, C-303/07.
19. Article 49 TFEU.
20. Article 63 TFEU.
21. *Aberdeen*, C-303/07, para. 25.
22. *Ibid.*, para. 63.
23. *Ibid.*, paras 63–64.
24. *Ibid.*, para. 65.
25. *Ibid.*, para. 66.

clearly rejected this though, as Finland chose not to tax recipient companies resident in Finland and therefore could not rely on this exception.[26]

The final exception raised is the preservation of the coherence of the tax system. This would require a direct link between the tax advantage concerned and the offsetting of that advantage by a particular tax levy.[27] Considering that the exemption awarded to the Finnish dividend recipients was not directly linked to the onward distribution and the subsequent taxation in the hands of the shareholders of the company, this argument was consequently rejected by the CJEU.[28]

Advocate General Mazák, in his AG Opinion,[29] stated that despite the SICAV not being an entity listed in the Directive 90/435, it could still rely on the fundamental freedoms established under the TFEU.

The Finnish government, on the other hand, argued that the SICAV was not comparable to a Finnish share company, due to differences in how the share capital operates and the taxation of the companies. Agreeing with the AG Opinion, the Court stated however that discrimination can only arise through the application of different rules to comparable situations or the application of the same rule to different situations.[30] The Court linked back to its *Denkavit* decision,[31] which had found that resident companies can be deemed to be comparable to non-resident companies.[32]

The key point, which reappears across multiple CJEU cases, is that companies/funds, cannot be deemed to be non- comparable based solely on them being non-resident in a given Member State.

[C] Santander

In *Santander*,[33] the Court provided its decision on the 10 May 2012 on a joint case brought forward by Santander Asset Management SGIIC SA, amongst others, against the French government.

The Administrative Tribunal of Montreuil (France), raised preliminary questions to the CJEU, in order to help to resolve the cases at hand. The cases concerned withholding tax being suffered on dividends distributed from French companies to non-resident UCITS and US investment funds.

The CJEU was requested to address two key questions:

(1) Does the shareholder need to be taken into account in addition to the UCITS (or US fund).

26. *Ibid.*, para. 67.
27. Aberdeen, C-303/07, para. 72.
28. *Ibid.*, para. 74.
29. *Aberdeen*, C-303/07, AG Opinion, EU:C:2008:742, para. 23.
30. *Aberdeen*, C-303/07, para. 32.
31. *Denkavit Internationaal and Denkavit France*, C-170/05, Judgment, EU:C:2006:783 (hereinafter '*Denkavit*').
32. *Ibid.*, para. 43.
33. *Santander*, Joined Cases C-338/11 to C-347/11.

(2) Under which conditions the withholding being suffered would be considered as being compliant with the principle of free movement of capital.

The Court again stated that the exceptions to the freedom of movement of capital were to be strictly interpreted so as to ensure the effectiveness of the initial rule.[34] Therefore, the discrimination, purely based on residency, was not acceptable.

This is based on Article 65(3) TFEU, which limits the application of the exception by stating that it shall not constitute a means of arbitrary discrimination or a disguised restriction on the free movement of capital and payments defined in Article 63 TFEU.[35] Therefore, governments needed to ensure that their rules take into account if a situation is objectively comparable or not.

The CJEU concluded that the tax situation of the dividend recipient's shareholders (i.e., the investors in the fund) was irrelevant for the purpose of determining whether or not the legislation is discriminatory.[36] This is due to the fact that the tax exemption granted to the French-resident UCITS was not conditional on their shareholders being taxed on the income distributed to them. Thereby, the criterion applied is discriminatory in itself. The comparison needs to be made by determining how the internal rules function and then by placing the treatment of non-residents against this base. If the local fund withholding tax rules only take into consideration the dividend recipient (i.e., the fund), then these rules for non-resident funds should only take into consideration the level of the non-resident fund.

The distinguishing criterion within the law was solely the place of residence of the UCITS/fund, therefore, the Court judged that the comparison should be performed at the level of the investment vehicle to analyse whether the legislation is discriminatory.[37]

Santander was thus crucial, as it established - beyond doubt - that a fund did not have to prove a loss at its investor level if the tax system did not consider this level when granting exemptions to a domestic fund.

Beyond this point, *Santander* was particularly interesting from a third-country perspective, as one of the funds was a third-country (US) fund. However, the Court did not specifically address the third-country dimension, as it was not raised,[38] and some doubt remained whether non-EU funds were to be seen in a different legal context. This doubt was cleared up in *Emerging Markets*.

It is also worth noting that the CJEU dismissed attempts by France to limit, on budgetary grounds, the effects of a negative judgment in time. Notwithstanding the substantial amount at stake, the CJEU referred to its previous case law on the subject, rejecting such limitations.[39]

34. *Ibid.*, para. 21.
35. *Ibid.*, para. 22.
36. *Ibid.*, para. 28.
37. *Ibid.*, para. 39.
38. *Ibid.*, para. 54.
39. *Ibid.*, para. 62.

[D] Emerging Markets

In *Emerging Markets*,[40] the Court provided its decision on the 10 April 2014 concerning the case brought forward by Emerging Markets Series of DFA Investment Trust Company, a US registered investment company ('US RIC') against the Polish government.

Poland required two conditions to be met in order to benefit from a withholding tax exemption on dividends paid to investment funds:

- The investment fund is operated in line with the law on investment funds.
- The investment fund's registered office is in Poland.[41]

Consequently, solely because of the fact that an investment fund is resident outside of Poland, it would not be able to benefit from the exemption of withholding tax on the dividends paid from a Polish company. This would entail a restriction of the free movement of capital.

The Polish government raised the concern about the comparability between a Polish resident investment fund and a US-resident investment fund, specifically regarding the similarity of the area of the business activity and how the business is carried out.

A manner of assessing whether the measures would be forbidden under Article 63 TFEU would be to review the result. If the measure discourages non-residents from making investments in a Member State or vice versa, then it would be forbidden.[42]

The Polish requirements listed above were declared definitively as violating the principle of Article 63 TFEU. Due to their automatic exclusion of investment funds not having their registered office in Poland, this has been deemed to be a discrimination against non-Polish investment funds.

Under certain circumstances, this discrimination would be permitted. For instance, under the 'grandfathering' principles of Article 64(1) TFEU, if it were a law that had been applicable prior to 31 December 1993,[43] which in this case was not applicable, as the discriminatory law was brought into effect in 1997.

Across the years and across multiple national governments, the debate has often arisen with regards to the level at which the comparability test should be performed. *Emerging Markets* offers the answer, notably that the comparability analysis has to be performed at the level of the investment fund/vehicle and not at the level of the investors,[44] where the domestic law being challenged only tests for exemption at the level of the investment fund. This reiterates the conclusion from *Santander* reviewed above.

Furthermore, it is often argued that unfair treatment is nullified by the application of a tax treaty between the source State and the recipient State, in which a credit or

40. *Emerging Markets*, C-190/12.
41. *Ibid.*, paras 40–41.
42. *Ibid.*, para. 39.
43. *Ibid.*, para. 45.
44. *Ibid.*, para. 63.

exemption method is foreseen. This means that the credit method could be applied by the investor concerning the withholding tax suffered on the dividends paid to the investment fund. This line of argument has been rejected in *Emerging Markets*,[45] as the tax treaty relief would need to completely neutralize any difference in tax treatment, which was not the case. This argument is further discussed in *Miljoen*, discussed below.

Another topic that frequently surfaces within the debates of comparability is the need for Member States to ensure that the funds are effectively comparable with regards to their level and form of supervision (as, for instance, the regulatory obligations contained in the UCITS Directive[46]). Part of the UCITS Directive relates to the exchange of information ('EOI') between Member States, an exchange which does not exist with third countries. However, the Court pointed out that the EOI in the UCITS Directive is for prudential reasons and concerns solely the activity of the investment funds in relation to UCITS – it does not ensure cooperation in relation to the area of taxation.[47] Therefore, the non-application of the UCITS Directive's EOI provisions in a third-country context was not accepted as a valid argument to distinguish third-country funds from EU funds. As the Court pointed out, accepting this argument would remove any practical effect of Article 63 TFEU in a third-country dimension. Unusually, the Court declined to follow the Advocate General's Opinion in this regard.

It is also worth noting that many tax treaties contain EOI clauses, permitting parties to the tax treaty to request information from their counterparties in relation to tax matters. This, in past experience, has worked successfully. This can be seen in the recent case law from Poland whereby the Polish tax authorities had been able to obtain sufficient comfort from the USs' Internal Revenue Service ('IRS') to rule positively for a US RIC obtaining a refund for the withholding tax it had suffered.[48]

[E] Miljoen

In *Miljoen*,[49] the Court provided its decision on 17 September 2015 concerning the case brought forward by three claimants, including J.B.G.T. Miljoen, against the Dutch government.

The case was interesting in that it concerned a Dutch tax system under which Dutch source dividends were subject to a 15% withholding tax when paid to both residents and non-residents. At first glance, no discrimination existed.

The discrimination challenged by the taxpayer was that for a Dutch taxpayer, the withholding tax was treated as a prepayment, with a potential refund of any excess. However, for a non-resident taxpayer, the withholding tax was definitive with no possibility of obtaining a refund.

45. *Ibid.*, para. 64.
46. *Ibid.*, para. 66.
47. *Ibid.*, para. 76.
48. *See* §6.03[C], *infra*.
49. *Miljoen*, Joined Cases C-10/14, C-14/14 & C-17/14, Judgment, EU:C:2015:608 (hereinafter '*Miljoen*').

The Dutch government argued that the situation of a resident and non-resident were not comparable, as the resident is taxed in the Netherlands, on all his income, whereas the non-resident is only taxed on his Dutch-source income.

The CJEU rejected this superficially plausible argument, pointing out that the entire system of taxation of a Member State, including relief from double taxation, needed to be taken into account in comparing a resident and non-resident[50] and in this case, the Dutch tax system clearly discriminated against the non-resident (no refund being available).

The Court also concluded that in relation to expenses that are directly linked to taxable income in a Member State, residents and non-residents of that Member State are in a comparable situation. Therefore, if that Member State denies non-residents the right to deduct such charges while allowing residents to do so, is detrimental for the non-resident and consequently constitutes an indirect discrimination on grounds of nationality.[51] In the case of a dividend being paid, the withholding tax suffered upon the distribution has an evident direct link to the dividend.

A number of governments made the argument that the difference in treatment of resident and non-resident taxpayers simply reflects the difference between the situations in which those taxpayers find themselves.[52] The Court held that this argument would only be valid if the difference in treatment relates to situations which are not objectively comparable.[53] The difference in treatment would then also not necessarily result in a better answer for resident recipients.[54] However, in the case at hand, the difference was not due to a different collection arrangement reflecting the difference between residents and non-residents, but due to an advantage granted to resident taxpayers which was not extended to non-resident taxpayers.[55]

In this case, there was no different collection arrangement, as both residents and non-residents were subject to withholding tax on dividends. However, subsequent to the levying of the withholding tax, the treatment in relation to the application of a refund for a resident taxpayer and a non-resident taxpayer differed.

The question was raised whether the restriction could be justified by the neutralizing effect of a double tax treaty. A double tax treaty can be considered to neutralize any negative impact, however the Court held that this would only be the case if the withholding tax suffered on a dividend distributed from one State to a non-resident of that State can be offset in full in the country of residence of that non-resident.[56] Basically, the end result would need to be that the resident and non-resident taxpayer receives the same net treatment and, in the end, the difference in treatment ceases to exist. In practice, this type of perfect offset rarely exists and was not found by the Court to exist in *Miljoen*.

50. *Ibid.*, para. 90.
51. *Ibid.*, para. 57.
52. *Ibid.*, para. 70.
53. *Ibid.*, para. 70.
54. *Ibid.*
55. *Ibid.*, para. 71.
56. *Ibid.*, para. 79.

[F] Key Conclusions

The persistence of governments in re-arguing the same points seems to reveal a certain desperation or a state of denial.

Based on the case law discussed above and various other cases, the message is clear: each country needs to perform an objective comparability test between their resident taxpayers and their non-resident taxpayers to determine if they are in comparable situations.[57] Once this is determined, they can then determine to which internal legal form the non-resident would be comparable to, in order to determine if a national law is compliant with European law, and, if it is contrary to European law, to make an adjustment to correct the distortion.

Santander and other CJEU decisions clearly state that the exceptions to the freedom of movement of capital are to be interpreted strictly. Therefore, discrimination, purely based on residency, is not acceptable. Repeatedly, governments have tried to apply the exceptions that are available to justify discrimination much more broadly than is intended, to the point of removing the effect of Article 63 TFEU outside the EU. This has been systematically rejected by the CJEU, however.

Over the last few years, many US RICs have started filing reclaims across a dozen countries in Europe. This has led to additional case law, both at local levels and the CJEU. These have been insightful as to the positions of the governments as well as the comparability tests that the respective countries have performed or did not perform. Below are a few key jurisdictions that are of particular interest, as these are at the forefront of this body of jurisprudence.

§6.03 A REVIEW OF NATIONAL COURT DECISIONS

[A] Finland

Finland is one of the most advanced in the application of Article 63 TFEU with regards to non-Member States, specifically for US RICs. Finland is currently the sole country in which litigation has successfully and completely been achieved for US RICs.

The initial case was Case 182/2/12, issued on 13 January 2015, and concerned a closed-ended US RIC.[58] The aim was to determine whether a US RIC would be deemed comparable to a Finnish mutual fund or to a Finnish limited company.

The Finnish Supreme Court stated that, based on internal law, an investment fund or limited company would be exempt from tax in Finland.

In light of this, the Finnish Supreme Court proceeded to carry out a comparison of the entities and determined which one most resembled the closed-ended US RIC. It was considered that due to two comparatives (specifically, that the US RIC was closed ended and had no variation in the number of shares), that the specific US RIC resembled a Finnish limited company.

57. On the different approaches to frame this comparability test, also with respect to investment funds in other EU countries, *see Tenore*, Chapter 7, *infra*.
58. Case 182/2/12 – Finnish Supreme Court Ruling.

We have since received many positive decisions from the Finnish courts and the tax authorities confirming different forms of US RICs as being comparable to either Finnish investment funds or Finnish limited companies. Both comparisons effectively result in the same (i.e., withholding tax is refunded to the US RICs concerned).

Since then, the Finnish tax authorities have put in place a process to remove the discrimination by permitting the paying agents to not withhold tax on dividends paid to US RICs. US RICs have been able to request tax cards, which the tax authorities have issued stating that the given fund is comparable to one of the vehicles mentioned and therefore no withholding tax should be levied.

This mechanism allows a significant reduction in work on behalf of the funds as they can have dividends exempt from withholding tax at source rather than having to proceed with reclaim procedures that are time consuming and costly for the tax authorities, the custodians, and the funds.[59]

[B] Sweden

Many investment funds, both European and US, have been pursuing cases in Sweden for over five years already. The claims have been made due to the difference in tax treatment, notably with regards to the withholding tax applied to dividends paid by Swedish companies to resident shareholders compared to the European and US investment funds. In December 2014, the Swedish Supreme Court, in the *Dodge & Cox Global Fund* case (Case 862-13),[60] conceded that a US RIC is deemed to be comparable to a Swedish investment fund.

A US RIC should be comparable to a foreign collective-investment undertaking, which is embedded in the Swedish Investment Funds Act. Under Swedish tax law, the main criterion for the discrimination arose due to the US RIC's residence.

The Swedish government considered that important points for comparability should be control, supervision, similar protection, permissible assets, and risk spreading. Furthermore, they argued that the supervision of a US RIC was not sufficient as to be authorized to operate *under Swedish law*. They suggested comparing US RICs instead to a Swedish special fund.

The taxpayer relied on the previous CJEU cases in which the Court had decided that, in order to be deemed to be objectively comparable, there was no need to be identical. Therefore, differences in legal form or the fact that there is no company identical in local law should not mean that a fund may not be objectively comparable. Furthermore, the taxpayer relied on *Santander* and the past comparison of US RICs to UCITS by applying Article 63 TFEU.

The Swedish Supreme Court upheld that the rules and regulation governing US RICs and the Swedish investment funds do not need to be nearly identical, nor does the presence of differences in *legal form* mean that these cannot be deemed comparable.

59. N.B. Since this chapter was first drafted, the Finnish have ceased refunds based on a recent internal law ruling, which in the opinion of the authors, is not on point. It illustrates however that any pretext will be used to avoid making refunds.
60. Dodge & Cox Global Fund, Case 862-13 – Swedish Supreme Court Ruling.

Furthermore, the fact that US RICs are not subject to the UCITS Directive does not mean that they cannot be deemed comparable, as third countries cannot be subject to a European Directive.

Therefore, based on the proof provided by the taxpayer, the Swedish Supreme Court ruled that the US RIC concerned was comparable to a Swedish investment fund. Consequently, the difference in tax treatment was found to be contrary to Article 63 TFEU.

The Court further found that many US RICs do not have to pay US income tax and, therefore, cannot benefit from a deduction for foreign taxes paid. As a result, the difference in tax treatment could not be neutralized by the application of the tax treaty in force between the United States and Sweden.

The Swedish Supreme Court ruled that overriding reasons in the general interest were not present due to the fact that:

- The tax treaty in force provided for an EOI clause which allowed the Swedish tax authority to verify any information provided by the US RIC.
- In Swedish law, there was no direct link between the taxation of the dividend distributed and the taxation at the level of the shareholders.
- As the Swedish government chose not to tax resident investment funds on Swedish source dividends, it could not rely on the need to ensure a balanced allocation of power to tax.

Following this, the Swedish tax authorities conceded defeat and had refunded a large portion of outstanding refunds due to US RICs. This came to an abrupt halt with the Case 4530-15 ruled by the Swedish Supreme Court on 18 March 2016. This case, unrelated to the discussion of the withholding tax suffered on dividends paid to US RICs, discussed the legal form of funds and their subsequent qualifications based on their legal form.

This resurrected the Swedish tax authorities' motivation to not refund withholding tax suffered by US RICs. The key conclusions of the case of the Swedish tax authorities were that those foreign funds, which are legal entities, would only be reimbursed if they were UCITS funds, effectively removing the application for funds resident in non-Member States.

We expect that this new line of argument will be overturned in due course as this is contrary to the CJEU case law established to date. It seems to be just a question of time until a new US RIC case arrives at the Swedish Supreme Court and will require a clarification with regards to the withholding tax suffered by US RICs. The Swedish Supreme Court will then need to take into account the previous refunds granted and clarify the application of Case 4530-15.

[C] Poland

Despite *Emerging Markets*, which dates back to 2014, it is only recently that this case law and other case law concerning Article 63 TFEU are finding application in Poland.

Poland is the newest Member State to have joined the ranks of countries acknowledging that US RICs may be comparable to their local investment funds.

Following *Emerging Markets*, the Polish tax authorities reached out to the IRS by applying the information-exchange clause available to them under the tax treaty in force between the United States and Poland. Following the information obtained, the Polish tax authorities proceeded with a comparability analysis, not with the aim of analysing if the systems (*UCITS v. US RICs*) are identical, but if they are similar.

The analysis resulted in the conclusion that there are no significant differences in the funds' operations. As the CJEU jurisprudence makes clear that the two types of funds should only be similar with regards to their nature and the regulation of their activities in order to be comparable, the conditions have been met.

Consequently, multiple tax offices have started, since December 2016, to reimburse past withholding tax suffered by US RICs. It is significant that multiple tax offices across the country are awarding the withholding tax refunds, as the Polish legal system does not follow the system of precedence with regards to its internal legal system, as is common in other legal systems. Therefore, it would appear that there is a global position being taken by all the Polish tax offices that US RICs (subsequent to a comparability analysis being done) can be considered as being comparable to Polish investment funds.

[D] Conclusions

The trends that we are witnessing across the dozen countries that we have analysed in order to recover withholding tax suffered by US RICs, is that each country, based on its budgetary situation and political system are in line with CJEU case law to differing degrees.

A few countries have already recognized that they were discriminating against US RICs. These have subsequently either amended their laws so that going forward the situation has been corrected, but they have not necessarily refunded any withholding tax suffered. Other countries have refunded withholding tax, but their laws remain in place and will only be corrected when requested to (i.e., application of a withholding tax card so as to benefit from an exemption at source, or a comparability analysis will be performed per refund request). The approaches differ per country, but the key item is that the difference in tax treatment is corrected.

Other countries (some more than others) are seeking to avoid complying with Article 63 TFEU with regards to its true meaning. These countries generally have been trying to drag out the process or to make the burden of proof so extensive that only large claims remain viable and smaller claims are dropped.

With the amounts involved, one can understand the high political interest in these cases and also the delicate balance of power/influence between the judicial system and the political system (notably, the Ministries of Finance/Treasury). However, despite political resistance, it is hard to imagine that, in the end, the judicial systems will not be obliged to acknowledge that the correct interpretation of Article 63 TFEU requires an elimination of most – if not all – differential withholding tax burdens.

A final point worth making is that no tax harmonization has occurred across the Member States forming the EU, consequently, the various tax systems differ, which means that in each Member State, a slightly different analysis needs to be performed, so as to determine whether a third-country investment fund is in a comparable situation to a local fund.

§6.04 WHAT'S NEXT?

The various issues and cases above beg the question of what will occur now within the various EU jurisdictions within which litigation is on-going and the local jurisdictions are still refusing refunds. Out of the dozen or so countries where discriminatory legal systems exist, and claims have been made that the authors have been involved in, only three have started refunding or offering relief at source.

Across the multiple cases, both at the CJEU level and in certain local jurisdictions, the path has been paved as to how to apply Article 63 TFEU and its limitations. The limitations are not as significant, though, as certain jurisdictions would like to assume, taking into account the arguments brought forward by governments at the level of the CJEU and repeatedly rejected.

The cost of applying Article 63 TFEU correctly, although, means that the Member States concerned would need to refund a significant amount of money that is already in short supply in many treasuries. The additional issue is that late interest is due on many of these potential refunds. These late-interest amounts are growing very quickly in certain countries, due to the large volume and value of claims, in addition to the lengthy time delay of certain refunds. Certain jurisdictions have claims outstanding dating back to 2007, so are facing interest costs for nearly ten years.

The sums are daunting to many Finance Ministries; however, it is an issue that is just getting worse, especially with the large volume of positive cases ruled by the CJEU and the ever-growing number of countries acknowledging that their system is discriminatory and either changing their rules going forward or providing an opportunity to prove comparability (in advance or after withholding tax has been suffered).

This leaves Finance Ministries with a conundrum to solve: repay the withholding taxes suffered rapidly and suffer political and/or budgetary consequences, or delay repayment and eventually have to pay vast late-interest amounts in addition to the refund. A direct application of Article 63 TFEU at the domestic judicial level (following for example, *Sanz de Lera and Others*[61]) might allow Finance Ministers a convenient way out of this 'interest trap'.

In many countries, the higher up a case is ruled, the higher the chances are that EU law is applied within the guidelines of the jurisprudence issued by the CJEU and, therefore, in line with EU law. Therefore, many jurisdictions are trying to reduce the number of claims at the level of the tax authorities or in their lower courts, by either

61. *Sanz de Lera and Others*, Joined Cases C-163/94, C-165/94 and C-250/94, Judgment, EU:C:1995:451, para. 48.

threatening large costs of litigation or trying to disprove comparability on procedural grounds.

The hope, though, is that, in time, the national courts (or the CJEU) will pronounce themselves in the various countries and obtain equal treatment for investment funds that are comparable to their resident Member-State peers.

CHAPTER 7

Investment Fund Taxation and Fundamental Freedoms: Four Approaches to Comparability

Mario Tenore

§7.01 INTRODUCTION

The Court of Justice of the European Union (CJEU) has dealt with taxation of investment funds in a number of decisions, and it has done so from the perspective of both the Residence State and the Source State. Nevertheless, the scope of the present chapter is to provide a critical analysis of the case law dealing with 'comparability' between domestic and foreign funds, with particular emphasis on the application of dividend withholding tax from the Source-State perspective.

For the purpose of analysing comparability from the Source-State perspective, the author has identified four different approaches enshrined in the case law of the CJEU, which are referred hereinafter as:

- the *ACT GLO/Denkavit* Approach;
- the Distinguishing Criterion Approach;
- the AIM Approach; and
- the Regulatory Framework Approach.

The CJEU has never mixed the four approaches it has developed over time and in the same sequence as listed above. There is no hierarchical relationship in the application of the four approaches, but, based on its case law, the CJEU's choice of approach appears a consequence of the manner in which relevant domestic law is framed. This stated, the present chapter elaborates on the four approaches, each separately illustrated *infra*.

§7.02 THE ACT GLO/DENKAVIT APPROACH: THE ABERDEEN CASE

The *ACT GLO/Denkavit* Approach has been consistently applied by the CJEU in almost all decisions that have dealt with the levying of withholding taxes by the Source State (both within and outside the area of investment funds). The *ACT GLO/Denkavit* Approach label takes into account two landmark decisions, namely *Test Claimants in Class IV of the ACT Group Litigation* (*ACT GLO*)[1] and *Denkavit International.*[2]

ACT GLO dealt with UK rules on relief of economic double taxation through the granting of an indirect tax credit. Such a credit was limited to domestic situations; that is to say, it was not extended to foreign shareholders receiving UK-sourced dividends, unless a tax treaty between the UK and the shareholders' Residence State otherwise provided. According to UK domestic rules, dividends paid to non-resident shareholders were not subject to tax. The issue under dispute was therefore whether the UK should have extended the imputation credit to foreign shareholders as well.

The CJEU clarified that foreign shareholders:

> [are] not in the same position, as regards the prevention or mitigation of a series of charges to tax and of economic double taxation, as the Member State in which the shareholder receiving the distribution is resident.[3]

In particular the CJEU ruled that:

> by granting the shareholder a tax advantage equal to the tax paid on those profits by the company making the distribution, would mean in point of fact that [the Source State] would be obliged to abandon its right to tax a profit generated through an economic activity undertaken on its territory.[4]

In the *ACT GLO* case, the CJEU ultimately found that the denial of the imputation credit in the hands of non-resident shareholders did not amount to a difference in treatment, because, in both domestic and cross-border situations, dividends were not subject to UK tax.[5] The lack of any UK income tax (i.e., 'a charge to income tax'[6]) on outbound dividends was, indeed, a key element in the CJEU's reasons for denying comparability between resident and non-resident shareholders and, thus, refusing to extend to the latter shareholders the entitlement to the imputation credit.

In reaching its conclusions, the CJEU noted, incidentally, that, contrary to the above:

> once a Member State, unilaterally or by a convention, imposes a charge to income tax not only on resident shareholders but also on non-resident shareholders in

1. *Test Claimants in Class IV of the ACT Group Litigation* (hereinafter '*ACT GLO*'), C-374/04, Judgment, EU:C:2006:773.
2. *Denkavit Internationaal and Denkavit France* (hereinafter '*Denkavit*'), C-170/05, Judgment, EU:C:2006:783.
3. *ACT GLO*, C-374/04, para. 58.
4. *Ibid.*, para. 59.
5. *Ibid.*, para. 62.
6. *Ibid.*, para. 68.

> respect of dividends which they receive from a resident company, *the position of those non-resident shareholders becomes comparable to that of resident shareholders.*[7]

The same line of reasoning was reiterated by the CJEU in *Denkavit Internationaal.*[8] That case dealt with the French system of taxation of dividends, according to which cross-border distributions were taxed while domestic distributions were exempt therefrom. The CJEU found that non-resident parent companies that did not have a fixed place of business in France were comparable to resident parent companies and non-resident parent companies that have a fixed place of business in France.[9] In finding comparability, the CJEU relied on the fact that, unlike *ACT GLO*, dividends paid to foreign shareholders were subject to tax in France, the Source State of the dividends, whereas the dividends received by resident parent companies were exempt. Accordingly, CJEU held that, because the French legislation had chosen to relieve residents of any liability to tax, the same relief had to be extended to non-residents.

In light of the foregoing, it can be said that the *ACT GLO/Denkavit* Approach subordinates the concept of comparability to the existence of a charge-to-tax applicable to dividends in the Source State, irrespective of the form that charge-to-tax takes.

The aforementioned decisions of the CJEU, however, did not relate to the area of investment companies. However, the approach taken therein was extended thereto by the CJEU in the *Aberdeen* case,[10] which dealt with Finnish rules applicable to outbound dividends paid to a Luxembourg company constituted in the legal form of a *société d'investissement à capital variable* (SICAV) and operating as an investment fund.

According to Finnish tax rules, dividends paid to the SICAV were subject to 20% withholding tax rate, reduced to 5% pursuant to the 1982 Luxembourg-Finland Income and Capital Tax Treaty.[11] On the other hand, dividends received by Finnish corporate entities were not taxable and Finnish investment funds were exempt from corporate income tax. thus, they were not taxable in relation to Finnish source dividends, either.

The Court reiterated that:

> once a Member State, unilaterally or by way of a convention, imposes a charge to income tax not only on resident shareholders but also on non-resident shareholders in respect of dividends which they receive from a resident company, the position of those non-resident shareholders becomes comparable to that of resident shareholders.[12]

7. *Ibid.*, para. 68 (emphasis added).
8. *Denkavit*, C-170/05, para. 35.
9. *Ibid.*, para. 36.
10. *Aberdeen Property Fininvest Alpha*, C-303/07, Judgment, EU:C:2009:377 (hereinafter '*Aberdeen*').
11. For a French version of said treaty, *see Loi du 25 novembre 1982 portant approbation de la Convention entre le Luxembourg et la Finlande tendant à éviter les doubles impositions en matière d'impôts sur le revenu et sur la fortune et du Protocole, signés à Luxembourg, le 1er mars 1982*, as amended.
12. *Aberdeen*, C-303-07, para. 43 (citing, *inter alia*, *ACT GLO*, C-374/04, para. 68, *Denkavit*, C-170/50, para. 35).

The CJEU concluded that, if a Member State has chosen to relieve resident parent companies of a series of charges-to-tax on the profits distributed by a resident subsidiary, it must extend that relief to non-resident parent companies that are in a comparable situation, since an imposition of that kind on those non-resident companies results from the exercise of its tax jurisdiction over them.[13]

The application of the *ACT GLO/Denkavit* Approach in the area of investment funds presupposes that: (i) foreign funds are treated like corporate entities subject to ordinary corporate taxation and (ii) the exemption from withholding tax granted by the Source State for domestic dividends is aimed at eliminating economic double taxation. A first corollary to this two-prong presupposition is that the *ACT GLO/Denkavit* Approach relies on substance-over-form, meaning that, for example, differences in the legal form between resident and non-resident entities are not relevant. In this regard, the *Aberdeen* Court stated that:

> the circumstance that in Finnish law there is no type of company with a legal form identical to that of a SICAV governed by Luxembourg law cannot in itself justify a difference in treatment, since, as the company law of the Member States has not been fully harmonised at Community level, that would deprive the freedom of establishment of all effectiveness.[14]

A second corollary to that presupposition is that the *ACT GLO/Denkavit* Approach applies regardless of the tax treatment of dividends in the shareholder's Residence State. With regard to latter point, the *Aberdeen* Court stated that:

> the circumstance relied on by the Finnish Government that the income of a SICAV is not taxed in Luxembourg, assuming that to be correct, does not create a difference between a SICAV and a resident share company which justifies different treatment as regards withholding tax on dividends received by those two classes of company.[15]

In the *Aberdeen* case, while maintaining the comparability between Luxembourg SICAVs and Finnish entities using the *ACT GLO/Denkavit* Approach, the CJEU rejected the argument put forward by one of the intervenors in the action, the Italian government, according to which, because Luxembourg did not tax the income at the level of the SICAV, the imposition of a series of charges-to-tax took place - not at the level of the SICAV, but only at that of its members - and, thus, would be avoided in the member's Residence State. This argument has been further developed by the CJEU in the *Santander* case (*see* below) in the framework of the distinguishing criterion illustrated below.

§7.03 THE DISTINGUISHING CRITERION APPROACH

The Distinguishing Criterion Approach is, to a large extent, specific to the case law dealing with taxation of investment funds. This CJEU first examined this approach in

13. *See*, *Denkavit*, C-170/05, para. 37.
14. *Aberdeen*, C-303/07, para. 50.
15. *Ibid.*, para. 61.

the *Aberdeen* case. As mentioned above, the Italian Government put forward an argument according to which the comparability analysis should have been shifted to the level of the dividend-receiving entity's members (i.e., the Court should consider the tax levied upon the latter with regard to the distributions made by the SICAV).

The same reasoning was put forward again in the *Santander* case,[16] which dealt with French taxation of dividends paid to foreign UCITS.[17] According to French rules, UCITS residents in France were granted an exemption from dividend withholding tax, while a dividend withholding tax was levied upon French-sourced dividends paid to non-resident UCITS.

The CJEU was asked whether comparability for a UCITS should be determined after taking into account any exemption applicable at the level of the investment vehicle only or by determining that any such exemption is coupled with a charge to income tax at the level of the shareholder, if and to the extent the UCITS distributes its proceeds. One of the French government's arguments was that UCITS are collective investment vehicles carrying out investment holding activities on behalf of their shareholders. As such, the French government argued, collective investment vehicles were tax neutral by their very nature and, therefore, comparability must be established by taking into account the position of the UCITS and of its shareholders together.

The CJEU held that comparability had to be determined at the level of the investment vehicle, emphasizing that the French dividend exemption depended solely on the tax residence of the investment vehicle. The tax residence of the UCITS was, therefore, the distinguishing criterion by which the contested tax measure determined the tax treatment of the fund. Being that this criterion operated at the fund level, the CJEU concluded that taxation at the level of the shareholders was not relevant. The CJEU stated that:

> where national tax legislation establishes a *distinguishing criterion for the taxation of distributed profits*, account must be taken of that criterion in determining whether the situations are comparable.[18]

Thus, in order for the Distinguishing Criterion Approach to apply, it is necessary to isolate, within the contested tax measure, the distinguishing criterion for the taxation of distributed profits. The Distinguishing Criterion Approach requires, accordingly, an interpretation of the domestic law of the Source State. This interpretation is decisive, because, according to the CJEU:

> *only the relevant distinguishing criteria established by the legislation in question must be taken into account* in determining whether the difference in treatment resulting from that legislation reflects situations which are objectively different.[19]

16. *Santander Asset Management SGIIC* (hereinafter '*Santander*'), Joined Cases C-338/11 to C-347/11, Judgment, EU:C:2012:286.
17. The acronym 'UCITS' stands for 'undertakings for collective investment in transferable securities'.
18. *Santander*, Joined Cases C-338/11 to C-347/11, para. 27 (emphasis added).
19. *Ibid.*, para. 28 (emphasis added).

Moreover, the *Santander* Court went on to say that:

> where a Member State chooses to exercise its tax jurisdiction over dividends distributed by resident companies *on the sole basis of the place of residence of the recipient UCITS*, the tax situation of the latter's shareholders is irrelevant for the purpose of determining whether or not that legislation is discriminatory.[20]

The CJEU put forward a number of arguments as to why the tax residence of the UCITS was the distinguishing criterion under the French tax rules at issue, specifically: (i) the dividend were exempt irrespective of any tax collected at the level of the shareholders (ii) the French-resident UCITS could indefinitely capitalize its dividend earnings and still qualify for dividend exemption treatment, and (iii) there was no link whatsoever between the exemption of dividends received by the UCITS, on the one hand, and the taxation of those dividends in the hands of the UCITS' shareholders, on the other.

The difference between the *ACT GLO/Denkavit* Approach and the Distinguishing Criterion Approach is rather subtle. As mentioned above, the application of the *ACT GLO/Denkavit* Approach in the area of investment funds presupposes that: (i) foreign funds are treated like corporate entities subject to ordinary corporate taxation and (ii) the exemption from withholding tax granted by the Source State for its domestic-sourced dividends aims at eliminating economic double taxation.

§7.04 THE AIM APPROACH

In the *Santander* case, the CJEU emphasized that the French legislation at issue did not aim to create a link between the treatment of the UCITS and that of its shareholders. That issue has now returned to the CJEU for further clarification in the pending Danish case, *Fidelity Funds*, C-480/16, in which the Danish court has asked the CJEU has the following question:

> Is a tax regime, such as that in the main proceedings, under which non-Danish undertakings for collective investment covered by Council Directive 85/611/EEC (the UCITS Directive) are taxed at source on dividends from Danish companies, contrary to Article 56 TEC (Article 63 TFEU) on free movement of capital or Article 49 TEC (Article 56 TFEU) on freedom to provide services, *where equivalent Danish undertakings for collective investment can obtain an exemption for tax at source, either because they in fact make a minimum distribution to their members in return for retention of tax at source, or technically a minimum distribution is calculated, on which tax at source is retained in relation to the undertakings' members?*[21]

The Aim Approach to comparability is not novel, at least in the area outside investment fund taxation.[22] In that latter area, the CJEU looked, for the first time, into

20. *Ibid.*
21. Request for a preliminary ruling from the Østre Landsret (Denmark) lodged on 5 September 2016 - *Fidelity Funds v. Skatteministeriet* (Case C-480/16) (2016/C 419/42) [2016] OJ C 419/32.
22. *Commission v. Finland*, C-342/10, Judgment, EU:C:2012:688, para. 36 (emphasis added, citations omitted); *Commission v. Estonia*, C-39/10, Judgment, EU:C:2012:282, para. 51.

the aim of domestic legislation in the *Orange European Smallcap Fund* case.[23] This case involved a Dutch investment fund, Orange European Smallcap Fund NV (OESCF), established in the legal form of a company with variable capital. OESCF invested in securities issued by Dutch and foreign entities, and its investors included both Dutch and foreign investors. According to Dutch law: (i) a Dutch fund was liable to tax, but its profits were taxed at a rate of 0%, provided that such profits were distributed to its shareholders within eight months; (ii) Dutch-sourced dividends received by a Dutch investment fund were subject to a withholding tax that was subsequently refunded to the Dutch investment fund with the result that Dutch-sourced dividends were not subject to tax at the fund level; (iii) foreign dividends carried a right to an amount (i.e., a 'concession'[24]) corresponding to the amount of the withholding tax levied in the foreign country that would have been deductible under the applicable tax treaty from income tax due in the Netherlands when the proceeds were received by individuals resident in the Netherlands (with regard to investment funds in which Dutch and foreign investors participated, the amount of which was calculated in proportion to the shares held by Dutch individuals); and (iv) distributions of proceeds by the investment fund were subject to withholding tax. In regard to a foreign recipient, the latter withholding tax could be reduced by an applicable tax treaty.[25]

The CJEU held that a provision that is aimed at achieving tax neutrality between direct investments and investment made through a fund is not discriminatory, at least to the extent that the refund of foreign withholding taxes applies only when the proceeds received by individual Dutch-resident investors were paid by companies residing in countries with which the Netherlands had a tax treaty (condition (iii), *supra*). Thus, in light of the aim pursued by domestic law (i.e., the achievement of tax neutrality between direct and indirect investments), the *Orange European Smallcap Fund* Court found that dividends received from a company that is resident in a country that had not concluded a tax treaty with the Netherlands could not be compared to a dividend received from a company resident in a country that had concluded a tax treaty with the Netherlands.[26]

Nevertheless, the Court held that a provision is discriminatory if it reduces the amount of the concession the investment fund is entitled to depends on the residence

---

23. *Orange European Smallcap Fund*, C-194/06, Judgment, EU:C:2008:289.
24. *Ibid.*, passim.
25. *Ibid.*, paras 3–12.
26. *Ibid.* According to the *Orange European Smallcap Fund* Court:

> 62. In fact, it is only as regards investments in the Member States with which the Kingdom of the Netherlands has concluded such a bilateral tax convention that, without the concession granted by the legislation at issue in the main proceedings, the decision to invest through the intermediary of a fiscal investment enterprise runs the risk of being less advantageous to a shareholder who is a natural person than direct investment.63. By contrast, as regards the Member States with which the Kingdom of the Netherlands has not concluded such a convention, the decision, by a natural person, to invest through the intermediary of such an enterprise does not involve the risk of losing a benefit which he could have enjoyed if he had chosen to invest directly in those Member States. Accordingly, that situation is not objectively comparable to the situation in which the Kingdom of the Netherlands has concluded such a tax convention.

of the investment fund's shareholders. Indeed, since the Netherlands decided to grant Dutch funds a concession for tax deducted abroad and to exercise its fiscal sovereignty over proceeds distributed thereby, regardless of the residence of the fund's shareholders, it should have extended the benefit of that concession to investment funds with foreign investors, too.[27]

The CJEU confirmed its use of the Aim Approach in *Pensioenfonds Metaal en Techniek*.[28] The case dealt with taxation of pension funds. Swedish pension funds were only subject to a so-called Tax-on-Yield (i.e., a tax on capital income), whereas foreign pension funds were subject to a withholding tax on Swedish-sourced dividends. The Tax-on-Yield was, in fact, a tax imposed on the income accrued based on the entire pension funds' activities, although its tax base was a deemed-income amount calculated on the basis of a pre-determined formula.

The *Pensioenfonds Metaal en Techniek* Court first found that the taxation affecting Swedish-resident pension funds had a different aim from that applied to non-resident pension funds.[29] In particular, in the context of occupational pension schemes, it said:

> the aim pursued by the national legislation at issue in the main proceedings, that is to say, the application of neutral taxation independent of the economic climate surrounding various kinds of assets as well as all the kinds of pension products concerned, which presupposes that pensions funds are taxed on the whole of the assets, cannot be attained in respect of non-resident pension funds.[30]

It went on to say:

> the neutrality of taxation in respect of the type of investment, sought by the legislation at issue in the main proceedings, presupposes the taxation of the whole of the taxpayer's invested capital, whatever the make-up of his investment portfolio.[31]

It finally concluded that such an aim could not be achieved in the case of a non-resident pension fund subject, in Sweden, only to the taxation of its income having its source in that Member State.[32] Accordingly, the CJEU concluded that 'in the light of the aim pursued by the national legislation, and of its purpose and content too, a non-resident pension fund is not in a situation comparable to that of a resident pension fund'.[33]

---

27. *Ibid.*, paras 79, 113.
28. *Pensioenfonds Metaal en Techniek*, C-252/14, Judgment, EU:C:2016:402.
29. Whereas Swedish-resident pension funds were taxed on the basis of their total income (calculated on the basis of their assets reduced by their liabilities) multiplied by a standard yield rate irrespective of the actual receipt of dividends in the course of the relevant tax year, foreign pension funds were only taxed on Swedish-sourced dividends in the particular tax year. *Ibid.*, paras 7–14.
30. *Ibid.*, para. 59.
31. *Ibid.*, para. 61.
32. *Ibid.*, para. 62.
33. *Ibid.*, para. 63. Interestingly the CJEU took a different position with regard to the comparability of foreign funds for purposes of deducting its expenses in para. 64 of the same judgment:

§7.05 THE REGULATORY FRAMEWORK APPROACH

The CJEU's fourth approach to comparability is the Regulatory Framework Approach, which can be regarded as a further development in the last two approaches discussed: the Distinguishing Criterion Approach[34] and the Aim Approach.[35]

The CJEU addressed the Regulatory Framework Approach in its *Emerging Markets* case,[36] in which the contested tax measure was a Polish dividend tax exemption available for 'undertakings for collective investment' whose 'registered office' was in Poland, another Member State, or the EEA. To qualify for the dividend exemption, an undertaking for collective investment had to satisfy, *inter alia*, the following requirements: (1) its sole business object must be to collectively invest its capital in transferrable securities, money market instruments, or the like, and it must raise its capital from the public, by public or private subscriptions; (2) it must have an authorization from the competent financial market supervisory authority of its home state; (3) its business must be monitored by the competent financial market supervisory authority of its home state; (4) it must have a depository for the safe-keeping of its assets; and (5) it must be subject to corporation tax on its entire income, irrespective of its source, in its home state.[37] In essence, the Polish legislation relied on the underlying framework for UCITS established by the European Union (EU)-level UCITS Directive.[38]

Obviously, US investment funds could not qualify for the Polish dividend tax exemption with regard to any Polish dividends it might receive since only investment funds regulated under the UCITS Directive with registered offices within the EU or EEA could qualify therefore. For US funds, which by their very nature could not satisfy the requirements, the question was whether they were in a 'legal and factual situation which is fundamentally different from that of investment funds established in the Member States of the European Union'.[39]

In *Emerging Markets* the Court looked to the relevance of the UCITS Directive in its assessment of comparability, as the UCITS Directive is one of the main, if not the main, European framework covering collective investment schemes. The UCITS

> 64. That being noted, it is important, moreover, to observe that, if the application of two different taxation methods to resident and non-resident pension funds is in this instance justified by the difference in situation of these two categories of taxpayers, the Court has previously held that, in relation to professional expenses directly linked to an activity that has generated taxable income in a Member State, residents and non-residents of that State are in a comparable situation (*Miljoen*, Joined Cases C-10/14, C-14/14, and, C-17/14, Judgment, EU:C:2015:608, para. 57).

34. *Supra* §7.03.
35. *Supra* §7.04.
36. *Emerging Markets Series of DFA Investment Trust Company*, C-190/12, Judgment, ECLI-:EU:C:2014:249 (hereinafter, '*Emerging Markets*').
37. *Ibid.*, para. 4.
38. Directive 2009/65/EC of the European Parliament and of the Council of 13 July 2009 on the coordination of laws, regulations and administrative provisions relating to undertakings for collective investment in transferable securities (UCITS) (recast) (Text with EEA relevance) [2009] OJ L 302/32, as amended (hereinafter the 'UCITS Directive').
39. *Emerging Markets*, C-190/12, para. 66.

Directive stipulates common rules to be used to determine types of investment funds. It envisages the approximation of the conditions of competition for UCITS at the EU-level, making it easier for a UCITS to market its units in other Member States and it adopts, as its cornerstone, the principle of mutual recognition, which grants investment funds a passport to invest in any other Member State. Apart from the UCITS Directive, investment funds can also be regulated under the AIFM Directive.[40] Alternative investment funds are funds that are not regulated at the EU-level by the UCITS Directive. They include hedge funds, private equity funds, real estate funds and a wide range of other types of institutional funds.

This being said on the regulatory aspects, the CJEU stated that:

> the fact that non-resident investment funds are not part of the European Union's uniform regulatory framework, set up by the UCITS Directive on the rules applicable to the formation and operation of investment funds within the European Union, as transposed into national law by the Polish law on investment funds, *cannot in itself be sufficient reason to find that the situations of those funds are in fact different.*[41]

The above statement shows that the non-applicability vis-à-vis non-EU funds of the same legal framework applicable to EU funds do not per se vitiate the comparability analysis. However, the CJEU pointed out that such a conclusion is only true insofar as:

> *the main criterion laid down by the national tax legislation at issue in the main proceedings is based on the place of residence of an investment fund,* enabling solely investment funds which are established in Poland to qualify for the tax exemption[.][42]

Nevertheless, the Court goes further and explains that:

> in this case[,] a comparison of the regulatory framework governing funds established in a non-Member country and the uniform regulatory framework applied within the Union is of no relevance, *in that such a comparison forms no part of the applicable legislation at issue in the main proceedings.*[43]

This last clause of paragraph 68 of the decision contains some important clarifications. Indeed, the CJEU seems to suggest that use of the Regulatory Framework Approach depends on the manner in which domestic law is construed.

More specifically, if the domestic law of the Source State only attributes relevance to the taxpayer's tax residence to assess the tax treatment of the fund, then the Regulatory Framework Approach does not apply. If, by contrast, the domestic law of the Source State is construed in such a way that – in addition to the taxpayer's tax residence – the regulatory status of the fund is taken into account, then its regulatory

40. Directive 2011/61/EU of the European Parliament and of the Council of 8 June 2011 on Alternative Investment Fund Managers and amending Directives 2003/41/EC and 2009/65/EC and Regulations (EC) No 1060/2009 and (EU) No 1095/2010 Text with EEA relevance [2011] OJ L 174/1, as amended (hereinafter the 'AIFM Directive').
41. *Emerging Markets*, C-190/12, para. 67 (emphasis added).
42. *Ibid.*, para. 68 (emphasis added).
43. *Ibid.*

framework becomes relevant to the comparability assessment that the Regulatory Framework Approach is brought to bear. This implies that, regardless of whether or not the foreign investment fund is compliant with either the UCITS Directive or the AIFM Directive, they could be a decisive element in the comparability analysis. And, using the Regulatory Framework Approach, foreign investment funds could well be considered comparable to domestic UCITS, to the extent the former comply with the UCITS Directive, with the consequence that non-EU investment funds would never have access to the protection of TFEU's fundamental freedoms.

The CJEU, indeed, has acknowledged this in its *Emerging Market* decision:

> Since the UCITS directive does not apply to investment funds established in non-Member countries, because they are outside the scope of European Union law, a requirement that such investment funds be regulated in the same way as resident investment funds *would deprive the principle of free movement of capital of any practical effect.*[44]

The CJEU, thus, is well aware that strictly following the Regulatory Framework Approach would ultimately lead to a conclusion that foreign investment funds would never be protected by the free movement of capital (in case of non-EU investment funds). However, this statement is only partly true, as the non-applicability of the Regulatory Framework Approach does not mean that such non-EU funds cannot benefit from the above-mentioned freedom. It merely implies that the comparability analysis should be carried out on the basis of the *ACT GLO/Denkavit* Approach, which relies on a general criterion. In such a case, however, the foreign fund (one that does not comply with any EU-legislative framework) should be regarded as being comparable to a domestic entity resident in the Source State. Once comparability is assessed, the existence of discrimination should be tested against the domestic rules applicable in the Source State to dividends paid to domestic entities.

§7.06 CONCLUSIONS

The case law on the comparability of investment funds from a Source-State perspective is rather settled, although the application of the four different approaches still requires some fine-tuning.

The application of the *ACT GLO/Denkavit* Approach, for example, is rather straightforward and does not generate any particular uncertainty. In order for it to apply, however, it is of utmost importance that, under the domestic law of the Source State, foreign investment vehicles are assimilated to a corporate vehicle (subject, in that Source State, to corporate income tax law[45]) and that the domestic exemption is aimed at eliminating economic double taxation.

44. *Ibid.*, para. 67 (emphasis added).
45. Indeed, this was a pillar of the Court's *Aberdeen* decision, in which it found no 'difference between a SICAV and a resident share company which justifies different treatment as regards withholding tax on dividends received by those two classes of company'. *Aberdeen*, C-303/07, para. 51.

When the *ACT GLO/Denkavit* Approach does not apply, as when the relevant domestic law pursues a different aim, the Distinguishing Criterion Approach and the Aim Approach must be tested as a complementary method.

Finally, the Regulatory Framework Approach will be applicable insofar as the regulatory status of the fund is taken into account as '*part of the applicable legislation*'.[46] The Regulatory Framework Approach does not apply if the fund is established outside the EU in which case the *ACT GLO/Denkavit* Approach should apply as a last resort method for establishing comparability.

46. *Emerging Markets*, C-190/12, para. 68.

CHAPTER 8
Funds and EU Tax Directives

*Katerina Pantazatou**

§8.01 INTRODUCTION

The many different types of funds make it very difficult to regulate them in a single and consistent manner. The funds', often, complicated structure as well as the different schemes they might adopt makes this undertaking all the more challenging. First steps towards this direction have emerged in the area of finance with the Undertakings for Collective Investment in Transferable Securities (UCITS) Directive[1] and the Alternative Investment Funds Directive (AIFM Directive).[2] More 'funds-specific' secondary law, such as the IORP (Institutions for Occupational Retirement Provisions) and the EuVECA (European Venture Capital Funds) is also available, yet it remains outside the scope of this contribution.[3]

---

* I would like to thank Werner Haslehner for comments. All errors remain my own.

1. Directive 2009/65/EC of the European Parliament and of the Council of 13 July 2009 on the coordination of laws, regulations and administrative provisions relating to undertakings for collective investment in transferable securities (UCITS) (recast) [2009] OJ L 302/32, as amended (hereinafter 'UCITS IV Directive').
2. Directive 2011/61/EU of the European Parliament and of the Council of 8 June 2011 on Alternative Investment Fund Managers and amending Directives 2003/41/EC and 2009/65/EC and Regulations (EC) No 1060/2009 and (EU) No 1095/2010 [2011] OJ L 174/1, as amended (hereinafter 'AIFM Directive').
3. Directive 2003/41/EC of the European Parliament and of the Council of 3 June 2003 on the activities and supervision of institutions for occupational retirement provision [2003] OJ L 235/10, as amended (hereinafter 'IORPs I') and Directive (EU) 2016/2341 of the European Parliament and of the Council of 14 December 2016 on the activities and supervision of institutions for occupational retirement provision (IORPs) [2016] OJ L 354/37 (hereinafter 'IORPs II') and Regulation (EU) No 345/2013 of the European Parliament and of the Council of 17 April 2013 on European venture capital funds Text with EEA relevance [2013] OJ L 115/1, as amended (hereinafter 'EuVECA Regulation').

Despite the existence of this fund-specific secondary legislation, no unique and commonly accepted definition of what is a 'fund' can be easily discerned. For classification purposes the most commonly used division of funds is the division into UCITS (Undertakings for Collective Investment in Transferable Securities) and non-UCITS (or Alternative Investment Funds) or the Collective Investment Vehicle (CIVs) and the non-CIVs, the latter including private equity funds, pension funds, sovereign wealth funds, real estate funds and hedge funds.

Given the complexity of the sector, the unanimity requirement and the consonant limited progress in the area of European Union (EU) tax legislation, it comes as no surprise that no specific EU tax legislation exists with regard to the taxation of funds. Hence, the taxation of funds can be governed (or at least affected) either by the 'funds-specific' directives coming from the finance sector or from the CJEU's case law and the application of the EU principles and the fundamental freedoms, or the tax treaties, or domestic law or finally the existing EU tax directives. This latter point will constitute the focus of this chapter; in specific, whether and if so, how, the existing EU tax directives impact on funds.

The chapter will first briefly discuss the tax implications of the 'funds-specific' directives and will proceed to analyse the Parent-Subsidiary Directive (PSD),[4] the Anti-Tax Avoidance Directive (ATAD),[5] the Directive on Administrative Cooperation in Direct Taxation (i.e., 'exchange of information') (DAC),[6] the Anti-Money Laundering Directive (AMLD)[7] and the Tax Merger Directive.[8] It will conclude by pointing out at

4. Council Directive 2011/96/EU of 30 November 2011 on the common system of taxation applicable in the case of parent companies and subsidiaries of different Member States [2011] OJ L 345/8, as amended (hereinafter the 'PSD').
5. Council Directive (EU) 2016/1164 of 12 July 2016 laying down rules against tax avoidance practices that directly affect the functioning of the internal market [2016] OJ L 193/1 (hereinafter 'ATAD I'), as amended by Council Directive (EU) 2017/952 of 29 May 2017 amending Directive (EU) 2016/1164 as regards hybrid mismatches with third countries [2017] OJ L 144/1 (hereinafter 'ATAD II', and collectively, ATAD I and ATAD II, are hereinafter 'ATAD').
6. Council Directive 2011/16/EU of 15 February 2011 on administrative cooperation in the field of taxation and repealing Directive 77/799/EEC [2011] OJ L 64/1 (hereinafter 'DAC1'), as amended by Directive 2014/65/EU of the European Parliament and of the Council of 15 May 2014 on markets in financial instruments and amending Directive 2002/92/EC and Directive 2011/61/EU (Text with EEA relevance) [2014] OJ L 173/349 (hereinafter 'DAC2'), as further amended by Council Directive (EU) 2015/2376 of 8 December 2015 amending Directive 2011/16/EU as regards mandatory automatic exchange of information in the field of taxation [2015] OJ L 332/1 (hereinafter 'DAC3'), as further amended Council Directive (EU) 2016/881 of 25 May 2016 amending Directive 2011/16/EU as regards mandatory automatic exchange of information in the field of taxation [2016] OJ L 146/8 (hereinafter 'DAC4'), as further amended by Council Directive (EU) 2016/2258 of 6 December 2016 amending Directive 2011/16/EU as regards access to anti-money-laundering information by tax authorities [2016] OJ L 342/1 (hereinafter 'DAC5', collectively, DAC1, DAC2, DAC3, DAC4, and DAC5, are hereinafter 'DAC').
7. Directive (EU) 2015/849 of the European Parliament and of the Council of 20 May 2015 on the prevention of the use of the financial system for the purposes of money laundering or terrorist financing, amending Regulation (EU) No 648/2012 of the European Parliament and of the Council, and repealing Directive 2005/60/EC of the European Parliament and of the Council and Commission Directive 2006/70/EC (Text with EEA relevance) [2015] OJ L 141/73, as amended (hereinafter the '4th AMLD').
8. Council Directive 2009/133/EC of 19 October 2009 on the common system of taxation applicable to mergers, divisions, partial divisions, transfers of assets and exchanges of shares concerning

the shortcomings of the existing legislative framework and will propose solutions as to how this can be rectified.

[A] Setting the Scene: Background

The main problem with regard to the taxation of funds lies in their very nature. As funds are hybrid entities, no unique approach with regard to their 'type' (contract, trust, company) can be established among the twenty-eight Member States and, hence, there is no consistency within the Union as to whether they should be treated as opaque or transparent entities. This inconsistency leads to a series of other residence-related problems, such as whether funds should be treated as 'persons', residents and whether they can be considered to be beneficial owners entitled to tax treaty benefits. Hence, the most common problem and challenge for the existing EU tax legislation is the assessment of whether the funds fall under the scope of the directives and whether they can qualify as a 'company' in accordance with the definitions provided therein. If answered in the positive, then funds can claim the benefits of the directives, but they will also have to comply with the relevant obligations stemming from the ATAD and the DAC.

A second set of problems with regard to funds, attributable to their different 'nature' is the potential of triggering cross-border double taxation, notably leading to one of the participants in this funds-tripartite relationship (assets/investment property, fund and end-recipient/investor) being taxed twice (at least) or not benefiting from any deductions, or conversely benefiting from mismatches and sometimes even non-taxation. In order for this problem to be tackled by the tax directives, two necessary pre-conditions should be met: First, that the fund(s) in question fall *ratione personae* under the scope of the directives and secondly that the involved Member States in this cross-border situation treat the fund in the same way (as opaque or transparent).

These are only a few of the fundamental problems the different treatment of funds may cause, and in principle, given their ongoing expansion, they should be treated immediately, ideally at the *legislative level*. Yet, before one demands legislative initiative, he should consider whether the existing EU tax (and non-tax but funds-specific) directives can, in fact, offer solutions to the aforementioned problems. First, the funds-specific directives and what they contribute to the tax-related questions are briefly examined.

[B] 'Funds-Specific Directives' and Their Contribution

Having regard to the aims and the scope of the UCITS IV and the AIFM Directives, which can be summarized to laying down common rules and requirements governing the authorization, activities and supervision of UCITS and AIFMs, it comes as no

---

companies of different Member States and to the transfer of the registered office of an SE or SCE between Member States [2009] OJ L 310/34, as amended (hereinafter the 'Tax Merger Directive').

surprise that no specific tax rules are included in either of them.[9] Legally based on Article 53(2) and 53(1) TFEU, respectively, and hence, upon following the ordinary legislative procedure, it was anticipated that no tax-related rules would be introduced.

To clarify this, the UCITS IV Directive specifically states that: 'This Directive should not affect national rules on taxation, including arrangements that may be imposed by Member States to ensure compliance with those rules in their territory.'[10] The AIFM Directive makes no reference either to tax rules, with the exception of the need for the existence of an agreement between the third country where the non-EU AIF and the home Member State of the authorized AIFM which fully complies with the standards laid down in Article 26 of the OECD on the effective exchange of information.[11]

Despite the absence of direct reference to tax rules, both directives have an indirect impact on taxation through the definition/appointment of the fund's (regardless whether it is UCITS or non-UCITS) tax residence when the management services move cross-border. Consequently, if the UCITS management moved to another Member State (other than the Member State where the UCITS was established), then for many Member States which rely on the real seat theory, the transfer of the UCITS place of effective management would imply also the change of the UCITS tax residence. This change could result in a different treatment of the UCITS depending on the perspective of the 'new' residence state and could accordingly narrow or expand the available tax treaty network and its associated benefits. It could, furthermore, even trigger taxation if the state of the management's residence treated the UCITS as opaque. Moreover, if the UCITS was treated as transparent in its 'incorporation state', then by reason of the transfer of the management company, it could, in principle, be confronted with additional taxation in the Member State from which the management company is operating, such as corporate taxation or stamp duties.[12] This transfer of seat finds applicability in the case of mergers, the taxation of which is regulated by the Tax Merger Directive.[13] This is probably the only point where the UCITS IV and the AIFM Directives indirectly interact with an EU tax directive in the context of the taxation of funds.

By the same token, it is possible that the cross-border transfer of the fund's management might, under certain conditions, trigger the recognition of a permanent establishment (PE) for the fund, where the management is located and by reference to the revenue generated by the UCITS or non-UCITS in that state.

9. The same applies to other funds'-specific Directives such as the IOPRs.
10. *See* UCITS IV Directive.
11. UCITS IV Directive, Arts 35 (2)(c) and 37.
12. Pascal Borsjé & Willem Specken, *Tax Implications of the Amended UCITS and the AIFM Directives: A General Overview from a Dutch Perspective*, 4 Derivatives and Financial Instruments 164, 166 (2012).
13. *See infra*, §8.06.

§8.02 THE PARENT-SUBSIDIARY DIRECTIVE

Qualifying as an entity under the PSD allows the companies involved to benefit from an exemption from withholding tax for dividends and other profit distributions by the subsidiary to their parent companies and hence avoid being taxed twice on the same income.

A first question that arises in the context of funds' taxation is whether funds qualify as 'entities' under the PSD. Article 2(a) of the PSD provides that:

> 'company of a Member State' means any company which: (i) takes one of the forms listed in Annex I, Part A; (ii) according to the tax laws of a Member State is considered to be resident in that Member State for tax purposes and, under the terms of a double taxation agreement concluded with a third State, is not considered to be resident for tax purposes outside the Union; (iii) moreover, is subject to one of the taxes listed in Annex I, Part B, without the possibility of an option or of being exempt, or to any other tax which may be substituted for any of those taxes.

The qualifying criteria are laid out in Annex I, where different Member States choose to either insert a residual clause that reads as companies 'constituted under the *[relevant]* law' and/or are 'are subject to *[national]* tax' or in addition to or alternative to that enumerate specific company types that fall under the Directive's scope.

The CJEU was asked to interpret the term 'company of a Member State' under the PSD. In the question of whether the list provided in Annex I is exhaustive, the CJEU has ruled in the affirmative. Hence, in the *Gaz de France* case the CJEU stipulated that 'the fundamental principle of legal certainty precludes the list of companies in point (f) of the annex to the directive from being interpreted as merely an indicative list, when such an interpretation does not follow from the wording or scheme of Directive 90/435'.[14]

In the cases where the Member States refer to specific company types that fall within the scope of the Directive, then, in principle, it should be clear whether a fund qualifies as a company for the PSD purposes. If for instance one Member State, like the Netherlands,[15] lists in the Annex a fund, then for it to benefit from the PSD it should also be treated as opaque by the same Member State. This way, the (cumulative) requirements of residence and subjection to tax, as provided in Article 2 PSD are fulfilled.

In the opposite scenario where a fund is not specifically listed in Annex I, but the Member State at issue uses also/only the residual clause of the constitution/incorporation under its national law and/or the subjection to tax requirement,[16] then, one should again consider whether that particular Member State treats the fund as fiscally transparent or as non-transparent. In the former scenario, the fund

14. *Gaz de France - Berliner Investissement*, C-247/08, Judgment, EU:C:2009:600, para. 38.
15. The Netherlands is the only Member State that lists investment and pension funds in Annex I of the PSD: 'fonds voor gemene rekening'.
16. The only country that uses only the incorporation residual clause is Lithuania.

should not be covered by the PSD, in the latter scenario, it *could* fall under the PSD scope.

The reason why funds, even if they are treated as opaque by a Member State, do not automatically fall under the Directive's scope is because in most cases the funds will benefit from tax exemptions in the state at issue. In this case, the '*subjection to tax*' requirement, as listed in Article 2(c) PSD, becomes of relevance.

While Article 2(c) PSD specifically states that, in order to qualify as company for the PSD purposes, the entity must be 'subject to one of the taxes listed in Annex I ... *without the possibility of an option or of being exempt*' (emphasis added), the recent judgment of the CJEU in the *Wereldhave* case came to clarify the 'subjection to tax' requirement of the PSD in particular in relation to zero tax rates.[17] In a judgment where the concept of the exemption in the PSD context was not fully clarified, the Court ruled that the criteria of the subjection to tax (positive criterion) and the non-exemption from tax (negative criterion) lead 'to the conclusion that the condition laid down in Article 2(c) of the directive does not merely require that a company should fall within the scope of the tax in question, but also seeks to exclude situations involving the possibility that, despite being subject to that tax, the company is not actually liable to pay that tax'.[18] The Court agreed with the AG's opinion and confirmed its previous case law by stating that companies which are subject to a zero tax rate are practically in the same situation as the one which Article 2(c) of Directive 90/435 seeks to exclude, that is to say, a situation in which it is not liable to pay that tax.[19]

In light of the almost universal tax exemption of funds or the effectively equivalent zero tax rate, one may reasonably wonder whether all funds are excluded from the PSD, regardless whether they are treated as transparent or not.[20] Given the strict wording of the Directive, it appears as if one could only resort to the four freedoms provisions.[21]

The different treatment of funds in different Member States, as well as the growing popularity of international groups of companies, create one additional problem that was, *inter alia*, the subject of dispute in the *Aberdeen* case.[22] The case concerned dividend distributions from a Finnish subsidiary to a parent in Luxembourg which had the form of a *société d'investissement à capital variable* (SICAV). Given the legal form of the parent company and the fact that SICAVs did not figure in the PSD Annex, neither were they subject to tax in Luxembourg, the question arose as to whether the group should benefit from exemption of withholding taxes in Finland upon the distribution of dividends from the subsidiary to the parent.

17. *Wereldhave Belgium and Others*, C-448/15, Judgment, EU:C:2017:180.
18. *Ibid.*, para. 32. For a comment on the shortcomings of the judgment *see*, Paolo Arginelli, *The Court of Justice of the European Union Interprets the 'Subject to Tax' Requirement Provided for in the Parent-Subsidiary Directive*, Kluwer International Tax Blog (20 March 2017) http://kluwertaxblog.com/2017/03/20/the-court-of-justice-of-the-european-union-interprets-the-subject-to-tax-requirement-provided-for-in-the-parent-subsidiary-directive/.
19. *Wereldhave Belgium and Others*, C-448/15, paras 33–34.
20. The only possibilities for subjection to tax I see here are: non-exempt opaque entities and transparent entities with an option for corporate taxation.
21. On the topic, *see* Mario Tenore's contribution in this book, Chapter 7, *supra*.
22. *Aberdeen Property Fininvest Alpha*, C-303/07, Judgment, EU:C:2009:377.

The CJEU ruled that since a company in the form of a SICAV does not satisfy the conditions set out in Article 2(1)(a) and (c) of that Directive, it does not fall within the scope of the PSD.[23] In such cases 'it is for the Member States to determine whether, and to what extent, economic double taxation of distributed profits is to be avoided and, for that purpose, to establish, either unilaterally or by conventions concluded with other Member States, procedures intended to prevent or mitigate such economic double taxation'.[24] The fact that the SICAV at issue did not fall under the PSD did not mean, therefore, that withholding tax could be imposed in Finland on the distribution of dividends. Instead, as the CJEU held in the *Aberdeen* case, the non-applicability of the PSD was rectified by the application of the freedom of establishment. The CJEU found that the fact that Finland did not recognize the legal form of a SICAV was irrelevant for comparability purposes.[25] Upon applying a 'subject-to-tax' approach and in the absence of any valid justifications the Court found that the difference in treatment between non-resident SICAVs and resident share companies with respect to the exemption from withholding tax on dividends distributed to them by resident companies constituted a restriction of freedom of establishment.[26]

The *Aberdeen* case provides yet another example of how the CJEU can rectify the absence of funds-specific or funds-related rules in secondary legislation through the use of the fundamental freedoms.[27] Certainly, in this particular case, adopting a broad formulation with regard to the companies included in the PSD Annex (using, thus, the generic criterion), instead of providing a specific list of companies covered, would increase the possibility of compliance with the fundamental freedoms. At the same time, the use of such a generic criterion is more likely to enhance the legal uncertainty between the Member States involved as to the meaning of the company. In addition to that, while Article 2 proviso of the requirements of 'residence' and 'subjection to tax' without the possibility of exemption should not be overlooked; reliance only on the explicit list of entities covered can lead to the opposite results than the ones the PSD intended to promote. As the *Aberdeen* case showed, it is possible that an entity, which is sufficiently similar, if not identical, to the legal forms covered, is excluded despite the fact that it ought to receive the same tax benefits as those granted in the PSD in order for its tax treatment not to be in conflict with the freedom of establishment.[28] It is doubtful whether the solution to such problems, which are very likely to arise in the funds' context, should be provided by the Member States through a (comprehensive) update of the Annex, or whether it should be left to the Court – provided that the case reaches it – to conduct an in-depth analysis of the characteristics of each of the involved entities in order to evaluate whether these resemble any of the companies listed in the Annex.

The PSD includes one specific provision on the treatment of hybrid entities that may apply to funds whenever they fall into that category. Article 4(2) concerns

23. *Ibid.*, para. 27.
24. *Ibid.*, para. 28.
25. *Ibid.*, para. 50.
26. *Ibid.*, para. 76.
27. For more on this, *see* Tenore, *supra* note 21.
28. Marjaana Helminen, *EU Tax Law – Direct Taxation*, 163 (2015).

subsidiaries that are treated as opaque in their residence state but as transparent in the parent company's state, upon assessment of the subsidiary's legal characteristics. The implication of this provision is that the Member State of the parent company may tax the parent company on its share of the profits of its subsidiary as and when those profits arise even if no distribution has taken place. In this case, it shall, however, refrain from taxing the distributed profits of the subsidiary.

Whenever funds qualify as hybrid entities, different tax problems may arise. To demonstrate such a problem, we could construe a hypothetical example whereby the fund is covered by the company term of the PSD and is treated as opaque by its residence state. Accordingly, in this scenario, the state of the investor, State A, treats the fund as opaque, the 'Fund state', State B, treats the fund as opaque, whereas the state of the asset/investment, State C, treats the fund as transparent (Figure 8.1). In this scenario, the question that reasonably arises is whether, upon the distribution of the dividend by State C to the fund (State B), the former state (State C) should grant the benefits of the PSD (exemption from withholding tax) with regard to this distribution.

Figure 8.1 Distribution of Dividends

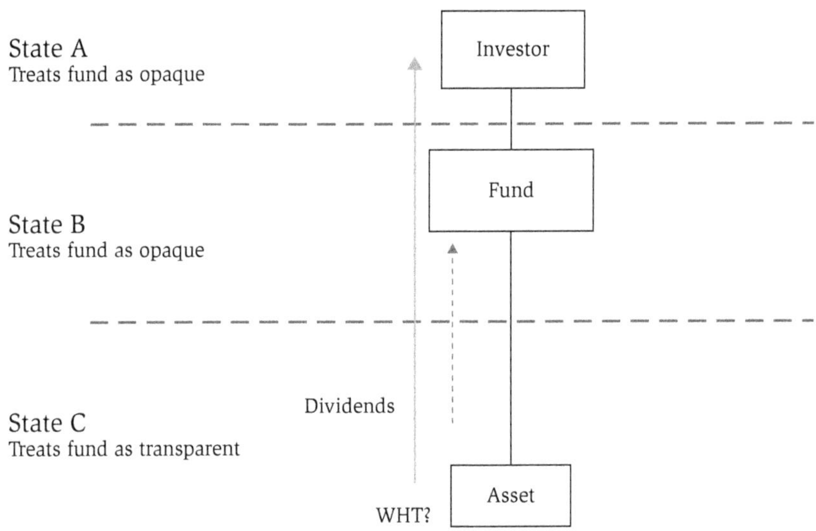

Could one possibility to effectuate this exemption under the PSD be by showing that State C pays a dividend to the investor's PE in State B, thereby triggering the PSD's scope under Article 1(1)(c) PSD? For the fund to be qualified as a PE, its profits should be taxed in the fund state (State B), and, therefore, State B should treat the fund as opaque. In this scenario, the payment of profit distributions to, and their receipt by, a PE of a parent company should give rise to the same treatment as that applying between a subsidiary and its parent. The first possible objection with regard to this scenario would arise by reference to the qualification of the 'fund' as a parent company in accordance with Article 3(1)(a) PSD.

In general, classic collective investment funds aimed at the retail market are not designed to be 'parent companies' - in terms of concentration and portfolio diversification - or to exercise management control functions over the companies, which they hold in their portfolios.[29]

In legal terms, the Court's understanding of the 'parent company' was provided in its judgment in the *Les Vergers du Vieux Tauves*,[30] where the CJEU essentially held - against AG Sharpston's opinion - that the concept of a 'holding in the capital' of a company in another Member State does not include the holding of shares in usufruct.[31] According to the Court, the concept of 'holding in the capital' refers to the legal relationship between a parent and a subsidiary, which did not exist in the *Les Vergers* case as the usufruct holder's position towards the subsidiary resulted solely from the right of usufruct that had been transferred to it by the owner of the shares.[32]

The starting point in order to answer the question of the 'parent company' in our example lies, hence, on the legal ownership of the distributed dividends. If the dividends the asset distributes are considered to be legally owned by the final investor then the fund would merely act as an intermediary - it would hold the dividends in 'usufruct', and hence the distribution at issue could not benefit from the PSD. In the opposite scenario, however, whereby the fund becomes the legal owner of the distributed dividends, which it distributes anew, then the PSD could apply in this distribution, as in the distribution from the fund to the final investor provided all previous hypotheses are met, and all other conditions of PSD are fulfilled.

In most cases, whether the fund at issue has the legal form of a company, or of a trust or of a contractual pool, the legal ownership of the dividends would remain with the fund, and hence, the aforementioned distribution would qualify as a distribution from a subsidiary to a parent company, provided all other conditions are met.

The same issues with regard to the effective exemption from the personal scope of the Directive arise also in the context of the Interest and Royalties Directive, all the more so given its more limited scope.[33]

§8.03 THE ANTI-TAX AVOIDANCE DIRECTIVE

Given the favourable tax treatment of different funds by almost all Member States, tax, and tax avoidance in specific, is not usually a key reason behind the location decision

29. Mark St Giles, Ekaterina Alexeeva & Sally Buxton, *Managing Collective Investment Funds* (2003).
30. *Les Vergers du Vieux Tauves*, C-48/07, Judgment, EU:C:2008:758.
31. *Ibid.*, para. 38. In interpreting Art. 3(1) of the PSD, the CJEU essentially ruled that Art. 3 'does not provide for the situation in which the parent company (Bepa SA) transfers to a third party (Vieux Tauves SA), in this case, to a usufructuary, a legal relationship with the subsidiary under which that third party might also be regarded as a parent company'.
32. *Ibid.*, para. 41.
33. Council Directive 2003/49/EC of 3 June 2003 on a common system of taxation applicable to interest and royalty payments made between associated companies of different Member States [2003] OJ L 157/49, as amended (hereinafter the 'Interest & Royalties Directive'). While the subjection to tax and residence requirements are also present in the Interest and Royalties Directive, its Annex comprising the types of companies covered is much more limited ratione personae in comparison to the Annex I of the PSD.

of the funds.[34] Hence, one could intuitively argue that the ATAD would have little relevance in the funds' context.

This intuition is confirmed by the ATAD's personal scope. Similar to the PSD, the application of the ATAD to funds becomes problematic by reason of the fact that the Directive itself explicitly or implicitly excludes entities like funds from its scope. As stated therein 'it is not desirable to extend the scope of this Directive to types of entities which *are not subject to corporate tax* in a Member State; that is, in particular, *transparent entities*'.[35] It thus appears that transparent entities are automatically excluded from the scope of the Directive. While the ATAD is applicable to all taxpayers *subject to* corporate tax (including PEs of third-country entities),[36] it provides no guidance as to whether opaque companies exempt from corporate tax fall within the Directive's subjective scope.[37] There are two possibilities to this. First, although technically unconvincing, would be the transposition of the *Wereldhave* case findings into the ATAD context. The existence of the subjection to tax requirement 'without the possibility of an option or of being exempt' in the PSD and the absence of such wording in the ATAD leaves little room for such a broad analogy, in particular since the ATAD and the PSD serve opposite purposes.[38] In such a scenario the tax-exempt funds would be 'equated' to not liable to pay tax and, hence, not subject to tax. Consequently, they would be excluded from the scope of the Directive. The second possibility would be to rely on a strict literal interpretation and consider that since opaque funds are technically subject to tax, they should fall within the scope of the Directive.

In either case and in light of the different treatment of funds among Member States, it remains questionable on which law one should rely in order to identify an entity/fund as transparent or not. Based on the textual interpretation of the preamble, it appears reasonable to assume that the law to be taken into account should be the law of the residence state of the fund. At this level, if the state of the fund treats the fund as opaque, then - at least at this level - the Directive seems applicable.

However, even if the fund were to be treated as opaque from its state of residence, it is likely that it would still not be covered by the ATAD because of the Directive's carve outs for 'financial undertakings'. According to the Directive, the term 'financial undertaking' includes, *inter alia*, both UCITS and non-UCITS.[39]

---

34. St Giles, Alexeeva & Buxton, *supra* note 29, at 68.
35. ATAD, Recital 4 (emphasis added).
36. *See* ATAD, Art. 1.
37. Such a scenario is very likely and can be found in Luxembourg in two different variations:

    (1) A non-taxable fund, i.e., one that is by definition not subject to corporate income tax (e.g., SICAV-SIF).
    (2) A fund that is tax-exempt for all practical purposes, although technically subject to corporate tax (e.g., SICAR, securitization company).

38. The exemption from tax requirement applies only in the definition of a CFC in the ATAD context (Art. 7).
39. *See* ATAD, Art. 2(5):

    > financial undertaking: (a) credit institution or an investment firm ... or an alternative investment fund manager (AIFM) ... or an undertaking for collective investment in

Financial undertakings, including UCITS and non-UCITS, *may*, thus, be excluded from the interest limitation rule,[40] and, under conditions, the CFC rules.[41] The freedom given to the Member States to decide whether to exclude or not financial undertakings from the aforementioned rules might create disparities within the internal market. These problems should not, however, be overstated, as for the ATAD to apply a series of unlikely to be met conditions should co-exist, including one and the same Member State opting out from the carve-out and treating the fund as opaque.

By reference to the interest limitation rule, even if the carve out for financial undertakings did not apply, as most investment funds are either tax exempt or treated as transparent or they are not leveraged at the level of the fund, the deductibility of interest should not be a main concern.[42] Similarly, it seems understandable that transparent funds do not fall within the scope of CFC legislation because of their 'flow through' basis. With regard to opaque funds, in practice it would be difficult for them to qualify as CFCs as the control test, as established in Article 7(1)(a) would be hard to satisfy.

The impact these rules might have on funds will largely depend upon the fund's type and investment and structuring strategy. In practical terms, all types of funds are operating in highly complex structures, often employing other structures or special purpose vehicles (SPV) for their purposes, or acting as umbrella funds consisting of several compartments.[43] Therefore, in both cases of the interest limitation rules and the CFC rules, the structure *beneath the fund* could be affected, impacting indirectly on the fund. In other words, these rules might concern the country where the fund's assets are located and depending on where they invest and how they are financed. The interest limitation rule, for instance, could affect more funds such as funds with investments in real estate (e.g., Real Estate Investment Trusts or REITs) when generating revenue from interest through mortgage loans, or funds that operate through vehicles that rely on debt financing.

---

transferable securities (UCITS) management company ...(d) an institution for occupational retirement provision falling within the scope of Directive 2003/41/EC of the European Parliament and of the Council (5); (e) pension institutions operating pension schemes which are considered to be social security schemes ...; an alternative investment fund (AIF) managed by an AIFM...; (g) UCITS in the meaning of Article 1(2) of Directive 2009/65/EC.

40. ATAD, Art. 4(7): 'Member States may exclude financial undertakings from the scope of paragraphs 1 to 6, including where such financial undertakings are part of a consolidated group for financial accounting purposes.'
41. ATAD, Art. 7(4): Where, under the rules of a Member State, the tax base of a taxpayer is calculated according to point (a) of paragraph 2, the Member State *may opt* not to treat financial undertakings as CFC if one third or less of the entity's income from the categories under point (a) of paragraph 2 comes from transactions with the taxpayer or its associated enterprises.
42. *See* Loyens & Loeff, *Q&A – What Is the Impact of the EU Anti-tax Avoidance Directive on Investment Funds?* Loyens & Loeff. www.loyensloeff.com/en-us/news-events/news/qa-what-is-the-impact-of-the-eu-anti-tax-avoidance-directive-on-investment-funds.
43. The investment fund organized as an umbrella scheme has separate sub-funds with segregated assets and liabilities. These sub-structures consist of different types of assets, are scattered in different geographic areas and are usually characterized by a different style of management.

In the context of the CFC rules, if one bypasses the problematic ownership issue – given that the ownership of the funds is in most cases quite dispersed and, hence, would not easily meet the ownership thresholds as set out in Article 7(1)(a) of the ATAD – one could potentially foresee an impact on opaque non-exempt or partly exempt funds, such the Luxembourg SICARs.[44] As with the case in the interest limitation rule, once again, the structures beneath the fund are not immune and may be treated as a CFC even if the fund is carved out.

The same applies with regard to Article 6 – the General Anti-Avoidance Rule (GAAR). While, once again, there is no discussion on the treatment of (investment) funds, this rule could have an impact on (non-UCITS and non-regulated) funds that are set up purely for tax purposes, provided all other conditions are met. The same would apply *mutatis mutandis* to structures beneath the fund. This would be, for instance, the case of a holding company or an SPV with limited physical and economic substance that is included in the fund's structure purely for tax purposes.

Whenever funds qualify as hybrid entities, their main purpose is not to benefit from the mismatches arising from this hybridity. Yet, it is likely that funds could fall under one of the two categories of hybrid mismatches provided in Article 9 ATAD. If withholding tax is imposed at asset level and the 'fund state' treats the fund as opaque, then it will typically allow for a deduction of the withholding tax from any tax levied at the 'fund level'. If, however, the 'investor state' treats the fund as transparent, then the deduction for the withholding tax raised at the 'asset level' may be provided there (at the investor level). The result of this hybrid mismatch will be the double deduction of the withholding tax at issue. While this double deduction would appear to be a problem; if this deduction is not followed by a refundable credit, the idea of tax neutrality that lies at the heart of the exemption of funds is not 'broken'. The solution to this is covered by the exception for double deductions that are matched by 'dual inclusion' income as provided in Article 2(9), as added by ATAD II.

While few Member States have already introduced interest deductibility restrictions in order to avoid the results of these hybrid mismatches, there is very little anti-avoidance legislation specifically targeting hybrid entities.[45]

44. Any *société d'investissement en capital à risque* (SICAR) constituted otherwise than as an ordinary limited partnership (*société en commandite simple*) is subject to Luxembourg income tax at the standard rate and may therefore benefit in principle from the Luxembourg tax treaty network, the EU parent-subsidiary directive and the Luxembourg provisions regarding participation exemption. However, SICAR income deriving directly from transferable securities (such as dividend distributions) is not included in the SICAR's chargeable tax base. In practice, this exemption attaches to the investment instruments most commonly held by private equity/venture funds. Where constituted as a public company or an incorporated limited partnership (both classified as *sociétés de capitaux*), income resulting from the sale or liquidation of such assets is also exempted from the SICAR's chargeable tax base. SICAR are also outside scope in terms of withholding tax and net wealth tax.

45. For details *see* Daniel Gutmann et al., *The Impact of the ATAD on Domestic Systems: A Comparative Survey*, 57 ET, n. 1, 2, and 19 (2017).

ATAD II came to extend the ATAD I rules on mismatches both *ratione personae* and *ratione materiae*. ATAD II extends the rules on hybrid mismatches and tax residency mismatches to all taxpayers that are subject to corporate tax in one or more Member States, including PEs in one or more Member States of entities resident for tax purposes in a third country.[46] Article 9a on reverse hybrid mismatches applies to all entities that are treated as transparent for tax purposes by a Member State.[47] While ATAD II introduces rules on reverse hybrid mismatches which should apply to all entities that are treated as transparent for tax purposes by a Member State, the newly inserted Article 9a(2) exempts from the application of the hybrid mismatches rules CIVs.[48] Consequently, by excluding CIVs from its scope, ATAD II would only apply to non-UCITS.

Whether directly or indirectly excluded, the Directive seems to premise its inapplicability to funds on the fact that the risk of tax avoidance is minimized as funds are effectively and in most cases tax exempt. In addition to that, the (apparent) presumption of no tax avoidance in connection to the funds could be explained, besides their exemption from tax, on grounds of their subjection to strict obligations to keep accounts on the income they receive.[49] Yet, funds could be indirectly affected by the ATAD provisions through the application of its rules to the structures beneath them (SICAVs, CIVs, employment of holding companies at a lower level).

§8.04 THE AUTOMATIC EXCHANGE OF TAX INFORMATION

The now-repealed EU Savings Directive was the first EU directive to introduce the automatic exchange of information between Member States.[50] Under this directive, automatic data transfer between EU Member States took place when interest payments were paid by paying agents to EU individual residents, keeping their savings in another Member State. According to the directive, distributions by UCITS were deemed to be of interest for the directive's purposes. Therefore, such distributions had to be reported by the UCITS or interested withholding tax had to be withheld by them.

Currently, the exchange of tax information in the EU is regulated by Council Directive 2011/16/EU ('DAC1') which succeeded and repealed the 1977 'Mutual Assistance Directive'[51] and sets out the procedures for the better cooperation between tax authorities in the EU. The EU Savings Directive was repealed on 10 November 2015. As the Directive was easily circumvented due to loopholes, the Commission proposed

46. ATAD II, Art. 1(1).
47. ATAD II, Art. 1(2).
48. ATAD, Art. 9 (a)(2) defines 'collective investment vehicle' as 'an investment fund or vehicle that is widely held, holds a diversified portfolio of securities and is subject to investor-protection regulation in the country in which it is established'.
49. On the funds' special accounting standards, *see* St Giles, Alexeeva & Buxton, *supra* note 29, at 261 et seq.
50. EU Savings Directive: Council Directive 2003/48/EC of 3 June 2003 on taxation of savings income in the form of interest payments [2003] OJ L157/38 (repealed in 2016).
51. Council Directive 77/799/EEC of 19 December 1977 concerning mutual assistance by the competent authorities of the Member States in the field of direct taxation, [1977] OJ L 336/15 (hereinafter: 'Mutual Assistance Directive').

in 2008 its amendment in order to extend information exchange by trusts, pensions, investment funds and 'other innovative financial instruments'.[52]

Prior to the Savings Directive's repeal, in December 2014, the European Council adopted DAC2, amending provisions on the mandatory automatic exchange of information between tax administrations and extending the scope of Directive 2011/16/EU both with regard to the procedure, the information and the income covered.

According to the Directive, any qualifying reporting financial institution is obliged to report information to the tax authorities on reportable persons and transactions. 'Financial Institutions' include, according to the Directive, a Custodial Institution, a Depository Institution, an Investment Entity or a Specified Insurance Company.[53] Following the definitions of what constitutes an 'Investment Entity' for the DAC2 purposes, one can easily infer that most investment funds qualify as 'Reporting Financial Institutions', and in some cases also as 'Custodial Institutions'.[54] Similarly in a FATCA context, (foreign/EU based) investment funds, mutual funds, intermediaries and private equity funds are also considered to be Foreign Financial Institutions (FFIs) and are obliged to report information about their United States account holders to the IRS.

The Directive considers, however, certain financial institutions as posing a low risk of tax evasion and, hence, those are excluded from the reporting obligations. These are referred to as 'Non-Reporting Financial Institutions' (NRFIs). DAC2 provides a definition thereof, which includes any financial institution that is:

> (b) a Broad Participation Retirement Fund; a Narrow Participation Retirement Fund; a Pension Fund of a Governmental Entity, ... (c) any other Entity that presents a low risk of being used to evade tax ... provided that the status of such Entity as a Non-Reporting Financial Institution does not frustrate the purposes of this Directive; (d) an Exempt Collective Investment Vehicle; or (e) a trust to the extent that the trustee of the trust is a Reporting Financial Institution and reports all information required to be reported pursuant to Section I with respect to all Reportable Accounts of the trust.[55]

In order to qualify as an NRFI, each of these funds must satisfy other requirements specified in the Directive, which include, *inter alia*, that the fund 'is generally exempt from tax on investment income, or taxation of such income is deferred or taxed at a reduced rate, due to its status as a retirement or pension plan'.[56]

Directive 2014/107/EU asked Member States to provide the Commission with a list of NRFIs and 'Excluded Accounts' under the Common Reporting Standards by end of July 2015.[57] Both NRFIs and 'Excluded Accounts', which are to be defined by the national law of the Member States, are excluded from reporting. In the list that the

52. Proposal for a Council Directive amending Directive 2003/48/EC on taxation of savings income in the form of interest payments, COM(2008) 727 final.
53. *See* DAC2, Annex 1, Section VIII (A) no. 3.
54. *See ibid.*, A (4) and (6).
55. DAC2, Annex I, Section VIII b.
56. DAC2, Annex I, Section VIII b, 5(c)(1).
57. DAC2, Art. 1(2)(e).

Member States gave to the Commission, wherever NRFIs were provided, they included notably different types of pension funds.[58]

§8.05 THE AMLD: TAX REPERCUSSIONS FOR FUNDS

Since the adoption of Directive (EU) 2016/2258 on the provision of access to anti-money-laundering information by tax authorities, the 4th AMLD has become relevant for tax purposes.

Trusts and financial institutions, including '(c) an investment firm as defined in point (1) of Article 4(1) of Directive 2004/39/EC' and '(4); (d) a collective investment undertaking marketing its units or shares;' fall under the scope of the Directive and are considered as 'obliged entities'.[59] Consequently, the Directive does not apply to non-corporate fund structures like unit trusts[60] or common contractual funds.[61] The 4th AMLD obliges investment funds to identify and verify the beneficial owners of its units or shares, whether they are direct investors/shareholders holding more than 25% of the shares or whether they use intermediary corporate entities to invest in the fund. In practical terms, this means that funds falling within the scope of the Directive need to conduct an analysis of their investors and shareholders to determine if a beneficial owner exists.[62] This exercise is more demanding for corporate funds, in particular where there are nominee arrangements in place and, hence, the fund is unlikely to hold the relevant information on beneficial ownership.[63]

The Member States must ensure that the information on beneficial ownership provided by the obliged entities is held in a central register in each Member State which is accessible to competent authorities and financial intelligence units (FIUs), obliged entities when carrying out customer due diligence measures and those who can demonstrate a 'legitimate interest' in that information.[64]

With the adoption of Directive (EU) 2016/2258, this information will become available to the national tax authorities, in an attempt to minimize tax avoidance by any potential 'hidden' beneficial owners.

---

58. Many Member States did not list any entities to be treated as NRFIs. See List of entities that are to be treated as NRFIs for the purposes of subparagraph B.1(c) of Section VIII of Annex I of Council Directive 2011/16/EU [2015] OJ C 362/13. Belgium included in its list in addition to pension funds also mutual funds ('*fonds communs de placement* or FCP))'.
59. 4th AMLD, Arts 2(1) and 3(2).
60. In this case the collective investment is constituted under a trust deed in order to establish a trust, an Anglo-American legal form.
61. In this case the invested capital is pooled as separate property, the ownership of which lies with the investment company in its capacity as a fiduciary or with the investors as co-owners.
62. Beneficial owner in the context of the 4th AMLD refers to 'any natural person(s) who ultimately owns or controls the customer and/or the natural person(s) on whose behalf a transaction or activity is being conducted.' For a list of who could constitute a beneficial owner and under what circumstances, *see* Art. 3(6) of the 4th AMLD.
63. Maples and Calder Update, *The Beneficial Ownership Regulations 2016: Implications and Recommended Actions for Funds*, Maples and Calder, https://www.maplesandcalder.com/fileadmin/uploads/maples/Documents/PDFs/The_Beneficial_Ownership_Regulations_2016__Implications_and_Recommended_Actions_for_Funds.PDF (last visited 1 July 2017).
64. 4th AMLD, Art. 30(3), (4), (5).

§8.06 THE TAX MERGER DIRECTIVE

The European Commission had already noted in 2006 that '[I]n the absence of a facilitating EU framework, fund mergers are complex, time consuming and expensive - where at all possible.'[65] This becomes all the more problematic with regard to cross-border funds' mergers because of the many differences in the treatment of funds. In order to, *inter alia*, facilitate cross-border fund mergers and address the problems that arise therefrom, the EU Commission suggested to amend the UCITS Directive. These efforts resulted in the revision of the UCITS legal framework until then and the adoption of the UCITS IV Directive.

Among the many problems that might arise in the context of cross-border fund mergers, the Commission also identified the possible adverse tax consequences for investors. While it noted that these problems should be eliminated and it acknowledged that most UCITS do not qualify for the Tax Merger Directive, it added that:

> As far as *taxation* of cross-border UCITS mergers is concerned, the Commission considers it preferable to build on relevant case law of the European Court of Justice. This route seems more promising than tabling proposals for tax harmonization which will require unanimous support of 27 Member States. On the basis of European Court of Justice case-law, the Commission will come forward with a Communication to clarify that national tax-arrangements should be extended to mergers involving funds domiciled in another Member State.[66]

Consequently, the regulation of the mergers of UCITS and non-UCITS funds is not comprehensively addressed neither in the UCITS IV directive nor in the tax merger directive, and the latter is examined first.

The qualifying companies under the Tax Merger Directive bear the same characteristics as the ones under the PSD. Article 3, thus, provides that for a company to fall within the scope of the tax merger directive, it has to take one of the legal forms listed in Annex I, Part A; be a resident of a Member State for tax purposes and (the company) be subject to one of the taxes listed in Annex I, Part B, without the possibility of an option or of being exempt, without the possibility of an option. With regard to the latter requirement, one could argue that in light of the similar wording used in the PSD and the Tax Merger Directive, the recent CJEU judgment that interpreted the 'subjection to tax' requirement as, effectively, a 'liability to tax' requirement can by analogy apply also to the personal scope requirements of the tax merger directive.[67] However, the different scope and rationale of the two directives (avoidance of double taxation for the PSD as opposed to ensuring that cross-border reorganizations are tax neutral for the Tax Merger Directive) would possibly point to a different conclusion. Indeed, different Member States have opted for a 'clear' subjection to tax solution, for instance, Italy and Spain only require that the company be viewed as a taxable person, while Sweden

65. EU Commission, White Paper on enhancing the Single Market Framework for Investment Funds, 15 November 2006.
66. *Ibid.*, at 6–7.
67. *Wereldhave Belgium and Others*, C-448/15.

requires that the company actually pay corporate tax in an amount that is not negligible.[68]

In view of these criteria, as with the PSD and as the Commission noted in its White Paper,[69] the applicability of the Tax Merger Directive to funds will be limited.

The Tax Merger Directive, however, includes provisions on hybrid entities that could apply to funds. With regard to the personal scope and the potential mismatches that might arise as a result of the different treatment of the hybrid entities, already in the preamble it is stated that:

> [W]hile the companies listed in Annex I, Part A are corporate taxpayers in their Member State of residence, some of them may be considered to be fiscally transparent by other Member States. In order to preserve the effectiveness of this Directive, Member States treating non-resident corporate taxpayers as fiscally transparent should grant the benefits of this Directive to them. However, Member States should have the option not to apply the relevant provisions of this Directive when taxing a direct or indirect shareholder of those taxpayers.[70]

Consequently, if an entity meets the Article 3 requirements, it will be considered a company and should be granted the benefits of the Directive, irrespective of the fact that another Member State may classify that entity as transparent for domestic tax purposes. These benefits, however, *may* be denied to the direct or indirect shareholders of funds that are treated as transparent by the other Member State.

An analysis of the tax merger directive or a comment on its shortcomings does not fall under the scope of this contribution. Instead, the focus will lay on the Tax Merger Directive provisions applicable to hybrid entities. A funds' cross-border merger by absorption is schematically presented in Figure 8.2. The different possibilities that may arise with regard to the treatment of the transferring fund as opaque or transparent are discussed below.

68. Simon Xuereb, *Addressing the Tax Consequences of UCITS IV Cross-Border Mergers in Europe: Extending the Merger Directive as a Solution? – Part 1*, 52 ET, 215, 222 (2012) with references listed therein.

69. *See supra* note 65.

70. Council Directive 2009/133/EC of 19 October 2009 on the common system of taxation applicable to mergers, divisions, partial divisions, transfers of assets and exchanges of shares concerning companies of different Member States and to the transfer of the registered office of an SE or SCE between Member States [2009] OJ L 310/34, as amended (hereinafter 'Tax Merger Directive'), Preamble Recital 8.

Figure 8.2 Funds' Cross-Border Merger by Absorption

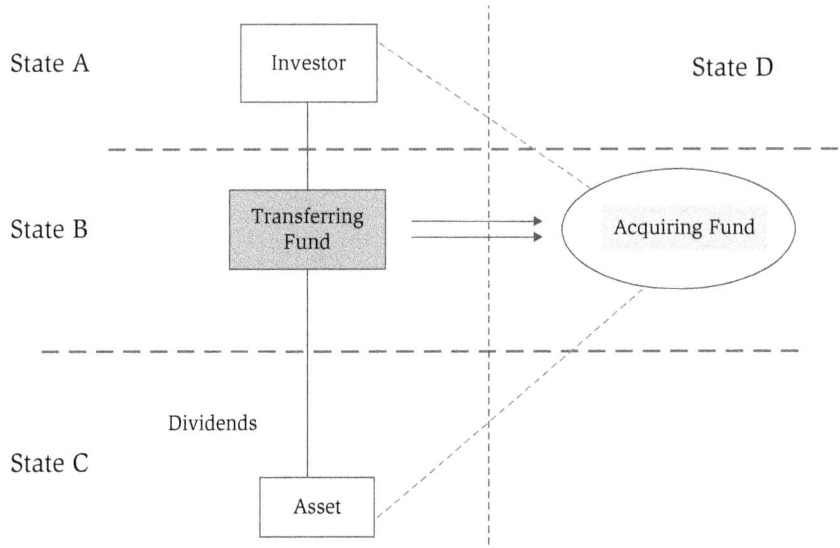

For the Tax Merger Directive's benefits to apply (tax deferral), a taxable event has to be recognized and then the merger itself has to trigger taxation. For instance, if the transferring fund is treated by State B as transparent, then the 'realized' capital gains are disregarded in the hands of the fund. In some cases, State B might also opt to provide for a deferral or exclusion of different types of income at either the fund or the investor level in order to provide tax benefits to the investment funds that would not typically be available through direct investment.[71] In all the aforementioned cases, the two possible outcomes would be either the non-recognition of the taxable event or the recognition and exemption of the transaction.[72]

Things are more straightforward if State B treats the transferring fund as opaque. Then, the merger-induced transfer of assets would be recognized as a taxable event, and the disposal of the assets would give rise to a taxable gain.

In either of the aforementioned scenarios where the 'exit' state considers that the exit of the transferring fund and its absorption by the acquiring fund gives rise to a taxable event and a deemed realization of gains (resulting from the deemed disposal of assets), the Tax Merger Directive does not restrict the 'exiting' state (State B) from imposing a tax.[73] However, depending on the type of taxation imposed (immediate, optional, provision of bank guarantees, etc.), the exit tax may be found to be incompatible with the fundamental freedoms in accordance with the CJEU case law.[74]

71. What Simon Xuereb calls the 'tax-advantaged prototype' in Xuereb, *supra* note 68, 219.
72. Simon Xuereb, *Addressing the Tax Consequences of UCITS IV Cross-Border Mergers in Europe: Extending the Merger Directive as a Solution? – Part 2*, 52 ET, 290, 291 (2012).
73. *Ibid.*
74. *See* for instance *DMC*, C-164/12, Judgment, EU:C:2014:20.

In the likely scenario that State B does not tax the fund (whether nominally or effectively) it allows capital gains to accumulate within the fund without being subject to tax. This results in the investors' deferral of tax liability until the taxable event occurs, i.e., the alienation of the investor's interest in the fund and the subsequent deemed disposal of the assets. In this scenario, State B facing the risk, by reason of the merger, of losing the right to tax the non-resident investor on any unrealized gains in the current value of the units may attempt to collect such tax due on the unrealized gain upon exit by way of imposing an exit tax.[75]

With respect to *shareholders/investors*, Article 8(1) of the Tax Merger Directive provides that:

> on a merger, division or exchange of shares, the allotment of securities representing the capital of the receiving or acquiring company to a shareholder of the transferring or acquired company in exchange for securities representing the capital of the latter company shall not, of itself, give rise to any taxation of the income, profits or capital gains of that shareholder.[76]

In these triangular cases, however, it is not only the perspective of the 'exiting' state (State B) that matters with respect to the hybrid entity's (the fund's) treatment. It is not unlikely in these hybrid situations that while State B treats the fund as opaque and as a corporate resident, the State of the investor (State A) treats the fund as transparent. In this case State A would tax the investor directly on his share in the fund as it arises. Article 4(3) of the Tax Merger Directive was inserted in 2007 in order to ensure that State A would still apply the Directive's benefits in this aforementioned scenario. Therefore, according to Article 4(3), a Member State, which considers a non-resident *transferring company* to be fiscally transparent and hence taxes the participants directly on their share in the company's profits as they arise, must refrain from taxing any income, profits or capital gains calculated by reference to the difference between the real values of the assets and liabilities transferred and their values for tax purposes.

While this provision is straightforward and resolves at least one type of mismatch, Article 11 of the Tax Merger Directive allows in our scenario State A to opt out of the Directive when taxing a direct or indirect shareholder of that company in respect of the income, profits or capital gains of that company.[77] If, however, State A exercises its right to tax the investor, then according to Article 11(2) it has to give relief for the

75. Xuereb, *supra* note 72, at 293.
76. Article 8(3) makes specific reference to another type of 'hybridity', that is, cases where a Member State considers the *shareholder* to be *fiscally transparent*. While this scenario is not unlikely in the context of funds, it is very remotely relevant for our funds-focused analysis and will thus not be addressed in this chapter. This more complicated scenario would materialize through the involvement of another State (State E) where an(other) investor with a shareholding in State A is resident. In this example, if State E considers the investor in State A to be fiscally transparent, then Art. 8(3) prohibits that residence State E to tax those persons on income, profits or capital gains from the allotment of securities representing the capital of the receiving or acquiring company to the shareholder.
77. Article 11(1) of the Tax Merger Directive reads as follows: 'Where a Member State considers a non-resident transferring or acquired company to be fiscally transparent on the basis of that Member State's assessment of the legal characteristics of that company arising from the law

tax which, but for the provisions of this Directive, would have been charged on the fiscally transparent company on its income, profits or capital gains, in the same way and in the same amount as that Member State would have done if that tax had actually been charged and paid. Consequently, the combination of these provisions can be summarized as follows: State A is in principle allowed to levy tax (by virtue of Article 11(1)), on the occasion of a merger or share exchange operation, in the amount of the difference between the tax it would levy itself on the capital gain becoming visible in the operation, and the tax that State B would levy on that gain if the latter were not precluded from levying tax by the Directive.[78]

Conversely, in the scenario where the investor's state (State A) considers the *receiving/acquiring fund* to be fiscally transparent (on the basis of its domestic law), it *shall have the right* not to apply Article 8(1), (2) and (3), that is, it has the right to tax the allotment of shares to the resident investors.[79] However, if it opts to do so, it must treat the non-resident fund as if it were a resident company. Consequently, it must tax the allotment of shares to the direct or indirect shareholders in the same way as if the operation was entirely domestic.[80] The same, non-discriminatory treatment would probably also be guaranteed under the fundamental freedoms and the CJEU's case law.

In the hybrid-specific provisions of the Directive, the assessment of the fund as transparent or opaque lies on the Member State of the investor/shareholder (State A). If State A assesses the non-resident fund as fiscally transparent on the basis of that Member State's (State A) assessment of the legal characteristics of the transferring or acquired fund (Article 11(1) and (2)) or of the acquiring or receiving fund (Article 11(3) and (4)) *arising from the law under which it is constituted*, - State B and State D respectively - then, it (State A) shall have the right not to apply the provisions of this Directive when taxing a direct or indirect shareholder of the fund in respect of the income, profits or capital gains of it. The Directive, thus, by making reference to the company or partnership law characteristics under which the fund is constituted does not consider as relevant (for the assessment of the fund as transparent or not by State A) the fiscal treatment of the fund in its respective state (B or D).

The treatment of the fund (whether it is treated as opaque or transparent) is not relevant for State C which, if it recognizes a change in the legal ownership of the assets, will probably consider this transfer as a taxable event.[81] In this case, and on the usually fulfilled condition, in this context, that the underlying assets are not considered as a PE of the fund, then their transfer does not fall within the scope of the Directive.[82]

---

under which it is constituted, it shall have the right not to apply the provisions of this Directive when taxing a direct or indirect shareholder of that company in respect of the income, profits or capital gains of that company.'

78. Ben J.M. Terra and Peter J. Wattel, *European Tax Law*, 517 et seq. (2012).
79. Tax Merger Directive, Art. 11(3).
80. Tax Merger Directive, Art. 11(4).
81. In a tax treaty context and pursuant to Art. 13 (1), (4) and (5) OECD MC, the taxability of the event by State C will depend of course on the nature of the assets, *see* Xuereb, *supra* note 72, at 291–292.
82. According to Art. 4(2)(b) of the Tax Merger Directive, the directive and its benefits apply only to those assets and liabilities of the transferring company which, in consequence of the merger, division or partial division, are effectively connected with a permanent establishment of the

§8.07 CONCLUSION

The analysis so far has demonstrated that 'funds' - both UCITS and non-UCITS - do not enjoy a particular place in the EU tax directives. On the contrary, in almost all cases, because of their hybrid nature and their non-subjection to tax, they are not even covered *ratione personae* by the Directives. Conversely, the fund-specific secondary law does not include any provisions with regard to the tax treatment of the funds. This fragmented approach that draws from the reliance on domestic law(s) with regard to the taxation of funds creates legal uncertainty and might give rise to 'clashes' between the indirect consequences of the 'finance-specific' directives and the tax directives.[83]

This absence should not come as a surprise. One of the difficulties in establishing a common legal framework with regard to the taxation of funds, in addition to the inherent difficulty in adopting any secondary legislation in direct taxation, lays on the many possible variations with regard to their legal form and the treatment of the fund by the Member States, its investment choices and its structures. As shown above, in most cases the Directives could be of use in the structures *beneath (or above)* the fund.

This finding is better demonstrated in the context of the ATAD. In this case, the *ratio legis* behind some funds' exclusion from the ATAD seems to be the belief that funds are not susceptible to tax avoidance and tax evasion. While there are good reasons to believe that, given the fact that most funds are either treated as transparent or tax exempted, it is doubtful whether all these funds should be *a priori* exempted. The danger of tax avoidance and/or tax evasion remains, however, present *above* or *beneath* the fund as the DAC shows. In contrast to the ATAD, in DAC2, effectively, only pension funds were found as posing a low risk of tax evasion and were, thus, excluded. Conversely, reporting financial institutions include seemingly all other types of funds, whether those are acting as investment funds or custodial or employ a depositary.[84] Hence, while the fund itself does not, in most cases, pose a direct risk of tax avoidance (or tax evasion), its structures can be employed by the shareholder/investor in order to avoid or to evade taxes.

---

receiving company in the Member State of the transferring company and play a part in generating the profits or losses taken into account for tax purposes.

83. *See* for example in the mergers case, *supra*, §8.06.

84. *See* similar the 4th AMLD, *supra*, §8.05.

PART III Funds in International Tax Law and Policy

CHAPTER 9

Non-collective Investment Funds under BEPS Action 6 Versus European Investment Fund Law

Dirk A. Zetzsche

§9.01 INTRODUCTION

Looking at collective investment schemes from a financial law perspective seems to stand in harsh contrast to the OECD's perspective as expressed in the materials to BEPS Item 6. While financial lawyers emphasize the *use* of collective investment schemes - for manifold-financial relationships involving individuals and intermediaries - the word *abuse* can be often found in the BEPS Item 6 materials.

In contrast to this perspective, this chapter argues that the apparent divide between financial law and tax law does not exist, or at least that it is overstated, *if financial law and tax law are properly applied*. For this purpose, it will first outline the OECD's approach to, and concerns with regard to, collective investment schemes in §9.02, and then the financial law's view on investment funds in §9.03. Based on these fundamentals, it will be argued in §9.04 that the OECD's position is suffering from definitional uncertainty; clarifying definitions, however, is far from easy. Drawing on almost a hundred years of financial law, it will be argued that the tax law's definitional uncertainty finds counterparts in financial law - and that it is advisable to employ the financial law's solutions to this uncertainty for remedying the definitional vagueness in tax law to avoid unnecessary structural complexity. Section §9.05 demonstrates how this could work highlighting similarities and differences between the tax and financial law concept of 'transparency' in the context of collective investment schemes. Section §9.06 concludes.

§9.02 THE OECD'S APPROACH

As stated in BEPS Item 6,[1] the OECD's main concern with regard to collective investment schemes is that:

- non-collective investment vehicles (non-CIV) funds may be used to provide treaty benefits to investors that are not themselves entitled to treaty benefits; and
- investors may defer recognition of income on which treaty benefits have been granted.

At the core of this concern is the OECD's definition of (CIV), since it delineates CIV from non-CIV funds. The BEPS Action Items rely on the definition of 'collective investment vehicles' provided in the 2010 OECD Report 'The Granting of Treaty Benefits with Respect to the Income of Collective Investment Vehicles.'[2] According to that definition, a collective investment vehicle:

- is widely held;
- holds a diversified portfolio of securities;
- is subject to investor-protection regulation in its home country;
- must consider limits of leverage;
- must not acquire controlling interests in portfolio companies; and
- manager has discretionary powers to manage the assets.

The role model under that definition is the UCITS (Undertaking for Collective Investment in Transferable Securities) as regulated by the UCITSD 2009/65/EC, as amended. In light of this, it is interesting to note which funds are not CIV within that definition. These include funds:

- where ownership is not widely held, in particular funds with a single or only a few investors;
- that either hold a concentrated portfolio of securities (i.e., one type of securities only) or that hold assets other than securities, in particular real estate, commodities; it is unclear whether the term 'securities' is to be construed broadly or narrowly. In the latter sense, a fund investing in derivatives and other non-securities financial instruments (such as hedge funds) would not qualify as CIV under the OECD's CIV definition;
- that employ leverage (such as hedge funds) or acquire controlling stakes in portfolio companies (such as private equity funds);

1. Cf. OECD/CTPA, BEPS Action 6 Preventing the Granting of Treaty Benefits in Inappropriate Circumstances Issued by Tax Treaties, Transfer Pricing and Financial Transactions Division, http://www.oecd.org/tax/preventing-the-granting-of-treaty-benefits-in-inappropriate-circumstances-action-6-2015-final-report-9789264241695-en.htm (accessed 17 January 2018).
2. *See* OECD, *The Granting Of Treaty Benefits With Respect To The Income Of Collective Investment Vehicles (Adopted By The OECD Committee On Fiscal Affairs On 23 April 2010)*, para. 33, https://www.oecd.org/tax/treaties/45359261.pdf (accessed 17 January 2018).

- that are not subject to investor-protection regulation in its home country; this particular concerns legal regimes that only provide for the private law form of a fund, without at the same time addressing investor concerns;[3]
- where the asset management strategy is determined by the investors themselves or other parties that follow the investors' request.

However, if all CIVs that do not meet the CIV definition were deemed 'non-CIV' for the purposes of BEPS Item 6, the objective of BEPS Item 6 would fail. For instance, even if there are just a handful of investors as long as the influence on the manager is reduced and the portfolio is diversified there is little ground for concern from a tax perspective. This is because in all of these cases the economic rationale for fund investing is sound: investors pool their funds with other investors in a CIV rather than investing directly in order to achieve diversification, professional investment management, liquidity, cost effectiveness and efficient reinvestment of income.

Further, the OECD definition is not precise as to whether the investor protection measures must apply to the manager or the fund. Modern financial law focuses on the manager rather than the fund, with the AIFMD – Europe's framework for managers of Non-UCITS funds – being the eminent example.[4] Finally, the Global Financial Crisis has made it obvious that a regulatory emphasis on funds holding securities only is inadequate; funds investing in infrastructure, as well as certain new and social ventures are equally desirable from a social perspective which is why recent European financial legislation granted European passports to funds focusing on these asset classes. Note that in all of these efforts inadequate or inconsistent taxation is mentioned as one of the main obstacles for smooth cross-border investing.[5]

As the BEPS Item & Working Group has recognized,[6] to which extent BEPS Item 6 applies to investment funds cannot be determined by looking at the 2010 OECD definition of CIV alone. In order to grant the necessary legal certainty, a further narrowing down of cases that provide a reason for concern, and a delineation from cases that do not is of the essence. Accordingly, the OECD continues 'to examine issues related to the treaty entitlement of non-CIV funds to ensure that the new treaty provisions included in the Report on Action 6 address adequately the treaty entitlement of these funds'.

Being aware that a transfer of harmonized European financial law to tax law faces methodological challenges, the legal certainty so crucial for setting up cross-border investment funds can be provided by and is ready to use in, European financial law.

3. Note that the OECD definition is not precise as to whether the investor protection measures must apply on the manager or the fund level. Modern financial law focuses on the manager rather than the fund.
4. *See* Dirk A. Zetzsche, *The Anatomy of European Investment Fund Law,* II.5. (12 April 2017), https://ssrn.com/abstract=2951681 (accessed 17 January 2018).
5. *See* for EuVeCa, Dirk Zetzsche & Christina Preiner, *EuVeCA Verordnung,* in Assmann, Wallach & Zetzsche, *Kapitalanlagegesetzbuch* (Cologne: Otto Schmidt, 2018), Vor § 337 KAGB para. 6 (with further references).
6. *See* OECD, *BEPS ACTION 6 Discussion Draft on non-CIV Examples,* 6 January 2017, p. 2, http://www.oecd.org/tax/treaties/Discussion-draft-non-CIV-examples.pdf (accessed 17 January 2018).

Focusing on what tax law can learn from financial law, we voluntarily disregard technical tax issues, cross-border transfer of information as well as Double Taxation Agreement matters.

§9.03 THE FINANCIAL LAW'S VIEW OF INVESTMENT FUNDS

Investment funds play a crucial role in between the capital supply side where asset owners - private investors from the retail sector or high net worth individuals, or professional investors such as pension funds, insurance undertakings, credit institutions and investment funds - look for investment opportunities and the capital demand side where SMEs, infrastructure and mature business look for capital at the most beneficial terms for them.

[A] Investment Fund as Network of Contracts

From a financial law perspective, investment funds are at the core a mere functional network of contracts set up and run by expert intermediaries, comprising:

- the *fund manager* (in Europe UCITS ManCo or AIFM) who makes the investment decision, but who is also obliged to manage risks and undertake the overall administration (bookkeeping, compliance, tax declarations, reporting, etc., but also valuation) on behalf of the fund. Further, many fund managers (and all UCITS ManCos) are commissioned with the sales of the fund units. Finally, the fund manager controls other service provides, such as the depositary, but also outsourcing partners, such as delegated asset managers, etc.;
- the *depositary* (in Europe a credit institution or investment firm) who holds the fund's assets in custody, or otherwise safeguards them, but also controls the fund manager, and exercises the issue and redemption of fund units. The depositary functions as the point of contact for money flowing to and from the investor, as asset separation rules seek to reduce the manager's access to the client's monies and assets; and
- the *investors* that invest in the fund.

Both intermediaries - fund manager and depositary - oversee each other's activities.[7]

The contractual structure between the three constituencies can legally be characterized as a triangle. The fund(s) is/are at the centre of this arrangement. This holds

7. Cf. Arts 22-26 UCITSD and Commission Delegated Regulation (EU) 2016/438 of 17 December 2015 supplementing Directive 2009/65/EC of the European Parliament and of the Council with regard to obligations of depositaries, OJ L 78/11, 24.3.2016; Art. 21 AIFMD and Ch. IV 'Depositary') of Commission Delegated Regulation (EU) No 231/2013 of 19 December 2012 supplementing Directive 2011/61/EU of the European Parliament and of the Council with regard to exemptions, general operating conditions, depositaries, leverage, transparency and supervision (AIFMD Implementing Regulation).

true even when in practice many services are delegated to specialized service providers or when funds are set up as an investment company that is available in corporate or partnership form (*see* Figure 9.1).

Figure 9.1 Investment Triangle

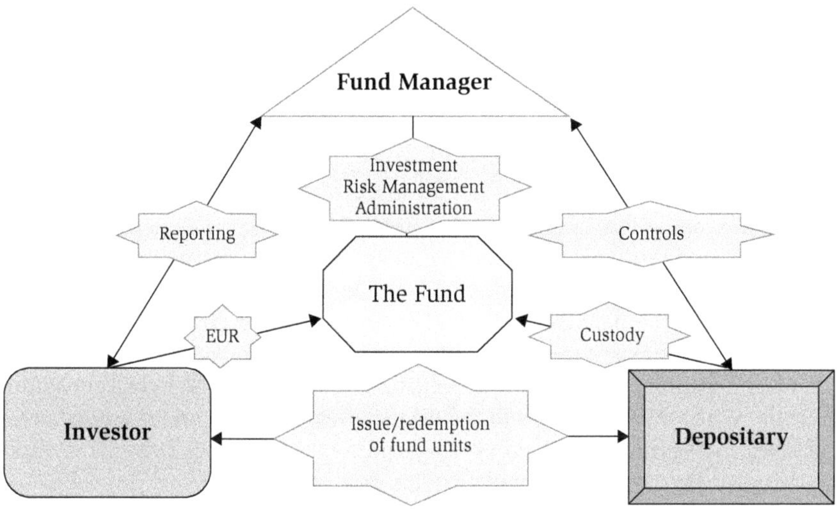

[B] Economic Rationale

The investment triangle shall ensure protection of investors by mandating the best possible check on the intermediary's agency costs, be it by 'stealing' (i.e., charging too high fees, or outright fraud) or by 'shirkung' (i.e., doing nothing, or less than what is possible to prepare and make the best possible decision for investors).

The investment triangle is not an innovation of the European legislature nor was it first established by European financial law. It can be traced back to the golden age of the first Dutch investment funds in the eighteenth century.[8] The triangle has only changed in minor ways over the centuries during its development within Swiss contractual funds and British Income Trusts in the nineteenth century, with the advent of French and Luxembourgish *Organismes de Placement Collectif* and German *Investmentfonds* and UCITS in the twentieth century and with the AIFs of the AIFMD of the early twenty-first century. If an organizational structure has survived for such a long time with no significant changes (and at first without mandatory law) despite the significant bargaining power of sophisticated investors, we may conclude that it can provide an effective balance between the interests of intermediaries and investors.

8. Cf. W.H. Berghuis, *Ontstaan en Ontwikkeling van de Nederlandse Beleggingsfondsen tot 1914*, 46 (Van Gorcum & Comp 1967); for a detailed account of investment fund's history *see* Dirk Zetzsche, *Prinzipien der kollektiven Vermögensanlage*, 275–430 (Tübingen: Mohr Siebeck, 2015).

Today, the investment triangle is part of European legislation for both retail and institutional fund managers.[9] However, we note that the AIFMD's adoption of the triangle structure necessitated some changes to the structure of AIFs in some countries.[10]

The rationale behind the investment triangle becomes obvious when taking into account the managers' and depositaries' capital requirements and returns from being engaged in a collective investment scheme. The manager's own investment in the fund is low, in relative terms although the returns may be quite large. For instance, a carried interest or performance premium could result in a very large return for the manager's key staff, while only investors suffer when fund management results in losses. Further, due to information asymmetry investors may face difficulties in taking legal action against fund managers.

By contrast, depositaries under European law are not allowed to benefit from the fund's performance as this creates a conflict of interest with its safekeeping and control obligations. The depositaries are subject to (quite high) bank capital requirements and can gain at best a low but stable return. If the fund investment fails, investors are inclined to pursue the bank with the higher likelihood of having their losses reimbursed. Depositaries aware of their position seek to intensify controls and make sure that fund managers act in line with the obligations laid down in the fund's constituting documents. While there are limits to the depositaries' liabilities under European law, the prospect of yearlong legal proceedings pushes depositaries towards a careful approach whenever risks are involved. This risk-averse depositary functions as a counter-weight to the fund manager's appetite for risk.[11]

The above is subject to two qualifications, however. First, we see fund managers focusing on the fund's administration and risk management only while the asset management and its positive potential is outsourced to external risk managers. In this case, the fund manager's incentive structure is similar to that of the depositary; depositaries and administrator-fund managers together keep tight control over the asset manager's activities. Second, the depositary triangle is ineffective at controlling the fund manager's activities when depositary and fund manager collude. For this reason, regulation was put in place to deal with conflicts in case the fund manager and depositary belong to the same group of companies.[12]

9. Cf. Arts 22–26 UCITSD; Art. 21 AIFMD.
10. *See* in particular, J. Siena, *Depositary Liability – A Fine Mess and How to Get Out of It*, pp. 531–572, and Dirk Zetzsche, *AIFMD, (Prime) Brokerage*, pp. 573–606 (2nd ed., Wolters Kluwer 2015).
11. *See* Dirk Zetzsche, *Prinzipien der kollektiven Vermögensanlage*, 507–535 (Tübingen: Mohr Siebeck, 2015).
12. *See* Arts 23, 24 Commission Delegated Regulation (EU) 2016/438 of 17 December 2015 supplementing Directive 2009/65/EC of the European Parliament and of the Council with regard to obligations of depositaries, OJ L 78/11, 24.3.2016.

[C] Minimum Substance as Precondition of the Investment Triangle

The investment triangle works best if both intermediaries involved - manager and depositary - can be held accountable for complying with their legal obligations. The triangle structure is less efficient if the two intermediaries involved do not properly engage to fulfil their duties. For that reason, economic wisdom suggests that the intermediaries shall have sufficient capital and resources invested as a precondition for being involved in the investment triangle. Only then can investors and financial supervisors hold the intermediaries accountable.

This economic rationale is backed-up by regulation. The regulatory requirement that shall ensure sufficient capabilities and resources for that purpose is the so-called substance requirement, or prohibition of letterbox entities deeply engrained in European financial law.[13] According to financial law,[14] all intermediaries involved in the investment fund must be able to justify its entire delegation structure, ensure that outsourcing does not prevent the effectiveness of supervision, and provide for sufficient resources and expertise at the 'effective place of management' which is the place of asset and risk management in the case of fund managers, and the place of safekeeping and custody in the case of depositaries. This requirement is not only detailed in plenty of rules surrounding the fund manager and the depositary, but also a key rationale for enforcing financial law.

A field of law where the minimum substance matters, in particular, is outsourcing. Due to Brexit, the importance of minimum substance has been discussed in particular in the context of poorly capitalized subsidiaries outsourcing value-creating services to well-capitalized mother or sister companies in other countries (most likely the UK).[15] A race to the bottom with regard to minimum substance would outsource profit opportunities to other entities (and, most likely, to other countries such as the UK), while the risks for investors and the economy remain in the country of authorization. Such an unbalanced move would be not only detrimental for the national economy, but it would also undermine the efficiency of supervision if subsidiaries were so poorly equipped by their parents that the supervisory or resolution authorities could not access assets and business links in a crisis, and reorganize the firm.[16] In this context, ESMA has reminded Member States of the need for the uniform application of

13. *See* Dirk Zetzsche, Drittstaaten im Bank- und Finanzmarktrecht in Gregor Bachmann & Burkhard Breig, Finanzmarktregulierung zwischen Innovation und Kontinuität in Deutschland, Europa und Russland (Tübingen, Germany: Mohr, 2014), at 86–90.
14. For AIF, *see* Art. 20(1) lit. a, e, f AIFMD, as detailed in Art. 82 of Commission Delegated Regulation (EU) No 231/2013 of 19 December 2012 supplementing Directive 2011/61/EU of the European Parliament and of the Council with regard to exemptions, general operating conditions, depositaries, leverage, transparency and supervision; in a less detailed manner, *see also* Art. 13 UCITSD.
15. *See* Matthias Lehmann & Dirk Zetzsche, Brexit and the Consequences for Commercial and Financial Relations between the EU and the UK, 27 Eur. Bus. L.J. 99 (2016); Matthias Lehmann & Dirk Zetzsche, How Does It Feel To Be a Third Country? The Consequences of Brexit for Financial Market Law, in Centre for International Governance Innovation (CIGI) & British Institute of International and Comparative Law (BIICL), Brexit (2018) at 117.
16. For more details, *see* Dirk Zetzsche, *supra* note 13 at 86–90.

European Union (EU) law and of avoiding regulatory and supervisory arbitrage.[17] In particular, ESMA warns against too generous outsourcing to British headquarters, which enables the creation of letterbox companies from which the whole EU market is served. The warning is important and meaningful, considering ESMA's coordinating function in applying financial law and its power to solve disputes between national supervisors, especially in the area of asset management and market infrastructure.[18]

As a minimum, the personnel of the subsidiary must be capable of coping with subsidiary's operative business, as well as providing its internal control system (comprising compliance, risk management and internal audit[19]) independently of the parent company.[20] In addition, the efficient enforcement of EU law requires that the branch's data and servers work independently of the parent company and keep functioning in case of a breakdown in the parent company. This implies the need for a suitable hierarchy of reading and editing rights, a diversified selection of providers, as well as operation guarantees bespoke to EU countries, for instance, in the area of cloud computing.

The summary of this discussion is evidence of one aspect important for tax law: *minimum substance is not only a concern in tax law, but also financial law.* And, the day-to-day business of financial law authorities is enforcing the prohibition of letterbox entities on the side of intermediaries, and if necessary revoke the license in the case that the intermediaries do not maintain the substance necessary for providing the services laid down in their contractual and financial law obligations. And, given the day-to-day contact between the financial law authorities and the supervised entities and intensive information flow from the latter to the former mandated in contemporary investment fund law,[21] we could assume that the former know what they do; it is safe to say that the financial law substance requirement is a bottom line on which tax law could rely.

17. Cf. ESMA, General Principles To Support Supervisory Convergence In The Context Of The UK Withdrawing From The EU, 31 May 2017, ESMA42-110-433.
18. Cf. Regulation (EU) No 1095/2010 of the European Parliament and of the Council of 24 November 2010 establishing a European Supervisory Authority (European Securities and Markets Authority), amending Decision No 716/2009/EC and repealing Commission Decision 2009/77/EC, 15 December 2010, [2010] OJ, L 331/84 (entered into force 16 December 2010) [hereinafter: 'ESMA Regulation'], Art. 19; Zetzsche & Eckner, *supra* note 5, § 7A para. 92; Zetzsche & Preiner, *supra* note 5, § 7B para. 105.
19. Cf. *MiFID II*, *supra* n. 9, Art. 16(2), 16(5); Commission Delegated Regulation (EU) 2017/565 of 25 April 2016 supplementing Directive 2014/65/EU of the European Parliament and of the Council as regards organizational requirements and operating conditions for investment firms and defined terms for the purposes of that Directive, 31 March 2017, [2017] OJ, L 87/1, Arts 22–24 (entered into force 20 April 2017).
20. ECB, *Relocating To The Euro Area (2017)*, www.bankingsupervision.europa.eu/banking/relocating/html/index.en.html (accessed 17 January 2018) ('Banks in the euro area should be capable of managing all material risks potentially affecting them independently and at the local level, and should have control over the balance sheet and all exposures').
21. *See*, for example, the details of information to be provided on a regular basis from the AFIM to national competent authorities laid down in the Annex to AIFMD Commission Implementing Regulation 2013/231. For a discussion, *see* Zetzsche, Arner, Buckley, Weber, *Europe's Big-Bang in RegTech*, forthcoming.

[D] Investor Passivity as Precondition of the Investment Triangle

Another concern addressed in the OECD's definition of collective investment vehicle is (undue) influence of investors on the fund's investment policy. The tax-law rationale is: if investors have influence on individual investment decisions the investment decisions could be designed to achieve tax rather than investment benefits.

With a slightly different angle, these concerns are mirrored in financial law. The regulatory requirement of third-party investment management excludes funds self-managed by investors and investment clubs whose investors participate in the making of investment decisions from the scope of undertakings of collective investments.[22] On the one hand, the rationale of the triangle structure is mandated in order to defend the passive investor who puts its trust into the intermediaries it has chosen and paid to make investment decisions on its own behalf. Given that there is more than one investor in the fund,[23] if the manager would follow one investor's orders, it would treat unequally the other investors that have simultaneously invested in the fund and put them potentially at a disadvantage. Further, the fees paid to manager and depositary for controlling each other would be wasted (although this waste may payout from an individual's perspective if the gains from tax benefits are greater than the losses incurred by the fees).

Again, the passivity requirement is laid down in regulation. In particular, the fund managers' discretion to make investment decisions independent from the investors - so-called Third Party Management requirement - is a crucial feature of the definition of European investment-fund law.[24] If the manager follows an investor's orders, it is not subject to regulation by the European investment-fund law laid down, in particular, in the UCITSD or AIFMD, but subject to the MiFID/MiFIR framework or no European financial law altogether.

Admittedly, various ways are discussed and practised to ensure *some* investor influence over the life cycle of an investment fund, ranging from appointment of a suitable investment advisor[25] over board appointments to investment committees with investor representatives.[26] But, the point we make here is sound: financial law fights the same fight as tax law, while trying to ensure that fund managers exercise their investment discretion rather than follow individual investor's orders.

---

22. The criterion of third party management is also applied by the ESMA in order to define the AIF, deriving it from the position of AIFM. *See* ESMA/2012/117, No. 34: 'The AIFM or internally managed AIF must have responsibility for the management of the AIF's assets. Investors have day-to-day no discretion or control over these assets.'
23. We will address Single Investor Funds *infra*, §9.04[A].
24. *See* Dirk A. Zetzsche, *The Anatomy of European Investment Fund Law*, V.1.d (12 April 2017), https://ssrn.com/abstract=2951681 (accessed 17 January 2018).
25. Regarding financial instruments, this refers to investment advice which is subject to authorization pursuant to Arts 1 and 3(1), second bullet point MiFID; advice concerning other assets as financial instruments (such as real estate, shares in ship vessels) is not subject to authorization under MiFID.
26. For details, *see* Dirk Zetzsche & Christina Preiner, Scope of the AIFMD, pp. 53–56 in Dirk Zetzsche, *AIFMD* (2nd ed., WoltersKluwer 2015).

[E] Irrelevance of the Legal Form as Precondition of the Investment Triangle

As a third precondition for the investment triangle, the legal form of the investment fund is deemed of so little relevance for financial law purposes that European financial law refrains from stipulating details of the legal form altogether. Rather, it is acknowledged that, depending on the legal tradition of the Member States, the investment fund could take the legal form of contract, trust, corporate and partnership, but also associations and foundations are accepted forms of the investment fund. But, the legal form chosen by the fund promoter, or the investors, respectively, by virtue of their investment decision, does not matter for regulatory purposes, i.e., for investor protection, prevention of systemic risk and the proper functioning of capital markets.

The European financial legislature has solved the integration and recognition of legal forms - which provides a major difficulty in cross-border taxation - with a radical solution: by simply disregarding the legal form and implementing a so-called *functional approach*: If a structure is a collective investment scheme for regulatory purposes[27] it will be subjected to the same financial law and regulation regardless of the legal form.

Since the private law of the Member States on investment funds is subject to the European law's *effet utile* requirement, the functional approach of European investment-fund law also shows effects on the Member States' private law. Accordingly, some modifications of private law are noticeable that are due to the functional approach. For instance, the directors of an investment company must exercise their fiduciary obligations with a view to protecting fund investors rather than pursuing the interests of the shareholders controlling the investment company.[28] Furthermore, European rules on conflicts of laws are influenced by the functional approach that is following from the fact that a split jurisdiction for multiple investment relationships within a fund is undesirable.[29] The results of this development is a specific law for investment funds - in disregard of the legal form, and in full recognition of the structural and organizational particularities of investment fund.[30]

If financial and private law do not assign major importance to the legal form anymore, but focus on a functional approach, it is an oddity that tax law which at its core shall reflect economic realities to remain efficient and counter tax arbitrage and

27. For details on the definition *see* Dirk Zetzsche & Christina Preiner, Scope of the AIFMD, pp. 50-63 in Dirk Zetzsche, *AIFMD* (2nd ed., WoltersKluwer 2015); Dirk A. Zetzsche, *The Anatomy of European Investment Fund Law*, V (12 April 2017), https://ssrn.com/abstract=2951681 (accessed 17 January 2018).
28. *See* Dirk Zetzsche, *Prinzipien der kollektiven Vermögensanlage*, 520-521 (Tübingen: Mohr Siebeck, 2015), with further examples.
29. For details, *see* Dirk Zetzsche, *Das grenzüberschreitende Investmentdreieck*, in Dirk Zetzsche & Matthias Lehmann, *Grenzüberschreitende Finanzdienstleistungen* (Tübingen: Mohr, 2018), § 7, pp. 199-264.
30. *See* Dirk Zetzsche, Prinzipien der kollektiven Vermögensanlage, 549-588 (Tübingen: Mohr Siebeck, 2015); Morley, John D., The Separation of Funds and Managers: A Theory of Investment Fund Structure and Regulation, 123 Yale L.J. 1228 (2014).

tax leakage still does. The differential tax treatment violates the general policy goal of treating economically similar structures similarly.[31]

§9.04 A FINANCIAL LAW SOLUTION TO BEPS ITEM 6 DEFINITIONAL ISSUES

The application of financial law concepts could result in greater certainty and tax law consistency with regard to two widely debated questions re BEPS Item 6,[32] in particular the details of the detailed Limitation on Benefits rule (so-called LOB rule) and the details of the more general Principal Purpose Test (so-called PPT rule). Both questions were so difficult and subject to the contracting parties' particularities that they did not make it into the final version of the BEPS Multilateral Instrument (MLI), resulting in a generic PPT test (in Article 7(1) MLI) and a simplified LOB rule (in Article 7(8–14) MLI). But, the discussion is ongoing since contracting parties can and will agree on a detailed LOB rule in combination with a more sophisticated PPT test (cf. Article 7(16) MLI).

The detailed LOB rule could provide a specific anti-abuse rule similar to LOB articles adopted in many tax treaties, for instance, those concluded by the US. The upside of a detailed LOB rule is the legal certainty stemming from precise criteria employed, while the downside is its openness to circumvention due to its formal character. The PPT rule seeks to grant more flexibility to the tax authorities than the LOB rules, in form and spirit similar to general anti-avoidance rules aimed at preventing treaty abuse and treaty shopping that may not be addressed adequately by the LOB rule due to the former's formal character.

As to the details of the LOB and PPT rules, a look towards financial law could provide some guidance.

[A] Designing the LOB Rule with a View to the 'Widely Held' Criterion

If we look at European financial law, what could the formal criteria of a detailed LOB rule look like?

First, we suggest drawing on the UCITS and AIF definition as provided for Article 1(2) UCITSD and Article 4(1)(a) AIFMD. If we relied on these definitions to narrow down the LOB Rule, all investment funds subject to the UCITSD and the AIFMD as well as their off-spins (EuVeCA, EuSEF, ELTIFR) should be deemed *regulated with a view to protecting investors*.

Further, funds regulated under the UCITSD and AIFMD are funds where the manager of the CIV has *discretionary powers* to manage the assets, as this is the gist of financial law's Third Party Management requirement. At the same time, a tax law

31. The OECD 2010 CIV paper (*supra* note 2) at 4.1. (p. 13), accounts for differential treatment with the (private and financial) legal differences, but since 2010 the landscape of European investment funds law has fundamentally changed due to the implementation of the AIFMD, the ELTIFR, the EuVECA-VO and the EuSEF-VO.
32. *See* Report on BEPS Action 6, paras 19, 25.

consistent with financial law would lead to giving up three criteria of the 2010 CIV definition: (1) holding a diversified portfolio of securities, (2) limits of leverage and (3) not acquiring controlling interests in portfolio companies.

Relying on the Third Party Management requirement of financial law and giving up the remaining three criteria of the 2010 CIV definition is acceptable from a tax policy perspective as long as we can assume that one otherwise fully taxable investor cannot design an investment policy tailor-made to its personal needs and instruct the fund manager to pursue such strategy. Such instructions are likely, only, if the one investor - rather than the fund manager or promoter - is dominating the fund structure. We argued above that legal domination of the fund is non-compliant with financial law, in particular the Third Party Management requirement. So, the true concern, if European investment-fund law applies is that economic incentives lead the fund intermediaries to pursue the one investor's - in contrast to all investors' - interest. Economic domination over the fund structure, however, occurs only if the one investor's invested amounts exceed by far the amounts invested by other investors. These concerns are the core of the 'widely held' requirement in the 2010 CIV definition.

Financial law does not address economic domination adequately: (1) A UCITS shall be distributed to the public, i.e., potentially an unlimited amount of unknown investors, but the UCITSD refrains from stipulating a minimum amount of investors and a minimum distributions of funds invested among investors. (2) An AIF must be potentially open to more than one investor, but no legal requirement prevents the existence of Single Investor Funds if the fund units are offered to one investor only. In ESMA's liberal view there are two cases where the assumption must be made that Single Investor Funds are AIFs:[33] (1) *Potential two-party investor funds:* One investor holds all of the funds' shares but, subject to the constitutive documents of the fund, another investor can acquire units of the fund, and (2) *Single Investor Funds which, when applying the transparency hypothesis, act on behalf of several investors:* Only one investor holds all of the fund's shares but this investor represents a variety of other investors who are thus indirectly associated with the fund. Examples include feeder-funds, trust funds or funds for insurance undertakings or pension funds that hold investment entities for a variety of policyholders or pensioners.

In light of this liberal financial law approach - even if we apply financial law definitions to tax law - tax regulators need to devote some attention to how to ensure that Third Party Management takes place not only on paper but also in practice. This is at the heart of the 2010 CIV definition's 'widely held' criteria.

An adequate definition of 'widely held' must take three aspects into account: (1) the number of investors; (2) the amount invested by each investor; and (3) the economic ('beneficial') ownership of each investor. This is because tax concerns could develop on each of the three levels: First, if only one or very few investors hold fund units economic domination over the structure is likely. Second, equally likely is

33. ESMA/2013/600, *Key concepts of the AIFMD* (24 May 2013), No. 17. This interpretation corresponds to the German definition of the investment fund prior to implementing the AIFMD, *see also* Dirk Zetzsche, *Prinzipien der kollektiven Vermögensanlage* 75–81, 140–143 (Tübingen: Mohr Siebeck 2015).

economic domination if one investor holds a very large stake (let us say 90%), regardless of how many other investors hold fund units. Third, economic domination of the structure could develop from re-concentration on sub-layers of the investment chain. For instance, even if a certain number of investors hold fund units in a balanced way (let us say each of them 10%), one investor could be legally entitled to ask the other investors to sell their fund units to the one investor upon demand, or the one investor could hold the majority of shares in the shareholder meetings of these other investors. In these and many more cases, the one investor's economic dominance over the fund structure is likely.

However, a closer look reveals that criteria (2) and (3) are really just one. This is because the amount invested could change immediately after the investment by virtue of a sale/purchase by the other investors. So what tax policy truly asks for is a constant sufficiently dispersed economic ownership (i.e., that the *number of investors and the economic ownership* need to be set in light of tax considerations only).

An efficient LOB rule would provide thresholds for each of the two criteria. How shall we set these thresholds? Let us assume an investor benefits from adding more equity and investing less in debt after taxes on interests have increased in the investor's home country. Under which conditions is a fund manager likely to invest more in equity once a single investor wishes so? From the perspective of game theory, requiring two investors with antagonistic interests that go beyond the generic joint interest of overall low taxation[34] would suffice to protect the Third Party Management requirement where the fund manager pursues a neutral investor interests rather than an individual investor's interest. The fund manager, avoiding liability for violating the Third Party Management requirement, would not pursue any individual investor's interest. In practice, a nasty deal following cooperation among the investors - leading to equally undesirable *joint* instructions aiming at both investors' overall low taxation - is the more likely the less investors are around. The risk of collusion to circumvent the 'widely held' and Third Party Management requirement diminishes with the number of investors truly independently invested in the fund.[35] If a clear majority stands on the other side (such as 80% of the capital invested), a fund manager will hesitate to adjust the investment strategy to pursue the interests of just one investor by (holding just 20%). Following this insight, and with a view to other international examples a *five investor, 20% threshold* is reasonable.

34. Such antagonistic interests could result, for instance, from different tax domiciles of both investors. Example: Investor A lives in a country where the tax rates on dividends are higher than on interest, while investor B lives in a country where the tax rates on interest are higher than on dividends.
35. If B is the benefit from violating the law and in order to violate the law you need N people to cooperate, and P is the cost (penalty) for each cooperating party, it would be rational to cooperate only if $B/N > P$; as N grows the utility from cooperation shrinks, rendering defection from collusion more likely.

[B] Role of the PPT Rule

The BEPS Item 6 PPT Rule (laid down in Article 7(1) of the BEPS MLI) is a broad sword indeed: Under the PPT rule, where the national tax authority establishes that one of the principal purposes of a fund structure is to obtain treaty benefits (e.g., to obtain tax relief, deferral or refund provided under the treaty), those benefits would be denied unless it can be established that it would be consistent with the object and purpose of the particular provisions to grant such benefits in those circumstances. When compared to traditional *fraus conventinis* clauses, the PPT rule is particularly dangerous in light of its broad wording that enables invoking the PPT rule already if *one* of the principal purposes is to obtain treaty benefits.[36] Taken as it is, no one will deny that tax considerations always play a role, albeit not always a central one, and even less in a strictly regulated environment when deciding upon a certain fund structure. If it remains as it is, national tax authorities would always be open to invoke the PPT rule.

However, if the LOB rule was drafted as suggested herein, the tax authorities' discretion to invoke the PPT rule would be limited by the legislative determinations set out in the LOB rule. This means that the PPT rule would be available only once the LOB rule does not apply; this would mean in the case of non-CIVs if the fund is either not regulated by European financial law (as laid out above) or if it is regulated when it is held by fewer than five investors holding (directly or indirectly) a 20% economic ownership each. In the first case, European financial law has nothing to say, but a brief look across Europe shows that various Single Investor Funds or Special Fund models governed by national law are established within the EU and EEA Member States.[37] In the second case, the tax and the financial law rationale are well aligned since where the Third Party Management principle is put at risk, tax and financial regulators should have a reason to take a closer look, or intervene where necessary.

We do not pretend that the application of the PPT rule, in practice, is without difficulties. Quite the opposite, it will touch upon one of the most difficult questions in investment fund law which is the delineation between 'investment' (EU), or 'securities' (US) respectively, on the one hand, and 'operating business' or 'commercial activity' on the other. While this is not the place to go into details,[38] it suffices to say that this discussion dating back to the 1930s and circulating around whether the non-controlling holding company is a fund or an operating business, has to lead to some degree of certainty that could be utilized for tax law purposes.

36. Cf. Reinout Kok, The Principal Purpose Test in Tax Treaties under BEPS 6, Intertax, Volume 44, Issue 5, pp. 407–411.
37. *See* Dirk Zetzsche, Fondsregulierung im Umbruch – ein rechtsvergleichender Rundblick zur Umsetzung der AIFM-Richtlinie (transl. Changing Paradigms In Fund Regulation? – A Comparative View On The Implementation of the AIFM Directive), Zeitschrift für Bankrecht und Bankwirtschaft (ZBB), 22–40 (2014).
38. *See* Dirk Zetzsche & Christina Preiner, *Scope of the AIFMD*, pp. 70–77 in Dirk Zetzsche, *AIFMD* (2nd ed., WoltersKluwer 2015); Dirk Zetzsche, *Prinzipien der kollektiven Vermögensanlage*, 147–178 (Tübingen: Mohr Siebeck 2015).

[C] And One Step Further ...

The easiest and from the perspective of European countries most certain and predictable solution would connect financial and tax law, in that all entities licensed under UCITSD and AIFMD and their offspring under the ELTIFR, EuVeCa, EuSEFR would be deemed CIV, while non-AIF non-UCITS funds (such as Single Investor Funds or Special Investor Funds) would be subject to a case-by-case review drawing on the PPT rule. For such as step a bilateral tax treaty is inadequate, while the BEPS MLI refrains from making such far-reaching stipulations for the good reason that financial law differs across countries that participate in the MLI. Hence, we argue in favour of legislative action on the EU level.

Admittedly, adopting a financial law concept for tax purposes would widen the OECD's CIV definition significantly, but in a consistent and predictable manner that: (a) furthers the efficiency of European cross-border capital markets, (b) opens new capital for desirable investments across Europe, (c) promotes EU-compliant regulated structures to the disadvantage of lesser regulated fund vehicles, (d) brings down the costs of tax advice, and (e) could be considered by national tax legislatures consistently within their national tax laws without opening new opportunities for tax arbitrage.

Together with the recognition that UCITS and AIF are CIV within the definition the EU and its Member States should implement on the European level one of two rules to apply uniformly across Europe, which is either a full 'transparency' status for the fund (i.e., disregarding the fund for tax purposes entirely) or a Taxable Entity Status with full tax exemptions, for all entities within the scope of the UCITSD and AIFMD, as defined above. While it does not matter which of the two rules is implemented, it matters that only one of the two rules is mandatory and that tax reporting on the respective fund's investment income is standardized across the EU/EEA. In turn, national tax legislators could and would respond to that uniform decision and make adjustments to their national tax laws accordingly.

This bold step would not only lead to significant simplification of cross-border fund taxation but would in the long run benefit tax collectors and investors alike: in line with the BEPS Item 6 policy approach, at least within the EU/EEA arbitrage opportunities would be limited to the national level, while investors would have a better and more transparent view on the European investment fund market, where investors' hunt for the best (i.e., most profitable) fund product is facilitated and unblurred by short-term and (if true) ever-changing and, thus, eventually costly tax arguments.

§9.05 CONCLUSIONS

(1) The OECD's pure, tax lawyer's views blurs established concepts, questions and indicated conclusions. Financial law definitions could help. Closer alignment of tax law and financial regulation is necessary.

(2) Concerns of financial and tax laws are closer than some – and in particular, the OECD BEPS Item 6 Action Plan – would assume. A fund 'managed' by

investors, a fund manager without 'substance' and overly tax-driven structuring are concerns both for tax and for financial law.

(3) OECD-style (country-by-country) tax agreements are harmful to the completion of the EU Single Market and competition on the merits inside the EU/EEA. A harmonized European tax regime for UCITS and AIF would be preferable. Such a harmonized tax regime could include either Tax Transparency or a Taxable Entity Status with full tax exemptions. If CIV tax treatment is harmonized on a European level and associated with uniform reporting requirements, Member States could adjust their national tax laws accordingly.

(4) But also, European investors would benefit from the alignment of European tax and investment fund law. Harmonization of the CIV definition and CIV tax treatment on the European level would remove barriers to cross-border fund investment in Europe, facilitate investor choice regarding fund products, channel investor funds to their most productive use and enhance the efficiency of the European capital markets.

CHAPTER 10

Treaty Entitlement of Funds in the Pre-BEPS World

Daniel Dürrschmidt

§10.01 INTRODUCTION

The application of tax treaties to 'collective investment vehicles' (CIVs) – how investment funds or 'undertakings for collective investment' (UCIs) are often referred to by tax experts[1] – has become an important issue since the funds industry became globalized. Thus, the Organisation for Economic Co-operation and Development (OECD) dealt with the subject and issued a report entitled 'The Granting of Treaty Benefits with Respect to the Income of Collective Investment Vehicles' (hereinafter the 'OECD 2010 CIV Report').[2] Its main considerations and proposals were not incorporated in the OECD Model Tax Convention on Income and on Capital (hereinafter the 'OECD Model'),[3] but in the commentaries published therewith (hereinafter the 'OECD Model Commentary').[4,5] The term 'CIVs' is, in fact, defined by the OECD for tax treaty

1. *See, e.g.*, OECD, *Model Tax Convention on Income and on Capital 2017*, OECD Model Commentary on Art. 1, para. 22 (2017).
2. OECD, *The Granting of Treaty Benefits with Respect to the Income of Collective Investment Vehicles*, 3 (para. 1) (2010). For more details on the OECD 2010 CIV Report, *see* Gijs K. Fibbe, *The 2010 Update of the OECD Commentary on Collective Investment Vehicles, in The Tax Treatment of Collective Investment Vehicles and Real Estate Investment Trusts* 45–71 (Hein Vermeulen ed., 2013).
3. OECD, *Model Tax Convention on Income and on Capital 2017 (Condensed Version)* (2017), available at http://dx.doi.org/10.1787/mtc_cond-2017-en (last accessed 10 January 2018; full version to be published in 2018).
4. The OECD Model includes, among other things, article-specific commentaries, and for the purposes of this Chapter, said article-specific commentaries will be referred to as the 'OECD Model Commentary' (if not referring to specific articles) or the 'OECD Model Comm. on Art. [*X*] [the relevant article]' together with the relevant paragraphs thereof, as appropriate.
5. *See* OECD Model Comm. on Art. 1, para. 22; OECD 2010 CIV Report, at 15 (para. 62).

purposes as 'funds that are widely-held [*sic*], hold a diversified portfolio of securities and are subject to investor-protection regulation in the country in which they are established'.[6] The definition may deviate from the definition of the term 'investment funds' for regulatory law purposes.[7] For the sake of clarity, the analysis in this chapter does not address issues related to real estate investment trusts (REITs),[8] pension funds, or non-CIV funds, such as private equity funds, each of which raises some specific issues that differ from those related to CIVs.[9]

CIVs, investors, and their investments may be located in different countries.[10] In particular, a CIV and its investors do not necessarily have to be based in the same country; they may be - and, within the European Union (EU), are possibly encouraged by regulatory law implementing the UCITS Directive[11] to be - resident in different countries.[12] Concerning the place of investment, investing abroad through a CIV enables its investors to take advantage of, *inter alia*, economies of scale,[13] and allows for risk diversification - a characteristic feature of CIVs[14] - across international markets.[15] The extent of globalization of a country's funds industry may depend on the country's size, since CIVs located in a relatively small country - such as Luxembourg - may have many foreign investors and may be forced to invest assets predominantly outside their home markets.[16]

6. *See* OECD Model Comm. on Art. 1, para. 22; OECD 2010 CIV Report, at 3 (para. 1).
7. *See* Isabelle Riassetto, *supra*, Chapter 1; and Dirk Zetzsche, *supra*, Chapter 9.
8. *See* OECD, *Tax Treaty Issues Related to REITS* (2008) (still the current position of the OECD on tax treaty issues related to REITs). That report was included in OECD Model Comm. on Art. 10, paras 67.1-67.7.
9. For this reason, the treatment of pension funds and non-CIV vehicles under tax treaties is not covered in the OECD's *Preventing the Granting of Treaty Benefits in Inappropriate Circumstances Action 6 - 2015 Final Report*, 15 (paras 11-14) (2015) (hereinafter 'OECD 2015 Inappropriate Circumstances Report'). Meanwhile, in 2017, specific provisions for 'recognised pension funds' were included in Art. 3(1)(i) and Art. 4(1), sentence 1 OECD Model.
10. *See* OECD Model Comm. on Art. 1, para. 22; OECD 2010 CIV Report, at 2-5 (paras 2, 5, 13-16); Bruno da Silva, *Granting Tax Treaty Benefits to Collective Investment Vehicles: A Review of the OECD Report and the 2010 Amendments to the Model Tax Convention*, 39 Intertax 195, 196 (2011); Alexander Rust, *Article 1: Persons Covered, in Klaus Vogel on Double Taxation Conventions*, 112, margin no. 29 (Ekkehart Reimer & Alexander Rust eds, 4th ed., Kluwer Law International 2015) (hereinafter '*Vogel*, 4th ed.'); Sabine Kirchmayr, *Seminar G: Collective Investment Vehicles*, 21 IStR 673 (2012); Giulia Letizia, *International Tax Issues in Relation to Cross-Border Investment Funds*, 43 Intertax 526, 529 (2015).
11. Directive 2009/65/EC of the European Parliament and of the Council of 13 July 2009 on the coordination of laws, regulations and administrative provisions relating to undertakings for collective investment in transferable securities (UCITS), [2009] OJ L 302/32, as amended by: Directive 2014/91/EU of the European Parliament and of the Council of 23 July 2014 amending Directive 2009/65/EC as regards depositary functions, remuneration policies and sanctions, [2014] OJ L 257/186 and Corrigendum to Directive 2014/91/EU of the European Parliament and of the Council of 23 July 2014 amending Directive 2009/65/EC (OJ L 257, 28.8.2014), [2016] OJ L 52/37 (collectively, the 'UCITS Directive').
12. *See* OECD 2010 CIV Report, at 5 (paras 14-16).
13. *See ibid.*, at 3 (paras 1, 4, 8); *see also* Patricia A. Brown, *Fifty Years of Tax Uncertainty: The Problem of International Neutrality for Collective Investment Vehicles, in* Vermeulen ed., *supra* note 2, at 19, 22-25.
14. *See* Riassetto, *supra* note 7; *see also* OECD Model Comm. on Art. 1, para. 22; OECD 2010 CIV Report, at 3 (para. 4).
15. *See* OECD 2010 CIV Report, at 4 (para. 7).
16. *See ibid.*, at 5 (para. 13); Da Silva, *supra* note 10.

It is important to note that tax consequences are not the only 'driver' for using cross-border investment structures. Regulatory law and corporate law are equally important.[17] For example, Luxembourg is an attractive place for the fund industry,[18] since, *inter alia*, its regulatory law is considered very flexible.[19] Nevertheless, tax consequences can significantly impact the investors' return on investment and the CIV's net asset value (NAV).[20] Therefore, they constitute an important criterion in the process of implementing an investment structure. In cross-border investment structures, in particular, international double taxation should be avoided.

The avoidance of international double taxation is the main purpose of tax treaties.[21] Countries with close economic relationships to other countries usually have a dense tax treaty network (e.g., Germany has concluded about one hundred tax treaties and is currently negotiating about fifteen more,[22] while Luxembourg has eighty-one treaties currently *en vigueur*[23] and is negotiating sixteen more, including two replacements for, and one amendment to, existing treaties).[24] Most tax treaties are

17. *See* Bundesregierung, *Entwurf eines Gesetzes zur Modernisierung des Investmentwesens und zur Besteuerung von Investmentvermögen (Investmentmodernisierungsgesetz)*, BT-Drucksache 15/1553, at 65 (para. 1) (2003).
18. The funds industry is an important business sector in Luxembourg. *See* Hans-Ulrich Lauermann & Christian Birker, *Investmentfonds im neuen DBA Luxemburg – ein Überblick*, 3 RdF 51 (2013). As of October 2017, the Association of the Luxembourg Fund Industry (ALFI) reported that net assets under management in Luxembourg funds were approximately EUR 4,135.7 billion. *See* www.alfi.lu/sites/alfi.lu/files/files/Statistics/Luxembourg/ouverture_section_statistique_chiffres_du_mois.pdf (last accessed 10 January 2018). This is a significant portion of the net value of assets managed by CIVs worldwide. *See* OECD 2010 CIV Report, at 4 (para. 6); European Fund and Asset Management Association (EFAMA), International Statistical Report Q-2 2017, Worldwide Regulated Open-ended Fund Assets and Flows, Trends in the Second Quarter of 2017, available at www.efama.org/Publications/Statistics/International/Quarterly%20%20International/170928_International%20Statistical%20Release%20Q2%202017.pdf (last accessed 10 January 2018). Generally, the funds industry has created many attractive jobs for employees. *See* OECD 2010 CIV Report, at 5 (para. 11).
19. *See* Bundesregierung, *supra* note 17, at 65; Lauermann & Birker, *supra* note 18, at 51; *see also* Johannes Höring, *Aktuelles Steuerrecht für Investmentvehikel mit Bezug zu Luxemburg*, 104 DStZ 319 (2016); Frank van Kuijk et al., *Tax Aspects of Luxembourg Specialized Investment Funds*, 40 Intertax 365 (2012).
20. *See* OECD Model Comm. on Art. 1, para. 29; OECD 2010 CIV Report, at 7 (para. 21), 12 (para. 48).
21. *See* OECD Model, *Introduction*, para. 3; OECD 2010 CIV Report, at 3 (para. 2), 13 (para. 50); United Nations, *Model Double Tax Convention Between Developed and Developing Countries*, Introduction, para. 1 (2011); Moris Lehner, *Grundlagen, in Doppelbesteuerungsabkommen: DBA. Kommentar*, margin no. 6 (Klaus Vogel & Moris Lehner eds, 6th edn, Verlag C.H. Beck 2015); Klaus Vogel & Alexander Rust, *Introduction, in Vogel*, 4th edn, *supra* note 10, margin no. 20.
22. *See* German Federal Ministry of Finance (*Bundesministerium der Finanzen*), Circular Letter dated 17 January 2018, Bundessteuerblatt I 2018, 239.
23. Administration des contributions directes du Grand-Duché de Luxembourg, *Conventions en vigueur*, at www.impotsdirects.public.lu/fr/conventions/conv_vig.html (last accessed 10 January 2018).
24. *Ibid.*, *Conventions en négociations*, at www.impotsdirects.public.lu/fr/conventions/conv_neg.html (last accessed 10 January 2018).

bilateral treaties; nevertheless, to facilitate their interpretation and application, the parties typically negotiate on the basis of 'model' tax conventions, some of which are proposed by international organizations (such as the OECD[25] or the United Nations (UN)),[26] while others simply reflect the opening gambit of a powerful potential signatory (such as Germany[27] or the United States).[28] This chapter will refer to the OECD Model, as it appears to be the most commonly used model tax convention.

The application of tax treaties to CIVs is complex[29] for several reasons. First, the domestic investment tax law of the Contracting States may vary significantly,[30] which differences are exemplified by the domestic tax law of Luxembourg[31] and of Germany.[32],[33] Differences in domestic tax law matter in terms of the application of tax treaties due to the interplay of domestic tax law and tax treaty law.[34] Second, the interpretation of tax treaties raises difficult legal issues with a view to the application to CIVs,[35] resulting in undesirable legal uncertainty.[36] Third, tax authorities from at

25. *See supra* notes 3 and 4.
26. UN, *Model Double Taxation Convention 2011* (2011), available at http://www.un.org/esa/ffd/documents/UN_Model_2011_Update.pdf (last accessed 10 January 2018).
27. German Federal Ministry of Finance (*Bundesministerium der Finanzen*), *Basis for Negotiation for Agreements for the Avoidance of Double Taxation and the Prevention of Fiscal Evasion with Respect to Taxes on Income and on Capital* (2013), available at http://www.bundesfinanzministerium.de/Content/DE/Standardartikel/Themen/Steuern/Internationales_Steuerrecht/Allgemeine_Informationen/2013-08-22-Verhandlungsgrundlage-DBA-englisch.pdf?__blob=publicationFile&v=4 (last accessed 10 January 2018).
28. US Department of the Treasury, *United States Model Income Tax Convention of February 17, 2016* (2016), at https://www.treasury.gov/resource-center/tax-policy/treaties/Documents/Treaty-US%20Model-2016.pdf (last accessed 10 January 2018).
29. *See* Klaus Vogel, *Double Tax Treaties and Their Interpretation*, 4 Int'l Tax & Bus. Law 1, 46 (1986); *see also* Brown, *supra* note 13, at 19.
30. *See* OECD 2010 CIV Report, at 7–8 (paras 25–28); Raymond C. Adema, *The Revised UCITS Directive (UCITS IV): A Missed Chance for Creating Common Rules on the Taxation of UCITS*, 41 Intertax 140 (2013); Brown, *supra* note 13, at 19, 25–27; Roland Ismer & Katharina Riemer, *Article 4: Resident, in Vogel*, 4th ed., *supra* note 10, margin no. 30; Giulia Letizia, *International Tax Issues in Relation to Cross-Border Investment Funds*, 43 Intertax 526, 529 (2015); Günther Strunk & Bert Kaminski, *Artikel 3, in Außensteuergesetz Doppelbesteuerungsabkommen Kommentar*, margin no. 17.1 (Günther Strunk, Bert Kaminski & Stefan Köhler eds, loose leaf, Stollfuss, 2015).
31. *See* Eric Fort & Philipp Jost, *supra*, Chapter 2.
32. *See* Heribert M. Anzinger, *supra*, Chapter 4 (on the current treatment of investment funds under German domestic tax law).
33. Besides tax treatment for income tax purposes, the treatment of CIVs and of investment managers under domestic and EU VAT law must also be analysed. *See* Marie-Isabelle Richardin & Charlène-Adline Herbain, *supra*, Chapter 3.
34. *See* Lehner, *supra* note 21, margin nos 68, 87 (on the relationship of domestic tax and tax treaty law, generally).
35. *See* OECD 2010 CIV Report, at 7 (para. 22); Edward Barret, *Aspects of the 2010 Update Other than Those Relating to Article 7 OECD Model Tax Convention*, 65 Bull. Int'l Tax'n 13 (2011); *see also* §10.02 and §10.03, *infra* (on the application of tax treaties to CIVs).
36. *See* OECD Model Comm. on Art. 1, para. 29; OECD 2010 CIV Report, at 7 (para. 21), 12 (para. 48); Brown, *supra* note 13, at 19, 27–36.

least two countries are involved,[37] which may result in diverging decisions and, as a consequence, international double taxation.[38]

The complexity of the application of tax treaties to CIVs concerns all areas of tax treaty application (§10.02). The first and most critical issue in this regard is 'treaty entitlement' for CIVs; in this context, due to similar factual consequences, one should also consider the 'beneficial ownership' concept and the treaty entitlement of investors (§10.03). In order to provide for legal certainty in terms of the application of tax treaties to CIVs, the contracting states may adopt special tax treaty provisions providing for treaty entitlement and beneficial ownership of CIVs (§10.04). Such provisions are, however, rare at the moment and, due to their design, cannot remove any uncertainty; further, EU law and the implications of the OECD/G20 project on encountering base erosion and profit shifting (the 'BEPS Project')[39] may impact the analysis of the application of tax treaties to CIVs and the design of special tax treaty provisions (§10.05). However, the implications of the BEPS Project do not concern treaty entitlement in the strict sense. As a consequence, the comments on treaty entitlement of CIVs presented herein remain, as a matter of principle, true. Changes in tax treaties triggered by the BEPS Project, in particular the inclusion of a 'limitation on benefits' (LOB) clause in Article 29(1) OECD Model, may, however, restrict tax treaty benefits for CIVs.[40]

§10.02 OVERVIEW OF THE APPLICATION OF TAX TREATIES TO A CIV

[A] General Remarks

The application of tax treaties requires treaty entitlement (§10.02[B]). As such, it does not, however, ensure avoidance of double taxation in any case since it only allows for the application of a tax treaty. Double taxation may only be avoided if the so-called distributive rules (§10.02[C]) and the so-called methods for the avoidance of double taxation (§10.02[D]) so provide. The interpretation and application of tax treaty provisions, other than those providing for treaty entitlement, may also raise complex legal issues that may be connected to those arising in relation to treaty entitlement, since the terms used in the provision stipulating treaty entitlement may also be used in other tax treaty provisions. Further, the application of provisions that do not provide for treaty entitlement in the strict sense, such as the so-called beneficial-ownership requirement, may have similar factual consequences as treaty entitlement. Against this

37. On the application of tax treaties to CIVs from a Dutch perspective, *see* Arnaud de Graaf, *Dutch Tax Treaty Policy for Pooled Investment Vehicles, in* Vermeulen ed., *supra* note 2, at 73, 76–92.
38. *See* Lorenzo Banfi & Francesco Mantegazza, *Italian Undertakings for Collective Investment: Overview of the Current Tax Framework and Potential Developments,* 50 Eur. Tax'n 359, 372 (2010); Lehner, *supra* note 21, margin nos 96–96a (on diverging decisions by the Contracting States' competent authorities).
39. Relevant documents and explanations are available at http://www.oecd.org/tax/beps/ (last accessed 10 January 2018) and http://www.bundesfinanzministerium.de/Web/DE/Themen/Steuern/Beps/beps.html (last accessed 10 January 2018).
40. *See* Daniel W. Blum & Erik Pinetz, *Limitation on Benefits: Application to Investment Funds, in Base Erosion and Profit Shifting (BEPS)* (Michael Lang, et al., eds, Linde 2016), at 247, 257.

background, before treaty entitlement in the strict sense is analysed, a brief overview of the tax treaty provisions relevant to the application of tax treaties to CIVs illustrates the application of tax treaties to such vehicles in general.[41]

[B] Treaty Entitlement (Personal Scope of Application)

Treaty entitlement concerns the personal scope of application of a tax treaty. Only taxpayers encompassed by a tax treaty may claim beneficial treatment under said tax treaty.

Article 1(1) OECD Model, determining the taxpayers covered by a tax treaty, reads as follows: 'This Convention shall apply to *persons* who are *residents of one or both of the Contracting States*' (emphasis added). Therefore, in order to be entitled to claim tax treaty benefits, CIVs must qualify as a 'person'[42] and as a 'resident of one or both of the Contracting States'.[43]

[C] Distributive Rules, Including the Beneficial Ownership Concept

The distributive rules, such as those included in Articles 6 through 22 OECD Model, do not affect the personal scope of application of a tax treaty, but allocate jurisdiction to tax with regard to specific types of income (e.g., income from immovable property, business profits, dividends, or interest) to one or two Contracting States.[44] The distributive rules apply if, *inter alia*, the conditions specified in the provisions - in terms of the taxpayer claiming tax treaty benefits and the income - are met.

By way of example, dividends are an important type of income for many CIVs. In turn, CIVs may distribute dividends to investors or pass dividends received from investments on to their investors. The roles CIVs may assume are reflected in Article 10 OECD Model, which provides for the allocation of jurisdiction to tax with regard to 'dividends', and it reads as follows:

> (1) Dividends paid by a *company* which is a *resident of a Contracting State* to a *resident of the other Contracting State* may be taxed in that other State.
> (2) However, dividends paid by a *company* which is a *resident of a Contracting State* may also be taxed in that State according to the laws of that State, but if the *beneficial owner* of the dividends is a *resident of the other Contracting State*, the tax so charged shall not exceed:

41. For a brief historic view, *see, e.g.*, Renk, *Subject II: Fiscal Problems Arising in Connection with Investment Trusts of International Character, in IFA General Report*, 47b Cahier de Droit Fiscal International (1962); Lynne J. Ed & Paul J. M. Bongaarts, *Subject II: The Taxation of Investment Funds, in IFA General Report*, 82b Cahier de Droit Fiscal International (1997).
42. *See infra* §10.03[B].
43. *See infra* §10.03[C].
44. *See* Lehner, *supra* note 21, margin nos 67, 76–86; Daniel Dürrschmidt *Artikel 6 bis 22, in* Vogel & Lehner eds, *supra* note 21, margin nos 1a–7c; Vogel & Rust, *supra* note 21, margin nos 62–63 (details concerning distributive rules).

a) 5 per cent of the gross amount of the dividends if the *beneficial owner* is a *company*[45] which holds directly at least 25 per cent[46] of the capital of the *company paying the dividends* throughout a 365 day period that includes the day of the payment of the dividend (for the purpose of computing that period, no account shall be taken of changes of ownership that would directly result from a corporate reorganisation, such as a merger or divisive reorganisation, of the company that holds the shares or that pays the dividend);
b) 15 per cent of the gross amount of the dividends in all other cases (emphasis added).

As a result, both the residence state of the shareholder and the residence state of the paying company may tax dividends. The latter, however, may only apply a tax rate limited to 5% or 15%, depending on, *inter alia*, the amount of the share in the capital of the paying company.

To be granted tax treaty protection under Article 10 OECD Model, a CIV must, at the very least, qualify as a 'resident of the other Contracting State';[47] in addition, it must qualify as the 'beneficial owner'[48] of dividend income to take advantage of the limitation of the withholding tax rate in the source state in general and as a 'company'[49] to benefit from the limitation of the withholding tax rate to 5%. In turn, in order to enable its investors to claim tax treaty protection, a CIV must qualify as a 'company'[50] or a 'company paying the dividends', which is a 'resident of a Contracting State', if it distributes or passes dividends on to its investors.

The beneficial-ownership concept,[51] according to which the recipient of income must be the so-called 'beneficial owner' thereof, prevents 'treaty shopping', which occurs if the recipient of income is interposed only to benefit from a tax treaty that otherwise would not apply.[52] It is part of the distributive rules, and, thus, technically related to specific items of income rather than to the 'treaty entitlement' of the taxpayer. Nevertheless, its factual consequences are similar to those of treaty entitlement if all or part of the income is allocated to another vehicle under the beneficial-ownership concept for tax treaty purposes. The beneficial ownership concept will not be replaced – and, therefore, not be superfluous – by the inclusion of an LOB clause in Article 29(1) OECD Model as a consequence of the BEPS Project.[53]

45. In the former version, the provision stated that the beneficial owner must not qualify as a 'partnership'. In Art. 10(2)(a) of the Germany/Luxembourg Tax Treaty, partnerships ('*Personengesellschaft*') and CIVs in the form of legal entities ('*Investmentgesellschaft*') are excluded.
46. *Ibid.*: the threshold amounts to 10%.
47. *See infra* §10.03[C].
48. *See infra* §10.03[D].
49. *See infra* §10.03[B].
50. *See ibid.*
51. *See* Angelika Meindl-Ringler, *Beneficial Ownership in International Tax Law* (2016).
52. *See* OECD Model Comm. on Art. 10, paras 12–12.7; OECD 2015 Inappropriate Circumstances Report, at 17 (paras 17–18); Wolfgang Tischbirek, *Artikel 10 bis 12, in* Vogel & Lehner eds, *supra* note 21, margin no. 12; Eric C.C.M. Kemmeren, *Preface to Articles 10 to 12, in Vogel*, 4th ed., *supra* note 10, margin nos 19–23; for a general explanation of 'treaty shopping', *see* Rainer Prokisch, *Artikel 1, in* Vogel & Lehner eds, *supra* note 21, margin no. 101.
53. *See* OECD 2015 Inappropriate Circumstances Report, at 24 (para. 5) (commentary on the LOB clause).

[D] Methods for the Avoidance of Double Taxation

Distributive rules do not avoid double taxation in all cases, but may allow both Contracting States to tax a specific item of income.[54] In such a case, the state in which the taxpayer is a resident must apply methods for the avoidance of double taxation on the basis of either Article 23A(1) or 23B(1) OECD Model, which provide for the so-called exemption or credit method, respectively.

Article 23A(1) OECD Model reads as follows:

> Where a *resident of a Contracting State* derives income or owns capital which, in accordance with the provisions of this Convention, may be taxed in the other Contracting State, the first-mentioned State shall, subject to the provisions of paragraphs 2 and 3, exempt such income or capital from tax (emphasis added).

The first sentence of Article 23B(1) OECD Model, on the other hand, reads as follows:

> Where a *resident of a Contracting State* derives income or owns capital which, in accordance with the provisions of this Convention, may be taxed in the other Contracting State, the first-mentioned State shall allow:
>
> a) as a deduction from the tax on the income of that *resident*, an amount equal to the income tax paid in that other State;
> b) as a deduction from the tax on the capital of that *resident*, an amount equal to the capital tax paid in that other State (emphasis added).

In order to benefit from the relevant obligation of the residence state, the CIV must, again, qualify as a 'resident of a Contracting State'.[55]

In some cases, a special regime applies if two Contracting States may tax a specific item of income. This particularly holds true for dividend income, which constitutes an important type of income of both for and from CIVs and which, according to Article 10(1) and (2) OECD Model, may be taxed in the residence state of the shareholder and of the paying company.[56] In such a case, the state the shareholder is a resident of must credit an amount equal to the tax that the source state levies. This outcome results from Article 23B(1) OECD Model, if the tax treaty provides for the credit method, or from Article 23A(2), sentence 1 OECD Model if it provides for the exemption method. The latter provision states that:

> [w]here a *resident of a Contracting State* derives items of income which, in accordance with the provisions of Articles 10 and 11, may be taxed in the other Contracting State, the first-mentioned State shall allow as a deduction from the tax on the income of that *resident* an amount equal to the tax paid in that other State (emphasis added).

54. *See* §10.02[C].
55. *See infra* §10.03[C].
56. *See* §10.02[C].

Irrespective of the applicable provision, if the shareholder is a CIV, it must qualify as a 'resident of a Contracting State'[57] in order to benefit from the crediting obligation of the residence state.

In the event of a tax-exemption under domestic investment tax law, the avoidance of double taxation at the level of a CIV raises specific issues that cannot be discussed in the context of treaty entitlement. They must be subject to a separate contribution.[58]

§10.03 TREATY ENTITLEMENT AND BENEFICIAL OWNERSHIP OF A CIV UNDER GENERAL TAX-TREATY PROVISIONS

[A] General Remarks

The previous overview of the application of tax treaties to CIVs[59] revealed that treaty entitlement is an essential condition for beneficial treatment under a tax treaty. In the absence of a special tax treaty provision in tax treaties modelled on the OECD Model,[60] Article 1 OECD Model[61] implies that treaty entitlement requires that CIVs qualify as 'a person' (§10.03[B]) and as 'a resident of a Contracting State' (§10.03[C]). Both terms are defined in the OECD Model. Further, a CIV must qualify as the 'beneficial owner' as provided for by some of the OECD Model's distributive rules[62] in order to be granted tax treaty benefits for specific items of income (§10.03[D]). If a CIV does not meet the conditions of treaty entitlement stipulated in a particular tax treaty, its investors, instead, may be entitled to claim tax treaty benefits (§10.03[E]).

[B] CIV as a 'Person'

The term 'person' is defined in Article 3(1)(a) OECD Model to include 'an individual, a *company* and *any other body of persons*' (emphasis added).[63] In turn, the term 'company', which is included in the definition of the term 'person', is defined in Article

57. *See infra* §10.03[C].
58. *See* Daniel Gutmann, *infra*, Chapter 13.
59. *See supra* §10.02.
60. *See* OECD 2010 CIV Report, at 7 (para. 22). Currently, many tax treaties do not yet have a special provision applying to CIVs. *See* Adema, *supra* note 30, at 141; Letizia, *supra* note 30, at 529. However, many recently concluded tax treaties do contain such special provisions. *See infra* §10.04.
61. *See* OECD Model Comm. on Art. 1, para. 23; OECD 2010 CIV Report, at 7 (para. 22); Florian Haase, *Treaty Entitlement of Investment Funds: The German Perspective*, 39 Intertax 337 (2011); Christian Schmidt & Daniel Blöchle, *Einkünfte aus Auslandinvestmentfonds bei Anwendung von Doppelbesteuerungsabkommen - Zugleich grundsätzliche Überlegungen zur Relevanz des Abkommensrechts beider Einkünftezurechnung*, 11 IStR 645, 648 (2002).
62. *See* OECD Model Comm. on Art. 1, para. 23; OECD 2010 CIV Report, at 7 (para. 22).
63. *See* OECD Model Comm. on Art. 3, para. 2; Daniel Dürrschmidt, *Artikel 3*, in Vogel & Lehner eds, *supra* note 21, margin no. 9; Prokisch, *supra* note 52, margin no. 2.

3(1)(b) OECD Model to mean '*any body corporate* or *any entity that is treated as a body corporate for tax purposes*' (emphasis added).[64]

If a CIV is incorporated and established in the legal form of a company under domestic company law, it constitutes a 'body corporate' and, therefore, qualifies as a 'company' and as a 'person' for tax treaty purposes.[65] The same should hold true if an unincorporated CIV – like under German investment tax law[66] – is deemed to be a taxpayer under domestic investment tax law,[67] since both the term 'any entity that is treated as body corporate for tax purposes', which is included in the definition of the term 'company', and the term 'any other body of persons', which is included in the definition of the term 'person', indicate that the term 'person' has a broad meaning.[68] Accordingly, even a simple contractual arrangement or a form of joint ownership may qualify as a 'person' for tax treaty purposes, if it is treated as a taxpayer under domestic investment tax law.[69] Further, the tax treatment a CIV receives under domestic tax law should also be decisive with respect to CIVs structured as a trust.[70] As a consequence, CIVs structured as a trust that are treated as taxpayers under domestic tax law should also qualify as a 'person' for tax treaty purposes. By contrast, irrespective of the legal form, any CIV that is not treated as a taxpayer under domestic tax law does not qualify as a 'person' for tax treaty purposes.[71]

[C] CIV as a 'Resident of a Contracting State'

The term 'resident of a Contracting State' is defined in Article 4(1), sentence 1 OECD Model and 'means any person who, under the laws of that State, is *liable to tax* therein

64. *See* OECD Model Comm. on Art. 3, para. 2; Dürrschmidt, *supra* note 63, margin no. 11; Prokisch, *supra* note 52, margin no. 2.
65. *See* OECD Model Comm. on Art. 1, para. 24; OECD 2010 CIV Report, at 7 (para. 24); Lauermann & Birker, *supra* note 18, at 52–53; Dürrschmidt, *supra* note 63, margin no. 16; Niccolò Pallesi, *Application of Tax Treaties to Investment Funds,* 9 Int. Law: Rev. Colomb. Derecho Int. Bogotá (Colombia) 87, 125 (2007); Franz Wassermeyer & Christian Kaeser, *Artikel 4, in Doppelbesteuerung DBA*, margin no. 27 (Franz Wassermeyer et al., eds, loose leaf, Verlag C.H. Beck, 2013).
66. German Investment Tax Act (*Investmentsteuergesetz*) § 6(1)(1), as amended by the German Investment Tax Reform Act (*Gesetz zur Reform der Investmentbesteuerung (Investmentsteuerreformgesetz - InvStRefG*) of 19 July 2016, BGBl. I 2016, 1730, and pre-amendment § 11(1)(1) thereof. *See* Anzinger, *supra* note 32.
67. *See* OECD Model Comm. on Art. 1, para. 24; OECD 2010 CIV Report, at 7 (para. 24); Dürrschmidt, *supra* note 63, margin no. 16; Joachim Englisch, *§ 11 InvStG, in Investmentgesetz Investmentsteuergesetz*, margin no. 83 (Hanno Berger, Kai-Uwe Steck & Dieter Lübbehüsen eds, Verlag C.H. Beck 2010); Kirchmayr, *supra* note 10, at 674; Lauermann & Birker, *supra* note 18, at 53; Pallesi, *supra* note 65, at 125; Klaus Zinkeisen & Andreas Walter, *Seminar F: Abkommensberechtigung von Investmentfonds*, 16 IStR 583 (2007); Wassermeyer & Kaeser, *supra* note 65, margin no. 27.
68. *See* OECD Model Comm. on Art. 1, para. 24; OECD Model Comm. on Art. 3, para. 2; OECD 2010 CIV Report, at 7 (para. 24); Dürrschmidt, *supra* note 63, margin nos 17–18; Rust, *supra* note 10, margin no. 30; Pallesi, *supra* note 65, at 125 (2007).
69. *See* OECD Model Comm. on Art. 1, para. 24; OECD 2010 CIV Report, at 7 (para. 24); Kirchmayr, *supra* note 10, at 674.
70. *See* OECD 2010 CIV Report, at 7 (para. 26); *see also* OECD Model Comm. on Art. 1, para. 24.
71. *See* Kirchmayr, *supra* note 10, at 674; Rust, *supra* note 10, margin no. 30; Wassermeyer & Kaeser, *supra* note 65, margin no. 27.

by reason of his domicile, residence, place of management or any other criterion of a similar nature' (emphasis added).[72] Pursuant to Article 4(1), sentence 1 OECD Model, the tax liability must be based on the domestic tax law of the state in which the taxpayer shall be deemed a resident within the meaning of the definition.[73] With regard to CIVs, as a matter of principle, this is the state in which the CIV is established.[74] According to Article 4(1), sentence 2 OECD Model, the term 'does not include any person who is liable to tax in that State in respect only of income from sources in that State or capital situated therein'. As a consequence, the 'liability to tax' referred to in Article 4(1), sentence 1 OECD Model must be unlimited and based on the taxpayer's worldwide income.[75] By way of exception, taxation may be limited to source income, if the concept of residence taxation is limited to source income in a Contracting State.[76]

The residency requirement is not only crucial for treaty entitlement[77] but may also be relevant for the distributive rules.[78] For example, both the recipient of dividends and the paying company must qualify as a 'resident of a Contracting State' (Article 10(1) and (2) OECD Model). The same holds true for the rules providing the methods for the avoidance of double taxation,[79] since only a 'resident of a Contracting State' may claim beneficial treatment under those rules (Article 23A(1) and 23B(1) OECD Model). By contrast, according to Article 24(1), sentence 2 OECD Model, the taxpayer does not have to meet the conditions of the residency requirement in order to claim non-discrimination thereunder, provided the taxpayer qualifies as a 'person' and a 'national of a Contracting State'.[80]

With regard to CIVs, the liability-to-tax requirement must be scrutinized carefully for two reasons. First, liability to tax requires that income is attributed to the CIV. Second, a tax exemption granted to a CIV under domestic tax law must not preclude liability to tax within the meaning of the definition. Against this background, one must, as the first step, determine whether a CIV is transparent or non-transparent for tax purposes before one can, as the second step, evaluate the impact of a tax exemption granted to a CIV.[81]

---

72. *See* OECD Model Comm. on Art. 1, para. 1; OECD Model Comm. on Art. 4, para. 1; Lehner, *supra* note 21, margin no. 11; Prokisch, *supra* note 52, margin no. 2.
73. *See* Lehner, *supra* note 21, margin no. 76.
74. *See* OECD Model Comm. on Art. 1, para. 25; OECD 2010 CIV Report, at 8 (para. 27). The OECD's view may be misleading since, as a matter of principle, a fund may be relocated and, as a consequence, be subject to the domestic tax law of another state.
75. *See* OECD Model Comm. on Art. 4, para. 8; Lehner, *supra* note 21, margin nos 76–77; Ismer & Riemer, *supra* note 30, margin nos 27, 37.
76. *See* OECD Model Comm. on Art. 4, para. 8.3; Lehner, *supra* note 21, margin no. 120; Ismer & Riemer, *supra* note 30, margin no. 42.
77. A CIV may also be a dual resident, in particular if it is remotely managed. Then, the so-called 'tie breaker' rule such as those included in OECD Model Art. 4(3) applies. *See* Raymond P.C. Adema, *Domicile Issues Arising from the Management Company Passport: A Comparison of the UCITS Regulatory Framework and Tax (Treaty) Law in* Vermeulen ed., *supra* note 2, at 185, 197–200.
78. *See* §10.02[C].
79. *See* §10.02[D].
80. *See* Gutmann, *supra* note 58.
81. *See* German Federal Fiscal Court *(Bundesfinanzof)*, Judgment, 6 June 2012, I R 52/11, Bundessteuerblatt II 2014, 240; OECD 2010 CIV Report, at 8 (para. 29); Daniel Dürrschmidt, *BFH, Urteil vom 6. 6. 2012 - I R 52/11: Abkommensrechtliche Ansässigkeit von steuerbefreiten*

Transparent vehicles, from the outset, cannot be liable to tax, since income is directly attributed to the investors under domestic tax law.[82] This holds true, *inter alia*, for Luxembourg's *Fonds Commun de Placement* (FCP) under its domestic tax law, as applied by its tax authorities.[83] By contrast, income generated by a CIV is attributed to the CIV, rather than to its investors, if it qualifies as an opaque or non-transparent investment vehicle. This is the case if it qualifies as a taxable entity due to its legal form such as, *inter alia*, Luxembourg's *Société d'Investissement à Capital Variable* (SICAV) or its *Société d'Investissement à Capital Fixe* (SICAF)[84] or the German *Investmentaktiengesellschaft* (InvAG). Further, it should hold true for investment vehicles that - like the German *Investmentfonds* under German domestic investment tax law[85] - are deemed to be a taxpayer under domestic investment tax law.[86]

The 'transparency principle'[87] or 'neutrality principle'[88] underlying domestic investment tax law should not impact the qualification of an investment vehicle as transparent or non-transparent. According to this principle, the overall tax burden with respect to a CIV's income, after the distribution to its investors, must equal the tax burden at the level of its investors in the event of a direct investment.[89] At least from a German perspective, it is not, however, a general or even an overriding principle, but

Investmentfonds und anderen steuerbefreiten Rechtsträgern, Internationale Wirtschafts-Briefe (IWB), 818, 819–820 (2012); Franz Wassermeyer, *Artikel 1, in* Wassermeyer et al., eds, *supra* note 65, margin no. 33b.

82. *See* OECD Model Comm. on Art. 1, para. 25; OECD 2010 CIV Report, at 8 (paras 28–29); Ralf Dremel, *Artikel 1, in Doppelbesteuerungsabkommen (DBA). Kommentar*, margin no. 81 (Jens Schönfeld & Xaver Ditz eds, Verlag Dr. Otto Schmidt 2013); Dürrschmidt, *supra* note 81, at 819–820; Wassermeyer, *supra* note 81, margin no. 33b; *see also* Wassermeyer & Kaeser, *supra* note 65, margin no. 27 (on CIVs in the legal form of a partnership).
83. *See* Administration des contributions directes du Grand-Duché de Luxembourg, Circulaire du directeur des contributions, L.G.-A. n° 61 du 12 février 2015, 3–4; *see also* Fort & Jost, *supra* note 31; Jean Schaffner, *infra*, Chapter 11.
84. *See* Administration des contributions directes du Grand-Duché de Luxembourg, Circulaire du directeur des contributions, L.G. - A. n° 61 du 12 février 2015, 4–6; *see also* Fort & Jost, *supra* note 31; Schaffner, *supra* note 83; for a German perspective, *see* Jürgen Staiger & Vanessa Köth, *Abkommensberechtigung einer französischen SICAV sowie des deutschen REIT zugleich Anmerkungen zum BFH-Urteil vom 6.6.2012*, 67 Betriebs-Berater (BB) 2915, 2919 (2012).
85. German Investment Tax Act, as amended, *supra* note 66, § 6(1)(1). *See* Anzinger, *supra* note 32.
86. *See* Dremel, *supra* note 82; Englisch, *supra* note 67, margin no. 84; Wassermeyer, *supra* note 81, margin nos 33a, 33b. This finding does not conflict with the fact that 'residence' within the meaning of Art. 4(1), sentence 1 OECD Model, may not be based on a fiction contained in domestic tax law. *See* Dürrschmidt, *supra* note 81, at 821; Dremel, *supra* note 82 (even with a deviating reasoning); *see also* Lehner, *Artikel 4, in* Vogel & Lehner eds, *supra* note 21, margin no. 120 (on 'liability to tax' in the context of the 'residence' requirement generally). The fiction does not affect the extent of income that is covered by the liability to tax or the criteria establishing the nexus to a contracting state, which constitutes the basis for taxation.
87. *See* Englisch, *supra* note 67, margin no. 20; Haase, *supra* note 61, at 338.
88. *See* OECD Model Comm. on Art. 1, paras 22 and 25; OECD 2010 CIV Report, at 3 (para. 1), 8 (para. 27), 13 (para. 50); Da Silva, *supra* note 10, at 196; Gijs K. Fibbe, *Changes to the OECD Commentary on Collective Investment Vehicles Proposed by the OECD Committee on Fiscal Affairs*, 64 Bull. Int'l Tax'n 138, 140–141 (2010); for a Luxembourg perspective, *see* Fort & Jost, *supra* note 31, and for a German perspective, *see* Anzinger, *supra* note 32.
89. *See* OECD 2010 CIV Report, at 3 (para. 1), 8 (para. 27); Englisch, *supra* note 67, margin no. 20.

rather a concept underlying a number of provisions of the former[90] German domestic investment tax law.[91]

If a CIV is non-transparent for tax purposes, but is tax exempt or subject to another preferential tax treatment under the domestic investment tax law, the impact of the tax exemption on the liable-to-tax requirement must be determined. According to a widespread view, a tax-exempt CIV is not liable to tax within the meaning of the definition of the term 'resident of a Contracting State' in Article 4(1), sentence 1 OECD Model, since it does not actually pay taxes.[92] A differing position, which is even more popular, argues that a tax exemption does not affect the CIV's liability to tax, if non-transparent investment vehicles are, as a matter of principle, liable to tax under the general provisions of domestic tax law, but could be tax exempt if certain conditions specified in the law are met.[93] This view is shared by the OECD in cases where the entity is not 'totally and unconditionally'[94] exempt from tax and the requirements for such exemption are 'sufficiently stringent'.[95] Relevant conditions may concern, for example, the entity's investment and distribution policy.[96] Such conditions may also be found in domestic investment law,[97] to which domestic investment

90. For an overview, *see* Anzinger, *supra* note 32.
91. *See* German Federal Fiscal Court *(Bundesfinanzhof)*, Judgment, 11 Oct. 2000, I R 99/96, Bundessteuerblatt II 2001, 22; German Federal Fiscal Court *(Bundesfinanzhof)*, Judgment, 7 Apr. 1992, VIII R 79/88, Bundessteuerblatt II 1992, 786; German Federal Fiscal Court *(Bundesfinanzhof)*, Judgment, 4 Mar. 1980, VIII R 48/76, Bundessteuerblatt II 1980, 453; Dürrschmidt, *supra* note 81, at 821; Dieter Lübbehusen, *Vor §§ 1 ff. InvStG, in* Berger, Steck & Lübbehüsen eds, *supra* note 67, margin nos 18–24; Zinkeisen & Walter, *supra* note 67, at 584.
92. *See* OECD Model Comm. on Art. 1, para. 27; OECD 2010 CIV Report, at 30 (para. 27); *see generally*, OECD Model Comm. on Art. 4, para. 8.7; *see also* Pallesi, *supra* note 65, at 129–131 (pointing out that, in such case, no double taxation, which is to be avoided by tax treaties (*see* §10.01), can occur).
93. *See* OECD Model Comm. on Art. 1, para. 26; OECD 2010 CIV Report, at 8 (para. 29); *see generally*, OECD Model Comm. on Art. 4, para. 8.7; German Federal Fiscal Court *(Bundesfinanzhof)*, Judgment, 6 June 2012, I R 52/11, Bundessteuerblatt II 2014, 240; Dremel, *supra* note 82; Dürrschmidt, *supra* note 81, at 822; Matthias Geurts, *Das DBA-Irland aus investmentsteuerlicher Sicht*, 20 IStR 573, 573 (2011); Friedhelm Jacob, *Das neue DBA Deutschland-Luxemburg 2012*, 21 IStR 749, 749–750 (2012); Friedhelm Jacob, *Highlights des neuen Doppelbesteuerungsabkommens Deutschland-Luxemburg 2012*, 14 SAM 167, 167–168 (2012); Friedhelm Jacob & Antje Hagena, *The Germany-Luxembourg Income and Capital Tax Treaty (2012)*, 66 Bull. Int'l Tax'n 530, 530 (2012); Friedhelm Jacob & Mathias Link, 21 IStR 963, 950 (2012); Lauermann & Birker, *supra* note 18, at 53; Prokisch, *supra* note 52, margin no. 19; Zinkeisen & Walter, *supra* note 67, at 583; Wassermeyer, *supra* note 81, margin no. 33a; Wassermeyer & Kaeser, *supra* note 65, margin no. 27; *see also* Michael Lang, *Die Besteuerung von Einkünften bei unterschiedlichen Personen aus dem Blickwinkel des DBA-Rechts*, 2000 SWI 527, 530 (2000) (general comments on the relevance of tax exemptions for determining residency for tax treaty purposes); *contra* Carsten Pohl, *Artikel 4, in* Schönfeld & Ditz eds, *supra* note 82, margin no. 25.
94. *See* OECD 2010 CIV Report, at 8 (para. 29).
95. *See* OECD Model Comm. on Art. 1, para. 26.
96. *See* OECD 2010 CIV Report, at 8 (para. 29).
97. This particularly applies to CIVs that are subject to the German domestic investment tax law: German Investment Tax Act, as amended, *supra* note 66, § 1(2) and (3) and pre-amendment § 1(1)(1) thereof. For the legal position prior to the recent reform, *see* Dürrschmidt, *supra* note 81, at 822; Englisch, *supra* note 67, margin no. 84; *contra* Haase, *supra* note 61, 341; Kirchmayr, *supra* note 10, at 675.

tax law often refers.[98] The OECD's position is preferable, as the phrase 'liable to tax' does not mean the same as the phrase 'subject to tax'.[99] Only the latter wording would require the taxpayer to actually pay taxes.[100] Further, the position may be supported by the design of provisions in domestic tax law that imply that a foreign CIV qualifies as a resident of a Contracting State for tax treaty purposes (e.g., with a view to dividend income that is covered by a distributive rule modelled on Article 10 OECD Model) irrespective of a tax exemption.[101]

Moreover, the EU tax directives do not suggest a different view.[102] According to the wording of Article 3(c) of the Merger Directive,[103] Article 2(a)(iii) of the Parent-Subsidiary-Directive[104] and Article 3(a)(iii) of the Interest and Royalties Directive,[105] a taxpayer claiming beneficial treatment under these directives must be 'subject to ... tax ... without ... being exempt'. Both requirements must be met at the same time.[106] That wording significantly differs from that in Article 4(1), sentence 1 OECD Model ('liable to tax'). Because of the different wording, a mere tax exemption should not rule out that a taxpayer may qualify as a 'resident of a Contracting State' for tax treaty purposes. By contrast, the Anti-Tax Avoidance Directive[107] has been, from the outset, of only

98. *See* OECD Model Comm. on Art. 1, para. 36; OECD 2010 CIV Report, at 19 (proposed para. 6.22); Zetzsche, *supra* note 7; for a German perspective, *see* Anzinger, *supra* note 32.
99. *See* Ismer & Riemer, *supra* note 30, margin nos 26, 29, 30.
100. *See* Da Silva, *supra* note 10, at 199; Fibbe, *supra* note 88, at 142–143; Ismer & Riemer, *supra* note 30, margin no. 24.
101. In German domestic tax law, such a provision is found in the German Income Tax Act (*Einkommensteuergesetz*), § 50d(3), sentence 5, and was found in the German Foreign Tax Act (*Außensteuergesetz*), § 7(7), prior to its amendment by the German Investment Tax Reform Act (*Gesetz zur Reform der Investmentbesteuerung* (*Investmentsteuerreformgesetz – InvStRefG*)) of 19 July 2016, BGBl. I 2016, 1730. *See* Lauermann & Birker, *supra* note 18, at 52 fn 19. The amendment of the latter was triggered by an amendment of the concept in the German investment tax law. *See* Deutscher Bundestag, *Beschlussempfehlung und Bericht des Finanzausschusses (7. Ausschuss)*, BT-Drucksache 18/8739, at 118. Besides, it is recognized that an unlimited tax liability may establish a specific status irrespective of whether or not a taxpayer actually pays taxes ('*statusbegründende Funktion*') that may also be relevant for tax treaty purposes. *See* Lehner, *supra* note 21, margin no. 82. However, since the recent reform of German domestic investment tax law, this argument has lost some of its vigor from a German perspective due to the limitation of the tax liability to 'source income'. *See* Anzinger, *supra* note 32.
102. *See* Katerina Pantazatou, *supra*, Chapter 8.
103. Council Directive 2009/133/EC of 19 October 2009 on the common system of taxation applicable to mergers, divisions, partial divisions, transfers of assets and exchanges of shares concerning companies of different Member States and to the transfer of the registered office of an SE or SCE between Member States, OJ L 310, 25.11.2009, pp. 34–46.
104. Council Directive 2011/96/EU of 30 November 2011 on the common system of taxation applicable in the case of parent companies and subsidiaries of different Member States, OJ L 345, 29.12.2011, pp. 8–16.
105. Council Directive 2003/49/EC of 3 June 2003 on a common system of taxation applicable to interest and royalty payments made between associated companies of different Member States, OJ L 157, 26.6.2003, pp. 49–54.
106. *See Wereldhave Belgium and Others*, C-448/15, Judgment, ECLI:EU:C:2017:180, para. 31; *Wereldhave Belgium and Others*, C-448/15, AG Opinion, EU:C:2016:808, para. 42.
107. Council Directive (EU) 2016/1164 of 12 July 2016 laying down rules against tax avoidance practices that directly affect the functioning of the internal market, OJ L 193, 19.7.2016, pp. 1–14.

minor relevance for CIVs,[108] so that it should not be employed for the interpretation of tax treaties with a view to their application to CIVs. In addition, the EU tax directives only apply if a taxpayer, 'under the terms of a double taxation agreement concluded with a third State, is not considered to be resident for tax purposes outside the Union' (Article 3(b) of the Merger Directive, Article 2(a)(ii) of the Parent-Subsidiary-Directive and Article 3(a)(ii) of the Interest and Royalties Directive). This condition is relevant for dual resident companies,[109] which are deemed to be a resident of one Contracting State for tax treaty purposes on the basis of the so-called tiebreaker rules, such as those contained in Article 4(3) OECD Model. It is an additional condition, and is independent from another condition, according to which the taxpayer must not be tax exempt. However, the former provision would be superfluous if a tax-exempt taxpayer could not, from the outset, qualify as a resident for tax treaty purposes. Finally, the rationale behind tax treaties and the EU tax directives is different. Even if both target the avoidance of double taxation, tax treaties allocate jurisdiction to tax regardless of the tax treatment of a taxpayer in the state entitled to tax, subject to specific provisions (so-called subject-to-tax clauses),[110] whereas the EU tax directives mainly aim at the avoidance of impediments in the internal market, which only occur in the event of (juridical or economical) double taxation.[111]

Even if a CIV is not totally tax exempt, there may be doubt with regard to the liable-to-tax requirement if - as under current German investment tax law after its recent reform[112] - a CIV's taxable income is limited to specific types of source income ('*inländische Einkünfte*'). In any case, a CIV cannot be regarded as a 'resident of a Contracting State' only to the extent it is liable to tax, since residency for tax treaty purposes cannot be split up.[113] The limitation of taxable income matters since, according to Article 4(1), sentence 2 OECD Model, liability to tax within the meaning of Article 4(1), sentence 1 OECD Model requires that the taxpayer's tax liability not be limited to 'income from sources in that State' (i.e., the state which the taxpayer is connected to due to criteria specified in the tax treaty), but unlimited (i.e., covering its worldwide income).[114] The exception, according to which taxation may be limited to

108. *See* Pantazatou, *supra* note 102.
109. *See* Georg W. Kofler, *Kommentar zur Mutter-Tochter-Richtlinie,* Artikel 2, margin no. 27 (2011).
110. *See* Lehner, *supra* note 21, margin nos 69–73; Vogel & Rust, *supra* note 21, margin nos 55–56 (each with further references).
111. *See Wereldhave Belgium and Others*, C-448/15, Judgment, ECLI:EU:C:2017:180, paras 25 and 35–41; *Wereldhave Belgium and Others,* C-448/15, AG Opinion, EU:C:2016:808, para. 45.
112. German Investment Tax Act, as amended, *supra* note 66 §6(2), sentence 1. *See* Anzinger, *supra* note 32.
113. *See* Pohl, *supra* note 93, margin no. 25; Ismer & Riemer, *supra* note 30, margin no. 21.
114. *See supra,* and, with a view to CIVs, Susann Kammeter, *Änderungen durch die geplante Reform der Investmentbesteuerung – vom Referentenentwurf (18.12.2015) bis zum Regierungsentwurf (24.2.2016) des InvStRefG,* 5 ISR 99, 103 (2016); Rainer Stadler & Martin Mager, *Der Regierungsentwurf des Gesetzes zur Reform der Investmentbesteuerung,* 54 DStR 696, 699–700 (2016).

source income if the concept of residence taxation is limited to source income in a Contracting State,[115] does not apply here, since residence taxation under German tax law is principally based on the taxpayer's worldwide income.[116] The fact that the legislature intended to limit taxation to income that Germany is allowed to tax under the principles of international law (*'völkerrechtliche Grundsätze'*)[117] may suggest that the tax liability of CIVs is not unlimited under German law.[118] However, the reference to the principles of international law seems to be inconsistent, since taxation on a worldwide-income basis may also be compatible with international law.[119] If the legislature, however, only considered restrictions based on the allocation of jurisdiction to tax in tax treaties, such restrictions would only exist if tax treaties actually applied to domestic CIVs. This would, however, suggest that domestic CIVs may be treaty entitled, meaning that they also qualify as a 'resident of a Contracting State' within the meaning of Article 4(1), sentence 1 OECD Model. By contrast, the fact that the German legislature seems to have acted on the assumption that, as a matter of principle, CIVs – at least foreign ones – may be entitled to claim tax treaty benefits, does not speak in favour of treaty entitlement for CIVs. The legislative assumption may be derived from the reasons given by the legislature for some of the specific provisions in the reformed German domestic investment tax law. First, the reason why capital gains resulting from the alienation of shares in a company under particular circumstances[120] do not constitute taxable income is that domestic CIVs might face disadvantages due to the fact that foreign CIVs may claim tax treaty benefits with regard to such capital gains.[121] Second, for the same reason (i.e., the avoidance of disadvantages for domestic CIVs[122]), the withholding tax rate applicable to income of CIVs is limited to 15%,[123] because tax treaties applicable to foreign CIVs usually provide for such a limitation.[124]

115. *See supra.*
116. German Income Tax Act, *supra* note 101, §2(1), sentence 1, and German Corporation Tax Act (*Körperschaftsteuergesetz*), §1(2).
117. *See* Bundesregierung, *Entwurf eines Gesetzes zur Reform der Investmentbesteuerung (Investmentsteuerreformgesetz – InvStRefG)*, BT-Drucksache 18/8045, at 54; Johannes Höring, *Entwurf eines Gesetzes zur Reform der Investmentbesteuerung ('Investmentsteuerreformgesetz - InvStRefG')*, 104 DStZ 383, 395 (2016); Heinz Kußmaul, Andreas Patzner, Florian Kloster & Tu Minh Bui, *Investmentbesteuerung vor der Zeitenwende - Grundlegende Systemänderungen in der konzeptionellen Besteuerung von Publikums-Investmentfonds*, 9 Ubg 596, 599 (2016).
118. *See* Marcus Helios & Alexander Mann, *Das Gesetz zur Reform der Investmentbesteuerung: Darstellung, Meinung und Handlungsempfehlungen*, 1/2016 DB Sonderausgabe 1, 11 (2016); Tilmann Kempf & Julius Hirtz, *Schwerpunkte des Referentenentwurfs eines Gesetzes zur Reform der Investmentbesteuerung*, 54 DStR 1, 2 (2016).
119. *See* Angharad Miller & Lynne Oats, *Principles of International Taxation*, margin nos 2.4, 3.1, 3.7, 4.1, 4.2 (5th ed., 2015); Roy Rohatghi, *Basic International Taxation Volume 2*, 15 (2nd ed., 2005); Harald Schaumburg, *Internationales Steuerrecht*, margin no. 6.2 (4th edn, 2017).
120. German Investment Tax Act, as amended, *supra* note 66, §6(5), no. 1, in conjunction with German Income Tax Act, *supra* note 101, §49(1), no. 2, lit. e, §17.
121. *See* Bundesregierung, *supra* note 117, at 74; Thomas Elser & Tobias Stiegler, *Inbound-Investments in deutsche Vermögensgegenstände nach dem Investmentsteuerreformgesetz*, 26 IStR 567, 569 (2017); Jann Jetter & Martin Mager, *Der Referentenentwurf eines Gesetzes zur Reform der Investmentbesteuerung*, 7 SteuK 23, 25 (2015).
122. *See* Bundesregierung, *supra* note 117, at 76.
123. German Investment Tax Act, as amended, *supra* note 66, §7(1), sentences 1 & 3.
124. *See supra* §10.02[C] (on the limitation of the tax rate applicable to dividend income).

Though, there is no indication that the legislature's assumption covers all types of foreign CIVs, including such that, in the state in which they are established, are only subject to tax with foreign source income like German domestic CIVs. Only in that case, the assumption could be employed for the interpretation of the liable-to-tax requirement, as – unlike a total tax-exemption – a limitation of a CIV's liability to tax to source income is still rather uncommon. Similarly, the design of the new law, which aims to avoid conflicts with EU law[125] and disadvantages for domestic CIVs,[126] does not necessarily mean that CIVs must be treaty entitled, since both aims can be achieved without treaty entitlement for German CIVs. Against this background, it is questionable whether the limitation to specific types of source income is either a partial tax exemption that would not rule out that a CIV may qualify as 'resident of a Contracting State' or, with a different consequence, a limitation of jurisdiction to tax within the meaning of Article 4(1), sentence 2 OECD Model.[127] It will be interesting to see how tax authorities and tax courts in Germany and other countries deal with the issue in the future.

[D] CIV as the Beneficial Owner

Besides treaty entitlement, some tax treaty benefits with regard to specific items of income (e.g., dividend income) may only be granted if the taxpayer qualifies as its beneficial owner.[128] It is important to address the beneficial-ownership concept here, even if it is not connected to the treaty entitlement of a taxpayer in the strict sense, but is instead connected to the income a taxpayer generates, since its factual consequences may be similar to those of treaty entitlement if the latter's prerequisites are not met.[129]

Given the purpose of the beneficial-ownership concept (i.e., the prevention of treaty shopping),[130] a CIV, in many cases, can be regarded as the beneficial owner of dividend income[131] if a taxpayer other than a CIV could be regarded as the beneficial owner under the same circumstances.[132] Basically, a CIV must be held widely and, therefore, the impact of a single investor on investment decisions is limited.[133] The fact

125. *See* Bundesregierung, *supra* note 117, at 1, 49, 53, 56, 72, 97, 144; Höring, *supra* note 117, at 395.
126. *See* Bundesregierung, *supra* note 117, at 74, 76, 84.
127. *See* Rainer Stadler & Jann Jetter, *Der Diskussionsentwurf zum Investmentsteuerreformgesetz (InvStRefG)*, 53 DStR 1833, 1835 (2015).
128. *See supra* §10.01, §10.02[A] and §10.02[C].
129. *See ibid.*
130. *See ibid.*
131. *See* OECD Model Comm. on Art. 1, para. 28; OECD 2010 CIV Report, at 9–10 (paras 31–35).
132. *See* OECD Model Comm. on Art. 1, para. 48; OECD 2010 CIV Report, at 23–24 (proposed para. 6.34).
133. *See* OECD Model Comm. on Art. 1, para. 28; OECD 2010 CIV Report, at 9–10 (paras 31–35); David Eberhardt, *Abkommensrechtliche Missbrauchsvermeidung bei Investmentvermögen*, 22 IStR 377, 378 (2013); Rust, *supra* note 10, margin no. 32.

that an investor in a CIV is treated like an investor who owns the underlying assets directly for tax purposes under domestic investment tax law[134] does not conflict with the view advanced here, because an investor holding a direct investment is in a different position when compared to an investor in a CIV, both economically and legally.[135] As a consequence, a CIV is often not a suitable vehicle for treaty shopping.[136]

This, however, might be different in the case of special investment vehicles, such as Luxembourg's *Fonds d'investissement spécialisés* (FIS) (or, in English, Specialized Investment Fund (SIF)) or Germany's *Spezialfonds*, as the number of investors is limited and can even be only one investor.[137] Here, investors can have a significant impact on the vehicle's investment decisions, making it more suitable for treaty shopping.[138]

[E] Treaty Entitlement of Investors

If a CIV is not entitled to claim tax treaty benefits under the treaty's general rules, it is common ground that the investors are entitled to claim tax treaty benefits; otherwise a tax treaty would have failed in its purpose of eliminating juridical double taxation.[139] If the CIV and the investors are located in different countries, the investors may claim the benefits granted by the tax treaty between the state where the investment is situated (the 'source state') and the state(s) in which the investors are resident.[140]

Under such an approach, administrative difficulties may, however, make investors refrain from claiming tax treaty benefits; given the number of investments a CIV may have and the relatively small share a single investor may have therein, the benefits of a claim related to a particular item of income may be rather insignificant.[141] Further, tax authorities would more than likely be overwhelmed by the number of claims made, if every investor in every non-treaty entitled CIV made a claim for tax treaty benefits.[142] Therefore, a CIV should be allowed to claim its investors' tax treaty benefits on their behalf, allowing an aggregated claim for its investors against tax authorities.[143]

134. *See supra* §10.03[C] (on the so-called transparency principle or neutrality principle).
135. *See* OECD Model Comm. on Art. 1, para. 28; OECD 2010 CIV Report, at 9–10 (para. 29); Da Silva, *supra* note 10, at 200–202.
136. *See* Eberhardt, *supra* note 133, at 378.
137. *See ibid.*
138. *See ibid.*
139. *See* OECD 2010 CIV Report, at 10 (para. 36); Wassermeyer, *supra* note 81, margin nos 33b–33d; *see also* Wassermeyer & Kaeser, *supra* note 65, margin no. 27 (on CIVs in the legal form of partnerships).
140. *See* OECD 2010 CIV Report, at 10 (para. 36).
141. *See* OECD Model Comm. on Art. 1, para. 41; OECD 2010 CIV Report, at 10 (para. 37); Rust, *supra* note 10, margin no. 30.
142. *See* OECD 2010 CIV Report, at 10 (para. 37).
143. *See* OECD 2010 CIV Report, at 10–11 (paras 38–40).

§10.04 SPECIAL TAX TREATY PROVISIONS FOR CIVS RELATED TO TREATY ENTITLEMENT AND BENEFICIAL OWNERSHIP

[A] General Remarks

Given its complexity, the interpretation of the relevant terms is neither unambiguous nor clear in every case,[144] resulting in undesirable legal uncertainty.[145] Further, the Contracting States may qualify CIVs differently.[146] For example, from a German perspective, many investment vehicles, including unincorporated investment vehicles, might be treated as a 'resident of a Contracting State' because the German Federal Fiscal Court (*Bundesfinanzhof*) stated that (foreign) non-transparent investment vehicles may qualify as a 'resident of a Contracting State' irrespective of a tax exemption.[147] By contrast, under its general rules, Luxembourg apparently only regards incorporated investment vehicles, such as SICAVs and SICAFs, as a 'resident of a Contracting State' for tax treaty purposes.[148]

Differences with respect to the qualification of CIVs may make a tax treaty appear unbalanced.[149] In order to overcome the difficulties mentioned, the OECD 2010 CIV Report and the OECD Model Commentary offered potential solutions.

[B] Content of Special Tax Treaty Provisions

Besides mutual agreement procedures targeted at the interpretation and application of the general tax treaty provisions to CIVs,[150] both the OECD 2010 CIV Report and the OECD Model Commentary recommend the inclusion of special tax treaty provisions that grant both treaty entitlement and beneficial ownership to CIVs.[151] The OECD's proposals, of course, may be adapted to the needs of the Contracting States.[152] Special tax treaty provisions do not constitute treaty entitlement for CIVs if the conditions of the general provisions are met, but do provide legal certainty[153] if the personal scope of application is clearly determined. Clarity can be achieved if a special tax treaty provision applies to investment vehicles covered by domestic investment tax law.[154] By

144. *See* OECD Model Comm. on Art. 1, para. 29.
145. *See supra* §10.01.
146. *See supra* §10.03[C].
147. German Federal Fiscal Court *(Bundesfinanzhof)*, Judgment, 6 June 2012, I R 52/11, Bundessteuerblatt II 2014, 240; *see also supra* §10.03[C].
148. *See supra* §10.03[C].
149. *See* OECD Model Comm. on Art. 1, para. 32; OECD 2010 CIV Report, at 13 (para. 50), 18 (proposed para. 6.18).
150. *See* OECD Model Comm. on Art. 1, para. 30.
151. *See ibid.*, para. 31; OECD 2010 CIV Report, at 18 (proposed para. 6.17). For examples of special tax treaty provisions in Luxembourg tax treaties, *see* Schaffner, *supra* note 83.
152. *See* OECD Model Comm. on Art. 1, paras 31–48; OECD 2010 CIV Report, at 12–24 (paras 48–62).
153. *See* OECD Model Comm. on Art. 1, para. 31; OECD 2010 CIV Report, at 12 (para. 48).
154. *See* OECD Model Comm. on Art. 1, para. 31; OECD 2010 CIV Report, at 18 (proposed para. 6.17).

contrast, only if a CIV is not entitled to claim tax treaty benefits under the general rules anyway, do special tax treaty provisions constitute treaty entitlement.

In addition to the general beneficial-ownership requirement included in the distributive rules,[155] special tax treaty provisions may contain additional mechanisms for the prevention of treaty shopping or other forms of improper use of a particular tax treaty through a CIV.[156] Beyond their role as anti-abuse provisions, such provisions may also be a clarification that CIVs are treaty entitled since they only make sense if a tax treaty applies to them.[157] An exception to anti-treaty shopping mechanisms may apply to publicly traded CIVs, as they normally cannot be used for treaty shopping.[158] However, such exception should not rule out treaty entitlement for CIVs in general or for publicly traded CIVs, since the rationale of the exception is that no treaty shopping can occur with respect to publicly traded CIVs. In anti-treaty shopping provisions, treaty entitlement or, more precisely, specific tax treaty benefits could be linked to the residence state of the investors.[159] For example, treaty entitlement or specific tax treaty benefits could be granted to a CIV (i) only to the extent that investors are a 'resident of the Contracting State' in which a CIV is established[160] or investors are entitled to equivalent tax treaty benefits on the basis of a tax treaty between the state where the income arises and the residence state of the investor,[161] or (ii) fully provided that the proportion of investors who are 'residents of a Contracting State' and, therefore, entitled to tax treaty benefits themselves, exceeds a threshold specified in the tax treaty.[162] Investors who are a 'resident of a Contracting State' in which the CIV is established or entitled to tax treaty benefits themselves within the meaning of such special tax treaty provisions may be referred to as 'equivalent beneficiaries'.[163] In practice, however, it might be difficult for CIVs to determine the proportion of equivalent beneficiaries if interests in them are transferred to other investors or held by intermediaries.[164]

Regardless of difficulties in determining the proportion of equivalent beneficiaries, this approach may be inconsistent if tax treaty benefits are granted to CIVs as such.[165] Given the aim of investment tax law, according to which the tax consequences

155. *See supra* §10.02[C].
156. *See* OECD Model Comm. on Art. 1, paras 33–34; OECD 2010 CIV Report, at 13–15 (paras 52–57), 18–19 (proposed paras 6.18–6.19).
157. *See* Eberhardt, *supra* note 133, at 378; Geurts, *supra* note 93, at 573–574; Martin Schraufl, *Limitation-on-benefits-Regelungen im Hinblick auf deutsches Investmentvermögen*, 13 PIStB 335, 335 (2011).
158. *See* OECD Model Comm. on Art. 1, para. 46; OECD 2010 CIV Report, at 14, para. 57; Eberhardt, *supra* note 133, at 378; *see also* §10.03[C].
159. *See* OECD Model Comm. on Art. 1, para. 37; OECD 2010 CIV Report, at 14 (para. 56), 18–19 (proposed paras 6.18–6.19).
160. *See* OECD Model Comm. on Art. 1, paras 35 and 40; OECD 2010 CIV Report, at 21 (proposed para. 6.26).
161. *See* OECD Model Comm. on Art. 1, paras 35 and 37; OECD 2010 CIV Report, at 14 (paras 55–56), 19–20 (proposed para. 6.21).
162. *See* OECD Model Comm. on Art. 1, para. 41; OECD 2010 CIV Report, at 14 (paras 55–56).
163. *See* OECD Model Comm. on Art. 1, para. 35; OECD 2010 CIV Report, at 19–20 (proposed para. 6.21).
164. *See* OECD 2010 CIV Report, at 6–7 (paras 19–21); Eberhardt, *supra* note 133, at 380–381.
165. *See* OECD 2010 CIV Report, at 14 (para. 56).

of an investment in a CIV should be neutral compared to the tax consequences of a direct investment,[166] only an equivalent beneficiary should be able to take advantage of tax treaty benefits without any reductions,[167] which may not be guaranteed under rules that link tax treaty benefits granted to a CIV, as such, to the proportion of equivalent beneficiaries. Investors that qualify as equivalent beneficiaries may not be able to take full advantage of tax treaty benefits in a case when tax treaty benefits are granted proportionally based on the extent that equivalent beneficiaries hold interests in the CIV.[168] In turn, investors who do not qualify as equivalent beneficiaries may profit indirectly from tax treaty benefits if other investors qualify as equivalent beneficiaries.[169] A combination of both approaches (i.e., tax treaty benefits are, as a matter of principle, granted proportionally, but only fully if the proportion of equivalent beneficiaries exceeds a threshold specified in the tax treaty)[170] would not remove the inconsistencies, either, but would generally facilitate the application of a tax treaty.[171]

These inconsistencies may be overcome if - as proposed by the OECD as an alternative approach - a CIV is not entitled to tax treaty benefits itself, but may claim tax treaty benefits on behalf of its investors (the 'look-through-approach'[172]).[173] This approach facilitates the administration of granting tax treaty benefits, so that not every single investor must claim tax treaty benefits on its own.[174] The CIV, though, would have to know - in detail - the countries in which its investors are resident at the time the income is generated. Treaty shopping should not be a problem under such an approach, since tax treaty benefits could only be claimed on behalf of investors who are entitled to such benefits.

In considering which approach to be chosen, the Contracting States should take into account the investment vehicles actually covered by the special tax treaty provision, as the look-through-approach and other anti-treaty shopping provisions linked to the residence state of the investors do not result in administrative difficulties in every case, particularly, if its ownership is sufficiently stable.[175] Irrespective of the approach chosen by the Contracting States, withholding taxes and administration of tax treaty benefits are of major importance with regard to compliance costs and the

166. *See* §10.03, *supra*.
167. *See* OECD Model Comm. on Art. 1, para. 37; OECD 2010 CIV Report, at 20 (proposed para. 6.23).
168. *See* OECD 2010 CIV Report, at 14 (para. 56).
169. *See ibid.*
170. *See ibid.*
171. *See* Eberhardt, *supra* note 133, at 380-381 (in favour of such an approach).
172. *See* OECD 2010 CIV Report, at 15 (paras 60-61).
173. *See* OECD Model Comm. on Art. 1, para. 42; OECD 2010 CIV Report, at 21-22 (proposed para. 6.28); *see also supra* §10.03[E] (on CIVs claiming tax treaty benefits on behalf of their investors when they are not entitled to them themselves).
174. *See supra* §10.03[E] (on CIVs claiming tax treaty benefits on behalf of their investors when they are not entitled to them themselves).
175. *See* OECD 2010 CIV Report, at 15 (para. 61).

CIV's rate of return.[176] Therefore, the relevant provisions must be designed in a way that can be applied easily.[177]

[C] Weaknesses of Special Tax Treaty Provisions for CIVs, Exemplified by the Provisions in the Germany/Luxembourg Tax Treaty

Special tax treaty provisions do not, however, mean that double taxation will be avoided in every case or that all uncertainty has been removed. Rather, such special tax treaty provisions may have weaknesses due to their design, particularly if there is a limitation on the scope of application. These weaknesses cannot be discussed in detail here, since the design of such provisions varies significantly.[178]

Nevertheless, to give an idea of some issues that might be raised by special tax treaty provisions, without anticipating details that are subject to a separate contribution in this volume,[179] attention is drawn to the Germany/Luxembourg Tax Treaty[180] signed on 23 April 2012. Paragraph 1 of the Protocol thereto[181] contains a special provision concerning the treaty entitlement of CIVs.[182] In contrast, its Article 10(2), sentence 1, letter (a) of the Germany/Luxembourg Tax Treaty, which, as a matter of principle, also applies to CIVs, is of minor importance with regard to treaty entitlement, since it concerns the distributive rule governing the tax treatment of dividend income.

Said Paragraph 1 reads as follows:

> (1) Ein nach dem Recht eines Vertragsstaates gebildetes *Investmentvermögen*, das aus dem anderen Vertragsstaat stammende Dividenden oder Zinsen bezieht, kann die in den Artikeln 10 und 11 dieses Abkommens vorgesehenen Beschränkungen des Besteuerungsrechts des anderen Vertragsstaats geltend machen, soweit die Anteile an dem Investmentvermögen von *in dem erstgenannten Staat ansässigen Personen* gehalten werden. Mit Anerkennung eines Anspruchs des Investmentvermögens erlischt das Recht der Anteilscheininhaber an diesem Investmentvermögen, einen Anspruch auf dieselbe Vergünstigung geltend zu machen.
>
> Im Sinne dieser Bestimmung bedeutet *Investmentvermögen*
>
> (a) in der Bundesrepublik Deutschland ein durch eine Kapitalanlagegesellschaft verwaltetes *Sondervermögen* im Sinne des Investmentgesetzes,
>
> (b) in Luxemburg ein *Investmentfond (fonds commun de placement)*.

176. *See ibid.*, at 6-7 (paras 19-21).
177. *See* OECD Model Comm. on Art. 1, paras 43-45; OECD 2010 CIV Report, at 20 (proposed paras 6.29-6.31).
178. For a Luxembourg perspective, *see* Schaffner, *supra* note 83.
179. *See ibid.*
180. *See* Abkommen vom 23. April 2012 zwischen der Bundesrepublik Deutschland und dem Großherzogtum Luxemburg zur Vermeidung der Doppelbesteuerung und Verhinderung der Steuerhinterziehung auf dem Gebiet der Steuern vom Einkommen und vom Vermögen, Bundesgesetzblatt 2012 II, pp. 1402, 1403.
181. According to Article 29 of the Germany/Luxembourg Tax Treaty, its Protocol is part thereof.
182. *See* Administration des contributions directes du Grand-Duché de Luxembourg, Circulaire du directeur des contributions, L.G. - Conv. D.I. n° 58 du 9 février 2015 (administrative guidelines from the Luxembourg tax authorities).

(2) *Investmentgesellschaften* können die in Artikel 10 und 11 vorgesehenen Beschränkungen selbständig geltend machen. Im Sinne dieser Bestimmung bedeutet *Investmentgesellschaft*
(a) in der Bundesrepublik Deutschland die *Investmentaktiengesellschaft*
(b) in Luxemburg
- die *Risikoanlagegesellschaft (société d'investissement en capital à risque [SICAR]),*
- die *Anlagegesellschaft mit variablem Kapital (société d'investissement à capital variable [SICAV])* und
- die *Anlagegesellschaft mit festem Kapital (société d' investissement à capital fixe [SICAF]).*

Die zuständigen Behörden können die Einzelheiten zur Durchführung dieser Bestimmung in gegenseitigem Einvernehmen regeln, um sicherzustellen, dass aufgrund dieser Bestimmung keine unberechtigten Erstattungen erfolgen (emphasis added; German sole authentic language).

According to the memorandum ('*Denkschrift*'), said Paragraph 1 was incorporated at the explicit request of Luxembourg,[183] which makes sense given the importance of the investment fund industry to Luxembourg.[184] However, these provisions seem to have a somewhat surprising content, since their scope of application is limited. It is not quite clear why the scope of application is limited and what the implications of those limitations are.

With regard to the personal scope of application, there are two categories of investment vehicles[185] said Paragraph 1 applies to:

- *Investmentvermögen* (often translated as a 'pool of assets'), including Germany's *Sondervermögen* under the *Investmentgesetz* (German Investment Act) that was subsequently replaced by the *Kapitalanlagegesetzbuch* (German Capital Investment Act),[186] and Luxembourg's *Investmentfond* ([FCP]).
- *Investmentgesellschaften* (investment companies), including Germany's *Investmentaktiengesellschaft* (InvAG), and Luxembourg's *Anlagegesellschaft mit variablem Kapital (société d'investissement à capital variable* [SICAV]) and *Anlagegesellschaft mit festem Kapital (société d' investissement à capital fixe* [SICAF]).[187]

183. *See* Bundesregierung, *Entwurf eines Gesetzes zu dem Abkommen vom 23. April 2012 zwischen der Bundesrepublik Deutschland und dem Großherzogtum Luxemburg zur Vermeidung der Doppelbesteuerung und Verhinderung der Steuerhinterziehung auf dem Gebiet der Steuern vom Einkommen und vom Vermögen*, BR-Drucksache 478/12, p. 23.
184. *See supra* §10.01.
185. *See* Eberhardt, *supra* note 133, at 382–383.
186. The reference to the German Investment Act (*Investmentgesetz*) in the Germany/Luxembourg Tax Treaty does not rule out the application of the Germany/Luxembourg Tax Treaty to CIVs governed by the German Capital Investment Act (*Kapitalanlagegesetzbuch*) since, as a matter of principle, a reference to domestic (tax or investment) law in a tax treaty is dynamic, meaning that it encompasses the law in force at the time the tax treaty is applied. *See* Lehner, *supra* note 21, margin no. 187. *See also* Dürrschmidt, *supra* note 63, margin no. 124. In particular, Article 3(2) OECD Model refers to domestic law, in particular domestic tax law, for the definition of terms used in a tax treaty. According to the explicit wording thereof, the reference is dynamic.
187. Luxembourg's *Société d'investissement en capital à risque* (SICAR) also qualifies as an investment company (*Investmentgesellschaft*), but a SICAR is not obliged to ensure risk

The investment vehicles covered by said Paragraph 1 are listed exhaustively.[188] Therefore, it does not apply to other investment vehicles, such as the Luxembourg investment vehicles for pension funds.[189] Further, the extent of treaty entitlement or, more precisely, of treaty benefits a CIV may claim depends on the legal form of the relevant investment vehicle. Paragraph 1(1) makes clear that *Investementvermögen* (pools of assets) are entitled to tax treaty benefits thereunder to the extent their investors are resident in the state in which the investment fund is established, while Paragraph 1(2) makes clear that *Investmentgesellschaften* (investment companies) are entitled to tax treaty benefits without restrictions linked to the residence of the investors.

Interestingly, the scope of the provision is not only limited with regard to the eligible investment vehicles, but also with regard to the types of income involved. According to the explicit wording, said Paragraph 1 only applies to dividends and interest covered by Articles 10 and 11 of the Germany/Luxembourg Tax Treaty.[190] Other types of income, such as income from immovable property, are not encompassed by the special tax treaty provision.[191]

Due to the restrictions in terms of the investment vehicles and the types of income covered by said Paragraph 1, one must determine whether the special tax treaty provision may preclude the general provisions of the Germany/Luxembourg Tax Treaty from governing the personal scope of application and the income covered in situations not covered thereby. According to the author's view, it does not.[192] Rather, Paragraph 1's special tax treaty provision mainly provides legal certainty.[193] In addition, with regard to *Investementvermögen* (pool of assets), it could (a) prevent treaty shopping through unincorporated investment vehicles (as a sort of LOB

diversification, meaning that it does not qualify as a CIV as defined by the OECD. *See* Alain Steichen, *Anhang DBA Luxemburg, in* Wassermeyer et al., eds, *supra* note 65, margin no. 147; *see also* Eric Fort, *Luxemburg, in Steuern in Europa, Amerika und Asien,* margin no. 301 (Annemarie Mennel & Jutta Förster eds, loose-leaf, NWB Verlag, 2014).

188. *See* Dirk Siegers, *Artikel 1 DBA Luxembourg, in* Wassermeyer et al., eds, *supra* note 65, margin no. 11; Alain Steichen, *Artikel 10 DBA Luxemburg*, in Wassermeyer et al., eds, *supra* note 65, margin no. 41.
189. For examples, *see* Alain Steichen, *Artikel 1 DBA Luxemburg, in* Wassermeyer et al., eds, *supra* note 65, margin no. 29.
190. *See* Eberhardt, *supra* note 133, at 382; Eric Fort, Jan Neugebauer & Clemens Willvonseder, *Änderungen im DBA Deutschland-Luxemburg Das neue Doppelbesteuerungsabkommen mit Luxemburg*, IWB 391, 399 (2012); Jacob, *supra* note 93, 21 IStR 749, 750; Jacob, *supra* note 93, 14 SAM 167, 168; Jacob & Hagena, *supra* note 93, 66 Bull Int'l Tax'n 530, 531–532.
191. *See* Jacob, *supra* note 93, 21 IStR 749, 750; Jacob, *supra* note 93, 14 SAM 167, 168; Jacob & Hagena, *supra* note 93, at 531–532. The terminology of the heading of Paragraph 1 of the Protocol to the Germany/Luxembourg Tax Treaty seems, at first glance, a bit unclear. It refers to the Germany/Luxembourg Tax Treaty in general ('*Zu dem Abkommen insgesamt*'), although it is limited to income covered by Arts 10 (Dividend) and 11 (Interest). However, in contrast to Paragraph 2 of the Protocol to the Germany/Luxembourg Tax Treaty, the heading of which explicitly refers to Arts 10 and 11 ('*Zu den Artikeln 10 und 11*'), Paragraph 1 of the Protocol to the Germany/Luxembourg Tax Treaty also provides for the 'treaty entitlement' of the investment vehicles specified in the provision.
192. This view is shared by Lauermann & Birker, *supra* note 18, at 53; Siegers, *supra* note 188, margin no. 12; *contra* Friedhelm Jacob, *supra* note 191, 21 IStR 749, 750–751.
193. *See* Siegers, *supra* note 188, margin no. 12.

clause[194]) or (b) if one does not believe *Investmentvermögen* (pools of assets) are entitled to tax treaty benefits, facilitate the claiming of such benefits on behalf of their investors.[195] Further, it clarifies that incorporated investment vehicles (such as *Investmentgesellschaften* (investment companies) are entitled to claim tax treaty benefits for themselves.[196] Against this background, it does not constitute treaty entitlement for the investment vehicles covered, if the general requirements of treaty entitlement are met. The clarifying character of such a provision, however, may change into a constituting character if, for example, amendments to domestic (investment) tax law, such as the abolition of the total tax exemption granted to CIVs provided for in German domestic investment tax law,[197] impact the tax treaty analysis.[198] The same holds true if a Contracting State does not grant tax treaty benefits to some forms of investment vehicles under the general rules.

Because of the restrictions mentioned, Paragraph 1's special tax treaty provision seems to be inconsistent, given its apparent purpose to promote Luxembourg as a location for CIVs, since its FCPs may only claim tax treaty benefits to the extent its investors are resident in Luxembourg.[199] Given its focus on international investors,[200] it seems, however, to be unlikely that Luxembourg FCPs will be able to claim tax treaty benefits on a large scale.[201] It is possible, though, in many cases, that foreign investors would not invest in Luxembourg FCPs directly, but would do so through a so-called master fund that - due to its legal form - might well benefit from beneficial treatment under Luxembourg's domestic (investment) tax and tax treaty law, particularly under Paragraph 1(2) of the Protocol to the Germany/Luxembourg Tax Treaty. Further details on Luxembourg fund structuring are not discussed here but are the subject of a separate contribution to this volume.[202]

Some weaknesses of special tax treaty provisions applicable to CIVs are mainly rooted in their design. They can be either practically irrelevant or eliminated through an amendment of the tax treaty. Other weaknesses may also result from the character

194. *See* Lauermann & Birker, *supra* note 18, at 53–54.
195. *See* Federal German Ministry of Finance (*Bundesministerium der Finanzen*), letter dated 24 March 2015, IV B 3 - S 1301-LUX/0-08, not officially published; summary available at 103 DStZ 502, 503 (2015); for more on the position of the German tax authorities, *see* Höring, *supra* note 117 at 319–321.
196. *See* Lauermann & Birker, *supra* note 18, at 53.
197. *See* Anzinger, supra note 32.
198. *See supra* §10.03[C].
199. *See* Steichen, *supra* note 189, margin no. 42. Further, weaknesses may not only occur with regard to 'treaty entitlement', but also with regard to the 'distributive rules'. In particular, the tax rate applicable to investment companies as receiving company is only limited to 15% rather than to 5% (Article 10(2)(1)(a) of the Germany/Luxembourg Tax Treaty). It is true that the goal of the provision to promote Luxembourg as a location for CIVs could be achieved better in case of a limitation to 5%. Nevertheless, it means a limitation of the tax rate. *See* Jens Schönfeld, *Die Besteuerung von Dividenden nach dem neuen DBA-Luxemburg*, 21 IStR 834, 835 (2012).
200. *See supra* §10.01.
201. *See* Lauermann & Birker, *supra* note 18, at 54.
202. *See* Geoffrey Scardoni, *infra*, Chapter 14.

of tax treaties as bilateral treaties.[203] Trilateral situations, which occur when a CIV, its investors, and its investments are located in different countries, may not be adequately treated in a bilateral tax treaty, since one country affected is not a party to the bilateral tax treaty between the other countries. Even if special tax treaty provisions could be designed in a way that covers trilateral situations,[204] this would 'only' be a bilateral (two-party) solution to a trilateral situation.[205] Further details on this issue are not discussed here, as trilateral situations do not generally concern treaty entitlement with regard to a bilateral tax treaty, but issues of the avoidance of double taxation,[206] that are subject of a separate chapter in this volume.[207] In any case, weaknesses of special tax treaty provisions in existing (bilateral) tax treaties cannot be eliminated easily since amendments can only be effected in a lengthy process.

§10.05 CONCLUSION AND IMPACT OF EU LAW AND THE G20/OECD PROJECT CONFRONTING BEPS

To sum up, the comments so far have revealed that the application of tax treaties to CIVs is a complicated area of tax treaty law. This particularly holds true for treaty entitlement. Awareness of the issue and the inclusion of special tax treaty provisions applicable to CIVs do not guarantee that all uncertainty is removed. While tax treaty issues, as such, are already complex, things may get even more complicated as areas of law other than tax treaty law may affect treaty entitlement for CIVs.

At first, due to the interplay of tax treaty law and domestic tax law,[208] any amendment of the legal framework of domestic investment tax law may impact the analysis of tax treaty law. Germany's recent reform of its domestic investment tax law, in the course of which the total tax exemption for CIVs was replaced by tax liability for CIVs with particular items of source income,[209] may serve as an illustrative example.[210]

Further, the implications of EU law must be considered. Such issues may concern the impact of EU law on tax treaties, in general,[211] and on the tax treatment of CIVs, in particular, taking into account State-aid law,[212] the EU fundamental freedoms,[213] and EU tax directives.[214] Even if most EU law issues are not specifically related to the

203. *See* OECD 2010 CIV Report, at 3 (para. 2), 11 (para. 44); Keith Lawson, *infra*, Chapter 12.
204. *See* OECD 2010 CIV Report, at 12, (para. 45) (for an example).
205. *See* OECD 2010 CIV Report, at 12 (para. 46).
206. *See* OECD 2010 CIV Report, at 11 (para. 44).
207. *See* Gutmann, *supra* note 58.
208. *See supra* §10.01.
209. *See* Anzinger, *supra* note 32.
210. *See supra* §10.03[C].
211. *See* Wolfgang Schön, *Doppelbesteuerung und EU-Recht, in Doppelbesteuerung: DBA Zum 75. Geburtstag von Prof. Dr. Dr. h.c. Franz Wassermeyer*, 7, 9–11 (Christian Kaeser ed., Verlag C. H. Beck 2015).
212. *See* Claire Micheau, *supra*, Chapter 5.
213. *See* Keith O'Donnell and Uljana Molitor-March, *supra*, Chapter 6, and Mario Tenore, *supra*, Chapter 7.
214. *See* Pantazatou, *supra* note 102.

application of tax treaties to CIVs, EU law may impact their design and application to CIVs. For example, mechanisms intended to prevent treaty shopping that link treaty entitlement and tax treaty benefits to the residence state of a CIV's investors may be incompatible with the case law of the Court of Justice of the European Union (CJEU) applying the fundamental freedoms.[215] In contrast, its case law holds that the fundamental freedoms do not oblige the EU Member States to grant most-favoured-nation treatment with regard to tax treaty benefits,[216] which might also hold true for special tax treaty provisions applicable to CIVs.[217]

Finally, as mentioned earlier,[218] treaty entitlement – in its strict sense – is not affected by the BEPS Project. Due to its far-reaching implications, it may, nevertheless, impact the tax treatment of CIVs in areas other than treaty entitlement. Without discussing details,[219] some relevant issues are briefly mentioned here. First, clarification that tax treaties are not only targeted at the avoidance of international double taxation, but also at the avoidance of double non-taxation,[220] may be relevant to the tax treatment of CIVs, because, as a matter of principle, CIVs can be used for tax avoidance. As a consequence, the LOB clause included in Article 29(1) OECD Model[221] may apply to CIVs, depending on their tax treatment under domestic tax law and under the relevant tax treaty.[222] Even if such a clause does not preclude treaty entitlement in the strict sense, the denial of tax treaty benefits may have the same factual consequences as a denial of treaty entitlement. Also, the so-called Principal Purpose Test (PPT) included in Article 29(9) OECD Model[223] may, as a matter of principle, be applied to CIVs. Second, the so-called multilateral instrument, which is to be established as

215. *See Orange European Smallcap Fund*, C-194/06, Judgment, EU:C:2008:289, paras 72–74, 79, 82–83, 94–95 (provisions in domestic investment tax law countering such restrictions).
216. *See D.*, C-376/03, Judgment, EU:C:2005:424.
217. *See* Fibbe, *supra* note 88, at 149–151 (an in-depth analysis of the issue).
218. *See supra* §10.01.
219. *See* Lawson, *supra* note 203.
220. *See* OECD Model, Title ('prevention of tax evasion and avoidance'), Preamble ('without creating opportunities for non-taxation or reduced taxation through tax evasion or avoidance') and Introduction, para. 16.1; OECD 2015 Inappropriate Circumstances Report, at 91 (paras 68–74). Avoiding double *non*-taxation has long been a purpose of tax treaties. *See* OECD 2010 CIV Report, at 3 (para. 2). However, as a consequence of the BEPS Project, it has been clarified and supported by specific anti-abuse provisions.
221. *See supra* §10.04[C], §10.02[C] (both CIVs and LOB clauses in general) and §10.04[C] (special LOB clause for CIVs in the Germany/Luxembourg Tax Treaty).
222. *See* OECD Model Comm. on Art. 29, paras 55–67 (specific provisions for CIVs); OECD 2015 Inappropriate Circumstances Report, at 15 (para. 9), 21 (proposed OECD Model Art. X(2)(f)), 32–35 (proposed OECD Model Art. X(2)(f) – detailed version and OECD Model Commentary thereon); Blum & Pinetz, *supra* note 40, at 253–270; Martha Isabel Rodriguez Daniels, *Limitation on Benefits and (non-)Collective Investment Vehicle*s, *in Preventing Treaty Abuse* (Daniel W. Blum & Markus Seiler eds, Linde 2016), 253, 259–270 (on CIVs in the context of the LOB clause in Article 29(1) OECD Model); *see also* Dremel, *supra* note 82 (on CIVs in the context of LOB clauses included in tax treaties prior to the BEPS Project-era OECD Model amendment).
223. *See* OECD 2015 Inappropriate Circumstances Report, at 54–55 (para. 26 and the proposed para. 7 of the Article containing the LOB clause, and the proposed paragraphs of the OECD Model Commentary thereon).

part of the BEPS Project,[224] might assist Contracting States in the future amending their tax treaties to adopt an LOB clause[225] or special tax treaty provisions applicable to CIVs.[226]

224. *See* OECD, *Report 'Developing a Multilateral Instrument to Modify Bilateral Tax Treaties–Action 15: 2015 Final Report'* (2015).
225. *See* OECD-sponsored Multilateral Convention to Implement Tax Treaty Related Measures to Prevent BEPS (not yet in force), Art. 7-Prevention of Treaty Abuse; *see also* Lawson, *supra* note 203.
226. *See supra* §10.04. Special tax treaty provisions applicable to CIVs are not yet included in the 'multilateral instrument'. However, it might be amended to do so in the future.

CHAPTER 11

Funds in International Tax Law: Examples from Luxembourg's Treaties

Jean Schaffner

§11.01 INTRODUCTION

The exclusive purpose of 'undertakings for collective investments' (UCIs) is the collective investment of savings acquired from the public while respecting the principle of risk diversification.[1] Luxembourg UCIs are not subject to corporate taxes, but are liable to an annual *taxe d'abonnement* (subscription tax) of 0.05 %[2] on the value of their net assets.[3] The amount of that subscription tax is reduced to 0.01 % for monetary UCIs[4] and for compartments and securities classes of UCIs reserved for institutional investors; certain other UCIs are completely exempt therefrom (i.e., funds of funds,[5] funds investing in micro-finance institutions and certain monetary funds (a) whose securities are reserved for institutional investors who invest exclusively in monetary market instruments and deposits with credit institutions, (b) whose portfolio-weighted residual maturity does not exceed ninety days, and (c) who enjoy the highest rating delivered by a recognized rating agency).

Traditionally, if a UCI has several compartments, the reduced subscription tax is reserved for the compartments that respect the investment policy set forth above (i.e., that meet the required criteria to benefit from such a reduction). Luxembourg's law also takes account of the existence of several classes of securities within the same

1. For a comprehensive description of Luxembourg's tax regime for Luxembourg funds, *see* Eric Fort & Philipp Jost, *supra*, Chapter 2.
2. The rate had been 0.06 % until a fiscal reform came into effect in 2002 pursuant to Art. 10, *la Loi du 21 décembre 2001 portant réforme de certaines dispositions en matière des impôts directs et indirects*.
3. Meaning, the value of its assets after deducting the amount of its debts.
4. Funds investing solely in monetary market instruments and cash deposits.
5. To avoid double submission to the subscription tax.

compartment. In such cases, the subscription tax exemption for certain monetary funds, and the 0.01% reduced fee, only apply to securities reserved for institutional investors.

Luxembourg's 15 June 2004 law regarding *Sociétés d'Investissement en Capital à Risque* or SICARs (venture capital companies)[6] also eliminated from the subscription tax for UCIs with securities reserved for pension institutions and for companies investing sums to provide pension benefits to their employees. The law's aim was to encourage the grouping of assets to optimize their management and, thus, deliver better pensions (pension pooling).

Schematically, UCIs can be divided into *Sociétés d'Investissement à Capital Variable* or SICAVs (investment companies with variable share capital) and *Fonds Communs de Placement* or FCPs (collective investment funds).[7] *Sociétés d'investissement à capital fixe* or SICAFs (investment companies with fixed capital) usually follow the same regime as SICAVs. We will not address herein other types of investment vehicles frequently used in Luxembourg (such as the SOPARFI, a fully taxable, financial participation company, which is an ordinary Luxembourg company, benefiting from the participation exemption with respect to dividends and capital gains on shares; the SICAR, which is a fully taxable company, investing exclusively in risk capital and otherwise exempt from income and capital gains on securities; and pension funds (ASSEP) and pension companies (SEPCAVs), as well as securitization companies).

Once, certain Luxembourg companies, governed by the now-abrogated law of 31 July 1929[8] and commonly known as '1929 holding companies', were also subject only to subscription tax and not to common taxes imposed on companies (e.g., corporate income tax, municipal business tax, and net wealth tax). The tax regime for such 1929 holding companies expired on 20 July 2006 and all remaining 1929 holding companies were only allowed to benefit from conditional grandfathering until 31 December 2010.

Sociétés de Gestion de Patrimoine Familial or SPFs (family estate management companies)[9] are subject to tax treatment that is similar to that of UCIs, as they are subject to an annual subscription tax, also calculated on the value of their net assets. The SPF replaced Luxembourg's former 1929 holding companies, which were abolished, as they were found to benefit from an unfair State-aid regime by the European

6. *Loi du 15 juin 2004 relative à la Société d'investissement en capital à risque (SICAR) et portant modification de la loi modifiée du 4 décembre 1967 relative à l'impôt sur le revenu ; la loi modifiée du 16 octobre 1934 concernant l'impôt sur la fortune ; la loi modifiée du 1er décembre 1936 concernant l'impôt commercial communal ; la loi modifiée du 12 février 1979 concernant la taxe sur la valeur ajoutée ; et la loi modifiée du 20 décembre 2002 concernant les organismes de placement collectif,* as amended.
7. *See further* Claude Kremer & Isabelle Lebbe, *Organismes de placement collectif et véhicules d'investissement apparentés en droit luxembourgeois* (2014).
8. *Loi du 31 juillet 1929 sur le régime fiscal des sociétés de participations financières* (Holding companies) (abrogated).
9. *Loi du 11 mai 2007 relative à la création d'une société de gestion de patrimoine familial* (SPF), as amended.

Commission. Initially, SPFs were prevented, as were the former 1929 holding companies, from receiving more than 5% of their total dividends from non-resident companies that were not considered to be fully taxable according to Luxembourg standards; they could, therefore, under those conditions, lose their tax status and became fully taxable. That condition, which potentially discriminated against investments in European Union (EU) companies, was abolished in 2012.

With regards to taxing investors, SICAVs are fiscally opaque. Their shareholders, in principle, are only taxable on dividends received from the SICAV itself during a distribution and on the capital gains they realize at the sale or repurchase of their shares. FCPs, *a priori*, are tax transparent; their investors are taxed directly on the underlying assets in the FCP, in view of investments made and income realized (*see infra*).

The application of tax treaties to UCIs is of fundamental importance. From a tax perspective, a UCI manager has no interest in investing in income generating products that bear an important withholding tax in their country of origin. As a UCI is subject only to an annual subscription tax in Luxembourg, such a foreign withholding tax could not be credited against the Luxembourg tax due and, thus, reduces the investment return all the more. If a UCI can benefit from the provisions of the particular tax treaty signed by Luxembourg, it is entitled to its withholding tax reductions and exemptions on dividends and interest from the other Contracting State arising therefrom. The tax impact, consequently, may be reduced or even eliminated.

§11.02 SICAVS

To be considered as a resident of a Contracting State under the OECD's Model Tax Convention on Income and on Capital,[10] on which most Luxembourg tax treaties are based, a 'person', under the laws of the State of which said person claims to be a resident, has to be liable to tax therein by reason of said person's domicile, residence, place of effective management, or any other criterion, and the term 'resident' excludes persons liable to tax in that State only in relation to income from sources in that State.[11] The term 'person' is defined in a very broad manner, and includes individuals, companies, and other bodies of persons,[12] so that this definition is generally met by investment funds. The exclusion of persons liable to tax based only on income from sources in their State of origin is aimed, for instance, at individuals taxed only on a remittance basis, but not on income derived from sources outside their country of residence and not otherwise repatriated.

We, therefore, can concentrate on liability to tax itself in the country of origin of the fund.

---

10. OECD, Model Tax Convention on Income and on Capital 2014 (Full Version) available at http://dx.doi.org/10.1787/9789264239081-en (last accessed 8 December 2017) (hereinafter 'OECD Model', and the commentary published therewith (the 'OECD Model Commentary')).
11. OECD Model Art. 3.
12. *Ibid.*, Art. 3.

To enable a SICAV to benefit from a tax treaty, it could first be argued that the Luxembourg treaties that follow the OECD Model cover the subscription tax. Article 2 OECD Model specifically states that the convention shall:

> apply to taxes on income and on capital imposed on behalf of a contracting State … irrespective of the manner in which they are levied. There shall be regarded as taxes on income and on capital all taxes imposed on total income, on total capital, or on elements of income or of capital … The existing taxes to which the Convention shall apply are in particular: … .[13]

The subsequent list of taxes is not restrictive, but may include other similar taxes. Income and wealth taxes not mentioned in the list, thus, may still be covered by the treaty.

This could also be the case for the subscription tax borne by SPFs and UCIs. It could, therefore, be said that, due to their liability to the subscription tax, UCIs can be fully taxable in the tax-convention sense.

Arguably, Luxembourg's subscription tax is similar to a wealth tax, as it applies to the UCI's net assets. Historically, however, the subscription tax was a tax on the negotiation (i.e., disposition) of shares and bonds issued by a company. Further, in case of a potential double taxation of certain assets, the treaty typically eliminates such double taxation for a wealth tax, but would not have a similar effect for a subscription tax. In other words, if a Luxembourg UCI has assets located in another Contracting State or, where, because of their specific nature, taxation rights would belong to the other Contracting State (for instance, with respect to shareholdings in real estate companies), typical Luxembourg tax treaties would not eliminate double taxation for Luxembourg's subscription tax, and its UCI would still be subject to the subscription tax on its worldwide assets, regardless of the potential application of a wealth tax in the other Contracting State.

An alternative approach assumes that the effective liability to a tax is not an essential condition for tax treaty protection. It is not necessary that the concerned entity actually be taxable; it is sufficient if it falls within the scope of the tax, even if it benefits from a subjective exemption.[14] This approach is shared by part of the doctrine according to which Article 4(1) OECD Model confines itself to requiring a link between the company and its State of origin and provides that the difference between a subjective exemption (e.g., for SICAVs and SPFs) and an objective exemption of certain income, such as the application of a parent-subsidiary regime, is often very difficult to determine.[15]

13. *Ibid.*, Art. 2.
14. Philippe Hoss, *Dans quel cadre national et international s'inscrit la fiscalité des actionnaires des OPCVM établis à Luxembourg: le point de vue des actionnaires luxembourgeois et étrangers*, ALFI Yearbook 45 (1994); Philippe Hoss & Patrick Kinsch, *Conventions fiscales internationales et organismes de placement collectif en valeurs mobilières, Colloque des groupements belgo-luxembourgeois et français de l'IFA*, 15–16 May 1992; Jean-Pierre Winandy, *Droit fiscal international et européen* 375 et seq. (2009).
15. Michael Lang, *Taxation of Income in the Hands of Different Taxpayers from the Viewpoint of Tax Treaty Law*, 55 Bull. Int'l Fiscal Documentation 596 (2001).

As indicated above, 1929 holding companies and SPFs, until the law of 18 February 2012,[16] could become subject to corporate income tax in any given year if they received a substantial amount of their dividends from tax-haven companies.[17] That shows not only that the corporate income tax exemption was linked to certain conditions and that there was the potential to lose the exemption in a given year, but also the potential to recover it in a subsequent period. As a consequence, such vehicles were potentially subject to corporation tax.

The application of subscription tax of SICAVs mirrors the SPF tax regime, although the restriction on dividends from tax havens was never extended to investment funds. SICAVs are collective bodies governed by Article 159 LIR,[18] and are liable to corporation tax if there is no specific exemption therefrom in Luxembourg's law on UCIs.

A contrario, if neither of the foregoing tax-residence analyses were established, the drafters of the tax treaties would not have felt the need to specifically state that the old 1929 holding companies did not, or that SICAVs do not, benefit from particular tax treaties.[19] Yet, such exclusions for holding companies can still be found in almost all of Luxembourg's tax treaties, except, in particular, those made with Romania, China, Tunisia, Uzbekistan, and Vietnam.

The China/Luxembourg tax treaty, pursuant to correspondence dated 20 and 30 August 1996, respectively, marked a step backwards, as the Chinese authorities wrote that, after careful deliberation, they did not want to grant treaty protection to 1929 holding companies. Thereafter, the Luxembourg tax administration ensured that SICAVs be able to benefit from certain tax treaties, which evidences the fact that it considers that the SICAVs can be viewed as Luxembourg tax residents and that this analysis has not unduly shocked the negotiators of the other Contracting State. It also follows that the shareholders of the SICAVs cannot, in principle, directly invoke the benefit of the tax treaty their State of residence has negotiated with the State from which the income of the SICAV is originating. As a SICAV is a corporate vehicle, a case for tax transparency seems unlikely.

16. *See Loi du 18 février 2012 portant modification de la loi du 11 mai 2007 relative à la création d'une société de gestion de patrimoine familial* (SPF).
17. Basically, subsidiaries which are subject to a corporate income tax burden of less than 50% of the corporate income tax they would bear under the Luxembourg income tax law on the same income and provided they are not covered by the EU parent-subsidiary directive.
18. Article 159 *Loi du 4 décembre 1967 concernant l'impôt sur le revenu*, as amended (Luxembourg's law concerning income tax, hereinafter 'LIR').
19. One can regret that Luxembourg SICAVs are not entitled to a withholding tax exemption on dividends paid to them by a Luxembourg company, as required by Art. 147 LIR. That lack of coherence is an inconvenience in the contractual framework. That disadvantage would disappear if SICAVS could opt in to liability to corporate income tax.

§11.03 COLLECTIVE INVESTMENT FUNDS (FCPS)

The situation is more complex for FCPs. First, opinions differ regarding the FCP tax regime.[20] Some authors, who refer to the official position of the Luxembourg authorities, argue that FCPs should be fiscally transparent,[21] such that its unitholders would be taxed on the FCP's profits, be they redistributed or capitalized. Taxation would be carried out according to the nature of the FCP's income[22] and not necessarily as a dividend. For others, FCPs should be treated as opaque entities, similar to SICAVs. Their unitholders would then be taxed only at the moment of profit distributions, which solution seems to be the result of Luxembourg's standard practice,[23] where investors only have taxable income when they receive it and not when it is generated by the FCP.

The opaque treatment of an FCP may, in particular, be upheld in view of the fact that tax transparency for an FCP is not confirmed by specific provisions in a tax code, but merely results from the fact that the FCP has no legal personality and is only a co-ownership of assets. However, under Luxembourg tax law, an FCP may also be considered as a separate taxable estate, within the meaning of Article 159(1)(A)(7)(b) LIR, which addresses *patrimoine d'affectation* (*Zweckvermögen*). This category encompasses estates managed with a specific goal, which would, in the case of FCPs, usually be the maximization of return generated by the invested money, based on the principle of risk diversification.

Another difficult issue for an FCP relates to the fact that it may be treated differently in various jurisdictions. It is all but sure that investors in a Luxembourg FCP will be able to treat the investment income received by the vehicle, which Luxemburg usually considers as tax transparent, as being directly allocated to them for their own tax purposes, including the nature of the underlying income (income or capital gains) and the availability of tax credits or the ability to deduct investment losses. The same applies from the perspective of the source state, where it is likely that some jurisdictions will consider the FCP as tax transparent while others will treat it as a tax-opaque entity, regardless of whether or not the state grants treaty protection to it.

Finally, another complex issue may result from the FCP's investment and distribution policy. There are, indeed, FCPs that capitalize their income and do not allocate it immediately to investors. In practice, the issue is whether the investors would nonetheless be taxable immediately upon realization of the income by the FCP

20. For an overview of the alternative theories and the possible approaches, *see* Jean Schaffner, *Application des conventions fiscales aux organismes de placement collectif luxembourgeois*, 1997 Agefi Luxembourg Monthly Report No. 788, 8 (1997).
21. Jean-Pierre Winandy, Claude Kremer & Eric Fort, *L'imposition des fonds de placement, Rapport luxembourgeois*, 82b Cahiers de droit fiscal international, 598 (1997); Claude Zimmer, *La fiscalité des organismes de placement collectif à Luxembourg, Séminaire AFBL-ALFI*, September 1995, 55; *see also* Winandy, *supra* note 14, at 420 fn. 5 (offers an interesting line of approach regarding collective investment funds management companies).
22. Investment income (dividend or interest), capital gain, and rental income.
23. Alain Steichen, *Précis de droit fiscal de l'entreprise* 239 (2013); Philip Warner & Marc Schmitz, *Luxembourg in International Tax Planning* 422 (2004); *see also* Alain Steichen, *Régime fiscal de la titrisation, in La titrisation* 75 (André Prüm ed., 2008).

or only upon distribution of this income at a later stage, and how they would be taxed on redemption (i.e., whether any redemption gain is treated as capital gain or is taxed in light of the proceeds used to finance such redemption (dividends, interest, etc.)), which may often be difficult to determine. Luxembourg's tax authorities lean towards tax transparency for FCPs, while admitting that such tax transparency tends to create practical difficulties.[24]

The answer to that tax-treatment question may influence the status of FCPs with regard to tax treaties. Indeed, if FCPs are opaque, they may benefit from Luxembourg tax treaties in the same way as SICAVs do, depending on the particular treaty. If, on the other hand, they are transparent, the FCP's investors may individually claim the protection of the tax treaty entered into by their State of residence with the state from which the income of the FCP is originating. The transparency of an FCP generates significant practical difficulties, particularly if the FCP does not provide its investors the relevant details on the nature of the income it collects. The taxpayer – the FCP's investor – or the tax administration would then have to determine what type of income it is, in order to be able to apply, for taxpayer taxation purposes, the appropriate tax regime. It is misleading to think that FCP investors will have been provided all of the necessary information about the qualification of the income they receive through the FCP and especially about the procedures to follow to benefit from the imputation of a withholding tax or the reimbursement of an excess amount of tax withheld therefrom.[25]

In addition, only a distributing FCP that systematically and immediately allocates its entire income to its investors could allow them to invoke the benefit of a tax treaty in all neutrality. The assertion of transparency would, in practice, mean the creation of a differentiation between capitalization FCPs and distribution FCPs.

The collection of income via an FCP that distributes the entire income received to its unitholder does not, in principle, cause a problem; the income is simply transiting through the FCP. In case of a capitalization FCP, however, unitholders of FCPs who set their income aside as reserves collect the returns on their investment only when they transfer their units of the FCP. Those unitholders do not control the FCP's investment decisions or its distribution policy. The question is open to whom any reduction for withholding tax benefits belongs – assuming that the State of source recognizes the transparency of the (capitalization) FCP and grants contractual protection to its investors. *A priori*, a contractual reduction or exemption of withholding tax on certain income primarily and directly benefits the FCP, not its unitholders. The concept of transparency, thus, causes a problem for a capitalization FCP. Furthermore, according to the fiscal law of the State of residence of the particular investors holding units of a capitalization FCP, it is not certain that the investors can benefit from a tax credit corresponding to the withholding tax levied on income generated by the FCP. If an investor's State of residence taxes its taxpayers on income capitalized at the level of the

24. Note II/1425-S38 HE/CG of 24 October 2001; *see also Circulaire du directeur des contributions, L.G. – A. n° 61 du 12 février 2015*, replaced by *Circulaire du directeur des contributions, L.G. – A. n° 61 du 8 décembre 2017* (hereinafter the 'Treaty Protection Circular').
25. Philipp Warner & Marc Schmitz, *Luxembourg International Tax Planning* 419 (2004).

FCP, including non-distributed income, the investor is probably taxed on the gross income retained by the FCP without being able to benefit from a tax credit.

Assuming that an FCP is not transparent, the source state must also grant the benefits of the tax treaty it signed with Luxembourg to the FCP (i.e., it has to adhere to Luxembourg's determination regarding the FCP's opacity and tax liability). To determine the right to treaty protection, the State of source would have to take into account, on the one hand, any discussions it may have had with Luxembourg's tax authorities during the treaty negotiations or later and, on the other hand, the elements that it will be provided by Luxembourg (e.g., a certificate of residence). If the Luxembourg authorities determine that one of its FCPs does not fall within the scope of a tax treaty, it is likely that the authorities of the other Contracting State will adopt the same position.

The Luxembourg approach to the negotiation of tax treaties relies on its willingness to explain the legal structure of Luxembourg UCIs and to try to convince the treaty partner that it would be appropriate for the treaty to include SICAVs. On the other hand, FCPs are almost automatically excluded from the scope of the treaty, despite certain theoretical arguments and, sometimes, ambiguous treaty clauses. For instance, in its Treaty Protection Circular, which provides a list of jurisdictions granting treaty protection,[26] the Luxembourg tax administration indicated that Ireland grants treaty protection to an FCP,[27] but that Luxembourg would not issue a certificate of residence for an FCP, as opposed to an SICAV. This is not very coherent. If SICAVs and FCPs are treated alike under a certain treaty, they should also be able to benefit from the same certificate of residence.

§11.04 EXPRESS PROVISIONS IN TAX TREATIES

As a preliminary remark, even if an investment fund is entitled to the benefits of a particular double tax treaty, that does not necessarily imply that it will be given a withholding tax exemption; rather, at least for dividends, the usual benefit is only the reduced rate applicable to individuals (typically 15%).

If a UCI is found to be fiscally residing in Luxembourg, the relevant tax treaty between Luxembourg and the other Contracting State in which the UCI has invested may still not be applicable, if said treaty contains a specific exclusion.[28] First, mention must be made of the cases of express exclusion, that is, when a specific treaty provision explicitly excludes UCIs. Such express exclusions appear, for example, in the 14 October 1996 Sweden/Luxembourg treaty and in the 5 April 1996 United States/Luxembourg treaty.

In addition, indirect exclusion cases exist (i.e., when the treaty protection is denied to holding companies and other companies subject to a similar tax treatment,

26. Treaty Protection Circular, *supra* note 24, §4(A).
27. *Ibid.*, §4(A)(a).
28. Keith O'Donnell & Samantha Nonnenkamp, *Fonds d'investissement et accès aux conventions préventives de la double imposition, in Droit Fiscal Luxembourgeois: Livre Jubilaire de l'IFA Luxembourg, 493* (André Elvinger et al., eds, 2008).

meaning those with annual tax burdens limited to Luxembourg's subscription tax). Such reference to companies only leaves the door open for FCPs, which are, by definition, not organized as companies, but their inclusion is unlikely as their tax transparency weakens their case for tax treaty protection. The Greece/Luxembourg treaty, for example, specifically excludes investment funds, although it refers to former legislation that was in place at the time the tax treaty was entered into. The US/Luxembourg treaty only excludes 1929 holding companies and all companies enjoying a similar tax treatment by virtue of Luxembourg legislation. That highlights the link that exists between, on the one hand, SPFs and the old 1929 holding companies and, on the other hand, SICAVs, when it comes to treaty protection.

Indirect exclusion cases among the various Luxembourg treaties present certain inconsistencies. Thus, regarding the Greek/Luxembourg treaty, the parliamentary documentation indicates that its implicit exclusion concerns all UCIs.[29] On the contrary, parliamentary documentation concerning the Japan/Luxembourg treaty explains that the express restriction applies to investment companies, so that, by contrast, FCPs might be targeted thereby.[30] Such an *a contrario* analysis of the parliamentary documents, however, is most likely inappropriate and is not necessarily in line with the Treaty Protection Circular.

Although the Treaty Protection Circular provides a list of jurisdictions granting treaty protection, there is no strict relationship between that list and the developments discussed in this chapter. The list is based on a relatively opportunistic approach, as Luxembourg is keen to ensure treaty protection on the basis of a mutual agreement with the other Contracting State whenever possible, so there may be situations where similar wordings in a treaty result in different conclusions in a mutual agreement procedure as to the application of the tax treaty to investment funds.

Another form of indirect exclusion arises if treaty protection can only be obtained if the relevant income is indeed taxable in Luxembourg. The main tax treaty of this kind is the France/ Luxembourg treaty of 1 April 1958. Article 10*bis* thereof obliges a person who wishes to benefit from the treaty provisions regarding dividends and interest to provide a certificate delivered by the tax authorities of his/her State of residence that confirms that the income in question is subject to direct tax in said State under its ordinary law conditions. Such a certification cannot, in any event, be obtained by a Luxembourg UCI. In addition, the France/Luxembourg treaty contains a specific exclusion aimed at the holding companies governed by the law of 31 July 1929.

Interestingly, the exclusion in the France/Luxembourg tax treaty not only targets holding companies, but also income paid by such companies to a French resident as well as any gains a French resident receives from the sale of shares in such a company. This means that France is not obliged to exempt, for instance, capital gains by a French resident on the sale of shares in a 1929 holding company. But, the exchange of letters containing such exclusion does, however, only address 1929 holding companies and other holding companies addressed by specific Luxembourg legislation, so that it should, in our view, not apply to investment funds.

29. Luxembourg doc. parl. 3663.
30. Luxembourg doc. parl. 3636.

Exclusion from treaty protection hits the UCI itself, but some double tax treaties, such as the treaty with Canada, extend this exclusion to income paid by the UCI to its own resident investors.

An exclusion may also result indirectly from certain clauses in a particular tax treaty, such as a limitation-on-benefits or LOB provision. Typically, under an LOB provision, taxpayers, even if residents of a Contracting State, are only entitled to treaty protection if they meet certain conditions that demonstrate a clear connection to the jurisdiction of origin and taxation therein. For instance, under the 'derivative benefit test', a taxpayer may only benefit from the relevant tax treaty if its investors are, themselves, residents of the same jurisdiction (or, in Luxembourg's case, if its investors are residents of an EU or a European Economic Area Member State). Investment funds typically have a broad investor base with investors having a variety of origins, such that the investment fund cannot meet this condition. The United States/Luxembourg treaty incorporates the first, and most important, of these clauses included in any Luxembourg treaty. Several others have followed, such as the Trinidad and Tobago/Luxembourg treaty, which contains a much simpler, condensed version.

In the Multilateral Instrument signed on 7 June 2017, Luxembourg has opted for the application of the principal purpose test, and not for the LOB, to avoid undue benefit of double tax treaties. On the other side of the spectrum are treaties that do not contain any exclusion towards the 1929 holding companies or UCIs (e.g., the recent Hong Kong/Luxembourg treaty dated 2 November 2007) and those that only exclude 1929 holding companies, but not other vehicles with a similar tax regime. These treaties do not rule out treaty benefits for UCIs. Certain other treaties target the law of 31 July 1929 as well as the other laws meant to govern holding companies. This wording does not allow for the exclusion of other entities benefiting from an exorbitant tax regime under common law, which include UCIs, as UCIs are not holding companies.

Finally, the 29 April 1994 Malta/Luxembourg treaty allows for the exclusion of companies benefiting from special treatment under the law or from an administrative practice of one of the contracting States. The authorities of both States agreed to say that this provision was aimed only at the holding companies of the 1929 law.

According to the Luxembourg tax administration, in its Treaty Protection Circular, a series of double tax treaties include clear wording confirming the application of the double tax treaty to Luxembourg's SICAVs.[31]

Certain Contracting States have specifically acknowledged the application of their particular tax treaty to Luxembourg SICAVs.[32] Interestingly, for four conventions, however, the Luxembourg tax authorities, in the Treaty Protection Circular, indicate that the availability of treaty protection is based on their own interpretation of the

31. Andorra, Armenia, Azerbaijan, Austria, Bahrain, Barbados, Brunei, China, Croatia, Czech Republic, Estonia, Finland, Georgia, Germany, Guernsey, Hong Kong, Isle of Man, Israel, Jersey, Laos, Liechtenstein, Macedonia, Malaysia, Malta, Mongolia, Monaco, Morocco, Panama, Poland, Portugal, Qatar, Romania, San Marino, Saudi Arabia, Serbia, Seychelles, Singapore, Slovak Republic, Slovenia, Thailand, Trinidad and Tobago, Tunisia, Turkey, United Arab Emirates, Uruguay, Uzbekistan, and Vietnam.
32. Denmark, Indonesia, Ireland, and Spain (only for UCITS).

particular convention and might be challenged by the other country: Finland, Kazakhstan, Slovakia, and Thailand.[33] In the explanations given in the Treaty Protection Circular, the authorities indicate that, while there is no formal inclusion of SICAVs, they may benefit from the treaty in case such inclusion is indirect, because the relevant exclusion only applies to 1929 holding companies and, perhaps, to SPFs. The authorities also indicate that, for certain other treaties, it has not been clearly indicated whether SICAVs can or cannot benefit from treaty protection, such as in the treaties with Bulgaria, Greece, Italy and South Korea; no residence certificate can be delivered for SICAVs under these treaties. Ideally, an exchange of letters or a mutual agreement procedure could clarify the positions of those authorities under these treaties, bearing in mind of course that Luxembourg favours treaty access for investment funds wherever possible.

A further difficulty may arise if a particular treaty specifically excludes the old legislation on investment funds (from 30 March 1988), but does refer to Luxembourg's subsequent laws (e.g., laws of 13 February 2007 or 1 December 2010). This is particularly true if the treaty was modified after the earlier law was abrogated and replaced by more recent legislation on investment funds. The Mauritius/Luxembourg treaty, for instance, only excludes 1988 investment funds. The Treaty Protection Circular, however, specifically includes Mauritius among those countries refusing treaty protection to Luxembourgish funds.

The United Kingdom, which had previously granted the benefit of the UK/Luxembourg tax treaty to SICAVs, withdrew such protection, in an apparent attempt to reduce the competitive advantage of Luxembourg SICAVs as compared to British investment structures.

Regarding Spain, only SICAVs under Part I (coordinated SICAVs) can benefit from treaty access; other SICAVs are assimilated to SPFs. The Spanish wording is not particularly helpful, as even non-coordinated SICAVs may find it useful to invest in the Spanish markets. Their exclusion from treaty protection may only be understood on the assumption that coordinated SICAVs more often have a very broad investor base, which makes them unlikely for tax planning vehicles.

Contrary to other, more recent tax treaties based on the OECD Model, the 1958 Germany/Luxembourg tax treaty did not make tax liability in the State of residence a condition of its concept of residence; rather, a company was considered a resident of the State in which its effective management office was situated. It followed, for example, that a company that maintained its effective management office in Luxembourg was considered a Luxembourg resident according to that treaty, even if it benefitted from a corporate income tax exemption there (such as an investment company with variable share capital). Luxembourg SICAVs, therefore, according to a previous version of the list provided by the Luxembourg tax authorities, would have benefited from the 1958 Germany/Luxembourg treaty.

The new Germany/Luxembourg treaty, dated as of 23 April 2012, on the other hand, has the most detailed provision currently included in any Luxembourg treaty: an

33. Treaty Protection Circular, *supra* note 24, §4(A)(c), esp. fn. 4 ('*Cette position peut être contestée par l'autre État.*').

investment fund constituted under the law of one of the two Contracting States that receives dividends or interest derived from the other Contracting State may invoke the restriction of the tax legislation of the other Contracting State set out in Articles 10 and 11 thereof, but only to the extent that the units of the fund are held by residents of the first-mentioned Contracting State. With the recognition of a claim by the investment fund, the right of the shareholder of the investment fund to claim the same benefit ceases.

For the purposes of this detailed provision, 'investment fund' means, in the Federal Republic of Germany, a fund managed by an investment company in the sense of the law for investments (*Investmentfonds*), and in Luxembourg an FCP. The new treaty also contains a provision that grants investment companies an independent right to benefit from its Articles 10 and 11. For the purposes of said provision, 'investment fund' means a German 'investment company' (*Investmentgesellschaft*) and a Luxembourg SICAR, SICAV or SICAF; all may benefit from reduced withholding tax rates.

The inclusion of Luxembourg SICAVs in both the 1958 treaty and in the new 2012 treaty is of utmost importance, as German promoters frequently use Luxembourg SICAVs to channel their investments. It also indirectly demonstrates that the tax regime for SICAVs is not a tool for tax evasion, but protects neutrality to avoid multiple taxation for investors bundling their investment in a common investment vehicle.

The new, 2012 Germany/Luxembourg treaty enables us to draw some preliminary conclusions: it requires a resident of a Contracting State to be subject to tax in that State, due to the taxpayer's residence, usual place of living, head office, or any other criterion of similar nature. That qualification raises the question of whether a person who is otherwise exempt from income tax (a SICAV for example) can, indeed, be treated as a resident thereunder. Tax liability pursuant to State legislation must refer to an abstract concept of 'tax liability' and a specific tax exemption granted to a resident does not affect the condition of residence. The reasoning according to which Luxembourg SICAVs are considered Luxembourg residents under the 2012 Germany/Luxembourg tax treaty is in line with the Luxembourg administrative practice in its relations with the other jurisdictions that have already entered into OECD Model-based tax treaties with Luxembourg. A Luxembourg SICAV may, for example, benefit from the advantages of several Luxembourg tax treaties that include a similar residence condition (e.g., treaties with Denmark, China, Morocco, and Portugal). Unlike those treaties, the 1958 German/Luxembourg treaty with Germany granted treaty protection to SICAVs, but tax liability in the State of residence was never a condition to benefit therefrom.

An amendment, dated as of 21 November 2011, to the 1995 Russia/Luxembourg treaty eliminated that treaty's initial exclusion of 1929 holding companies and UCIs (SICAVs/Fs) from the benefits thereof, unless one of the main objectives of the structure is to obtain the benefits of the tax treaty (i.e., an anti-abuse rule).[34] The amended treaty retains the provision that grants the State in which the real estate is located the exclusive right to tax shares of a company investing predominantly in such

34. Diederik Ingen Housz & Frank van Kuijk, *Luxembourg Moves Up Among the Leading Jurisdictions Holding Russian Investments*, 40 Intertax 573 (2012).

real estate, but clarifies that such provision does not apply to any gains that a pension fund or a similar entity draws from the disposal of its shares in such a company. For real property funds, a decision of the Russian finance minister, dated 14 March 2013,[35] confirms that, from Russia's perspective, if a collective investment fund invests in Russian real estate and its units are owned by a Luxembourg company, the income received by the unitholder is considered taxable in Russia as real estate income. According to the Luxembourg authorities, however, Russia denies treaty protection to UCIs in general.

A specific provision with regard to the application of the tax treaty to UCIs appears in the protocol to the Seychelles/Luxembourg treaty dated as of 4 June 2012. The protocol indicates that a UCI that is a legal entity in the State in which it is established is considered a resident of said Contracting State and the beneficial owner of the income it receives, which is per se a very favourable provision for Luxembourg funds. Moreover, if a UCI is not considered a legal entity for tax purposes (which would be the case for an FCP), such entity is assimilated to an individual residing in the Contracting State in which it is established and is deemed to be the beneficial owner of the income it receives. In other words, a Luxembourg FCP may also enjoy protection under the Seychelles/Luxembourg tax treaty, regardless of the residency of its unitholders; thus, it will benefit from the rules provided therein for individual (rather than corporate) beneficial owners, particularly the 10% reduced withholding tax on any dividends coming from the other Contracting State.

Other recent treaties with Luxembourg follow the same approach: the Andorra, Guernsey, Jersey, Croatia, and Isle of Man treaties all have protocols that provide that collective investment vehicles (CIV) that are established in a Contracting State and are treated as a body corporate for tax purposes therein shall be deemed to be a resident of said Contracting State. Moreover, a collective investment vehicle that is established in a Contracting State that is *not* treated as a body corporate for tax purposes therein is also deemed to be a resident thereof as well as the beneficial owner of the income it receives. Hence, these treaties apply to tax-transparent investment vehicles and assimilate them to individuals, while investment funds set up as legal entities directly benefit from the treaty's reduced or super-reduced withholding tax rate in case of substantial shareholding by the fund in the distributing subsidiary. The Andorra/Luxembourg treaty extends treaty access not only specifically to investment funds, but also to pension funds.

The protocol of the Isle of Man/Luxembourg treaty adds an additional remark (in italics) at the end of the first paragraph, which reads:

> A collective investment vehicle which is established in a Contracting Party and that is not treated as a body corporate for tax purposes in that Contracting Party shall be considered as an individual who is resident of the Contracting Party in which it is established and as the beneficial owner of the income it receives. *However, this provision shall not prevent the other Contracting Party from taxing its residents if they receive income from such a collective investment vehicle (Isle of Man).*

35. IBFD Tax News Service, 2 April 2013.

This comment confirms the taxation of investors in their country of residence (the Isle of Man), which appears to be a more or less obvious assumption about the tax transparency of FCPs in both Contracting States.

In addition, most of these treaties specifically confirm beneficial ownership, regardless of the distribution policy of the fund.

The protocols to the Taiwan/Luxembourg and Sri Lanka/Luxembourg treaties are limited to the first sentence quoted above:

> A collective investment vehicle which is established in a Contracting Party and that is treated as a body corporate for tax purposes in that Contracting Party shall be considered as a resident of the Contracting Party in which it is established and as the beneficial owner of the income it receives.

Hence, these treaties only cover SICAVs and SICAFs, while the other treaties mentioned above also encompass FCPs. No rule, however, has been provided in these two treaties for UCIs without legal personality. It should be noted that, in the Sri Lanka/Luxembourg treaty, the reference to the status of 'legal entity for tax purposes' goes beyond the definition of a 'person' in Article 3(1)(a) OECD Model, but is nonetheless supposed to target companies.

Furthermore, the Taiwan/Luxembourg treaty uses the concept of 'territory' instead of 'Contracting Party' for political reasons due to its particular relationship with China.

The Saudi Arabia/Luxembourg and Tajikistan/Luxembourg tax treaties use the following provision:

> A collective investment vehicle which is established in a Contracting Party is considered a resident of that Contracting Party where it is established and the beneficial owner of the income it receives.

This includes SICAVs, SICAFs, and FCPs. For instance, the Tajikistan/Luxembourg treaty states that an undertaking for collective investments established in a Contracting State is considered a resident of this State and the beneficial owner of the income received pursuant to the articles on dividends, interest and fees. The same approach applies to Taiwan/Luxembourg treaty. This contractual precision, thus, has the effect of avoiding any discussion on the status of 'beneficial owner' of a UCI, regardless of its distribution policy.

As for the Singapore/Luxembourg treaty, the Contracting States agree that a collective investment vehicle is a resident of a Contracting State if, under the domestic laws of that Contracting State, it is liable to tax therein by reason of its domicile, residence, place of management, or any other criterion of a similar nature and a collective investment vehicle is also considered liable to tax if it is subject to the tax laws of that contracting State but is exempt from tax only if it meets all the requirements for exemption specified in the tax laws of that Contracting State. That particular wording raises an interesting question as to whether an FCP may be considered a resident of Luxembourg, despite the fact that it is generally viewed as tax transparent. However, as an FCP may be considered a person under the Singapore/Luxembourg treaty and is subject to the same tax treatment as a SICAV, an

FCP may indeed be determined to be a resident under similar conditions. Thus, treaty protection should be made available to an FCP as well. Nevertheless, the Treaty Protection Circular does not list the Singapore/Luxembourg treaty as one that is specifically available to FCPs.

The United Arab Emirates/Luxembourg treaty does not include any specific exclusion eliminating Luxembourg investment funds from treaty protection. However, its protocol lists a whole series of Emirati institutions, in particular those linked to its government, for which treaty protection is available. Interestingly, Luxembourg was not successful in its attempt (or, perhaps, has not bothered to attempt) to include Luxembourg investment funds in that protocol.

The Czech Republic/Luxembourg treaty uses the following provision:

> For the purposes of the first sentence of paragraph 1 of Article 4, it is understood that the term 'resident of a Contracting State' also includes a fiscally non-transparent person (including a collective investment vehicle) that is established in that State according to its laws even in the case where the income of that person is taxed at a zero rate in that State or is exempt from tax there.

This comment confirms that the specific tax status of a Luxembourg fund is not relevant.

The protocol of the Estonia/Luxembourg treaty specifically lists SICAVs, SICAFs, SICARs, and FCPs as residents.

§11.05 THE NEW OECD APPROACH

The OECD launched a study on tax treaties' application to investment funds in 2009; one of its conclusions was that either the funds or their investors (if the entity is tax transparent) should be able to benefit from the tax treaties. Its Committee on Fiscal Affairs (CFA) also proposed a modification to the OECD Model Commentary, to give states the ability to propose wording that would allow the application of a bilateral tax treaty to an investment fund,[36] but only for those funds that have a significant number of investors[37] and having sufficiently diversified assets. However, the CFA's proposed rule, which was included by the OECD in the 2014 revision of the Model, excludes most private equity funds and hedge funds from benefitting from these new rules. Its objective, therefore, is to allow fiscal neutrality between direct investments owned by 'small' savers and similar investments owned by them via funds.[38]

36. *The Granting of Treaty Benefits with Respect to the Income of Collective Investment Vehicles*, Public Discussion Draft, 9 December 2009; *see* Gijs Fibbe, *Changes to the OECD Commentary on Collective Investment Vehicles Proposed by the OECD Committee on Fiscal Affairs*, 64 Bull. Int'l Tax'n 138 (2010); Nigel Johnston, *Collective Investment Vehicles*, 66 Bull. Int'l Tax'n 383.
37. Bruno da Silva, *Characterization and Tax Treaty Issues of Collective Investment Vehicles: A Review of the OECD Report and the 2010 Amendments to the Model Tax Convention, in 2010 OECD Updates: Model Tax Convention and Transfer Pricing Guidelines – A Critical Review* 70 (Dennis Weber & Stef van Weeghel eds, 2011).
38. Mary Bennett, *La mise à jour 2010 du modèle de convention fiscal de l'OCDE*, 39 Droit Fiscal 18 (2010).

According to the OECD Model Commentary, an investment fund, under certain conditions, must be found to be a resident of a Contracting State, even if that fund is de facto non-taxable. The form of the undertaking for collective investment is not important in this respect. Similarly, UCIs subject to tax on a reduced base or at a specific rate, as the case may be, can also benefit from the tax treaties. Alternatively, the OECD suggests that Contracting States apply a transparency approach and thereby allow the residents of the State in which the UCI is situated to directly benefit from its tax treaties. The OECD wishes to ensure a broad application of tax treaties in order to decrease the cases of double taxation. The OECD, however, is conscious of the fact that this position may not be easy for all states entering into tax treaties to accept.

It is particularly complicated to determine who actually benefits from the tax treaty's application to an investment fund. If the fund capitalizes its income, and if treaty protection is allocated on a proportional basis depending on its qualifying investors, a partial reduction of withholding tax would benefit all investors, even those located in other jurisdictions or not otherwise qualifying for a lower rate. If the fund is a tax transparent entity, if the residence states of the various investors tax such investors directly, it will be difficult for such investors, in any event, to demonstrate what withholding tax has been applied to their income share so that they can enjoy any credit of said withholding tax against their domestic tax liability.

For that reason, the OECD Model Commentary proposes alternative solutions, for example, suggesting that only UCIs that are residents in the same state as their investors be allowed to rely on the tax treaties entered into by that state (or, indirectly, the investors themselves, by transparency) or limiting its new tax-treaty rules to UCIs that distribute their entire income.

From Luxembourg's perspective, all of these OECD Model Commentary solutions are not satisfactory, given that most Luxembourg investment funds have investors who are not residents of Luxembourg. Luxembourg is the number one jurisdiction for investment funds in Europe and number two worldwide, second only to the United States. The investor base of Luxembourg funds, therefore, is very broad, such that any solution in which only funds having Luxembourg-resident investors benefiting from treaty protection simply does not take into account the diversified nature of such investors and the fact that their investments are not made for tax purposes, but mainly with the intent to benefit from Luxembourg's sophisticated fund management in an experienced environment.

These explanations were included in Article 6.9, following the OECD Model Commentary on Article 1, and in furtherance of the modifications of the OECD Model.[39]

39. Hein Vermeulen, *Suggested Treaty Benefits Approaches for Collective Investment Vehicles (CIVs) and Its Investors Under the OECD MTC 2010 Update*, 39 Intertax 248 (2011); Bruno da Silva, *Granting Tax Treaty Benefits to Collective Investment Vehicles: A Review of the OECD Report and 2010 Amendments to the Tax Model Convention*, 39 Intertax 195 (2011); Jacques Wantz & Jean Schaffner, *Luxembourg Investment Funds: A Status Report*, 51 Eur. Tax'n 2 (2011).

§11.06 PRACTICAL ISSUES

The ultimate question, in relation to treaty protection or benefits for Luxembourg investment funds, is whether the Luxembourg authorities will deliver a certificate of residence for that purpose. A separate, but equally important question, is what Luxembourg administrative entity should be contacted to get such a certificate - its direct tax authorities (*Administration des contributions directes*) or its indirect tax administration (*Administration de l'enregistrement et des domaines*). Logically, any request for a residence certificate should first be addressed to the funds' supervisory administration, the indirect tax administration, which is in charge of the subscription tax. But, a certificate delivered by the indirect tax administration may not be sufficient for the other Contracting State, because it does not come from the authority that has neither the taxes specifically covered by the treaty within its competence nor the authority to negotiate tax treaties. A double certification, therefore, may be necessary. The direct tax authorities take the position that the residence certificate must be issued by the Sociétés VI tax office, which is responsible for finance companies. Moreover, except for the RAIF, as mentioned below, any request for a certificate of residence must be accompanied by a certificate from the financial sector supervisory authority (*Commission de surveillance du secteur financier* or CSSF), which was initially interpreted as meaning that the applicant can only be a SICAV (which is subject to its supervision). The authorities add that in German-Luxembourg relationships, the certificate of residence must specifically indicate that the applicant is not covered by the law of 31 July 1929 on holding companies.

The Sociétés VI tax office is also entitled to deliver a certificate of residence to a SICAV receiving income from a state that has neither accepted nor clearly rejected the treaty protection of the statutory UCIs.[40] The State of source will then, on a case-by-case basis, be able to allow or deny the benefit of the treaty.

Quite surprisingly, the Luxembourg tax administration indicates that it will not deliver certificates of residence to an FCP, even if treaty protection is granted by the other residence country, because it considers FCPs to be tax-transparent. Thus, a tax-transparent vehicle may not, in the Luxembourg tax administration's view, be a resident of the Contracting State in which it is established; this approach is surprising as it ignores both the particular nature of investment funds when it comes to treaty protection and the similarities between SICAVs and FCPs in this context.

Finally, more recent vehicles such as the reserved alternative investment fund (RAIF) and the specialized investment fund (SIF) must be assimilated to SICAVs because they must follow the same tax regime, as they are, legally, investment funds. The delivery of certificates of residence must be available to these new vehicles, too, even if, for an RAIF, there is no need for prior CSSF approval before its launch. The 2017 version of the Treat Protection Circular confirms that for a RAIF, the residence certificate is requested by the fund or its custodian.

40. Except for treaties with Bulgaria, Greece, Italy, and South Korea, as indicated by the Treaty Protection Circular.

§11.07 OUTLOOK

Based on the foregoing, there are several different ways Luxembourg could ensure broader treaty access for investment funds. One possibility would be to change its tax regime for Luxembourg investment funds, to make them fully taxable. This would be like the Belgian approach, where investment funds are fully taxable, but on a reduced base consisting of abnormal advantages granted to their managers and investors.

Luxembourg courts have already recognized the Belgian approach, by considering that a Belgian investment fund could have access to the European parent-subsidiary directive. The European parent-subsidiary directive is indeed applicable to all taxpayers subject to corporate income tax, without any option and without possibility of an exemption. According to the Luxembourg tribunal, taxation (without exemption) on a low basis is sufficient in this respect, under the condition that this regime is not optional, as such a tax system is not akin to an exemption.[41]

Introducing new or distinct tax regimes, in particular in combination with other regimes such as the application of an optional full taxation on a reduced tax base, might however be subject to criticism under the EU State-aid rules. Indeed, tax measures aimed at ensuring tax neutrality for investments in collective investment funds are not viewed as selective under the EU State-aid rules, when such measures do not have the effect of favouring certain UCIs or certain types of investment, but solely reduce or eliminate double economic taxation. On the contrary, the coexistence of several tax regimes for investment funds may induce such selectivity if the various regimes cannot be justified by the logic of the tax system to which they belong.[42]

Another approach Luxembourg could take would be to change the nature of its subscription tax, as this tax is close to a net wealth tax. However, historically, the subscription tax was a tax on the negotiation of securities; it is also not certain whether the application of wealth tax to a taxpayer is sufficient to make it, in all instances, a resident of a country. In particular, certain Contracting States do not have a wealth tax, hence it is possible that subjecting the investment fund to a wealth tax would not be sufficient to recognize tax residency for a Luxembourg fund.

41. *Tribunal administratif*, 15 February 2012, n° 27587.
42. *See* Notice from the European Commission on the notion of State aid as referred to in Art. 107(1) of the Treaty on the Functioning of the European Union (2016/6262/01). *See* further Micheau, *supra* Chapter 5.

CHAPTER 12

Treaty Entitlement of Funds in the Post-BEPS World

Keith Lawson

§12.01 INTRODUCTION

This chapter's topic is 'Treaty Entitlement of Funds in the Post-BEPS World.' 'Funds' here refer to collective investment vehicles ('CIVs') as that term is used in various reports issued by the Organisation for Economic Co-operation and Development (the 'OECD').[1]

Reflecting upon this topic, the author realized that he was being asked to predict the future. In fact, and fortunately, the task is only to make predictions on one (albeit very important) issue, rather than on the several other issues of concern for the global funds industry. Those other tax issues facing today's global funds industry include: the OECD's Treaty Relief and Compliance Enhancement ('TRACE') project,[2] the OECD's Base Erosion and Profit Shifting ('BEPS') initiative,[3] the OECD's Common Reporting

1. More specifically, the OECD's Report – *The Granting of Treaty Benefits with Respect to the Income of Collective Investment Vehicles*, http://www.oecd.org/tax/treaties/45359261.pdf (last accessed 25 September 2017 and hereafter the 'CIV Report') – defined CIVs as 'funds that are widely-held [*sic*], hold a diversified portfolio of securities and are subject to investor-protection regulation in the country in which they are established.' CIV Report, para. 4. Funds that are not treated as CIVs in the CIV Report (and that are not addressed in this Chapter) include 'investments through private equity funds, hedge funds or trust or other entities that do not fall within the [CIV Report's] definition of CIV.' *Ibid.*
2. For more information thereon, *see* the OECD website, http://www.oecd.org/ctp/exchange-of-tax-information/aboutthetracegroup.htm (last accessed 25 September 2017) and http://www.oecd.org/ctp/exchange-of-tax-information/treatyreliefandcomplianceenhancementtrace.htm (last accessed 7 December 2017).
3. For more information thereon, *see* the OECD website, http://www.oecd.org/ctp/beps/ (last accessed 7 December 2017).

Standard ('CRS'),[4] financial transaction taxes ('FTTs'),[5] the Pan-European Pension Product ('PEPP') proposal,[6] and Article 63 litigation.

So, what is my prediction for treaty entitlement in the post-BEPS world? There are at least three possible answers, the first two of which involve famous sayings attributed to a very famous American baseball player named Yogi Berra.[7]

- The first possible answer involves Yogi's famous quote: 'It's like déjà vu, all over again.' In other words, nothing changes in the post-BEPS world. Were that the full answer, there would be little, if anything to add to Daniel Dürrschmidt's excellent chapter on 'Treaty Entitlement for Funds in a *Pre*-BEPS World.'[8]
- The second possible answer involves Yogi's famous quote: 'It's tough to make predictions, especially about the future.' Were that the full answer, the chapter could end here.
- The third possible answer, which this chapter will explore further, is the response often given by an American tax lawyer to an interesting question: 'It depends.' So, with a little 'Yogi' and almost thirty years of experience as a tax lawyer working in Washington with our fund industry association, here we go.

There are four distinct aspects to my 'it depends' answer. First, it is essential to consider what has changed - as a result of both the specific standard set out by the OECD in BEPS Action 6[9] and the post-financial crisis scrutiny of the financial services industry. Second, we must review the overarching industry themes - such as the need for tax certainty and practical solutions. Third, we absolutely must keep in mind the concerns of governments in general and of treaty negotiators in particular - such as protecting the tax base and having reliable solutions. Finally, I will discuss what I see as the way forward. Will we succeed along the path I envisage? It depends.[10]

4. OECD, *Common Reporting Standard, in Standard for Automatic Exchange of Financial Account Information in Tax Matters* (2014) (last accessed 7 December 2017).
5. https://ec.europa.eu/taxation_customs/taxation-financial-sector_en.
6. https://ec.europa.eu/commission/news/new-pan-european-personal-pension-products-2017-jun-29_en.
7. Yogi played for the New York Yankees and retired when I was a young boy growing up in Washington and supporting a much less successful team. You have Werner to thank for these, I hope amusing quotes, as he mentioned to me at dinner last night that he was in Chicago a few weeks ago when the Chicago Cubs baseball team won what we in the US call the 'World Series'. This result was particularly significant for 'the Windy City' as the last celebration of a Cubs World Series Championship occurred well over 100 years ago, on 14 October 1908. I add this random fact only to provide comfort to those readers who are unfamiliar with the psyche of the long-suffering Cubs' fans and who, therefore, may think that the sides *they* support are *historically* inept. Not so!
8. Daniel Dürrschmidt, *supra*, Chapter 10.
9. http://www.oecd.org/tax/preventing-the-granting-of-treaty-benefits-in-inappropriate-circumstances-action-6-2015-final-report-9789264241695-en.htm (last accessed 12 December 2017).
10. In the spirit of 'cultural' exchange, here are a few more Yogi quotes that could have been in my opening remarks: 'When you come to a fork in the road, take it.' ... 'You can observe a lot by just watching.' ... 'It ain't over till it's over.' ... 'The future ain't what it used to be.' ... 'If the world were perfect, it wouldn't be.' ... and 'I never said most of the things I said.' *See, e.g., Yogi-isms*, Yogi Berra Museum & Learning Center, http://yogiberramuseum.org/just-for-fun/yogisms/

§12.02 WHAT HAS CHANGED?

The two big changes that will impact treaty entitlement for funds, as noted above, are the OECD's BEPS Action 6 and the increased scrutiny of regulated funds (as members of the much larger financial services industry). The best way to appreciate these changes, however, requires us to start with the day (17 February 2005) when I first met my now good friend Keith O'Donnell, from ATOZ, who gave very insightful opening remarks this morning.

[A] The OECD's CIV Report

[1] Putting the CIV Report (and BEPS Action 6) in Context

Tax-treaty entitlement issues for funds made their way onto the OECD's agenda near the conclusion of the OECD's work on treaty entitlement issues for partnerships. As I heard the story, someone at an OECD Working Party 1 ('WP1') meeting (where treaty policy issues are discussed) said something like, 'If you think partnership treaty issues are complicated, you should look at treaty issues for funds.' As a result of this comment, a business delegation, of which Keith and I were active participants,[11] was formed to meet with WP1 in a claustrophobically small conference room in the basement of the old OECD building. During this meeting, we strongly encouraged the OECD to develop an international consensus for ensuring that fund investors receive appropriate treaty relief.

This 2005 subterranean meeting led, in 2006, to the OECD's formation of the 'Informal Consultative Group on the Taxation of Collective Investment Vehicles and Procedures for Tax Relief for Cross-Border Investors' (the 'ICG'). The business delegates to the ICG, including Keith and me, met frequently over the next two years (alone, with the OECD Secretariat, and/or with the government delegates) to craft the report that was approved by the OECD's Committee on Fiscal Affairs (the 'CFA') in January 2009 for public comment. That CFA adopted that report, with relatively minor CFA modifications, on 23 April 2010 and is now known colloquially as the '2010 CIV Report' (and generally, for the remainder of this chapter, as 'the CIV Report').[12] Subsequently, on 22 July 2010, the OECD Model Commentary on Article 1[13] was

(last accessed 25 September 2017); For the Win, *The 50 Greatest Yogi Berra Quotes*, USA Today Sports, http://ftw.usatoday.com/2015/09/the-50-greatest-yogi-berra-quotes (last accessed 25 September 2017).

11. The business delegates at the 2005 meeting represented the Belgian, Canadian, French, German, Irish, Italian, Luxembourgish, Swiss, British, and American fund industries. Also participating were representatives from EFAMA (the European Fund and Asset Management Association) and the Business and Industry Advisory Committee to the OECD (BIAC).
12. CIV Report, *supra* note 1.
13. OECD, *Model Tax Convention on Income and on Capital 2014 (Full Version)* http://www.oecd.org/tax/treaties/model-tax-convention-on-income-and-on-capital-2015-full-version-9789264239081-en.htm (hereafter the 'OECD Model') (last accessed 20 November 2017) The discussion of CIV issues begins with para. 6.8, on page C(1)-5 (page 105 of the 'read online' version of this document).

amended to include the new Paragraphs (6.8–6.34) that address the OECD's consensus view regarding cross-border issues relating to CIVs.

Importantly, the Final Report on BEPS Action 6[14] specifically references the CIV Report and emphasizes that 'there was general support for the conclusions'[15] reached therein. Moreover, and as discussed in greater detail below, the limitation on benefits ('LOB') rule included in the BEPS Action 6 Final Report 'dealt with the application to CIVs in a way that reflected the conclusions of the CIV Report.'[16] Consequently, 'there was no need for additional changes to the report on Action 6 in order to address issues related to collective investment vehicles, even though it was also agreed that the implementation of the recommendations of the TRACE project were important for the practical application of these conclusions'.[17]

[2] Some High-Level Observations about the CIV Report

The conclusions of the CIV Report are very significant to the post-BEPS world. Without revisiting in great detail Daniel's observations from earlier today, here are some high-level observations about the Report and its effect in the post-BEPS environment.

First, some (in my view, incorrectly) view the Report as 'flawed' because it offers government officials (including treaty negotiators) multiple options for providing treaty relief to fund investors. Those holding this 'flawed' view believe that a 'one-size-fits-all' approach is preferable (although, presumably, they also believe that all funds should receive treaty benefits in all cases).

One aspect of this 'one-size-fits-all' perspective is based upon the indisputable fact that different countries' tax regimes approach CIV taxation with a common 'tax neutrality' objective: to prevent double-taxation of the CIV's income (at the fund and investor levels) and thereby place CIV investors in a tax position comparable to that of direct investors in securities. This tax neutrality objective is achieved in different countries by (1) exempting their funds from tax, (2) imposing only a *de minimis* tax on their funds, or (3) providing that their funds are fully taxable, but then allowing a deduction for amounts distributed to the funds' investors. If all such tax regimes effectively provide the same 'no-tax-at-the-fund-level' treatment, as I understand this view, either all funds should receive treaty relief or none should receive it.

Despite this common tax neutrality objective, and as noted in the Report, there are important legal and factual differences in how funds in different countries are organized and operated. More specifically, funds take different legal forms, are distributed in different ways, and operate under different requirements for making (or not) distributions to investors. These differences, as explained below, can be important (particularly to treaty negotiators) when determining whether a fund is entitled to

14. *Preventing the Granting of Treaty Benefits in Inappropriate Circumstances, Action 6 – 2015 Final Report,* http://www.oecd.org/tax/preventing-the-granting-of-treaty-benefits-in-inappropriate-circumstances-action-6-2015-final-report-9789264241695-en.htm. (Last accessed 25 September 2017; hereafter, in the footnotes, 'the Final Action 6 Report.'
15. *Ibid.*, para. 9.
16. *Ibid.*
17. *Ibid.*

treaty relief in its own right (including after application of an LOB rule such as in US tax treaties) or whether treaty relief must be based, instead, upon the eligibility of the funds' investors. A brief review of the relevant treaty requirements – that the claimant be (i) a person, (ii) a resident of the Contracting State, and (iii) the beneficial owner of the income it receives – explains, I submit, the need for the options:

- The OECD Model Tax Convention (OECD Model)[18] defines a 'person' to include 'an individual, a company and any other body of persons'.[19] 'Company,' in turn, is defined as 'any body corporate or any entity that is treated as a body corporate for tax purposes'.[20] The Report explains that some funds clearly are persons (because they are companies),[21] others generally are viewed as persons (because the country in which they are organized treats them as resident taxpayers),[22] while others (such as those organized as a form of joint ownership) clearly are not persons.[23]
- The OECD Model Tax Convention defines a resident as a 'person who, under the laws of that State, is liable to tax therein by reason of his domicile, residence, place of management or any other criteria of a similar nature'.[24] The Report notes that, under the principles of Paragraph 8.5, OECD Model Commentary on Article 4, a person may be liable to tax and, therefore, a resident, even if tax is not imposed on that person.[25] Importantly, however, the Report emphasizes that the manner in which tax neutrality is achieved affects the treaty analysis.[26] A fund that is 'tax transparent' under the laws of its country of organization cannot meet the resident requirement while one that is opaque will be treated, under the principles of Paragraph 8.5, as a resident.[27] Because some countries take the view that a person exempt from tax cannot be liable to tax, as noted in Paragraph 8.6, OECD Model Commentary on Article 4, the Report notes that it would be prudent to address this issue in treaty negotiations with any country that adheres to the 'not-liable-to-tax-if-tax-exempt' view.[28]
- The third general treaty-eligibility requirement demands that the claimant be the 'beneficial owner' of its income, but the term 'beneficial owner' is not defined in the OECD Model. Instead, this requirement turns on how the term is defined under the laws of the country in which the investment is made (the 'Source Country'). Without getting into the details, the Report effectively urges countries to treat funds as the beneficial owners of their income because they

18. OECD Model, *supra* note 13.
19. *Ibid.*, Art. 3(1)(a).
20. *Ibid.*, Art. 3(1)(b).
21. CIV Report, *supra* note 1, para. 25.
22. *Ibid.*, para. 26.
23. *Ibid.*, para. 25.
24. OECD Model, *supra* note 13, Art. 4(1).
25. CIV Report, *supra* note 1, para. 29.
26. *Ibid.*
27. *Ibid.*
28. *Ibid.*, para. 30.

are not acting as 'intermediaries,' 'agents,' or 'nominees' for their investors.[29] Rather, the funds (through their managers) maintain total control over the funds' portfolio investment decisions - subject to any restrictions placed on them in their governing documents. Thus, the fund *is* the true owner of its income.

The differences, discussed very briefly above, regarding the extent to which funds organized and operated in different ways satisfy (or not) these three treaty-entitlement requirements, provide ample support for the need to provide different mechanisms by which fund investors receive, either directly or indirectly, the treaty relief to which they are entitled.

My second 'high level' observation about the Report is that it argues - very forcefully - for providing 'practical and reliable procedures'[30] by which a fund could claim treaty relief for its investors if the fund cannot claim this relief in its own right. Importantly, a treaty that would provide relief if an eligible investor purchased a security directly, but does not provide such relief if the investment is made through a fund, is a treaty that has failed its purpose of eliminating double taxation.[31]

The administrative difficulties of forcing fund investors to make individual claims in their own right with respect to each eligible income item received by their fund, however, would effectively deny treaty relief in essentially every situation. The typical fund has many thousands of investors (sometimes even hundreds of thousands or more!) and holds scores (if not hundreds or thousands!) of different securities simultaneously.[32] As a result, the typical benefit to any one investor of treaty relief with respect to any one income item (such as a dividend) would be very small, while the cost of recovering that benefit would be substantial. Only when all of the claims can be bundled and advanced as one claim by the fund, is it feasible for treaty relief to be pursued for fund investors (and, even then, the cost of processing the claim can be high, relative to the amount of the tax benefit).

[3] A Quick Review of the Optional Provisions Added to the Commentary

Given the many references in the BEPS Action 6 Final Report to the CIV Report and the changes to the OECD Model Commentary on Article 1,[33] it is useful to quickly summarize the Commentary's optional suggestions for treaty language that clarify the treaty eligibility of CIVs.

29. As noted in the Final Action 6 Report (*supra* note 14, para. 18), the beneficial owner concept was introduced in the Model Tax Convention in 1977 to address treaty shopping concerns by intermediaries acting as agents or nominees for their customers who own the assets (such as securities) on which income is received.
30. CIV Report, *supra* note 1, para. 39.
31. *Ibid.*, para. 36.
32. *Ibid.*, para. 37.
33. OECD Model, *supra* note 13.

Paragraph 6.17 treats CIVs as treaty entitled in their own right.[34] Some government delegates to the ICG supported this paragraph only for 'domestically distributed' CIVs (i.e., ones in which at least 'most' of the investors are residents in the same state as the state in which the CIV is established) that distribute their income periodically (e.g., annually).

Paragraphs 6.21 and 6.26 provide strictly proportionate relief. The first such 'proportionate relief' paragraph, Paragraph 6.21, provides relief to the extent that the CIV's investors are residents of any State with which the Source Country has a treaty that provides for withholding tax relief that is at least as low as the rate provided by the treaty with the CIV's State of establishment; this standard is known as the 'equivalent beneficiary' standard.[35] Paragraph 6.26, the second 'proportionate relief' paragraph, provides relief 'only to the extent that the beneficial interests in the collective investment vehicle are owned by residents of the Contracting State in which the collective investment vehicle is established'.

Paragraph 6.27 was added because of concerns that the 'purely proportionate' approach of Paragraphs 6.21 and 6.26 would impose substantial administrative burdens on CIVs to determine the treaty eligibility of *each* investor in the CIV. Under this alternative 'threshold relief' provision, a CIV would be fully entitled to treaty relief so long as at least a specific percentage of the CIV's investors (as agreed by the treaty partners) would have received treaty relief if investing directly. This paragraph effectively could be used to implement a treaty that limited relief to entities (such as CIVs) that needed a minimum percentage of 'eligible' investors to be treaty entitled in their own right (i.e., an LOB rule).

Yet another paragraph (Paragraph 6.28) would allow for a pure 'look through' approach for certain types of CIVs, such as those owned predominantly or exclusively by investors (such as pension funds) that would be exempt from tax or eligible for a substantially reduced rate in the Source Country if investing directly.

Finally, a paragraph (Paragraph 6.32) would provide that a CIV that is publicly traded could be eligible for treaty relief without regard to the residence of its investors. The Commentary notes that '[T]his provision has been justified on the basis that a publicly-traded [*sic*] CIV cannot be used effectively for treaty shopping because the shareholders or unitholders of such a CIV cannot individually exercise control over it.'[36]

34. Paragraph 6.17 could be used to clarify that a CIV 'shall be treated ... as an individual that is a resident of the Contracting State in which it is established and as the beneficial owner of the income it receives.' CIV Report, *supra* note 1.
35. 'Equivalent beneficiary' would be defined in para. 6.21(b)(ii) to mean 'a resident of the Contracting State in which the CIV is established, and a resident of any other State with which the Contracting State in which the income arises has an income tax convention that provides for the effective and comprehensive information exchange who would, if he received the particular item of income for which benefits are being claimed under this Convention, be entitled under that convention, or under the domestic law of the Contracting State in which the income arises, to a rate of tax with respect to that item of income that is at least as low as the rate claimed under this Convention by the CIV with respect to that item of income.' CIV Report, *supra* note 1.
36. *Ibid.*

All of these provisions (other than the look-through provision of Paragraph 6.28) effectively treat the CIV as an individual who is a resident and the beneficial owner of its income. The importance of this treatment will become apparent when we discuss the application to CIVs of the Final BEPS Action 6 Report.

[B] BEPS Action 6

[1] The Government Mindset and the BEPS Action 6 Objectives

The title of the BEPS Action 6: 2015 Final Report - Preventing the Granting of Treaty Benefits in Inappropriate Circumstances - is instructive of the government mindset. Moreover, any remaining doubt about this mindset is removed by the first sentence of the Executive Summary: 'Action 6 of the OECD/G20 [BEPS] Project identifies treaty abuse, and in particular treaty shopping, as one of the most important sources of BEPS concerns.'[37]

Treaty shopping is described in the Final Report as involving 'strategies through which a person who is not a resident of a State attempts to obtain benefits that a tax treaty concluded by that State grants to residents of that State'.[38] Clear guidance is not provided, however, regarding what it means to 'attempt' to obtain treaty benefits inappropriately.

One other objective of BEPS Action 6, as noted in the BEPS Action Plan, is to prevent 'double non-taxation.'[39] As noted in the preliminary remarks to the Commentary on the Article of the OECD Model Tax Convention concerning the entitlement to treaty benefits (added by the Final Action 6 Report), intent is not a necessary requirement for application of the Action 6 LOB-type provisions. Specifically, Paragraph 3.2 of the preliminary remarks provides:

> The provisions of the Article seek to deny treaty benefits in the case of structures that typically result in the indirect granting of treaty benefits to persons that are not directly entitled to these benefits whilst recognising that in some cases, persons who are not residents of a Contracting State may establish an entity in that State for legitimate business reasons. Although these provisions apply regardless of whether or not a particular structure was adopted for treaty-shopping purposes, the Article allows the competent authority of a Contracting State to grant treaty benefits where the other provisions of the Article would otherwise deny these benefits but the competent authority determines that the structure did not have as one of its principal purposes the obtaining of benefits under the Convention.[40]

37. *See* Final Action 6 Report, *supra* note 14, at 9.
38. *Ibid.*
39. *Action Plan on Base Erosion and Profit Shifting*, OECD, https://www.oecd.org/ctp/BEPSActionPlan.pdf, (last accessed 25 September 2017), 19. *See also,* Final Action 6 Report, *supra* note 14, at 91.
40. *See* Final Action 6 Report, *supra* note 14, at 23.

[2] The Specific Action 6 Requirements

[a] In General

The BEPS 6 Final Report contains three distinct parts (following the Executive Summary and Introduction). Section A, which contains most of the discussion, concerns treaty provisions and/or domestic rules to prevent the granting of treaty benefits in inappropriate cases. Section B clarifies that tax treaties are not intended to be used to generate double non-taxation. Section C discusses tax policy considerations that, in general, countries should consider before deciding to enter into a tax treaty with another country.

Action 6 addresses treaty considerations through a 'minimum standard' that provides implementation flexibility. The standard first includes a recommendation for a 'clear statement [in tax treaties] that the States that enter into a tax treaty intend to avoid creating opportunities for non-taxation or reduced taxation through tax evasion or avoidance, including through treaty shopping arrangements'.[41] In addition, the standard recommends the adoption of either a specific anti-abuse rule (the LOB rule) in Part (i) of Section A or a general anti-abuse rule based on the 'principal purpose' of a transaction or arrangement (the principal purpose test or 'PPT' rule) in Part (ii) of Section A, or both.[42]

The LOB and PPT rules, the Final Report notes, each have strengths and weaknesses. While the LOB rule is objective and, therefore (at least arguably), provides more certainty, its focus on treaty shopping limits its usefulness to other forms of treaty abuse. The PPT rule, on the other hand, is subjective and therefore requires a factual analysis in each situation of the principal purposes of the transaction or arrangement. While a combination of the LOB and PPT rules might be useful in some cases, the Final Report recognizes that the combination may not be appropriate or necessary for all countries such as when the countries already have domestic anti-abuse rules such as economic substance or substance over form. Importantly, the Final Report also recognizes that:

> the LOB rule will need to be adapted to reflect certain constraints of policy choices concerning other aspects of a bilateral tax treaty between two Contracting States (e.g.[,] policy choices concerning the treatment of collective investment vehicles).[43]

[b] The LOB Rule

The LOB rule limits treaty benefits to residents that are 'qualified persons'. Among the categories of 'qualified persons' are individuals, certain publicly listed entities, certain pension funds, and 'other entities that meet certain ownership requirements'.[44]

---

41. *Ibid.*, at 9.
42. *Ibid.*
43. *Ibid.*, at 19.
44. The Final Action 6 Report also allows for 'certain collective investment vehicles' to be treated as 'qualified persons.' *Ibid.*, at 21. The CIV issues are discussed, *infra*, in §12.02[C].

In some cases, the Final Report provides both 'simplified' and 'detailed' versions of possible treaty language. The 'simplified version' of the publicly traded companies and entities provision would apply 'if the principal class' of a company's shares or 'the beneficial interests' of a person other than a company are 'regularly traded on one or more recognized stock exchanges'. The more detailed version of this provision restricts the exchanges on which the shares/interests can trade or requires that the company's/entity's primary place of management and control be in the Contracting State of which it is a resident. A separate eligibility provision in the detailed version would be of little use to funds, as it would require that at least 50% of the value of the shares to be held by five or fewer companies that also would meet the publicly traded test.

[c] The PPT Rule

The PPT Rule is provided by Paragraph 7 of the Entitlement to Benefits Article. Specifically, Paragraph 7 provides that:

> Notwithstanding the other provisions of this Convention, a benefit under this Convention shall not be granted in respect of an item of income or capital if it is reasonable to conclude, having regard to all relevant facts and circumstances, that obtaining that benefit was one of the principal purposes of any arrangement or transaction that resulted directly or indirectly in that benefit, unless it is established that granting that benefit in these circumstances would be in accordance with the object and purpose of the relevant provisions of this Convention.[45]

[3] The Treatment of CIVs under Action 6

[a] The LOB Rule

The BEPS Action 6 Final Report has numerous provisions that deal expressly with CIVs under an LOB Rule. First, and perhaps foremost, the Final Report includes the possibility that a CIV would be included expressly within the definition of qualified person (Paragraph 2(f)).[46] The footnote to this possible provision on CIVs provides that: 'This subparagraph should be drafted (or omitted) based on how collective investment vehicles are treated in the Convention and are used and treated in each Contracting State; see the Commentary on the subparagraph and paragraphs 6.4 to 6.38 of the Commentary on Article 1.'[47] As explained above, the Commentary on Article 1 provides several drafting suggestions for clarifying CIV treaty eligibility. With the exception of the 'look-through' provision (in Paragraph 6.28), all of the provisions treat the CIV as an individual.

45. *See* Final Action 6 Report, *supra* note 14, at 55.
46. *Ibid.*, at 21.
47. *Ibid.*, at 32.

The Final Report notes that a 'special rule' expressly treating a CIV as a qualified person might be needed, such as when the CIV otherwise cannot satisfy the qualified person definition (Paragraph 2 of the Entitlement to Benefits Article) or is not engaged in the active conduct of a business (Paragraph 3 of that article). The reasons given in the Final Report for why a CIV might not satisfy either Paragraph 2 or 3 include:

> the interests in the CIV are not publicly traded (even though these interests are widely distributed); these interests are held by residents of third States; the distributions made by the CIV are deductible payments; and the CIV is used for investment purposes rather than for the 'active conduct of a business' within the meaning of paragraph 3.[48]

The Final Report, as it generally adopts the recommendations of the CIV Report, also includes detailed language along the lines of the Article 1 Commentary (in Paragraphs 6.8 through 6.34) that was added following adoption of the CIV Report. These provisions would be available for use in treaties that did not previously address the treaty eligibility of CIVs for situations in which the Contracting States agree that the CIV should be treated as a resident and the beneficial owner of its income.

[b] The PPT Rule

The Final Report also provides the option of addressing BEPS Action 6 concerns by adopting the subjective PPT. Specifically, Paragraph 7 of the Entitlement to Benefits Article of the OECD Model Tax Convention provides that:

> Notwithstanding the other provisions of this Convention, a benefit under this Convention shall not be granted in respect of an item of income or capital if it is reasonable to conclude, having regard to all relevant facts and circumstances, that obtaining that benefit was one of the principal purposes of any arrangement or transaction that resulted directly or indirectly in that benefit, unless it is established that granting that benefit in these circumstances would be in accordance with the object and purpose of the relevant provisions of this Convention.[49]

Guidance also is provided by the Final Report on the words and phrases 'benefit,' 'that resulted directly or indirectly in that benefit,' 'arrangement or transaction,' and 'one of the principal purposes'. Most importantly, the Final Report is clear that these phrases are 'deliberately broad'[50] and should be 'interpreted broadly'.[51] In applying the 'principal purpose' test, the Final Report notes:

> It is important to undertake an objective analysis of the aims and objects of all persons involved in putting that arrangement or transaction in place or being a party to it. ... It should not be lightly assumed, however, that obtaining a benefit

48. *Ibid.*
49. *Ibid.*, at 55.
50. *Ibid.*, at 57.
51. *Ibid.*

> under a tax treaty was one of the principal purposes of an arrangement or transaction and merely reviewing the effects of an arrangement will not usually enable a conclusion to be drawn about its purposes. Where, however, an arrangement can only be reasonably explained by a benefit that arises under a treaty, it may be concluded that one of the principal purposes of that arrangement was to obtain the benefit.[52]

The Final Report includes several examples, including one involving a CIV, of how the PPT is intended to apply. Given the specificity of this example (Example D) and the implications (or not) for factual variations, it is provided here in full:

> Example D: RCo, a collective investment vehicle resident of State R, manages a diversified portfolio of investments in the international financial market. RCo currently hold 15 per cent of its portfolio in shares of companies resident of State S, in respect of which it receives annual dividends. Under the tax Convention between State R and State S, the withholding tax rate on dividends is reduced from 30 percent to 10 percent.
>
> RCo's investment decisions take into account the existence of tax benefits provided under State R's extensive tax Convention network. A majority of investors in RCo are residents of State R, but a number of investors (the minority investors) are residents of States with which State S does not have a tax Convention. Investors' decisions to invest in RCo are not driven by any particular investment made by RCo, and RCo's investment strategy is not driven by the tax position of its investors. RCo annually distributes almost all of its income to its investors and pays taxes in State R on income not distributed during the year.
>
> In making its decision to invest in shares of companies resident of State S, RCo considered the existence of a benefit under the State R-State S tax Convention with respect to dividends, but this alone would not be sufficient to trigger the application of paragraph 7. The intent of tax treaties is to provide benefits to encourage cross-border investment and, therefore, to determine whether or not paragraph 7 applies to an investment, it is necessary to consider the context in which the investment was made. In this example, unless RCo's investment is part of an arrangement or relates to another transaction undertaken for a principal purpose of obtaining the benefit of the Convention, it would not be reasonable to deny the benefit of the State R-State S tax treaty to RCo.[53]

Because of the relatively limited scope of Example D, which was included first in the BEPS Action 6 2014 Deliverable,[54] and in response to questions issued by the OECD thereafter,[55] ICI Global specifically requested a second example of more general applicability. ICI Global also expressed concerns about the unilateral application of the PPT rule by an individual country.

52. *Ibid.*, at 57–58.
53. *Ibid.*, at 60–61.
54. *Ibid.*, at 72–73.
55. *Follow up Work on BEPS Action 6: Preventing Treaty Abuse (Public Discussion Draft 21 November 2014 – 9 January 2015*, OECD, http://www.oecd.org/ctp/treaties/discussion-draft-action-6-follow-up-prevent-treaty-abuse.pdf (last accessed 25 September 2017).

ICI Global's PPT comments, from the letter submitted to the OECD on 8 January 2015, are reproduced here:

> Questions 12-14 – PPT Rule Relief
>
> A PPT applied unilaterally by a government could create substantial uncertainty for CIVs. As discussed in the CIV Report, CIVs have a keen interest in tax certainty[,] as they typically must determine each day the value of their assets and liabilities to price their CIV interests. For a CIV to price its interests, it needs to know each day how much foreign tax it will owe on the income and gain from its cross-border investments.
>
> We submit that a PPT should be applied only upon the agreement of both Contracting States. At a minimum, effective and expeditious mechanisms for reviewing PPT application – such as administrative procedures that involve committees of experts and mandatory arbitration – are essential for CIVs to gain the requisite certainty. These mechanisms serve at least two purposes. First, their availability may limit inappropriate application to CIVs of a PPT. Second, when a PPT is applied inappropriately, these mechanisms – particularly if they are applied expeditiously – will shorten the period of uncertainty.
>
> We support strongly mechanisms for resolving unilateral application of a PPT. These mechanisms will assist CIVs in ascertaining expeditiously their tax liabilities on cross-border investments.
>
> Question 17 – List of examples in the Commentary on the PPT Rule
>
> We also recommend that CIVs generally be exempt, expressly or effectively, from any principal purpose test. Example D, on pages 72-73 of the BEPS Action 6 2014 Deliverable, provides an excellent starting point for effecting this recommendation. The CIV in this example makes investment decisions that 'take into account the existence of tax benefits provided under [the CIV's residence country's] extensive tax convention network'. Taking into account a treaty between the CIV's residence country and a country in which the CIV invests, the Example states, 'alone, would not be sufficient to trigger [the PPT]'. Because '[t]he intent of tax treaties is to provide benefits to encourage cross-border investment ... it is necessary to consider the context in which the investment was made'. In conclusion, the example provides, 'unless [the CIV's] investment is part of an arrangement or relates to another transaction undertaken for a principal purpose of obtaining [treaty benefits], it would not be reasonable to deny the benefit of the ... treaty to [the CIV]'.
>
> While very helpful, this example's application is limited because it assumes: (1) that a majority of the CIV's investors are resident in the CIV's country of residence and (2) the CIV distributes annually to investors almost all of its income and pays residence-country tax on any amounts retained. The example, on its face, does not apply to most globally distributed funds or to any fund (even if distributed only within a single country) that retains, rather than distributes, its income.
>
> We recommend that any final report on BEPS Action 6 include a second example in which a majority of the CIV's investors are resident in any country with which the Source Country provides treaty relief comparable to that provided to the treaty partner. This recommendation effectively would embed into the PPT the equivalent beneficiary approach that we submit is essential to provide appropriate treaty relief to globally distributed CIVs.
>
> We likewise recommend that the example apply to a CIV that retains, rather than distributes, its income. Without this change, the investors in a 'non-distributing'

CIV will suffer double taxation – first when the CIV receives income and a second time when the investor disposes of his/her CIV interest. At a minimum, an example with the assumptions we recommend above should be provided for those countries that support equivalent beneficiary treatment and seek to prevent double taxation (as opposed to preventing only double taxation that occurs within a single year).

Our recommendations are being advanced because the widely held CIVs covered by the CIV Report and the BEPS Action 6 2014 Deliverable are designed to assist individual investors, particularly those of moderate means, in saving for long-term needs such as retirement. Globally distributed CIVs, as discussed above, serve a wide range of important objectives; tax manipulation is not one of them. Any concern about potentially abusive arrangements should be addressed by including in the PPT examples a specific illustration of the concern; one such concern would be a CIV organized in a treaty country and distributed predominantly, and purposefully, only within countries that do not have treaties with the source countries in which the CIV invests. Factors that would support this abusive principal purpose would include: (1) an investment objective that targets countries with which the expected investor base does not receive treaty relief; and (2) promotional materials that highlight the ability to receive treaty benefits that would not be received by investing in the source countries directly or through other investment vehicles.[56]

[C] The Increased Focus on the Financial Services Industry and on Funds

The CIV Report, which was designed to simplify the process by which funds receive treaty relief, to date has not led to the sea change in treaty application that the ICG's members desired. While several recent individual treaties clarify fund eligibility, the number of treaty-related disputes may have increased as well. Certainly, there is additional scrutiny in some countries regarding when treaty relief should be provided.

The catalyst for this additional scrutiny of fund treaty eligibility, I submit, has very little to do with 'inappropriate' treaty claims being filed by funds. Some additional scrutiny, in fairness, may be attributable to the thorough consideration given by the CIV Report to the differences in how funds are organized and operated and the intermediated nature of many funds' distribution processes. Nevertheless, the CIV Report was quite clear that procedures should be implemented to address fully any governmental concerns about these differences.

In my view, the biggest catalyst for the additional scrutiny given to funds relates to what has been called 'the worst financial crisis in global history, including the Great Depression'.[57] The CIV Report had the misfortune of being crafted as the 'financial crisis' was unfolding in September 2008. The result of the 'financial crisis' has been

56. Letter from Keith Lawson, Senior Counsel, Tax Law, ICI Global, to Marlies de Ruiter, Head of Division, Tax Treaties, Transfer Pricing and Financial Transactions, Centre for Tax Policy and Administration, OECD 7–8 (8 January 2015) *available at* www.ici.org/pdf/28653.pdf (last accessed 12 December 2017).

57. Tim Worstall, *Ben Bernake: The 2008 Financial Crisis Was Worse Than the Great Depression*, Forbes (27 August 2014) *available at* http://www.forbes.com/sites/timworstall/2014/08/27/

additional scrutiny (which is fair)[58] and scapegoating (which is not)[59] of the financial services industry - both in its own right and as part of the global MNE economy.

One other development that has slowed progress on implementing the CIV Report's recommendations is BEPS itself. Since the BEPS Action Plan was announced in 2013, government officials have spent countless hours addressing quite admirably the many impediments to consensus positions on the fifteen action items. One consequence of this success, however, has been precious little attention to other important issues. Perhaps now, with BEPS somewhat in the rear view mirror, attention can be turned to implementing the CIV Report's recommendations - which were supported by the OECD in the BEPS Action 6 Final Report.

Thus, it is time to dig deeper into the prediction I have been asked to make: What will be the treaty entitlement of funds in the post-BEPS world?

§12.03 OVERARCHING INDUSTRY THEMES

The fund industry's major treaty-eligibility themes are certainty, neutrality, and practicality. Before discussing these themes in detail, particularly given that they are interrelated, a brief summary of each may be useful.

Certainty, in some respects, is the most important theme. Specifically, because interests in funds may be purchased and sold every day, and the transaction price is determined based upon the value of the funds' underlying assets, funds must estimate the value of their tax claims. The greater the uncertainty, the more difficult this valuation process. Certainty also makes it easier to explain to potential investors the consequences of withholding taxes on their after-tax returns. Finally, withholding agents, such as local bank subcustodians, may insist on certainty before claiming treaty relief for their fund clients. Certainty obviously is enhanced when tax relief is provided 'at source' (when the dividend is paid) rather than available only through a 'reclaim' process to recover previously withheld amounts.

Neutrality has two aspects. First, equal withholding tax treatment for funds organized and operated in different countries addresses competitive concerns that otherwise may result in treaty relief being denied because of reciprocity concerns. Second, fund investors are treated unfairly unless they have the same access to treaties whether they invest through a fund or directly. Thus, neutrality is sought between different countries' funds on the one hand and between fund investors and direct investors in the same underlying securities on the other hand.

---

ben-bernanke-the-2008-financial-crisis-was-worse-than-the-great-depression/#5dbb148277c0 (last accessed 25 September 2017).

58. The CRS, for example, reflects a thoughtful approach (albeit with technical issues still to be addressed) to respond to legitimate concerns about taxpayers' deliberate efforts to use financial instruments to avoid paying tax due.

59. The political rhetoric surrounding the FTT is a classic example of scapegoating. Although the FTT is designed to apply to those entities that 'caused' the financial crisis, funds had nothing to do with the crisis and yet would be taxed under the proposal being considered in the EU. Importantly, fund investors suffered just like other members of the general public and yet would bear the full cost of any tax imposed on their funds.

Practical approaches for receiving the treaty relief negotiated by a fund's government is essential. At-source relief, as noted above, is preferable to reclaim-process relief. Without practical approaches - and this is particularly the case when reclaims must be filed - the relief available in theory is just that: theoretical relief.

These themes lead all members of the global fund industry to support strongly the CIV Report's recommendations and, as discussed further below, effective TRACE implementation.

[A] Certainty

[1] The Importance of Certainty

Certainty is extremely important for funds and their investors - and not just on tax matters. Funds need certainty that their portfolio trades will settle on time and at the agreed price. Likewise, fund investors need to know that their purchase and sale orders will be processed correctly and on time - as the value of a fund's interests will fluctuate with the markets in which the fund invests. The processes that funds follow every day to determine accurately the value of their assets are developed carefully, performed tirelessly, and monitored closely.

Minimizing potential uncertainties, on tax and other matters, is essential for the daily valuation of a fund's net assets (the per-unit amount of which is known as the 'net asset value' or 'NAV'). If the fund cannot recover taxes for which relief should be available under a treaty, the fund investors - through no fault of the fund - will pay or receive too much for their units/shares if recorded, but ultimately unrecovered, tax recoveries are material to the fund's NAV.

Certainty of tax benefits also is important in marketing a fund to potential investors. If two funds otherwise are comparable, the deciding factor in purchasing a fund could be eligibility to receive tax treaty benefits. Obviously, withholding tax impacts negatively a fund's after-tax return.

Withholding taxes are less problematic to the extent that a fund's investors can claim credits relatively easily against their home-country tax for foreign withholding taxes. For globally distributed funds, where the fund's investors reside in a country other than the one in which the fund is organized, foreign tax credits generally are not available in the investors' home country.

Withholding taxes always are problematic for investors, such as pension funds, that are treated by the Source Country as tax-exempt. In this case, the withholding tax in all cases reduces the investors' return.

Many believe that funds' marketing potential increases to the extent they can inform potential investors that treaty benefits apply.

Certainty, finally, is important to the custodians filing treaty claims for their fund clients - particularly when relief is provided at source (when the dividend is paid). Because global custodians typically will be a government's first point of contact if the government concludes that treaty benefits should not be provided, these custodians are rightly worried that they effectively will be responsible for repaying the government for amounts 'wrongly' claimed. The subjective PPT Rule, as discussed below, will create uncertainty for global custodians unless comfort is received (such as through fairly detailed administrative guidance) that funds do not raise PPT concerns.

[2] Factors That Lead Funds to Book a Treaty Claim (or Not)

How do funds address the present uncertainty in whether treaty relief ultimately will be received? It depends on how the funds are organized and operated and whether practical solutions are likely to be available.

Those funds that clearly satisfy the 'person' and 'resident' requirements for treaty relief generally will include in their net assets the treaty relief to which they are entitled by the treaty's terms. I say 'generally' because there are several situations in which these funds do not 'book' the 'receivable' – or, in certain situations, may reverse a previous inclusion. The most common situations are when a source country either (1) changes its position, such as because of reciprocity concerns, regarding beneficial ownership, (2) imposes new 'proof' requirements (perhaps in response to perceived inappropriate behavior by investors generally) that cannot be met as a practical matter, or (3) provides relief only if claimed at source (and a fund has not completed the required paperwork before the dividend is paid). A less common situation, that unfortunately does arise, involves a country flatly ignoring its treaty responsibilities.

For funds that cannot satisfy the 'person' and 'resident' requirements, such as because the fund is tax transparent, treaty-provided tax relief typically will be included in NAV calculations only when eligibility is clear in the treaty itself or in administrative guidance. Thankfully, as a result of the CIV Report and the hard work of the local fund industries and their governments, relief is becoming available a bit more frequently.

[3] Getting Clarity

So, what happens when there is uncertainty regarding whether treaty relief will be provided? The parties supporting the funds in recovering treaty relief, in the order in which they generally become engaged, are the funds' global custodians, their accounting firms and outside counsel (sometimes), their trade associations, and their governments.

The first indication of a reclaim problem typically will come from the global custodian that, based upon conversations with the local subcustodian in the Source Country, advises that the Source Country has rejected a claim; perhaps the rejection will request supporting documentation (such as 'proof' that the fund's investors are treaty entitled in their own right). Typically, once the global custodian becomes concerned that the issue is industry-wide, and not just a single documentation failure or a single misinformed government agent, the global custodian will contact industry bodies (such as the Association of Global Custodians, the AGC). Others, sometimes outside advisors and almost always a fund's industry association, will become involved in the effort to coordinate an industry-wide response.

ICI and ICI Global, for example, work closely with the AGC, their outside counsel, and the AGC's members when industry-wide issues arise. The ICI and three AGC members first jointly retained counsel to address a specific country's rejections of treaty claims in 1989. Our most recent ICI Global-AGC joint effort, involving counsel retained in 2016, is ongoing.

Industry interaction with governments takes different forms. In some countries, coordination with residence country governments is ongoing. When a problem is administrative (proof-related), governments typically choose not to intervene (as they have their own administrative procedures and would not appreciate other governments challenging them). In contrast, when an issue reaches the 'effective denial of treaty relief' stage, because no practical route exists to satisfy a country's administrative procedures, government-to-government discussions are much more likely. Sometimes, as in the situations mentioned briefly above, the industry association engages directly with the foreign government - while advising its residence country government along the way. In other situations, the industry association only provides support to its residence country government. In yet other situations, both the industry association and the government are involved (generally separately) in discussions with the foreign government.

Individual funds and their outside advisors are kept advised of the status of all industry-wide issues. This information is necessary so that each fund can make its own decision about whether or not there is sufficient certainty to book a receivable for the tax recovery to be claimed. The information regarding progress (or not) on industry-wide issues also is necessary to making any decision about writing off (reversing) a tax reclaim that no longer is viewed as recoverable. Difficult issues arise regarding how, consistent with accounting principles and shareholder fairness, to write off these amounts.

For all of the above reasons, tax certainty is extremely important for funds.

[B] Neutrality

Neutrality also is an important theme for funds. Competitive issues (between different countries' funds or between funds and those selling securities directly to investors) arise unless funds effectively are treated the same as direct investors. Competitive imbalances make it less likely that investors will achieve fully their investment goals.

Competitive imbalances create a practical problem in that governments sometimes object (with or without the instigation of their local fund industry) to 'unbalanced' treatment. Reciprocity considerations may arise if, for example, Country A's government is providing treaty relief to Country B funds while its own (Country A) funds are not receiving treaty relief from Country B. While there may be sound tax policy differences (such as how the different countries' funds are organized and operated) for the different results, reciprocity issues often have political dimensions. Treaties, being bilateral arrangements, always are subject to interpretation and (at least potentially) abrogation. Moreover, all treaties eventually are renegotiated.

Funds that are persons and residents – particularly those that are distributed only within their country of organization – have a strong 'reciprocity' interest in ensuring the other countries' funds also are treaty-eligible (either directly or on behalf of their investors). Among other things, as 'domestically sold' funds are not competing across borders for 'foreign' customers, they have no potential 'competitive advantage' to protect. This lack of a competitive advantage concern helps explain the strong industry support for the CIV Report and the options it provides for giving all funds an avenue for pursuing treaty relief.

[C] Practical Solutions

Treaty relief that is available only in theory denies fund investors a benefit that their governments have negotiated for them. Thus, the fund industry has a keen interest in practical solutions. Importantly, such solutions are offered by the CIV Report and by the changes to the Commentary to Article 1 of the OECD Model Tax Convention, which ensure that a fund that is not treaty-entitled in its own right should be permitted to claim treaty relief on behalf of its eligible investors.[60]

The CIV Report offers several practical solutions to the difficulties funds have in establishing the identity and tax residence of each underlying investor. Because of the large number of investors in a fund, and the frequency with which they purchase and redeem/sell their interests, as noted above, proving investor eligibility with precision can be a practical impossibility. A few sentences from the Commentary to Article 1 of the OECD Model Tax Convention illustrate the mindset that governments should take in addressing CIV treaty-eligibility proof issues:

- Contracting States should be willing to accept practical and reliable approaches that do not require such daily tracing.[61]
- In many countries, the CIV industry is largely domestic, with an overwhelming percentage of investors resident in the country in which the CIV is established. ... It may be appropriate, for example, to assume that a CIV is owned by residents of the State in which it is established if the CIV has limited distribution of its shares or units to the State in which the CIV is established or to other States that provide for similar benefits in their treaties with the Source State.[62]
- In other cases, interests in the CIV are offered to investors in many countries. Although the identity of individual investors will change daily, the proportion of investors in the CIV that are treaty-entitled is likely to change relatively slowly. Accordingly, it would be a reasonable approach to require the CIV to collect from other intermediaries, on specified dates, information enabling the CIV to determine the proportion of investors that are treaty-entitled. This information could be required at the end of a calendar or fiscal year or, if

60. CIV Report, *supra* note 1, para. 6.16.
61. *Ibid.*, para. 6.29.
62. *Ibid.*, para. 6.30.

market conditions suggest that turnover in ownership is high, it could be required more frequently, although no more often that the end of a calendar quarter.[63]

- An alternative approach would provide that a CIV that is publicly traded in the Contracting State in which it is established would be entitled to treaty benefits without regard to the residence of its investors.[64]

[D] Support for the CIV Report's Recommendations and TRACE Implementation

The fund industry obviously supports wholeheartedly the CIV Report's recommendations. Support also is wholehearted for the TRACE Implementation Package. Among other benefits of TRACE, treaty relief would be provided at source. The resulting high degree of tax certainty would be extremely beneficial to funds and their investors.

§12.04 GOVERNMENTAL CONCERNS

Governments – during the CIV Report consultation, during the BEPS consultation, and in various meetings to address specific withholding tax issues – have expressed several concerns with how treaties should be applied to funds. These concerns range from 'treaty negotiator' concerns (such as preserving negotiating position, preventing treaty abuse, or preventing double non-taxation of income) to 'technical requirement' concerns (such as when a fund is not treaty-entitled in its own right) to 'administrative' concerns (such as proving eligible investors or preserving revenue). Although the concerns are somewhat interrelated, it is helpful to think about them separately as we prepare to consider the way forward.

[A] 'Treaty Negotiator' Tax Policy-Related Concerns

Treaty negotiators rightly take very seriously the tax policy rationales for tax treaties and the need to maximize the benefit to resident taxpayers when it negotiates treaties and later administers their operation. Because of the relatively unique nature of funds, these concerns can present challenges for providing funds and their investors with appropriate treaty relief.

[1] The 'Preserving the Ability to Negotiate a Treaty' Concern

One government concern, as explained in Paragraph 3.1 of the preliminary remarks to the commentary on the Article concerning the entitlement to treaty benefits, is the need to preserve a State's ability to negotiate treaty relief for its own residents. Specifically:

63. *Ibid.*, para. 6.31.
64. *Ibid.*, para. 6.32.

> Allowing persons who are not directly entitled to treaty benefits (such as the reduction or elimination of withholding taxes on dividends, interest or royalties) to obtain these benefits indirectly through treaty shopping would frustrate the bilateral and reciprocal nature of tax treaties. If, for instance, a State knows that its residents can indirectly access the benefits of treaties concluded by another State, it many have little interest in granting reciprocal benefits to residents of that other State through the conclusion of a tax treaty.[65]

[2] *The (Related) 'Treaty Shopping' Concern*

Governments, as illustrated quite clearly by the BEPS Action 6 Final Report, are very concerned about treaty shopping. This concern, in its purest form, suggests that an investor never should be able to receive a tax treaty benefit that would not be available if he/she made an investment directly.

Thankfully, this 'purest form' concern is not reflected in the Action 6 minimum standard. The LOB test has no minimum requirement for eligible investors if a fund is publicly traded and only a minimum of 50% eligible investors if an otherwise-eligible fund is not publicly traded. The PPT Rule, on the other hand, does not provide any objective test; the Rule's subjective standard arguably would allow a fund to receive treaty benefits even if none of its investors were treaty eligible in their own right.

Some in industry have suggested that funds never should violate the PPT rule because investors do not 'control' the funds' investments and therefore, when investing, never could have a principal purpose of gaining an 'inappropriate' tax benefit. Unfortunately, the PPT rule examples provided in the Final Report are not this expansive; indeed, the CIV-specific example included in the Final Report (Example D, discussed above) applies only to domestically sold funds that make current distributions.

Moreover, even if funds 'generally' should not be viewed as violating the PPT rule, situations could arise in which even 'favourably inclined governments' would have PPT rule concerns. The example discussed during the conference, while perhaps unrealistic, illustrates one aspect of the PPT rule's potential ambiguity. Specifically, assume an attractive Source Country that imposes fairly substantial withholding taxes on dividends and capital gains, and has a very limited treaty network. Governments adopting a PPT approach very likely would be concerned were an asset manager to establish a fund in a 'treaty-eligible' country and then market it extensively in countries that do not have treaties with the Source Country. This concern would be even more pronounced if the fund's marketing materials highlighted the tax advantages that were available *only* through this fund. Notwithstanding that the Source Country might be a very attractive investment destination and that the fund provides superior investment performance, the marketed tax advantage very well might be enough for some/most/all governments to have PPT rule concerns.

The lack of guidance regarding how the PPT rule will be applied to funds may (or may not) lead to interpretive issues in the future. Certainly, the example immediately

65. Final Action 6 Report, *supra* note 14, at 22.

above (even ignoring the limited nature of the CIV Example in the Final Report) suggests that some governments may believe that more definitive PPT Rule guidance may be needed to distinguish 'good' CIV situations from 'bad' ones.

[3] The 'Deferral' Concern

The CIV Report devotes a separate section to policy issues involving 'potential deferral of income'.[66] As explained in the Report, some governments believe that 'benefits to the CIV should be limited to the proportion of the CIV's investors who are currently taxable on their share of the income of the CIV, similar to the approach taken with respect to partnerships'.[67] Other governments, conversely, 'take the view that, even if the investor is not taxed currently on the income received by the CIV, it will be taxed eventually, either on the distribution, or on any capital gains if it sells its interest in the CIV before the CIV distributes the income'.[68] These governments also note that the risk of deferral is limited because of the Source Country's withholding tax (generally at a 10%–15% rate) and the fact that many countries tax investment income at approximately the same rates. Moreover, these countries point to anti-deferral rules that often result in 'rolled-up' income nevertheless being taxed currently in investors' residence countries.

[4] The 'Equivalent Beneficiary' Concern

One last 'treaty negotiator' tax policy-related concern is that treaty benefits should be available under a bilateral treaty only to the extent that investors are resident of one of the two treaty partners. Governments holding this concern reject the CIV Report's option of also providing treaty benefits under bilateral treaties to 'equivalent beneficiaries'. To my knowledge, this concern arises only to the extent that an LOB test is being applied.

The equivalent beneficiary approach is essential for globally distributed funds – and, in my view, is clearly the much better tax policy answer. This approach limits treaty benefits to investors in any country with which the Source Country (1) has a treaty that (2) provides withholding tax relief at the same or lower tax rate. As all of the 'equivalent-beneficiary-eligible' investors would receive the treaty benefit if investing directly or through a 'domestically sold' fund, it is very unclear (at least to me) why relief should be denied if they invest instead through a globally distributed fund.

For funds treated by the Source Country as fiscally transparent, and therefore entitled to relief only to the extent of the eligible investors on whose behalf claims are filed, there would appear to be no tax policy rationale for rejecting the equivalent beneficiary approach. Certainly, there is no LOB issue for the fiscally transparent fund; the only LOB issue would arise with respect to entities investing in the fund.

66. CIV Report, *supra* note 1, Section 4.3.
67. *Ibid.*, para. 58.
68. *Ibid.*, para. 59.

Even for funds treated by the Source Country as opaque, and therefore claiming treaty benefits on their own behalf, the rationale for rejecting the equivalent beneficiary standard is (at least for me) elusive. If a country has determined that it will provide treaty relief if at least 50% of a fund's interest are held by eligible investors resident in the treaty partner, and the Source Country provides equivalent benefits to residents of other countries, where is the harm of treating all such eligible investors as 'good' for bilateral treaties? Perhaps the 'response' is that bilateral treaties are bilateral. I submit that this is not a sufficient policy rationale for denying treaty benefits to fund investors who would be eligible if investing directly. Certainly, this result violates the 'tax neutrality' theme that is so important to the fund industry.

[B] 'Technical Requirement' Concerns

As the CIV Report notes, some funds are not treaty-eligible in their own right or are not treated, under a Source Country's domestic tax rules, as beneficial owners. These concerns, as explained in the CIV Report, can be addressed through express treaty language and/or memoranda of understanding clarifying that these funds are claiming on behalf of their investors and must provide reliable proof of these investors' treaty eligibility.

[C] 'Administrative' Concerns

Finally, there are governments' 'administrative' concerns. These concerns call out for thoughtful discussion between funds and governments on the one hand and between governments on the other hand to ensure that funds have practical solutions while governments have solutions that are reliable.

[1] The 'Revenue' Concern

Without (hopefully) putting a too-overly cynical point on this concern, lower-level government officials charged with providing tax relief only to eligible investors are less concerned with tax policy matters and more concerned with not 'giving away' tax revenues. Thus, they often apply treaty provisions very literally (and strictly). Funds and/or their advocates often need to elevate 'revenue concern' issues to policy-making officials to reach practical solutions that 'protect the treasury' while ensuring that the treaty operates as intended.

[2] The Proof Concern: AKA 'Reliable Solutions'

At the end of the day, government officials want 'reliable' solutions to the concerns discussed above. The CIV Report is quite clear, however, that 'reliable' solutions do not involve daily tracing of individual fund investors. The required degree of 'reliable solution precision' should turn on the extent to which legitimate tax policy concerns arise in the CIV context. As the CIV Report expressly limits its conclusions to 'funds that are widely held, hold a diversified portfolio of securities[,] and are subject to investor-protection regulation in the country in which they are established,'[69] the tax policy concerns that might arise were other types of funds at issue simply do not exist.

§12.05 THE WAY FORWARD

[A] In General

Finally, we get to the prediction stage of this chapter. So, what will be the treaty entitlement of funds in the post-BEPS world? Well, it depends.

For funds to get the treaty benefits that the industry firmly believes are important, at least three things must happen:

(1) Funds and their national and global industry associations must be effective advocates for practical and reliable solutions. An important aspect of this first point – one that cannot be over-emphasized – is that funds must understand (and address fully) the legitimate tax policy concerns raised by governments.
(2) Governments must recognize that funds are unique investment vehicles for the general public;[70] they are not crafted (or marketed) to meet the tax planning needs of wealthy investors. The funds (CIVs) that are the focus of this Chapter present tax policy considerations that generally are quite distinct from those raised by BEPS for other types of entities.
(3) While acknowledging the legitimacy of many concerns raised since the financial crisis began, governments must strive to ensure that the benefits arising from the economic growth attributable to more efficient capital investment are available to all.

All three of these things are possible; indeed, the industry advocacy effort is extensive and ongoing. Getting governments to the 'right' answer on fund treaty eligibility issues will take time – less for some and more for others.

The path forward, nevertheless, is clear.

[B] Implement the CIV Report

Countries should embrace the protections provided by the CIV Report, as the fund industry urges, and adopt the Report's recommendations through updated treaty provisions, memoranda of understanding, or appropriate administrative guidance. These recommendations are fully consistent with, and were supported in, the BEPS Action 6 Final Report.

69. *Ibid.*, para. 4.
70. In the US, for example, over 93 million Americans invest in these funds. *2015 Facts at a Glance*, *in* ICI, *2016 Investment Company Fact Book*, inside front cover (56th ed., ICI Publishing 2016), https://www.ici.org/pdf/2016_factbook.pdf (last accessed 25 September 2017).

The interesting question is how the CIV Report's options will be implemented. Funds that are treaty entitled in their own right should experience fewer treaty-eligibility difficulties as governments move from the recent 'BEPS-centric' environment to one that allows for tax policy consideration of other issues. Most particularly, opaque funds that are domestically sold and distribute their income to investors currently present few (if any) of the governmental concerns discussed above. The most significant issue, which at the moment is most prevalent in only a small number of countries, concerns beneficial ownership. Educating government officials who were not involved in the CIV Report about the wisdom of the CIV Report recommendations, such as for (at most) quarterly testing, is essential. Progress on these issues for treaty-entitled funds will ensure a strong foundation for solutions for globally distributed funds.

Globally distributed funds have at least two distinct routes for receiving the treaty relief to which their investors are entitled. The first route involves continuing to advance treaty eligibility through treaty negotiations and memoranda of understanding. The Luxembourgish government, for example, has been an effective advocate for its industry in several recent situations.

The second route involves modifying how globally distributed funds are organized and operated on a going-forward basis to address any remaining intractable governmental concerns. I am not suggesting that this route *should* be necessary, only that it may be worth considering if important source countries with large and robust capital markets continue to impose treaty-eligibility requirements that globally distributed/income-retaining funds cannot meet.

One such modification would be for a fund - or a fund class - to distribute (either voluntarily or through a legislative/regulatory change) its income annually to its investors. To the extent that countries move towards adopting 'anti-deferral' regimes that eliminate any tax benefit of investing in a 'roll-up' fund, this change should be unnecessary (as the income is taxed currently without distribution) and would have little practical effect. Moreover, the experience in the US is that most investors automatically reinvest their distributions.[71] Thus, the cost of making actual distributions (at least to a class of investors not subject to anti-deferral provisions) is relatively insignificant.

A second such modification, that presumably would be somewhat more easily achievable for newly organized funds (and somewhat less so for new investors in existing funds), would involve creating some investor-specific identifier based upon residence country. This identifier could be based upon a 'residence code' for each investor, using separate share/unit 'classes,' or Block Chain technology. A newly organized fund, for example (at least in theory), could add a tax-residency code to each new shareholder record (e.g., a 'Germany code,' a 'France code') and require each intermediary to do likewise. Importantly, the residence identifier would not require an

71. For 2015, the last year for which complete data was available as this chapter was being finalized, US equity fund investors reinvested 95.7% of distributed capital gains and 93.1% of distributed ordinary (dividend) income. https://www.ici.org/research/stats/mf_disthttps://www.ici.org/pdf/2017_factbook.pdf, tables 29 and 30).

intermediary to disclose to the fund the identity (name, address, etc.) of the customer; the only information provided would be the tax residence for the shares held by each (unidentified) investor.

Because of the additional cross-border investor reporting requirements being adopted to meet the OECD's CRS, governments should have great confidence that investor residency-country information is correct. Thus, it may be 'relatively' easy for a fund to establish (such as on an annual or quarterly basis) the percentage of its units held by residents of each country with which a Source Country has treaties. This approach also could be used by existing funds (as funds' intermediaries also are subject to the CRS).

This level of precision, importantly: (1) is not contemplated by the CIV Report (in part because the resulting substantial burden would be disproportionate to the limited potential for some unintended tax benefit); (2) would be expensive (at least initially) to implement; and (3) therefore should *not* be required for globally distributed funds to receive treaty benefits.

I add this point only to suggest that all hope is not lost, necessarily, if some countries refuse to adopt the CIV Report's recommendations for practical and reliable solutions. A lot more thinking needs to take place before sound business judgments can be reached about the practicality – on a cost/benefit basis – of pursuing these possible changes.

[C] Implement TRACE

Governments should adopt the TRACE implementation package. TRACE provides governments with all of the assurances they need that treaty relief is being provided only to eligible investors. Moreover, as TRACE is *entirely* voluntary, financial services firms and industries have no responsible basis for opposing TRACE. Those financial institutions that find the benefits to their clients outweigh the costs of becoming Authorized Intermediaries, and thereby wish to gain access to TRACE's many benefits (including at source relief), should be allowed to do so.

[D] Clarify the PPT Rule's Application to Funds

The one post-BEPS area that seems particularly problematic – particularly from a global custodian perspective – is the potential uncertainty arising from the subjective PPT Rule. We are not far enough down the post-BEPS route to know whether a global consensus will develop that funds do not raise PPT concerns (or, at a minimum, gain some guidance regarding the types of funds that raise concerns and how those concerns can be addressed). Given my many years of experience representing the fund industry in tax treaty eligibility disputes, and my involvement over the past ten years representing funds at the OECD on these issues, I am perhaps less sanguine than others that industry-acceptable guidance will be issued soon.[72]

Without clear guidance, global custodians may well be reluctant to claim at-source relief in any country adopting the PPT Rule – as their deep pockets will be the first ones picked should a country decide that a fund had a 'bad' principle purpose. Because of the costs, and uncertainty, arising when funds must file for tax reclaims, at-source relief is highly preferable.

[E] Final Thoughts

Final thoughts (in a few short bullet points):

- Funds need practical solutions (that are reliable).
- Governments need reliable solutions (that are practical).
- Global custodians (and funds) need certainty.
- All of this is possible – so long as funds and governments work together to understand each other's concerns and needs.
- Because the fund industry is determined to work with governments to reach an outcome that is mutually agreeable, the outlook is bright (at least in the medium term).

72. ICI Global, for example, urged that the multilateral instrument (MLI) crafted by the OECD to implement BEPS Action 15 allows countries to specify in a memorandum how they believe the BEPS Action 6 minimum standards for treaty eligibility should be applied to CIVs resident in their jurisdictions. This information would be posted on the OECD's website similarly to how country-specific tax residency guidance is provided on the OECD's automatic exchange of information (AEOI) website. Unfortunately, this suggestion was not accepted by the OECD.

CHAPTER 13

Non-discrimination of Funds and Double Taxation Relief

Daniel Gutmann

§13.01 INTRODUCTION

Funds are generally non-taxable entities under the domestic law of the state where they are established, because either corporate income tax applies to them at a zero rate or because they are transparent for tax purposes.

However, when a fund established in one state receives a payment from a resident of another state, the latter may levy a withholding tax on that payment. That withholding tax generally arises because the domestic legislation of the source state does not provide a specific exemption for non-resident funds and the particular tax treaty in place between the relevant states does not eliminate the withholding tax. Accordingly, the combination of domestic law and treaty law leads to the conclusion that a non-resident fund is required to pay tax on the payment, while a resident fund would not have paid any tax at all. The first question tackled in this chapter is whether this different treatment constitutes illicit discrimination by virtue of tax treaties or other instruments.

A second problem is also likely to arise in the residence state of the fund. Indeed, it may well be that when a fund receives foreign-sourced income that has already been taxed at source abroad, the way the resident state grants double taxation relief may differ according to the residence of the investors in the fund. The question is, therefore, whether this discriminatory way to relieve double taxation is contrary to a specific legal norm.

§13.02 THE PERSPECTIVE OF THE SOURCE STATE

Where a payment is made to a non-resident fund and is subject to withholding tax in the source state (while a similar payment would not have been taxable in a purely domestic situation), the first question is obviously which norm is likely to apply in order to counter the discriminatory effect of such a tax.

In a situation in which the law of the European Union (EU) is applicable (which presupposes, at a minimum, that the source state is a Member State of the EU), one may wonder about the extent to which fundamental freedoms demand that the withholding tax be eliminated. It is well known that the Court of Justice of the European Union (ECJ) has already taken favourable positions on this issue.[1] However, this chapter does not deal with EU-law aspects relating to discrimination against funds (which are tackled by Tenore as well as O'Donnell and Molitor-March in their own chapters in this book).[2] Let us, therefore, focus on a treaty approach to this question. For this purpose, we will refer to the OECD's Model Tax Convention on Income and on Capital ('OECD Model').[3]

Discrimination may be caused by two different types of causes: either the source state does not apply a treaty exemption for any applicable withholding tax because it denies treaty benefits to the non-resident fund[4] (probably on the ground that the fund is not liable to tax within the meaning of Article 4 OECD Model and, therefore, is not a resident under treaty law); or the source state does recognize that treaty benefits are applicable to the non-resident fund, but its withholding tax is superior to nil, while a comparable fund having its residence in the source state would have been tax exempt. In both circumstances, the question will be whether the non-discrimination principle enshrined in Article 24 OECD Model may compel the source state to refrain from taxing the payment to the non-resident fund.

Article 24(1) OECD Model provides:

> Nationals of a Contracting State shall not be subjected in the other Contracting State to any taxation or any requirement connected therewith, which is other or more burdensome than the taxation and connected requirements to which nationals of that other State in the same circumstances, in particular with respect to residence, are or may be subjected. This provision shall, notwithstanding the provisions of Article 1, also apply to persons who are not residents of one or both Contracting States.

1. *See, notably, Santander Asset Management SGIIC,* Joined Cases C-338/11 to C-347/11, Judgment, EU:C:2012:286.
2. *See supra* Chapter 6 and Chapter 7.
3. OECD, *Model Tax Convention on Income and on Capital 2014 (Full Version),* available at http://dx.doi.org/10.1787/9789264239081-en (last accessed 20 November 2017).
4. The question whether funds should be entitled to treaty benefits has been highly debated. *See, e.g.*: Daniel W. Blum & Erik Pinetz, *Treaty Entitlement of Investment Funds in Light of BEPS Actions 2 and 6*, 18 Derivatives & Fin. Instruments (2016); Moritz Scherleitner, *Thoughts on the Potential Effects of the OECD/G20 BEPS Action Plan on Collective Investment Vehicles – Part I*, 70 Bull. Int'l Tax'n 601 (2016); Giulia Letizia, *International Tax Issues in Relation to Cross-Border Investment Funds*, 43 Intertax 526 (2015); Patricia A. Brown, *Fifty Years of Tax Uncertainty: The Problem of International Neutrality for Collective Investment Vehicles*, *in The Tax Treatment of CIVs and REITs* 19 (Hein Vermeulen ed., 2010).

In order to implement Article 24 OECD Model in the situation at hand, it is necessary to overcome several hurdles, which are presented below in the form of questions.

- Is it possible to apply Article 24 although funds may not be eligible for tax treaty benefits?
  The answer, in principle, is yes, as the last sentence of Article 24(1) OECD Model provides that the 'provision shall, notwithstanding the provisions of Article 1, also apply to persons who are not residents of one or both Contracting States'. It should be possible, therefore, to apply Article 24 OECD Model to funds that are not 'residents' under treaty law, as long as they are 'nationals' of the other Contracting State.
- Are funds 'nationals of a Contracting State'?

According to Article 3(1)(g) OECD Model:

> For the purposes of this Convention, unless the context otherwise requires:
>
> ...
>
> (g) The term 'national', in relation to a Contracting State, means: (i) any individual possessing the nationality or citizenship of that Contracting State; and (ii) any legal person, partnership or association deriving its status as such from the laws in force in that Contracting State.

Where funds are legal persons, which is often (but not always) the case, there is no reason why they should be excluded from the concept of 'nationals of a Contracting State'. This reasoning was implicitly followed by a French Court of Appeal, in a case involving a Dutch pension fund that was taxed on its capital gain on French real estate when a similar domestic fund would have been tax-exempt under French tax law. The court had no problem applying the non-discrimination principle set out in Article 25 of the relevant tax treaty (dated 25 March 1973 between France and the Netherlands) to alleviate the tax imposed on the Dutch fund.[5] It is worth mentioning, in this respect, that the second paragraph of that Article 25 contained a definition of a 'national' modelled on the OECD Model's concept thereof.[6]

- *Can non-resident funds be subject to any taxation that is more burdensome than the taxation to which nationals of the source state 'in the same circumstances, in particular with respect to residence,' are subjected?*

5. Cour d'appel administrative de Paris, 6 December 2007, n° 06PA03370, *Fondation Stichting Unilever Pensioenfunds Progress*, Revue de jurisprudence fiscale 4/08, n° 409; for more on this case, *see* Daniel Gutmann, Stéphane Austry & Pierre Le Roux, *Le traitement fiscal des fonds de pension étrangers*, 2008 Revue de jurisprudence fiscale 337. The *Conseil d'État* (the French Administrative Supreme Court) did not accept an appeal of this decision (Conseil d'État, 27 October 2008, n° 313135).
6. The fact that the definition of the concept of 'national' was inserted in Art. 25 of the France/Netherlands Treaty comes as no surprise. Let us recall that the definition of 'nationality' used to be found in Art. 24 OECD Model before it was moved, in 1992, to Art. 3 on treaty definitions.

Paragraph 7 OECD Model Commentary on Article 24 provides in this respect that:

> The expression 'in the same circumstances' refers to taxpayers (individuals, legal persons, partnerships and association) placed, from the point of view of the application of the ordinary taxation laws and regulations, in substantially similar circumstances both in law or in fact.

Paragraph 17 of said Commentary, however, further provides that:

> Since Paragraph 1 of Article 24 prevents different treatment based on nationality but only with respect to persons or entities 'in the same circumstances, in particular with respect to residence', it is, therefore, important to distinguish, for the purposes of that paragraph, a different treatment that is solely based on nationality, from a different treatment that relates to other circumstances and, in particular, residence.

Let us try to use these OECD Model Commentary indications to ponder whether non-resident funds and resident funds are placed 'in the same circumstances' and are 'comparable' by nature. While the methodological approach to comparison is always difficult to determine, it seems reasonable to proceed in the following way. First, one should try to identify the legal features of resident tax-exempt funds, which should serve as the starting point for comparison.[7] One should, for instance, wonder whether the tax exemption that is granted to them depends upon the fulfilment of certain regulatory requirements, a specific investment risk profile, one or more specific types of assets invested in, whether they are open-ended or close-ended, etc. Once (and if) this analysis has allowed a better identification of the types of entities that enjoy exemption under domestic law, one should then assess whether such features are broadly possessed by non-resident funds and, if so, the 'same circumstance' requirement for the application of Article 24 should be considered as fulfilled.

It is important to observe, at this stage, that comparability of situations does not mean identity. This point has been made clear in an EU-Law context by the ECJ in its *Emerging Markets* decision.[8] It is also the position of the French *Conseil d'Etat* (its Supreme Court), which decided (albeit for the purpose of implementing EU-law principles) that a non-resident, not-for-profit entity should be deemed comparable to a domestic entity although the managers of the former received a remuneration for their activities, and even though the existence of such a remuneration would disqualify the entity as 'not-for-profit' under a strict domestic approach. The underlying reasoning is that comparability requires the fundamental features of two entities to be comparable in the light of the objective pursued by the legislature or regulator, but does not go as far as requiring that the two entities function exactly in the same way, in the absence of any harmonization of company/civil law systems.

This last question is probably the hardest one to answer. Assuming that a non-resident fund can be considered to be in the 'same circumstances' as a resident

7. For an interesting reflection on the methodological approach to comparison (from an EU-law perspective), *see* Giampaolo Genta, *Dividends Received by Investment Funds: An EU Law Perspective – Part 2*, 53 Eur. Tax'n 141 (2013).
8. *Emerging Markets Series of DFA Investment Trust Company*, C-190/12, Judgment, EU:C2014:249.

fund, how is one to ascertain whether the different treatment applied to that fund is solely based on 'nationality' and not on residence? One possible to answer could be that there is, in fact, no way to demonstrate that the discrimination of a non-resident fund is based on its nationality rather than on its residence, which answer relies on the idea that, as long as the alleged discrimination is based on the fund's incorporation or registration in another state, it is, *ipso facto*, based on its residence. As Paragraph 17 OECD Model Commentary on Article 24 states, under the domestic law of many countries, incorporation or registration constitutes *the* criterion, or one of *the* criteria, for determining the residence of companies for the purpose of Article 4 OECD Model.

It is not, however, certain that this interpretation of Article 24 OECD Model should systematically prevail. In some countries, case law provides examples of a court's recognition that discrimination based on the place of incorporation should be analysed as discrimination based on nationality.[9]

In still other countries, one may observe that case law seems to accept that residence and nationality can be, in certain circumstances, equivalent, with the result that Article 24(1) OECD Model would seem to have a very broad scope of application. If the problem was to be raised in France, a fund would have a strong claim to the benefits of that non-discrimination principle, on the ground that French case law has already made it clear that nationality and residence converge for the purpose of implementing Article 24 OECD Model, provided that the entity's different treatment was based on the location of its head office. Here is an interesting example of a case where the problem explicitly arose.[10] A Greek public entity with a non-profit activity sold a piece of real estate located in France and was obliged to pay a tax on the capital gain it derived from such sale. It then claimed a refund thereof on the ground that a similar public entity engaged in a non-profit activity, having its head office in France, would not have been subject to the capital gain tax. It argued that the imposition of the capital gain tax on it was, therefore, contrary to Article 22 of the French/Greek tax treaty of 21 August 1963; that article incorporated a non-discrimination clause based on Article 24 OECD Model. The *Conseil d'Etat*, the French Supreme Court accepted the Greek entity's argument, stating that the domestic rules that subjected the non-resident public entity's capital gain created a difference in treatment that 'is grounded, as far as legal persons are concerned, on the location of their *head office which determines their nationality*'.[11] Interestingly, the *rapporteur public* (the French equivalent of an Advocate General), Ms Cortot-Boucher, explicitly contemplated the opposite interpretation

9. *See, e.g.*, Niels Bammens, *The Principle of Non-Discrimination in International and European Tax Law* 79 (2012) (commenting on Transvaal Special Income Tax Court decision of 10 March 1992 (54 SATC 456 (T)) (South Africa)). He also commented on the 's-Hertogenbosch Court of Appeal of 13 December 2002 (00/2337, Vakstudie Nieuws (2003), 12.2.10) (*id.*, at 80) where discrimination based on the place of incorporation was considered discrimination based on nationality.
10. Conseil d'État, 5 July 2010, n° 309693, *Pinacothèque d'Athènes*, 2010 Revue de droit fiscal n° 44, comm. 543, concl. Emmanuelle Cortot-Boucher, comment by Frédéric Dieu.
11. Author translation of 'la différence de traitement qu'instaurent ces dispositions est fondée, s'agissant des personnes morales, sur le lieu de *leur siège social qui détermine leur nationalité*'. The opinion of the *rapporteur public*, Ms Cortot-Boucher, before the *Conseil d'Etat* is very interesting in this respect as it provides examples of tax provisions that have given rise to earlier

of the non-discrimination clause in the tax treaty, whereby a different treatment, based on the location of the head office, would have been found to be based on residence. She, however, suggested that the Court not follow that line of reasoning on the ground that:

> this would end up depriving the non-discrimination clauses in tax treaties of any effect with respect to legal entities, while nothing explicitly indicates that this had been the intention of their authors.[12]

Whether this trend in French case law is orthodox or not with respect to the real intention of the OECD Model's drafters may certainly be discussed. As one author rightly explains:

> nationality and residence need to be distinguished for purposes of article 24, as the clauses protecting against discrimination based on residence and nationality should be understood as mutually exclusive.[13]

While the developments above have only focused on the interpretation of Article 24 OECD Model, one might lastly wonder whether other international instruments could be implemented in the same situation. In particular, it should be recalled that Article 14 European Convention on Human Rights ('ECHR') provides:

> the enjoyment of the rights and freedoms set forth in this Convention shall be secured without discrimination on any ground such as sex, race, colour, language, religion, political or other opinion, national or social origin, association with a national minority, property, birth or other status.

Moreover, Article 1, Protocol No. 1 ECHR establishes that 'every natural or legal person is entitled to the peaceful enjoyment of his possessions'. When read together, these two provisions were held by the *Conseil d'Etat* to be a valid basis on which to challenge any unjustified discrimination created by domestic tax law or by bilateral tax treaties. For instance, the Conseil d'Etat already decided that a provision of the French/Monaco tax treaty was compatible with Article 14 ECHR, when read together

case law with respect to discrimination on the ground of nationality and/or residence. One may note, for instance, that discrimination based on the fact that a company 'does not have an establishment in France' was regarded as based on residence, not on nationality (*Conseil d'État*, 15 December 2004, n° 257337, *min. c. sté de Promotion écologique*, 2005 Revue de droit fiscal n° 23, comm. 469, concl. Laurent Olléon). *Compare also* the position of the *Cour de cassation* in its decision of 28 February 1989 (n° 87-14900, 1989 Revue de droit fiscal n° 19, comm. 943), which is described in-depth in Bammens, *supra* note 9, at 99. Bammens also discussed the French case law (*ibid.*, at 118).

12. Conseil d'État, 5 July 2010, n° 309693, *Pinacothèque d'Athènes*, *supra* note 10, § 2 [author translation].
13. Werner Haslehner, *Nationality Non-Discrimination and Article 24 OECD Model: Perennial Issues, Recent Trends and New Approaches*, in *Non-Discrimination in Tax Treaties: Selected Issues from a Global Perspective* 13 (Pasquale Pistone & Dennis Weber eds, Vol. 14 EC & Int'l Tax L. Series, IBFD 2016). This author further observes that if residence and nationality were to converge for companies, it would be impossible to understand why Arts 24(3) and 24(5) OECD Model refer to discrimination based on *residence*.

with Article 1, Protocol No. 1, ECHR.[14] It is also worth mentioning that Protocol No. 12 ECHR, which entered into force in 2005 (although it has not been ratified by all the parties thereto), contains another general non-discrimination principle that, contrary to the current Article 14 ECHR, is independent and non-accessory.

The idea of relying on the ECHR to protect investment funds from discriminatory withholding taxes may seem odd at first blush. It is, however, interesting to note that the question of whether discrimination based on residence is admissible under the ECHR is not new. As observed above, Article 14 ECHR contains a list of grounds on which discrimination is prohibited, such as sex, race, colour, or 'other status'. The meaning of the expression 'other status' has been very controversial; some authors have pointed out that the European Court on Human Rights ('ECtHR') has diverging interpretations thereof.[15] Generally, the ECtHR holds that a difference in treatment must be based on a personal characteristic ('status') by which persons or groups of persons are distinguishable from each other,[16] but certain other judgments seem to give less weight to the requirement that a 'personal characteristic' be at stake.[17] In any case, there is no doubt that the ECHR applies to discrimination based on residence, which the ECtHR made very clear in its *Carson* decision,[18] in which it tried to reconcile its lines of reasoning to provide more consistency in its case law. After recalling its earlier case law on the meaning of the expression 'other status', it concluded that a 'place of residence constitutes an aspect of personal status for the purposes of Article 14'.[19] Subsequent ECtHR judgments have confirmed this conclusion.[20]

It remains to be seen whether tax discrimination based on residence remains acceptable in light of the ECtHR's doctrine on the 'margin of appreciation' left to the ECHR's signatories. Moreover, it will be necessary to verify whether such discrimination can rely on an 'objective and reasonable justification', in the ECtHR's words. One, however, cannot ignore that, even if Article 24 OECD Model might not apply due to a strict interpretation of the concept of discrimination based on nationality, other instruments, such as the ECHR, may be brought into play insofar as they prohibit unfair discrimination based on residence.

14. Conseil d'État, 11 April 2014, n° 362237, *M. Giorgis*, 2014 Revue de droit fiscal n° 21, comm. 342, concl. Edouard Crépey, comment by Charles Louit.
15. Janneke Gerards, *The Discrimination Grounds of Article 14 of the European Convention on Human Rights*, 13 Hum. Rts. L. Rev. 99 (2013).
16. ECHR, 7 December 1976, *Kjeldsen, Buk Madsen and Pedersen v. Denmark* A 23 (1976), App. Nos. 5095/71, 5920/72, 5926/72, 1 EHRR 711.
17. *See* Gerards, *supra* note 15, at 105 et seq.
18. ECHR, 16 March 2010, *Carson and Others v. United Kingdom*, App. No. 42184/05, 51 EHRR 13.
19. *Ibid.*, § 71.
20. *Sekerovic and Pasalic v. Bosnia and Herzegovina*, 8 March 2011, App. No 5920/04; *Zammit Maempel v. Malta*, 22 November 2011, App. No. 24202/10; *Vuckovic and Others v. Serbia*, 28 August 2012, App. No. 17153/11; *Efe v. Austria*, 8 January 2013, App. No. 9134/06; *Schindler v. United Kingdom*, 7 May 2013, App. No. 19840/09.

§13.03 THE PERSPECTIVE OF THE RESIDENCE STATE

Discrimination issues may also occur from the perspective of a fund's residence state. Let us consider the following case: a company established in State A pays a dividend to a fund established in State B. State A levies a withholding tax on that dividend. The fund in State B is subject to corporate income tax at that rate of 0% and, thus, cannot use, itself, the available tax credit to offset any resident state tax liability. Assuming that the resident state taxes the fund's distribution of profits to its investors ('unitholders'), two techniques may be used to relieve any double taxation when the fund distributes profits to its unitholders: the State B tax credit available to the fund can be transferred to its unitholders or the withholding tax levied in State A can be refunded to the State B fund at a later stage.

[A] Transfer of Tax Credit to Investors

Let us consider the first technique (i.e., transferring the tax credit to the fund's investors). Normally, when a tax credit is transferred to a fund's investors in State B (i.e., in the fund's residence State), the amount thereof is typically equal to the tax credit the investor would have enjoyed if it had received the income directly from the source state (State A). The unitholder, therefore, may invoke the State A/State B tax treaty to determine the amount of the available tax credit.[21] Let us observe that the transfer of the tax credit to the investors in State B may be granted either by State B's legislation or by virtue of a specific provision in the State A/State B tax treaty. There may, indeed, be a provision in that State A/State B treaty that provides for a transfer of the tax credit corresponding to the initial withholding tax levied by State A to the fund's unitholders in State B. Nonetheless, such a clause does not go so far as to allow a tax credit to unitholders residing in a third country ('State C'). Only investors who are residents of State B qualify for that tax credit.

If, however, the investor in the fund is a resident of State C, State B may treat the situation in two different ways. One approach uses a 'flow-through' approach, meaning that State B deems the fund to be a fiscally transparent entity, with the effect that any fund income sourced in State B will be attributed directly to any fund investors residing in State C. This approach does not create any discrimination, at least from State B's perspective. Indeed, State B's legislation does not make the tax treatment of investors of State C less favourable than that of any of the fund investors residing in State B.

The other approach that State B could adopt involves State B applying a withholding tax on the amount distributed to State C resident fund investors. If State B then reduces the amount of its withholding tax by the initial tax credit given to the fund for the withholding tax levied on it by State A), no discrimination takes place between investors residing in State B and those residing in State C. However, if State B does not

21. This is the French practice for income received by French SICAVs (*see* Administrative guidelines published online at *Bulletin Officiel des Finances Publiques-Impôts*: BOI-RPPM-RCM-10-40, §§80 et seq.).

offset that initial tax credit against its withholding tax on the fund's distribution, the outcome will be that the fund's investors residing in State C are worse off than its investors who reside in State B.

Can such discrimination be considered contrary to Article 24 OECD Model? The State B/State C treaty may indeed be applicable, on the ground that the payment is made by a State B fund to a State C resident. In our hypothetical case, State B is the source state and it applies different treatment to payments made to its own residents and to residents of the other Contracting State. Nevertheless, the main problem remains: Is such discrimination based on nationality? In most cases, the practical answer will be 'no', as the reason why State B refuses to offset the tax credit on the withholding tax levied on the State B fund's distribution to its State C unitholders will generally be that the beneficiaries of the distribution are 'residents' of State C, not that they have State C nationality (as State C nationals residing in State B would receive the same treatment as State B nationals residing in State B). The discrimination at stake is, therefore, attributable to the distribution recipient's residence rather than to its nationality, which may block the implementation of Article 24 OECD Model.

[B] Refund of the Withholding Tax to the Fund

If State B refunds, to the fund itself, the withholding tax levied by State A when the fund distributes its income to its unitholders, discrimination may occur if the refund is limited in proportion to the payments made to its unitholders who are residents in State C. In this case, the fund, itself, is personally discriminated against because the amount of its refund depends upon the residence of its unitholders. This situation may be compared to the situation that gave rise to the ECJ's *Orange European Smallcap Fund* case,[22] where it found Dutch legislation to be incompatible with the freedom of capital movement.

Would Article 24(5) OECD Model apply in such a case?

This is an interesting theoretical question, as it illustrates how the non-discrimination standards adopted by EU law and those proposed by the OECD Model interrelate and may converge in some circumstances.[23]

From a technical perspective, let us recall that Article 24(5) OECD Model states:

> Enterprises of a Contracting State, the capital of which is wholly or partly owned or controlled, directly or indirectly, by one or more residents of the other Contracting State, shall not be subjected in the first-mentioned State to any

---

22. *Orange European Smallcap Fund*, C-194/06, Judgment, EU:C:2008:289. *See* Hans van den Hurk et al., *Dutch Withholding Tax Rules as Applied to FIIs Partially Incompatible with EU Law*, 36 Intertax 410 (2008).
23. For an interesting reflection on this question, *see* Niels Bammens, *The Non-Discrimination Analysis Under the OECD Model as Compared to the EU Fundamental Freedoms*, *in International Tax Law: New Challenges to and from Constitutional and Legal Pluralism* 97 (Joachim Englisch ed., 2016).

> taxation or any requirement connected therewith which is other or more burdensome than the taxation and connected requirements to which other similar enterprises of the first-mentioned State are or may be subjected.

In a situation where investors of State C control the fund, nothing seems to prevent said Article 24(5) from applying. The same seems to hold true in case residents of State C are in a non-controlling position, as Article 24(5) OECD Model does not require the enterprise to be controlled. Rather, its capital must only be 'wholly or partly owned or controlled' by residents of the other Contracting State (State C for our purposes). As long as the withholding tax refund is limited to the portion that corresponds to the interest of non-controlling investors in State C, there is a case for the implementation of Article 24(5) OECD Model.

§13.04 CONCLUSION

In conclusion, it appears that although Article 24 OECD Model may be used in a number of situations that are not covered by EU law, the main hurdle to its implementation relates to the nationality requirement enshrined in its first paragraph. Whether the ECHR could be an additional standard to take into account in tax treaty law is a more open question, but certainly deserves future reflection.

CHAPTER 14

Practical Tax Aspects of Fund Structuring in Luxembourg

Geoffrey Scardoni

§14.01 INTRODUCTION

Structuring a fund is complex for a variety of reasons. When launching a fund, its promoters must consider not only the tax burden of a structure but also the relevant regulatory framework applicable thereto, the political and economic stability of the relevant jurisdiction, and the relevant currency controls.

This chapter, however, is confined solely to domestic and international tax considerations relevant for launching a Luxembourg fund. Furthermore, its goal is to choose one investment vehicle as an example, rather than consider the numerous types of funds available in Luxembourg. The vehicle chosen is a non-regulated alternative investment fund (an 'AIF') that invests in real estate in Europe.

The rationale behind this choice is that regulated funds, such as undertakings for the collective investment of transferable securities ('UCITS'), have existed for a long time and most of the tax aspects have already been addressed in great detail.[1] As the success of AIFs continues its growth, they are subject to more relaxed regulation and can now invest in a wider range of eligible investments.[2]

1. *See, e.g., UCITS Handbook* (Christian Szylar ed., ISTE 2012); Jean Schaffner, *Droit Fiscal International* (Promoculture/Larcier, 2005); Claude Kremer & Isabelle Lebbe, *Collective Investment Schemes in Luxembourg* (Oxford University Press, 2d ed. 2014); Marc Schmitz & Philip J. Warner, *Luxembourg in International Tax* (IBFD, 3d rev. ed. 2015); Tomi Viitala, *Taxation of Investment Funds in the European Union* (IBFD, 2005); *Investment Funds* (Samuel Kay ed., Sweet & Maxwell, 3d ed. 2016).
2. Danielle Sougné, *Fund Industry in Luxembourg: A Practitioner Guide*, 28–32 (Éditions Larcier, 2013).

Moreover, when compared to a typical private equity structure, real estate investments often require more-complex tax structuring and, thus, are of more interest, at least for the purposes of this chapter.

The analysis below commences by identifying the general tax aspects of fund structuring that should be considered for a given scenario. It is followed by an analysis of solutions available for each phase of the structuring, namely: (i) a preliminary analysis focusing on the choice of fund vehicle; (ii) an analysis of domestic tax considerations, mainly in order to determine the repatriation route and the Luxembourg tax burden of the particular structure; (iii) an analysis of international tax considerations that mainly depend on the laws, as well as the practices, of the jurisdictions in which the targeted assets and/or investors are located.

§14.02 OVERVIEW OF GENERAL TAX ASPECTS OF FUND STRUCTURING

[A] Proposed Case Scenario

As mentioned above, this chapter focuses on an AIF investing in real estate in Europe. For this proposed scenario, we assumed that the group of fund promoters would like to establish a closed-end fund in Luxembourg that invests in properties (commercial and residential) in France, the United Kingdom, and Germany, with such investments to be held for five to ten years. The pool of investors consists of individuals and legal entities, as well as some other investment funds.

During the fund's lifetime, its management will be delegated to an authorized alternative investment fund manager (the 'AIFM'). The AIFM shall, in turn, outsource some functions to professional investment advisors.

Several of the key individuals (usually at the level of the investment advisors) will be entitled to a share of certain excess profits upon exit from the structure (so-called carried investors). Debt financing from banks for acquisition of the targeted assets is expected. Yearly income from the assets will first service the bank debt and any remaining income will be distributed to the investors.

The above facts are referred to as the 'Case'.

[B] General Tax Aspects to Be Considered

This chapter focuses on main tax points that should be addressed when structuring a fund. It is intended neither to be exhaustive nor to give a clear-cut answer to points in question. In terms of fund structuring, there is no 'one-size-fits-all' answer. Solutions to the highlighted questions will always depend on specific facts and circumstances.

In the Case, we can determine the following main actors: (i) regular and carried investors, (ii) the fund, (iii) the targeted assets, and (iv) the AIFM (together with its investment advisor(s) relating to the fund). These actors will be present in most of the practical cases but the composition may vary.[3]

The main goal for investors is to invest in a structure that is tax neutral to the largest extent possible. In other words, it is reasonable for any investor to expect that investing via any fund should not worsen its tax position when compared to a situation in which it/he/she invested directly in a targeted asset.[4]

Bearing in mind the actors involved along with the main goal of investors, the relevant tax analysis for fund structuring can be broken down into the following layers.

[1] Preliminary Analysis

Before proceeding with an analysis of specific tax aspects, one must first make sure that as much information as possible is collected about the investment policy of a fund, its investors, and its potential targets. In practice, based on the information collected, both the regulatory and tax specialists develop an initial fund structure.

[a] Choosing a Fund Vehicle

From a tax perspective, the choice would typically be between a transparent entity and an opaque entity.

A transparent entity, itself, is not subject to taxation. For Luxembourg tax purposes, a transparent entity is deemed not to exist and its shareholders are viewed as directly holding the assets of the fund.[5]

With regard to an opaque entity, on the other hand, there are two possibilities: it may be either: (i) a normally taxable entity or (ii) provided certain requirements are met, an entity benefitting from a specific tax regime, with all or some types of its income exempt from taxation.[6] Such classification is accepted not only in Luxembourg but also in most countries.

While tax neutrality for the fund itself can easily be achieved by providing a special tax regime, however, in some cases, it might still be beneficial for the entire structure to establish a fund that is a normally taxable company to ensure that it has access to double tax treaties. A fund benefitting from a specific tax regime may not necessarily be eligible in this respect.

One should also pay attention to the hybrid treatment of vehicles. There are a number of instances in which a tax-transparent fund for Luxembourg tax purposes may be treated as an opaque fund for one or more of the other jurisdictions involved (i.e., those of the targeted assets and/or investors) and vice versa. Such situations should be

3. Tom Alabaster, *Global Investment Funds: A Practical Guide to Structuring, Raising and Managing Funds*, 8, 19–20, 23–24 (Globe Law & Business Ltd., 2016).
4. For further details, *see* Viitala, *supra* note 1, at 331–335; Alabaster, *supra* note 3, at 43.
5. Article 175, Luxembourg's *Loi du 4 décembre 1967 Concernant l'Impôt sur le Revenu*, as amended (Luxembourg's law concerning income tax, hereinafter 'LIR'); Alain Steichen, *Précis de Droit Fiscal de l'Entreprise*, 229–233 (Éditions Saint Paul, 4th ed. 2013).
6. Alabaster, *supra* note 3, at 43–45.

carefully monitored, as otherwise undesired tax consequences may arise in Luxembourg and/or such other jurisdictions.

[b] Choosing a Holding Vehicle for Investments

Depending on the location of the targeted asset(s), third-party financing needs, and the timing of the contemplated disinvestment, it may be more efficient to establish separate holding/acquisition vehicles for each investment.

Separate holding vehicles can be desirable for purposes of third-party financing or management incentive plans, as well as for a relevant investment and, more generally, for segregating the various assets. When the fund is a tax-transparent entity (or an opaque, tax-exempt entity) choosing an interposed holding that is a normal taxable entity can also present the advantage of having an entity potentially being able to claim treaty benefits or the protections offered by European Union ('EU') directives.

[C] Domestic Tax Considerations

A key feature of domestic tax considerations is that they are driven mainly by local tax legislation and practice. However, as detailed below, some international elements in the analysis may still be present to a limited extent.

One can distinguish the following domestic tax considerations.

[1] Repatriation Structure

The goal, here, is to structure the repatriation to the largest extent possible as return on equity instruments, free of withholding tax. Due to how countries differentiate between debt and equity return, dividends and capital gains will generally benefit from tax relief while interest will be fully taxable.[7]

At the same time, one should keep in mind that payments of dividends by a normally taxable Luxembourg company will be subject to a 15% withholding tax unlike interest payments which are not subject to any withholding tax.

When the fund vehicle is structured as a normally taxable entity, withholding tax on dividends will have to be taken into consideration (since it is not always creditable at the level of the investors, the alternative repatriation routes, and potential for mitigation of the withholding tax may need to be investigated).

---

7. *See Tax Treatment of Interest for Corporations* (Otto Marres & Dennis Weber eds, IBFD 2013); *Taxation of Companies on Capital Gains on Shares Under Domestic Law, EU Law and Tax Treaties* (Guglielmo Maisto ed. IBFD 2013); Wolfgang Schoen, *The Distinct Equity of the Debt-Equity Distinction*, September 2012 Bull. Int'l Tax'n, Working Paper of the Max Planck Institute for Tax Law and Public Finance No. 2014-08, available at https://ssrn.com/abstract=2444648.

[2] Corporate Taxation of a Luxembourg Acquisition/Holding Vehicle

As mentioned above, in many instances, holding/acquisition vehicles may be established in Luxembourg. It is important to consider the Luxembourg tax burden related to these vehicles in terms of corporate income tax (a possibility of the application of the tax exemptions on the income received), net wealth tax ('NWT') (monitoring the wealth/cash held by these vehicles), and withholding tax mitigating that could apply on dividend distributions to the fund.

[3] Arm's Length Remuneration for the Management Company and the Investment Advisors

The management company and professional investment advisors are usually entitled to an annual remuneration for their services. The level of this remuneration should be determined at arm's length and should be checked on a case-by-case basis.

[4] Value Added Tax Treatment of Management and Advisory Services

A fund or its general partner (if the fund is organized as a limited partnership) will generally be registered for value added tax ('VAT') purposes.[8] However, management fees payable by a fund to its manager should be exempt from Luxembourg VAT[9] and any advisory fees paid to external advisors should also be exempt from Luxembourg VAT.

This exemption does not mean that all services rendered to the fund are exempt. Moreover, the VAT exemption does not mean that no VAT leakage arises within the fund structure (especially at the level of the professional investment advisors). VAT costs, therefore, deserve special attention and should be carefully reviewed.

[D] International Tax Considerations

International tax considerations require the assistance of the relevant foreign tax advisors. In the rapidly changing international tax environment, it becomes outmost importance to coordinate structuring with specialists of all implicated jurisdictions. These considerations must be addressed at the early stages of the structuring, as they may affect the manner in which the fund platform is structured in Luxembourg.

In our view, the main international tax aspects involve the following.

---

8. Article 4, *Loi du 12 février 1979 Concernant la Taxe sur le Valeur Ajoutée*, as amended (Luxembourg law concerning value added tax, hereinafter 'VAT Law').
9. *Ibid.*, Art. 44(1)(d)(iv).

[1] International Tax Considerations of the Targeted Assets

As mentioned above, a holding vehicle may be needed if the fund is a tax-transparent entity. However, in many instances, a separate acquisition vehicle will also be necessary to facilitate exit, to attract bank financing, and/or to ring-fence potential liabilities.

If the targeted assets are held by entities located outside of the EU or if EU Directives cannot be applied, it is necessary to check if the benefits of existing double tax treaties are available. In such cases, it is not sufficient to examine just the interpretation of the applicable treaty from the standpoint of the jurisdiction where the fund/holding vehicle is located; rather, the analysis must be carried out from the perspective of the jurisdictions of the targeted assets, as well.

[2] Foreign AIFM

When an AIFM is located in a foreign jurisdiction, said jurisdiction may claim the presence of a permanent establishment ('PE') of the managed Luxembourg fund.[10] This issue should be reviewed during the structuring phase to ensure that no adverse tax consequences arise during the lifetime of the structure.

[3] Deductibility of Interest and Hybrid Mismatches

As mentioned above, in general, countries distinguish differences between the tax treatment of dividends and interest.

Interest is commonly viewed as a tax-deductible expense while dividends are not. However, dividends tend to qualify as a tax-exempt income unlike interest.

Given such differentiation, it is clear from an investor perspective that the most attractive solution would be to obtain both (i.e., a tax deduction for the payment of interest and an exemption of the dividend income received).[11]

Due to the international nature of most fund platforms, such hybrid treatments are quite possible. For instance, one legal instrument (without even taking into consideration any tax advantages) may be classified as debt for the purposes of the source country (i.e., the country of the payor) but as equity in the country of the income recipient (and the reverse treatment can also occur). Such discrepancies typically result from instruments having characteristics of both debt and equity.

10. *See* Alabaster, *supra* note 3, at 45–47 regarding the advantages of being a European AIFM. However, a tax risk relating to AIFMs is to be managed for tax purposes: often one jurisdiction of AIFM may consider that the fund is managed by the AIFM and as such is a tax resident of such jurisdiction.
11. Sven-Eric Bärsch, Taxation of Hybrid Financial Instruments and the Remuneration Derived Therefrom in an International and Cross-Border Context (Springer, 2012).

As highlighted above, such diversified characteristics of an instrument may be used not only for tax purposes (i.e., to achieve a hybrid advantageous tax treatment) but also for other legal/economic reasons (often driven by capitalization requirements).

Therefore, when dealing with fund structuring, one should ensure the qualifications of the various payments made within a structure (i.e., interest versus dividends). The potential impact of anti-abuse rules should also be assessed.

If any interest is paid to the fund at the level of the target jurisdiction, any limitations on interest payments should also be considered. In particular, many countries have rules that result in reclassification of excessive interest payments as dividends (the so-called thin capitalization rules). Thin capitalization relates to excessive debt financing of an entity and the rules for such determination vary from a country to country.

The outcome of the application of thin capitalization rules is that interest which is deemed excessive under the domestic law of the payor which will be requalified as dividend. Such requalification may entail in general: (i) non-deductibility of such excessive interest by a payor and (ii) application of a dividend withholding tax.

Therefore, deductibility of interest where relevant should be confirmed.

[E] International Tax Considerations for the Investors

A fund typically has two types of investors: (i) regular and (ii) carried interest investors. Regular investors will be normally exposed to the success of the investments, while carried investors will only be entitled to a specific incentive if the fund is successful.[12]

A detailed analysis of above tax considerations in the light of the facts of the Case is provided below.

[1] Preliminary Analysis

[a] Choosing a Fund Vehicle

As highlighted above, it is reasonable for investors to expect that investing through a fund will not put them in a less-advantageous tax position compared to investments made directly. A first step to achieve the above-mentioned goal would be to use a tax-neutral Luxembourg fund vehicle. The tax neutrality of a particular fund vehicle may, in general, be derived from its legal nature, from a specific tax regime stipulated by law, or from an exemption for one or more types of income earned by a fund. In Luxembourg, the following tax-neutral vehicles are commonly used:

12. Andrew Metrick & Ayako Yasuda, *The Economics of Private Equity Funds*, 23 Rev. Finote Stud. 2303 (2010).

[i] Tax Neutrality Derived from the Legal Nature of the Vehicle

In Luxembourg, a number of entities (including virtually all partnerships) are treated as tax transparent for Luxembourg tax purposes. In particular, the Luxembourg legislature specifically stated, in its tax law, that a general partnership (*société en nom collectif* or 'SNC'), a limited partnership (*société en commandite simple* or 'SCS'), a special limited partnership (*société en commandite spécial* or 'SCSp') should all be treated as tax-transparent entities for tax purposes. It is also worth noting that both the SNC and SCS have legal personality, unlike the SCSp.

Generally, tax-transparent funds do not have access to the benefits or protections of EU Directives or double tax treaties.

[ii] Tax Neutrality Derived from Specific Tax Regimes

Some funds established as opaque entities may benefit from specific tax regimes. For instance, the Specialized Investment Fund ('SIF')[13] or the Reserved Alternative Investment Fund ('RAIF'), with features similar to those of the SIF[14] benefit from a subjective exemption. That means that taxes applicable in Luxembourg to a regular taxpayer are not imposed on SIFs (or RAIFs with the features of SIFs) established in Luxembourg.

Funds benefitting from that subjective exemption usually do not have access to the benefits or protections of EU Directives. Access to the benefits or protections of double tax treaties, on the other hand, must be assessed on a case-by-case basis.

[iii] Tax Neutrality Derived from an Exemption for Specific Types of Income

At first glance, tax-transparent funds or funds benefitting from a specific tax regime ensuring full tax neutrality may appear to be the most appropriate solution for the structure. However, depending on the type of income to be realized by the fund during its lifetime and at exit, it might be preferable to establish a normally taxable vehicle in Luxembourg that benefits from an exemption of a certain type of income (the so-called objective exemption).

For instance, if the fund will only realize dividends and capital gains and such dividends and capital gains are exempt in Luxembourg under its domestic participation exemption regime,[15] there might be no need to establish a transparent/exempt fund.

13. Articles 66, 68 & 69, *Loi du 13 février 2007 relative aux fonds d'investissement spécialisés*, as amended (Luxembourg law on specialized investment funds).
14. Articles 46–47, *Loi du 23 juillet 2016 relative aux fonds d'investissement alternatifs*, as amended (Luxembourg law regarding reserved alternative investment funds).
15. Article 166 LIR and *Règlement grand-ducal du 21 décembre 2001 portant exécution de l'article 166, alinéa 9, numéro 1 de la loi modifiée du 4 décembre 1967 concernant l'impôt sur le revenu* (Luxembourg regulation implementing Art. 166 LIR).

An additional advantage for companies that benefit from an objective exemption is that they may have access to the benefits or protections of EU Directives and double tax treaties. Whether such access is available must be verified on a case-by-case basis.

A normally taxable financial-holding company (*Société de Participations Financières* or 'SOPARFI') generally has access to the benefits or protections of the EU Directives and double tax treaties, while a company investing in risk capital (*Société d'investissement en capital à risqué* or 'SICAR') may, in some instances, be refused such benefits.[16] Hence, the first question that arises with respect to our Case is which of the above vehicles is the best fit. In practice, the final choice is typically driven by a combination of tax and regulatory factors.

The default choice, typically, would be to establish the AIF in Luxembourg as an SCSp (*société en commandite spéciale*) as this tax-neutral entity is the most flexible from the corporate and regulatory perspectives.[17] Luxembourg introduced the SCSp in 2013, which was inspired by the common law limited partnership, which offers great contractual freedom.[18]

For the Case, we would choose the SCSp as a starting point, it being understood at the outset that there may be other factors that ultimately push us towards a different type of entity (whether tax or regulatory). Indeed, we always strongly recommend combining any tax analysis with the views the regulatory specialists.

[b] Choosing a Holding Vehicle

The tax-transparent SCSp will not be eligible for the benefits or protections offered by double tax treaties or EU Directives. Although one might consider applying double tax treaties and EU Directives directly to the investors of a fund, in practice, that solution is likely to be quite complex to implement, as investors are, themselves, frequently tax-exempt entities or tax-transparent entities or are simply not able to claim treaty protection for investments through a transparent fund.

Since interposed holdings, in most instances, will be required for business and/or legal reasons, we would, in the present Case, choose to interpose a second Luxembourg entity, this time a normally taxable entity, below the SCSp ('HoldCo').

16. *See Loi du 15 juin 2004 relative à la Société d'investissement en capital à risque (SICAR)*, as amended (Luxembourg law regarding SICARs); Kremer & Lebbe, *supra* note 1, 696-701; *Circulaire du directeur des contributions L.G. - A. n° 61 du 12 février 2015* (Luxembourg circular regarding certificates of residence for collective investment vehicles).
17. A Luxembourg limited partnership (*société en commandite simple* or SCS) could be considered an alternative to SCSp, but investors generally prefer SCSps (as they are similar to common law types of partnerships that are more familiar to investors).
18. *See*, in this respect: Patrick Mischo & Paul Berna, *Clarification of the Tax Treatment of Limited Partnerships*, 55 Eur. Tax'n 215 (2015); Pierre-Antoine Klethi, *Administrative Circular on Taxation of Luxembourg Limited Partnerships Is a Welcomed First Step*, 17 Derivatives & Finote Instruments No. 3 (2015); Alabaster, *supra* note 3, at 236.

[F] Domestic Tax Considerations

[1] Financing Structure

One of the most important questions to tackle when structuring a fund is how to stream the financing into the structure. In general, the classic dilemma would be a choice between equity and debt, or perhaps a mix of both.

As mentioned, in typical tax systems the following distinctions are usually made: (i) capital gains are taxed at preferential tax rates; (ii) dividends may be taxed at preferential tax rates, but are not a deductible expense for tax purposes and may be subject to domestic withholding tax; (iii) interest is fully taxable income, but constitutes a tax-deductible expense and may not necessarily be subject to withholding tax.

As such differences exist in most countries, they naturally affect the economic choices of the investors as to how they want to invest in given structures. While the general idea was that interest and dividends should have the same effect economically (dividends as non-deductible payments and non-taxable/taxable at preferential rates, interest as deductible and taxable), in practice – due to cross-border situations (i.e., interaction of different tax systems) and withholding taxation of dividends – differences between the two exist and affect the choice of financing by the investors.[19]

Investors, thus, tend to seek tax deductions in the form of interest payments in the jurisdiction of the targeted asset while simultaneously realizing dividends and capital gains on their investments in the fund. Following this logic, one may conclude that it is better to invest equity in the fund and to finance the acquisition of the targeted assets through debt via holding/acquisition vehicles. However, in practice, such a straightforward solution can be difficult to implement.

In our Case, with respect to the repatriation structure, one should project various scenarios while taking into account the investors' preferences. The questions to be asked of the different actors would typically be:

- Investors: What are the preferred types of income – interest income and/or dividends and/or capital gains?
- Targeted assets (potentially held by holding/acquisition vehicles): is leverage needed and if so, to which extent may it be used?

For most real estate investments, we should also take into account that regular income from real estate will first be used to service its bank debt, if any. The question remains how to distribute the income remaining after payments of the bank interest and fees up the chain.

In general, if investors are not subjected to taxation (for instance, most of the pension funds will be tax-exempt entities), they may be indifferent with respect to realization via interest or dividends. However, in practice, because the investors may

19. *See* Wolfgang Schön et al., *Debt and Equity: What's the Difference? A Comparative View*, Max Planck Institute for Innovation & Competition Research Paper Series, Paper No. 09-09, September 2009. Available at https://papers.ssrn.com/sol3/papers.cfm?abstract_id=1457649## (last accessed 14 November 2017).

be a mix of both tax-exempt and subject-to-tax entities (as it is in the Case), a structure should be designed to address the interests of both types of investors.

Bearing in mind the above, one solution that meets the interests of both types of investors is financing a structure with debt to the extent such financing is acceptable to the jurisdictions of the assets or holding/acquisition vehicles. For a closed-end fund, the amount of debt should help to upstream the rental income as a repayment of principal over the life of the fund. Repayment of the principal amount of the debt should be a tax-neutral event at all layers of the structure. It is worth noting that Luxembourg does not impose any withholding tax on arm's length interest payments.[20] However, payments of interest may not be the preferred repatriation route for any taxable investors, as interest would typically be included in their taxable basis. It should also be noted that some investors might be taxed on accrued interest even if it is not distributed by the fund.

With regards to the exact level of indebtedness, one should carefully analyse the various limitations on the deductibility of interest (i.e., thin capitalization rules). Luxembourg tax law, for example, does not contain any specific thin capitalization rules that prescribe a certain debt-to-equity ratio to be met by companies subject to tax in Luxembourg. In practice, however, a debt-to-equity ratio of 85:15 is generally applied by the tax administration in relation to the acquisition of participation (and, to a lesser extent, properties).[21] Aside from the Luxembourg ratio, the general leverage of the structure will be determined in line with thin capitalization rules of the targeted jurisdictions.

Once the calculated debt financing is determined, one should keep in mind the consequences of dividend distributions. As an SCSp is deemed not to exist for Luxembourg tax purposes, our HoldCo will be deemed to be held directly by the SCSp's investors. Thus, any dividend distribution from HoldCo to the SCSp will be viewed as if it made it directly to the investors of the SCSp and, thus, may be subject to Luxembourg's 15% withholding tax.[22] Therefore, in combination with debt funding, the following should also be considered in order to manage any withholding tax exposure in Luxembourg:

- We could divide the capital of HoldCo into classes of shares. In that case, HoldCo could reduce its share capital through redemption and cancellation of one or more class(es) of its shares. Upon such redemption or cancellation, the amounts distributed to its shareholders should be qualified – for Luxembourg tax purposes – as a partial liquidation of HoldCo and, thus, such distributions should not be subject to Luxembourg withholding tax.[23]
- In the alternative, we could determine whether any of the investors in our fund may be eligible for tax credits in their home jurisdiction. However, in practice, this alternative is rarely used, as the investors may not be able to use the tax

20. Article 146 LIR in combination with Art. 97(1) LIR.
21. Schmitz & Warner, *supra* note 1, at 112.
22. Articles 146 & 148 LIR.
23. Articles 101 & 146 LIR in combination with Art. 97(1) LIR; Schmitz & Warner, *supra* note 1, at 177, 183–184.

credit or the timing differences between the moment of withholding and the use of the tax credit may not be attractive, as it can create a cash flow disadvantage for them.

- Withholding tax 'leakage' in Luxembourg can be fully eliminated if the investors benefit from Luxembourg's withholding tax exemption.[24] That exemption applies if the investors of the SCSp meet the following conditions:[25]
- the investor is a company covered by Article 2 of the amended Parent-Subsidiary Directive or is a company located in a treaty jurisdiction and subject to tax at a rate comparable to Luxembourg's income tax rate and applicable on a taxable basis similar to the one in Luxembourg;[26] and
- at the time of the dividend, the investor has held its interest in the paying entity for an uninterrupted period of at least twelve months (or undertakes to continue to hold that interest until an uninterrupted period of at least twelve months has elapsed), which interest must be either: (a) a direct participation of 10% or more of the paying entity's nominal paid up capital; or (b) in the event of a lower percentage participation, a direct participation having an acquisition price of at least EUR 1,200,000.

For the Case, since it might be difficult to assess whether contemplated investors qualify or will qualify for Luxembourg's withholding-tax exemption and whether they are eligible for a tax credit elsewhere, the classes of shares alternative should be chosen as the safest route.

To sum up, the structure for the Case may be financed with: (i) up to 85% debt, as repayment of the principal, if needed for repatriation, should be a tax-neutral event at all levels of the structure and (ii) 15% or more equity, where the capital of HoldCo is divided in classes of shares (to provide for the possibility of repatriation of the partial liquidation proceeds because they are not subject to withholding tax). Finally, any constraints existing in the country where the real estate or an acquisition vehicle is located should also be taken into account to determine the most appropriate financing at the level of HoldCo.

[2] Taxation of a Luxembourg Holding/Acquisition Vehicle

[a] Corporate Income Tax

It is also important to consider the tax burden of any interposed holding vehicle. In our Case, HoldCo – established as a Luxembourg SOPARFI – will be subject to Luxembourg's corporate income tax (*impôt sur le revenu des collectivités* or 'CIT') at a rate of

24. Articles 146 & 147 LIR.
25. For purposes of this chapter, only the most commonly used scenarios of qualifying investors were chose note. Otherwise, the withholding tax exemption regime is broader.
26. For more detail, *see* Schmitz & Warner, *supra* note 1, at 174, 243–248.

20.33% (including a 7% surcharge for Luxembourg's unemployment fund). It will also be subject to Luxembourg's municipal business tax (*impôt commercial communal* or 'MBT') at a rate of 6.75% assuming the SOPARFI is incorporated in the city of Luxembourg.[27]

As detailed earlier, Luxembourg tax law does not contain any debt-to-equity ratio provisions. Nevertheless, when loans are made between related parties or when related parties guarantee the repayment of debtor's obligations for loans made by third parties and such loans are used for financing participations, Luxembourg's tax administration tends to apply a debt-to-equity ratio of 85:15. The interest rate on loans within this ratio should be arm's length interest rates. Moreover, financing the acquisition of a participation to a greater extent with debt might be acceptable, as long as the interest on the total debt cannot be considered as excessive.

If a normally taxable Luxembourg company is borrowing funds from or lending funds to affiliated parties, it will fall within the scope of Luxembourg's transfer pricing rules under Articles 56 and 56*bis* LIR and the Luxembourg tax administration's circular of 27 December 2016 (Luxembourg's 'TP rules').[28]

Such TP rules apply to a group of companies whose principal activity is something other than holding activities consists of intra-group financing transactions, which are defined as the granting of loans or advances to associated companies refinanced by any financial means. The definition of associated companies is very broad, including any participation, direct or indirect, in the management, control, or capital of another company.

In order to meet the 'substance' requirements of Luxembourg's TP rules, the Luxembourg company's management meetings should be held, in person, in Luxembourg. Moreover, the majority of the managers of the Luxembourg company should be Luxembourg residents or persons professionally domiciled in Luxembourg. The attendance of managers in Luxembourg when taking decisions should be documented, for instance, with plane tickets, hotel receipts, etc., so that the relevant managers are able to provide evidence of their physical presence and attendance in Luxembourg if ever required. The books and records of the Luxembourg company should be kept in Luxembourg at its registered office.

The Luxembourg company should also realize an arm's length margin based on both a functional and a credit risk analysis. For the purpose of the computation of the arm's length margin, a transfer pricing report should be drafted that includes a full description of the transfer pricing methodology applied, as well as a detailed analysis thereof and any further information that supports the methodology used.

27. Rates were current as of 15 November 2017.
28. Available at: www.impotsdirects.public.lu/content/dam/acd/fr/legislation/legi16/circulairelir561-56bis1-27122016.pdf (last accessed 14 November 2017).

[b] Net Wealth Tax

SOPARFIs are subject to an annual NWT (*'impôt sur la fortune'*), which is levied at a rate of 0.5% on its net wealth as of 1 January of each year. A reduced rate of 0.05% applies for taxable net wealth exceeding EUR 500,000,000.[29]

Certain assets, such as participations qualifying for Luxembourg's participation exemption regime or foreign real estate assets, are exempt from the NWT basis. To qualify for the Luxembourg participation exemption for NWT purposes, the participation must represent either: at least 10% of the share capital of the subsidiary's share capital or have an acquisition value of at least EUR 1,200,000. There is no minimum holding period requirement for this exemption.[30]

[c] Participation Exemption Regime

According to Article 166 LIR and the amended Grand-Ducal Decree of 21 December 2001, dividends, liquidation proceeds, and capital gains are exempt from tax, provided the following requirements are met:

- the subsidiary is: (i) a company covered by Article 2 of the amended Parent-Subsidiary Directive or (ii) a company located in a treaty jurisdiction and subject to tax at a rate comparable to Luxembourg's income tax rate on a taxable basis similar to the one in Luxembourg;[31] and
- at the time when the income is received or the capital gain is realized, the Luxembourg company has held (or, for dividends, has committed to hold) for an uninterrupted period of at least twelve months, a direct participation representing at least 10% of the subsidiary's share capital (including share premium); or, in the event of a lower percentage participation, the participation had an acquisition price of at least EUR 1,200,000 for dividends and liquidation proceeds, or EUR 6,000,000 for capital gains.

Typically, SOPARFI investments in acquisition vehicles are structured so that any income received by the SOPARFI is tax exempt under Luxembourg's participation exemption regime.

Foreign properties directly owned by a SOPARFI are also typically acquired so as to be exempt from Luxembourg's NWT under the relevant tax treaty.

29. Article 8(1) *Loi sur l'impôt sur la fortune du 16 octobre 1934 - (Vermögenssteuergesetz)* (Luxembourg net wealth tax). Rates are current as of 15 November 2017.
30. §60 *Loi du 16 octobre 1934 concernant l'évaluation des biens et valeurs - (Bewertungsgesetz)* (Luxembourg valuation law).
31. For more detail, *see* Schmitz & Warner, *supra* note 1, at 243–248.

[3] Funding HoldCo

For our Case, as noted above, it seems that funding our HoldCo with: (i) 85% of plain vanilla debt and (ii) 15% equity (i.e., shares and possibly share premium) is a workable solution. Since SOPARFIs typically also fall within the scope of Luxembourg's TP rules, the total amount of equity invested therein will be decided on the basis of the transfer pricing report, as there should be a certain amount of equity at risk for the financing activities.

As regards the capital structure of HoldCo, we recommend using the multiple classes-of-shares mechanisms in order to benefit from Luxembourg's partial liquidation regime. As detailed above, the proceeds allocated to the investors upon (partial) liquidation of an entire class of shares (i.e., repurchase of that class of shares followed by the cancellation of those shares) are not typically subject to Luxembourg withholding tax.

[a] Arm's Length Remuneration for the General Partner/AIFM/Advisors

Special attention must also be given to the remuneration provided to the various actors in terms of management/consulting fees, especially when such actors are not located in Luxembourg; foreign tax authorities will often assess whether a proper amount of the global fee paid by the fund is taxable income at the level of the advisors having contributed to the creation of the added value. A functional analysis has to be carried out to determine the proper remuneration of the various entities (e.g., the General Partner of a transparent fund vehicle, the AIFM, and its advisors) depending on the functions and added value of each actor.

[i] VAT Treatment of Management and Advisory Services

Article 135(1)(g) of Directive 2006/112 (the 'VAT Directive')[32] provides for an exemption from VAT for management of special investment funds as defined by each Member State ('VAT Exemption for Management'). That provision explicitly confers on the Member States the right to define the concept of 'special investment funds' that benefit from the VAT Exemption for Management in their jurisdiction. However, it is worth noting that the Member States' domestic VAT legislation varies significantly in this respect.[33] Furthermore, the Member States have not adopted a uniform approach to the

32. Said Art. 135(1)(g) replaced Art. 13B(d)(6) of Sixth Council Directive 77/388. The references made by the authors, the ECJ, and the Advocates General to Art. 13B(d)(6) of Sixth Council Directive 77/388 were kept for the purposes of the present analysis.
33. Liesbet Nevelsteen & Rob van den Plas, *Undertakings of Collective Investment and VAT in the EU*, 14 Int'l VAT Monitor 456 (2003); George Michie, *Value Added Tax on Financial Services in the European Union, in IFA General Report*, 88b Cahiers de Droit Fiscal International 43–83 (2003).

application of the VAT Exemption for Management in cases in which the management services are outsourced to third parties.[34]

The ambiguity with respect to: (i) the interpretation of the concept of special investment funds (the management of which is VAT exempt) by different Member States and (ii) the application of the VAT exemption for management of special investment funds to third parties to whom management services are outsourced has led to a number of ECJ cases that have been decided in the last twenty years.[35]

Unfortunately, the legal history of the Sixth VAT Directive offers no clues for the interpretation of that concept of 'special investment funds'.[36] Thus, in practice, for a definition of special investment funds, most Member States refer to their domestic financial legislation.[37] However, as mentioned above, said domestic legislation differs significantly and, thus, controversial positions are still possible among the Member States. Therefore, it appears justified that the ECJ took an active role in interpreting the concept of 'special investment funds'.

The first ECJ case to actually deal with the concept of the management of special investment funds was *Abbey National* in 2006.[38] Another case, *JP Morgan Fleming Claverhouse Trust plc,*[39] provided further guidelines as regards the interpretation of the concept special investment funds. In that case, the ECJ explained that the discretion of the Member States in defining 'special investment funds' does not - in any way - permit them to select certain funds located on their territory and grant them exemption and exclude other funds from that exemption.[40] Accordingly, Article 13B(d)(6) of the Sixth VAT Directive, thus, only grants the Member States the power to define, in their domestic law, the funds that meet the definition of 'special investment funds' and that power must be exercised in light of: (a) the objective pursued by the Sixth VAT

34. Nevelsteen & van den Plas, *supra* note 33.
35. The following matters are beyond the scope of the present analysis: (i) assessment of national legislation of each Member State in the light of the VAT Directive and existing ECJ case in order to determine as to whether the VAT exemption for management of investment funds is implemented correctly; (ii) overall assessment of effectiveness of VAT exemption for management of investment funds; and (iii) assessment of proposals of changes of the current VAT/ UCITS legislationote For more detail on the above-referenced topics, *see*, e.g., (a) Thiess Buettner & Katharina Erbe, *Revenue and Welfare Effects of Financial Sector VAT Exemption* (2013) (available at www.sbs.ox.ac.uk/sites/default/. files/Business_Taxation/Events/conferences/symposia/2012/buettner.pdf) (last accessed 14 November 2017); (b) Arthur Kerrigan, *The Elusiveness of Neutrality – Why Is It So Difficult To Apply VAT to Financial Services?*, 21 Int'l VAT Monitor 103 (2010); (c) Christian Amand, *VAT on Financial Services: The Unanswered Questions'*, 9 ERA Forum 357 (2008); and (d) Peter R. Merrill, *VAT Treatment of the Financial Sector, in The VAT Reader: What a Federal Consumption Tax Would Mean for America* 163 (R. Goulder et al., eds, Tax Analysts, 2011).
36. Joep Swinkels, *Special Investment Funds and VAT*, 17 Int'l VAT Monitor 247 (2006).
37. Nevelsteen & van den Plas, *supra* note 33.
38. *Abbey National*, C-169/04, Judgment, EU:C:2006:289.
39. *J.P. Morgan Fleming Claverhouse Investment Trust plc and The Association of Investment Trust Companies*, C-363/05, Judgment EU:C:2007:391.
40. *Ibid.*, para. 41.

Directive and (b) the principle of fiscal neutrality of the common system of VAT.[41] As regards the principle of fiscal neutrality, the ECJ further clarified that:

> the principle of fiscal neutrality, on which the common system of VAT established by the Sixth Directive is based, precludes economic operators carrying out the same transactions from being treated differently in relation to the levying of VAT. That principle does not require the transactions to be identical. According to settled case-law that principle precludes, in particular, treating similar goods and supplies of services, which are thus in competition with each other, differently for VAT purposes (citations omitted).[42]

Last, but not least, is the case *Fiscale Eenheid X,*[43] whereby the ECJ, in addition to the findings discussed above, stated:

> investments covered by the UCITS Directive and subject in that context to specific State supervision, on the one hand, and funds which, without being collective investment undertakings within the meaning of that directive, display characteristics identical to theirs and thus carry out the same transactions or, at least, display features that are sufficiently comparable for them to be in competition with such undertakings, on the other, must be regarded as exempt special investment funds within the meaning of that provision (citations omitted).[44]

The Court also made reference to Advocate General Villalón's opinion[45] and concluded that only investment funds that are subject to specific Member State supervision can be subject to the same conditions of competition and will appeal to the same circle of investors. Those other types of investment funds may, therefore, at least in principle, be eligible for the exemption in Article 13(B)(d)(6) of the Sixth VAT Directive, if the Member State provides for specific Member State supervision of those funds, too.

Furthermore, it is common knowledge that, in order to improve its competitiveness, the investment fund industry outsources a large portion of its value chain to specialized players. This creates an environment in which VAT costs or exemptions arise as a matter of course. In fact, outsourcing may be imposed by legal and regulatory constraints (e.g., custodian or depositary services focusing on the supervision and safeguarding of the assets of the fund) or may arise from organizational decisions, such as outsourced services rendered by specialized firms (e.g., administrative agents, transfer agents, distributors, sub-distributors, and paying agents).[46]

Following the ECJ's 1997 judgment in *SDC,*[47] one can reasonably assume that outsourced services are covered by an exemption if, viewed broadly, they form a distinct whole and are specific to, and essential for, an exempt transaction.[48] However,

41. *Ibid.*, para. 43.
42. *Ibid.*, para. 46.
43. *Fiscale Eenheid X,* C-595/13, Judgment, EU:C:2015:801.
44. *Ibid.*, para. 47.
45. *Fiscale Eenheid X,* C-595/13, AG Opinion, EU:C:2012:697.
46. Laurant Grencon & Christophe Plainchamp, *New VAT Context for the Investment Fund Industry,* 9 Derivatives & Finote Instruments 82 (2007).
47. *SDC v. Skatteministeriet,* C-2/95, Judgment, EU:C:1997:278.
48. *Ibid.*, para. 66.

the mere fact that a constituent element is essential for completing an exempt transaction does not guarantee a conclusion that the service that such element represents is exempt.[49]

The first ECJ case specific to outsourcing of investment funds was *Abbey National*,[50] which challenged the charging of VAT on the services rendered by the trustees (i.e., depositaries) of a number of authorized unit trusts and by the authorized corporate directors (the 'ACDs') of the investment companies, as well as the administration and accounting services delegated by the ACD of one of the investment companies to, and which were then rendered by, a third-party company.

The *Abbey National* Court determined that, although Article 13(B)(d)(6) of the Sixth VAT Directive did not contain a detailed definition of the term 'management of special investment funds', the term did incorporate portfolio management as well as the administration of the undertakings for collective investment themselves, which concerns functions *specific* to those undertakings, such as those listed in Annex II to the UCITS Directive (the list is not exhaustive).[51] However, it does not include the services corresponding to the functions of a depositary because they do not concern the management of undertakings for collective investment, but concern the control or supervision of their activities.[52]

Finally, the *Abbey National* Court, in line with its earlier *SDC* decision,[53] decided that services rendered by third-party managers can fall under Article 13(B)(d)(6) of the Sixth VAT Directive, because the exemption is defined according to the nature of the services provided and not according to the person supplying or receiving them.[54] If, viewed broadly, they form a distinct whole, are specific to, and essential for, the management of investment funds, services rendered by third-party managers are covered by the exemption.[55]

In *GfBk*,[56] the ECJ clearly stated that:

> advisory services concerning investment in transferable securities, provided by a third party to ... the manager of a special investment fund, fall within the concept of 'management of special investment funds' for the purposes of the [VAT] exemption laid down ..., even if the third party has not acted on the basis of a mandate.[57]

It is worth noting that this case was difficult to decide because asset management services are typically understood to include not only the identification of investment opportunities but also the authority to act upon such opportunity by acquiring or disposing of assets on behalf of its clients within the mandate granted to the asset

49. Ruud N.F. Zuidgeest, *Treatment of Outsourced Elements of Payment Transactions under EU VAT*, 22 Int'l VAT Monitor 105 (2011).
50. *Abbey National*, C-169/04.
51. *Ibid.*, para. 64.
52. *Ibid.*, para. 65.
53. *SDC v. Skatteministeriet*, C-2/95.
54. *Abbey National*, C-169/04, paras 65–66.
55. *Ibid.*, para. 70.
56. *GfBk*, C-275/11, Judgment, EU:C:2013:141.
57. *Ibid.*, para. 33.

manager. In the case of investment advisory services, on the other hand, the advisor typically only identifies investment opportunities available to his client and then advises the client thereof, leaving the decision whether to follow such advice (or not, as the case may be) to be taken by the client.[58] There is, arguably, a rather fine line between the two categories of services. However, as mentioned above, the question has been resolved by the ECJ: investment advice provided to a fund manager whose fund management services are VAT exempt also fall within the scope of the exemption.[59]

The ECJ also referred to conditions under which outsourced services, as established in *Abbey National*, can benefit from the VAT exemption (i.e., the advisory services must form a 'specific and essential part' of the management of the investment fund).[60] In the *GfBk* case, the ECJ held that the direct advice given regarding the purchase or sale of transferable securities has an intrinsic connection to the management of the investment fund.[61] Hence, investment managers may indeed outsource part of their management functions including investment advice without losing the VAT exemption provided that the conditions set in the ECJ cases are met.

Unfortunately, the system of exemptions of management services of funds from VAT is not fully harmonized between the various EU members. Therefore, a fund structure must be analysed globally with respect to its VAT position. As regards our Case, based on the criteria set forth above, one could decide that, in principle, the 'special investment funds' for VAT purposes may include AIFs. The Luxembourg legislature, to avoid any doubt, specifically included, in Article 44(91)(9d)(9iv) of the VAT Law, a VAT exemption for an AIF's management services. However, in other Member States, the approach may differ and, thus, must be checked on a case-by-case basis.

Furthermore, the fees charged by the AIFM and by any foreign investment advisors should also be exempt from a VAT in Luxembourg.

Finally, since our Case concerns a real estate fund, for the purposes of our VAT analysis, one must also consider the possibility that the fund's investment advisors will charge their fees directly to the real estate acquisition and management vehicles that manage the fund's real estate assets. In particular, if the latter charge VAT on their rental services, the VAT position within the fund structure may further be improved, as the services will ultimately benefit from the VAT deductibility deriving from the real estate operations.

As regards HoldCo, while its interposition (in addition to an acquisition company) should be neutral (as fees would generally flow through this entity to the acquisition vehicles), timing and business considerations may not always lead to a perfect mirroring situation.

As a last VAT point, HoldCo must assess whether it will be an active holding when managing the real estate acquisition and management vehicles to be able to

58. *The Tax Treatment of CIVs and REITs* 490 (Hein Vermeulen ed., IBFD 2014).
59. *GfBk*, C-275/11, para. 33.
60. *Abbey National*, C-169/04, paras 70–72.
61. *GfBk*, C-275/11, paras 23–24.

benefit from the *Larentia + Minerva* decision[62] and, thus, be able to deduct input VAT. However, in the specific case of Luxembourg, it remains unclear as to whether a Luxembourg holding company may benefit from a deduction of the input VAT.

[G] International Tax Considerations

An analysis of the international tax aspects of any particular fund is certainly the most sophisticated part of fund structuring, at least from the tax perspective. In our Case, there are at least four jurisdictions concerned (Luxembourg, Germany, the United Kingdom, and France), but this number, in practice, could easily reach ten or more. That means that one must ensure coordination of a number of different tax specialists and lawyers in order to develop the final fund structure that is as tax neutral as possible.

We provide, below, a high-level view of the international tax considerations relevant for our Case. It is worth noting that we only touch the tip of the iceberg, as in reality, a full analysis would be far more elaborate.

[1] Tax Considerations of the Jurisdictions Where the Targeted Assets Are Located

In practice, an acquisition vehicle will be needed in most scenarios, as such a vehicle facilitates the exit of the asset from the fund. A separate acquisition vehicle (in addition to a holding company) may also be preferred, due to bank financing and/or to ring-fence potential liabilities.

Thus, one of the first considerations to investigate is the best acquisition vehicle from the points of view of both Luxembourg and the foreign jurisdiction (i.e., where the proposed real estate asset is located). In practice, a foreign tax specialist would already have an opinion as to how the inbound real estate investment may be best structured, but in light of the latest anti-base erosion and anti-tax avoidance developments, one should cautiously verify how the structure will withstand any contemplated changes in the near future.

The starting point of the discussion will usually be whether the EU Directives and/or double tax treaties will apply. Both are efficient tools for eliminating or reducing the withholding tax on dividends and/or interest arising in the jurisdiction of the acquisition vehicle.

However, in 2015, general anti-abuse rules were introduced into the Parent-Subsidiary Directive, which target artificial tax arrangements and double non-taxation of income derived from hybrid instruments. Further, in 2016, the OECD released a multilateral instrument (as part of its BEPS programme) that, if adopted by the relevant countries, may impact the applicability of double tax treaties to holding companies and acquisition vehicles. Therefore, any current discussion regarding structuring fund investments via holding and acquisition companies will always involve substance

62. *Larentia + Minerva*, C-108/14, Judgment, EU:C:2015:496.

requirements, the business rationale for the interposition of the various companies, and the entitlement to income as the beneficial owner within the meaning of the treaties. Analysis of the deductibility of interest expenses (if the acquisition vehicles are debt-financed) may also be part of this discussion.

For the purpose of our Case, it is assumed that the best choice for the acquisition vehicle will be: (i) a Luxembourg SOPARFI for each acquisition real estate in Germany and the United Kingdom and (ii) a French OPCI (a collective investment scheme specializing in real estate) for each acquisition of real estate in France.

Those choices are for illustrative purposes only and are driven, in our Case, mainly by the fact that the type of income concerned is income from real estate. For such income, in many cases, the exclusive right of taxation is allocated to the jurisdiction in which the real estate is located. In other words, the choice of acquisition vehicle may be rather flexible, unless there is an attractive regime for a domestic vehicle (such as the OPCI in France).

Finally, taking into consideration the Case's preferred repatriation structure (as detailed above), the acquisition vehicles will need to be debt-financed.

§14.03 FOREIGN AIFM

When an AIFM is located in a foreign jurisdiction, that jurisdiction might claim that the Luxembourg Fund has a PE therein.[63] Whether or not that is likely in any particular situation is a question to be raised with the tax specialists in that jurisdiction. For the purposes of our Case, however, we assume that the AIFM is located in Luxembourg, so this risk is not relevant.

Nevertheless, as the risk of inadvertently establishing a PE in another jurisdiction is always a factual one, it is important to ensure that the managers of the AIFM indeed reside in Luxembourg and that the AIFM has proper expertise and infrastructure to supervise services to be provided by the investment advisors.

A careful, prior review of the substance of the fund structure as a whole is typically done with the relevant tax and regulatory specialists to avoid surprises.

[A] Investor Tax Considerations

In practice, a fund will be structured in a way that allows as many investors as possible to attain a tax-neutral position when investing therein. However, some investors may have specific subjective preferences and/or may originate from jurisdictions having specific domestic legislation (e.g., U.S. investors). Such investors will tend to have their own tax and regulatory advisors reviewing their exposure/risks on investments in the fund. To address such concerns, a so-called feeder vehicle is frequently interposed between the fund and its investors, which is an investment vehicle for certain

63. *See* Alabaster, *supra* note 3, at 45–47 (regarding advantages of being a European AIFM). However, a tax risk relating to AIFMs is to be managed as for tax purposes often a jurisdiction of AIFM may consider that a fund is managed by AIFM and as such is a tax resident of this jurisdiction note.

investors, established either as a transparent or an opaque entity, chosen specifically to invest in the relevant fund structure.

Carried investors (i.e., fund investors entitled to certain excess profits) typically use their own carried vehicle to invest into the fund structure, but carried investors benefitting from a specific carried interest regime may choose to invest directly in the fund. Here again, such carried investors generally have their own tax advisors to review their tax position in the relevant fund.

[B] Fund Structure Chart for Our Case

Finally, Figure 14.1 depicts the final fund structure our analysis established as best for our Case.

Figure 14.1 Diagram of Fund Structure

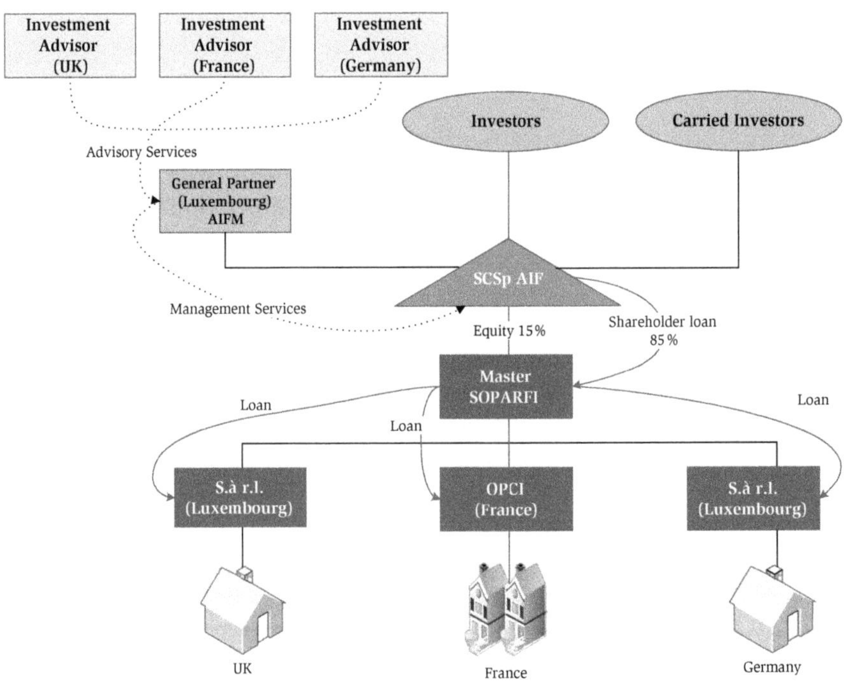

EUCOTAX Series on European Taxation

(1) Peter HJ Essers, Guido JME de Bont & Eric CCM Kemmeren (eds), *The Compatibility of Anti-Abuse Provisions in Tax Treaties with EC Law,* 1998 (ISBN 90-411-9678-1).
(2) Gerard TK Meussen (ed.), *The Principle of Equality in European Taxation,* 1999 (ISBN 90-411-9693-5).
(3) Michael Lang (ed.), *Tax Treaty Interpretation,* 2001 (ISBN 90-411-9857-1).
(4) Pasquale Pistone, *The Impact of Community Law on Tax Treaties: Issues and Solutions,* 2002 (ISBN 90-411-9860-1).
(5) René Offermanns, *The Entrepreneurship Concept in a European Comparative Tax Law Perspective,* 2002 (ISBN 90-411-9887-3).
(6) Michael Lang & Mario Züger, *Settlement of Disputes in Tax Treaty Law,* 2002 (ISBN 90-411-9904-7).
(7) Carlo Pinto, *Tax Competition and EU Law,* 2003 (ISBN 90-411-9913-6).
(8) Michael Lang, Hans-Jörgen Aigner, Ulrich Scheuerle & Markus *Stefaner, CFC Legislation, Tax Treaties and EC Law,* 2004 (ISBN 90-411-2284-2).
(9) Mattias Dahlberg, *Direct Taxation in Relation to the Freedom of Establishment and the Free Movement of Capital,* 2005 (ISBN 90-411-2363-6).
(10) Michael Lang, Judith Herdin & Ines Hofbauer, *WTO and Direct Taxation,* 2005 (ISBN 90-411-2371-7).
(11) Dennis Weber, *Tax Avoidance and the EC Tray Freedoms: A Study of the Limitations under European Law for the Prevention of Tax Avoidance,* 2005 (ISBN 90-411-2402-0).
(12) Félix Alberto Vega Borrego, *Limitations on Benefits Clauses on Double Taxation Conventions,* 2005 (ISBN 90-411-2370-9).
(13) Michael Lang, Josef Schuch & Claus Staringer, *ECJ-Recent Developments in Direct Taxation,* 2006 (ISBN 90-411-2509-4).
(14) Reuven S. Avi-Yonah, James R. Hines Jr. & Michael Lang, *Comparative Fiscal Federalism. Comparing the European Court of Justice and the US Supreme Court's Tax Jurisprudence,* 2007 (ISBN 978-90-411-2552-1).
(15) Christiana HJI Panayi, *Double Taxation, Tax Treaties, Treaty-Shopping and the European Community,* 2007 (ISBN 978-90-411-2658-0).
(16) Dennis Weber, *The Influence of European Law on Direct Taxation: Recent and Future Developments,* 2007 (ISBN 978-90-411-2667-2).
(17) Michael Lang & Pasquale Pistone, *The EU and Third Countries: Direct Taxation,* 2007 (ISBN 978-90-411-2665-8).
(18) Oskar Henkow, *Financial Activities in European VAT: A Theoretical and Legal Research of the European VAT System and Preferred Treatment of Financial Activities,* 2007 (ISBN 978-90-411-2703-7).
(19) Michael Lang (ed.), *Tax Compliance Costs for Companies in an Enlarged European Community,* 2008 (ISBN 978-90-411-2666-5).

(20) Michael Lang (ed.), *Source versus Residence. Problems Arising from the Allocation of Taxing Rights in Tax Treaty Law and Possible Alternatives*, 2008 (ISBN 978-90-411-2763-1).
(21) Ioanna Mitroyanni, *Integration Approaches to Group Taxation in the European Internal Market*, 2008 (ISBN 978-90-411-2779-2).
(22) Rolf Eicke, *Tax Planning with Holding Companies. Repatriation of US Profits from Europe:Concepts, Strategies, Structures*, 2008 (ISBN978-90-411-2794-5).
(23) Peter Essers et al. (ed.), *The Influence of IAS/IFRS on the CCCTB, Tax Accounting, Disclosure and Corporate Law Accounting Concepts: 'A Clash of Cultures'*, 2008 (ISBN 978-90-411-2819-5).
(24) Tonny Schenk-Geers, *International Exchange of Information and the Protection of Taxpayers*, 2009 (ISBN 978-90-411-3142-3).
(25) Raymond Adema, *UCITS and Taxation: Towards Harmonization of the Taxation of UCITS*, 2009 (ISBN 978-90-411-2839-3).
(26) Michael Lang, Jianwen Liu & Gongliang Tang (eds), *Europe–China Tax Treaties*, 2010 (ISBN 978-90-411-3216-1).
(27) Michael Lang, Pasquale Pistone, Josef Schuch & Claus Staringer (eds), *Procedural Rules in Tax Law in the Context of European Union and Domestic Law*, 2010 (ISBN 978-90-411-3376-2).
(28) Sjaak J.J.M. Jansen, *Fiscal Sovereignty of the Member States in an Internal Market: Past and Future*, 2011 (ISBN 978-90-411-3403-5).
(29) Dennis Weber & Bruno da Silva, *From Marks & Spencer to X Holding: The Future of Cross-Border Group Taxation*, 2011 (ISBN 978-90-411-3399-1).
(30) Claus Bohn Jespersen, *Intermediation of Insurance and Financial Services in European VAT*, 2011 (ISBN 978-90-411-3732-6).
(31) Sabine Heidenbauer, *Charity Crossing Borders: The Fundamental Freedoms' Influence on Charity and Donor Taxation in Europe*, 2011 (ISBN 978-90-411-3813-2).
(32) Michael Lang, et al., *The Future of Indirect Taxation: Recent Trends in VAT and GST Systems around the World*, 2012 (ISBN 978-90-411-3797-5).
(33) Harm van den Broek, *Cross-Border Mergers within the EU: Proposals to Remove the Remaining Tax Obstacles*, 2012 (ISBN 978-90-411-3824-8).
(34) Michael Lang, et al. (eds), *Tax Treaty Case Law around the Globe – 2011*, 2012 (ISBN 978-90-411-3876-7).
(35) Dennis Weber (ed.), *CCCTB: Selected Issues*, 2012 (ISBN 978-90-411-3872-9).
(36) Daniël Smit, *EU Freedoms, Non-EU Countries and Company Taxation*, 2012 (ISBN 978-90-411-4041-8).
(37) Rita de la Feria, *VAT Exemptions: Consequences and Design Alternatives*, 2013 (ISBN 978-90-411-3276-5).
(38) Karin Simader, *Withholding Taxes and the Fundamental Freedoms*, 2013 (ISBN 978-90-411-4842-1).
(39) Madeleine Merkx, *Establishments in European VAT*, 2013 (ISBN 978-90-411-4554-3).
(40) Carla De Pietro, *Tax Treaty Override*, 2014 (ISBN 978-90-411-5406-4).

(41) G.K. Fibbe & A.J.A. Stevens (eds), *Hybrid Entities and the EU Direct Tax Directives*, 2015 (ISBN 978-90-411-5942-7).
(42) Gerard Staats, *Personal Pensions in the EU*, 2015 (ISBN 978-90-411-5953-3).
(43) Michael Lang & Ine Lejeune (eds), *VAT/GST in a Global Digital Economy*, 2015 (ISBN 978-90-411-5952-6).
(44) Massimo Basilavecchia, Lorenzo del Federico & Pietro Mastellone (eds), *Tax Implications of Environmental Disasters and Pollution*, 2015 (ISBN 978-90-411-5611-2).
(45) Cristina Trenta, *Rethinking EU VAT for P2P Distribution*, 2015 (ISBN 978-90-411-6137-6).
(46) Marie Lamensch, Edoardo Traversa & Servaas van Thiel (eds), *Value Added Tax and the Digital Economy: The 2015 EU Rules and Broader Issues*, 2016 (ISBN 978-90-411-6612-8).
(47) Raffaele Petruzzi, *Transfer Pricing Aspects of Intra-Group Financing*, 2016 (ISBN 978-90-411-6732-3).
(48) Mario Grandinetti (ed.), *Corporate Tax Base in the Light of the IAS/IFRS and EU Directive 2013/34: A Comparative Approach*, 2016 (ISBN 978-90-411-6745-3).
(49) Bruno da Silva, *The Impact of Tax Treaties and EU Law on Group Taxation Regimes*, 2016 (ISBN 978-90-411-6905-1).
(50) Michael Lang, Alfred Storck & Raffaele Petruzzi (eds), *Transfer Pricing in a Post-BEPS World*, 2016 (ISBN 978-90-411-6710-1).
(51) Marta Papis-Almansa, *Insurance in European VAT: Current and Preferred Treatment in the Light of the New Zealand and Australian GST Systems*, 2017 (ISBN 978-90-411-8360-6).
(52) Wolfgang Speckhahn, *Real Estate Investment Trusts In Europe: Europeanising Tax Regimes*, 2017 (ISBN 978-90-411-8360-6).
(53) Frank J.G. Nellen, *Information Asymmetries in EU VAT*, 2017 (ISBN 978-90-411-8837-3).
(54) Erik Ros, *EU Citizenship and Direct Taxation*, 2017 (ISBN 978-90-411-8584-6).
(55) Werner Haslehner, Georg Kofler & Alexander Rust (eds), *EU Tax Law and Policy in the 21st Century*, 2017 (ISBN 978-90-411-8815-1).
(56) Claudia Sanò, *National Legal Presumptions and European Tax Law*, 2018 (ISBN 978-90-411-6613-5).
(57) Christoph Marchgraber, *Double (Non-)Taxation and EU Law*, 2018 (ISBN 978-90-411-9410-7).
(58) Dennis Weber & Jan van de Streek (eds), *The EU Common Consolidated Corporate Tax Base: Critical Analysis*, 2018 (ISBN 978-90-411-9233-2).
(59) Werner Haslehner (ed.), *Investment Fund Taxation: Domestic Law, EU Law, and Double Taxation Treaties*, 2018 (ISBN 978-90-411-9669-9).

www.ingramcontent.com/pod-product-compliance
Ingram Content Group UK Ltd.
Pitfield, Milton Keynes, MK11 3LW, UK
UKHW020240290926
15470UKWH00002B/640

9 789041 196699